Development

Education at SAGE

SAGE is a leading international publisher of journals, books, and electronic media for academic, educational, and professional markets.

Our education publishing includes:

- accessible and comprehensive texts for aspiring education professionals and practitioners looking to further their careers through continuing professional development

- inspirational advice and guidance for the classroom

- authoritative state of the art reference from the leading authors in the field

Find out more at: **www.sagepub.co.uk/education**

Child
Development
a practical introduction

Kevin Crowley

Los Angeles | London | New Delhi
Singapore | Washington DC

Los Angeles | London | New Delhi
Singapore | Washington DC

SAGE Publications Ltd
1 Oliver's Yard
55 City Road
London EC1Y 1SP

SAGE Publications Inc.
2455 Teller Road
Thousand Oaks, California 91320

SAGE Publications India Pvt Ltd

B 1/I 1 Mohan Cooperative Industrial Area
Mathura Road
New Delhi 110 044

SAGE Publications Asia-Pacific Pte Ltd
3 Church Street
#10-04 Samsung Hub
Singapore 049483

Editor: Jude Bowen
Editorial assistant: Rachael Plant
Production editor: Thea Watson
Copyeditor: Gary Lister
Proofreader: Rose James
Indexer: Avril Ehrlich
Marketing manager: Catherine Slinn
Cover design: Wendy Scott
Typeset by: C&M Digitals (P) Ltd, Chennai, India
Printed and bound in Great Britain by
CPI Group (UK) Ltd, Croydon, CR0 4YY

Library of Congress Control Number: 2013940960

British Library Cataloguing in Publication data

A catalogue record for this book is available from
the British Library

ISBN 978-1-84920-136-0
ISBN 978-1-84920-137-7 (pbk)

This book is dedicated to my wife Jacqui and
my children Amy and Ioan.

Contents

Tables

About the Author

Dr Kevin Crowley is a Principal Lecturer in Psychology at the University of South Wales. He has published research papers in a number of areas of child development, including bilingual language and literacy development, and play and learning in the early years.

Acknowledgements

I would like to express my thanks to the following for their support and encouragement when I was writing this book:

- My colleagues in the School of Psychology at the University of South Wales
- Jude Bowen and her team at SAGE
- And last but certainly not least, my wife Jacqui and my children Amy and Ioan

All words in **bold** are key terms explained in the glossary at the end of the book.

Introduction to Child Development

 Why you should read this chapter

This book focuses on the study of child development from birth to 8 years. From our own observations of children, we are all aware of the tremendous changes that take place during this period: in the space of a few years, not only do children grow in the physical sense, they also acquire skills in language and communication, the capacity to think and reason about the world, and skills in social interaction. The study of child development is not just fascinating in its own right; knowledge gained from studying development can also impact on many practical issues regarding the care, education and wellbeing of children. This book presents an overview of research and theory in various aspects of child development, but before we look at these, this chapter and Chapters 2 and 3 will aim to provide some basic context for the study of development as a whole. In this chapter we will look at some basic issues in child development and some of the broad theoretical approaches to understanding development.

(Continued)

(Continued)

By the end of this chapter you should

- be aware of the various domains of development that are of interest to researchers in this field
- understand some basic issues in the study of development including the role of nature versus nurture, and whether development proceeds in a continuous or discontinuous manner
- be aware of the different theoretical approaches to development including psychoanalytic, learning theory, cognitive-developmental, ethological and evolutionary psychology, and bioecological approaches
- have a basic understanding of some specific theories from the various approaches.

The nature of development

Development can be seen as the way in which individuals grow and change over the course of their lifespan and this can take place in different domains: *biological*, which includes features such as physical growth and developments in motor skills; *cognitive*, which refers to changes in thought processes such as memory, reasoning and problem solving, imagination, and creativity and language; *emotional*, where the focus is on changes in emotional experience and understanding; and *social*, which refers to changes in our understanding of ourselves and other people and how we relate to others. While the division of development into different domains may be useful from the point of organising our own thinking about the nature of development, it is important also to recognise that development itself is a holistic process and each domain influences and is influenced by the others. For example, development in a child's motor skills, such as crawling and reaching and grasping (physical development), will allow them to explore both their environment and the objects in this environment, leading to a greater understanding of their surroundings (cognitive development).

A central issue in development is the **nature** versus **nurture** debate, in other words, the relative roles played by biological and genetic factors as opposed to environmental factors in shaping development. Nature refers to the role of biology and genetics and nurture to the role of experience and other environmental factors. Advocates of the nature position see development as a process of **maturation**, with physical and psychological change unfolding according to a genetically predetermined 'plan' inherited from our parents. The nurture viewpoint sees development occurring as a result of **learning**. Hall (1883) was a strong proponent of the role of nature in development, and very much influenced by evolutionary theory. This can be seen in his theory of play, in which he argued that children's play emerged in a way that reflected the evolutionary history of the human species. For Hall, children's play was essentially acting out this history, for example an infant crawling reflected a point in human evolution when humans walked on all fours. On the other hand, Watson (1930) took the view that environmental experiences and learning were of most importance and claimed that he could use the environment to shape the development of any child:

> *Give me a dozen healthy infants, well-formed and my own specified world to bring them up in, and I'll guarantee to take any one at random and train him to become any type of specialist I might select – doctor, lawyer, artist, merchant-chief, and yes, even beggar-man and thief, regardless of his talents, penchants, tendencies, abilities, vocations and race of his ancestors.* (Watson, 1930: 104)

Watson's views on the role of the environment will be covered later in this book.

Today, most theorists do not take a rigid position on the role of nature and nurture and see development occurring through the interplay of both factors. For example, it is widely accepted that babies are born with different temperaments which can be classed as 'easy' or 'difficult', and there is likely to be an inherited basis for either. However, research by Thomas and Chess (1986) has also indicated that the nature of the parenting received by babies is also important in the long-term development of temperament and a difficult baby will not necessarily grow into a difficult child or adult. Sensitive caregiving can alter the temperament of the child. Another interesting issue is the extent to which abilities and behaviour are **canalised** (Waddington, 1975), in other words, are strongly influenced by genetic factors, or are amenable to environmental influences. The development of motor skills in infants would be an example of a strongly canalised process, as all infants will eventually roll over, reach for objects, sit up, crawl and walk, and it would take extreme circumstances to alter this pattern. On the other hand, personality characteristics such as temperament and intelligence, while having a genetic component, are seen as less strongly canalised and can be altered by the environment in which the infant is raised.

Another aspect of development that has been subject to debate is whether it proceeds in a **continuous** or **discontinuous** manner. Continuous development implies a gradual but smooth pattern of change over time. Essentially, babies and children are seen as having the same basic capacities as adults and changes take place in the efficiency and complexity of their abilities until they reach the mature, adult levels. Change is then essentially *quantitative* in nature. Just as children grow taller and can run faster as they get older, their psychological characteristics also change in the same way, for example they can remember more and their thought processes become more complex and sophisticated. The alternative discontinuous view is that development proceeds as a series of abrupt changes and with each change the child moves to a more advanced level of functioning. In this view, the child moves through a series of **developmental stages**, and with each new stage the child's behaviour, abilities or thought processes are *qualitatively* different to what they were in the preceding stage.

Theories of development

A theory is essentially a set of organised observations that are used to explain an interesting phenomenon. There are a number of broad theories of child development and some of these will be reviewed in this section. These will include *psychodynamic, learning, cognitive-developmental, ethology and evolutionary psychology,* and *bioecological* theories.

Psychodynamic theories

Psychodynamic theories have their roots in the work of Sigmund Freud whose views stemmed from his experiences of treating individuals suffering from a variety of neuroses. Freud concluded that human development is essentially driven by conflict. We have basic aggressive and sexual instincts that need to be satisfied, but we live in a society where such instincts have to be controlled and restrained. Development was therefore about seeking a balance between satisfying basic drives and adapting to the reality of our situation. Freud (1917) proposed that the human personality is made up of three components: the **id**, the **ego** and the **superego**. The id is present from birth and its sole purpose is the satisfaction of our basic urges. It operates according to the **pleasure principle** and seeks immediate gratification of our needs and Freud believed that the infant was dominated by it. However, as we develop, our instincts come into conflict with reality and we need to restrain the impulses of the id, and this leads to the emergence of the ego. The ego operates according to the **reality principle** in that it seeks to satisfy our basic drives but in a desirable and socially acceptable manner. The final component we develop is the superego and this occurs during the preschool years when children take on their parent's moral values as their own. The superego acts as the child's conscience and allows them to know when they have done wrong without the need to be told by an adult, thus they are enabled to feel guilt and shame over their unacceptable conduct. Freud viewed healthy development as achieving a balance between the three conflicting components of personality. The id communicates basic needs, the superego demands that we behave in a morally acceptable manner and the ego attempts to satisfy the demands of the id but in ways that are acceptable to the superego.

Based on his observation that many of his patients neurotic symptoms revolved around childhood sexual conflicts that they had repressed, Freud viewed sex as the most important instinct. This led him to propose his **psychosexual theory**, its basic premise being that development proceeded in a series of stages in which the sexual instinct shifted to different **erogenous zones** in the body. The first stage in Freud's theory was the **oral stage**, in which pleasure is centred on the mouth and behaviours such as sucking, chewing and biting were sources of pleasure. The next stage is the **anal phase** and this occurs around the second year of life and involves pleasure becoming focused on the processes of urination and defecation. A potential source of conflict here is the desire to satisfy these bodily functions immediately, clashing with the parent's desire to toilet-train the infant. The child then moves on to the **phallic stage** when they are between 3 and 6 years old: it is around these ages that sexual pleasure becomes centred on the genitals. During this stage an important conflict occurs in which the child sexually desires the opposite-sex parent. This is accompanied by feelings of jealousy towards the same-sex parent and also a fear of punishment from them. In boys this conflict is called the **Oedipus complex** and in girls the **Electra complex**. The conflict is eventually resolved by the child identifying with the sex-role characteristics and moral standards of the same-sex parent. The next stage is the **latent stage** in which sexual impulses are suppressed and channelled into intellectual and social activity and this leads to further development of the superego. Finally during puberty, the child reaches the **genital stage** in which sexual desires reawaken and the adolescent must learn to express these in socially appropriate ways. If development is successful, sexual desires will be satisfied by seeking to form relationships with peers, leading to marriage and the raising of children.

Freud's theory has few followers today, and from a scientific point of view it is difficult to test empirically: how can one test the notion that healthy development is characterised by the ego successfully balancing the demands of the id and the superego? However, in terms of stressing the importance of early experiences for later development, the basic ideas of Freud are influential.

Erikson's psychosocial theory

Erikson (1963) was influenced by Freud but came to place less emphasis on sexual urges and more on the role of social and cultural factors. He saw development as involving the interaction between the individual's biological (somatic) processes, mental (ego) processes and wider societal influences arising from our membership of '...*groupings of geographical and historical coherence: family, class, community, nation*' (Erikson, 1963: 30).

Erikson, like Freud, proposed that development occurred in a series of stages, but unlike Freud, whose theory saw development as being complete by adolescence, he saw it as a lifelong process whereby its stages extend into adulthood and old age. He viewed these stages as occurring in a fixed, orderly sequence. At each stage of development, he argued that the individual is confronted with an age-related task or **psychosocial crisis** related to biological maturation and the social demands being faced by the individual at a particular point in their life. The successful resolution of each crisis led to healthy developmental outcomes.

The first stage in Erikson's theory lasts from birth to when the child is around 1 year old and is termed **basic trust versus mistrust.** In this stage, infants must learn to trust others to care for them. If they do not (possibly due to poor caregiving), then they may come to view people as being unreliable and untrustworthy and this may have implications for future relationships. The next stage occurs between the ages of approximately

1 and 3 and is called **autonomy versus doubt**. Here the child begins to use their emerging mental and motor skills to become more independent and autonomous, for example being able to dress and feed themselves. A child who fails to achieve this autonomy will begin to doubt their abilities and feel a sense of shame. **Initiative versus guilt**, the third stage, takes place when the child is around 3 to 6 years old and is when they start to develop a sense of initiative, a desire to master their environment but do so in a socially appropriate way. Sometimes their goals or activities conflict with those of the parents and other family members and these conflicts may result in feelings of guilt. Successful resolution of this crisis lies in striking a balance between the child's sense of initiative and the demands to behave appropriately. This stage is followed by **industry versus inferiority** (aged approximately 6 to 12) wherein the child seeks to master the various intellectual and social challenges that occur during this period of life, such as doing well at school and establishing good peer relationships. The industrious child will acquire the academic and social skills to feel self-assured and failure to acquire these will lead to feelings of inferiority and incompetence. The next stage, **identity versus role confusion**, occurs from around 12 to 20 years of age and the developmental task for the individual at this stage is to achieve a sense of their own identity. Adolescents who fail to achieve this or let others determine their identity will remain confused about who they are and their role in society. The years of young adulthood (approximately 20 to 40 years of age) are dominated by **intimacy versus isolation**. The challenge of this stage is to establish close friendships and a loving relationship with another person. The individual's success in resolving past crises (learning to trust others, developing social skills and making friends) will determine their success in resolving this crisis and failure to develop close friendships and form an intimate relationship will lead to feelings of isolation. During middle adulthood (aged around 40 to 65), individuals pass through the **generativity versus stagnation** stage. The main concern here is to be productive in work and/or family life. A failure or inability to express oneself in this way leads to feelings of stagnation and a lack of a sense of accomplishment. During old age, the adult enters the stage of **ego integrity versus despair**. In this stage, we look back at and assess our lives. The individual who has successfully resolved the previous psychosocial crises will see life as having been productive and meaningful, leading to a sense of integrity, while those who resolved the stages in a negative fashion will see life as a series of unfulfilled promises and missed goals leading to feelings of despair and gloom.

Erikson's theory has the strength of widening the scope of psychodynamic theories beyond a concern with basic biological urges and not seeing development as a process that ends during adolescence. However, it has been criticised for being vague about the causes of development such as the experiences that are necessary for resolving the various psychosocial conflicts. As with Freud, the theory is also difficult to test empirically. Erikson's theory can be seen as a largely descriptive theory of the role of maturation and social influences on development, without clearly specifying how or why this development takes place (Shaffer and Kipp, 2010).

Learning theories

Learning theories began with the work of John Watson who, as we saw earlier, was a strong proponent of the view that it is nurture rather than nature that is the strongest influence on development. Watson saw development as a process of learning and is regarded as the founder of an approach to psychology called **behaviourism**.

Watson's classical conditioning

Watson was concerned with creating an objective science of psychology that focused on directly observable events (behaviour) rather than unobservable, hypothetical constructs such as the id and the ego. He was strongly influenced by the work of the Russian physiologist Ivan Pavlov. While conducting research on the digestive systems of dogs, Pavlov noted that the mere appearance of a food bowl was sufficient for the dogs to start salivating, and decided to investigate if other stimuli could be used to elicit this response. He found that if he paired the presentation of food with an environmental stimulus such as a light, eventually the light on its own would be sufficient to elicit salivation. The light had changed from being a neutral stimulus to being a **conditioned stimulus** and salivation had become a **conditioned response** to the light. This is the basis of a form of learning called **classical conditioning** in which a particular stimulus becomes associated with a particular response. Watson applied these notions to human behaviour and rejected the notion of behaviour developing in stages, and instead saw it as a continuous process of change shaped by people's environmental circumstances.

Watson's most famous demonstration of this view is the case of 'little Albert' (Watson and Raynor, 1920), wherein a gentle white rat was presented to Albert, a 9-month-old boy who crawled towards the rat and played with it. At a later stage, Watson presented the rat to the boy and accompanied this with a loud, unpleasant noise and eventually the presence of the rat on its own was enough to elicit a fear response from the child, who had come to associate the rat with the unpleasant noise. On the basis of findings such as these, Watson concluded that the environment was the main factor in development, with children learning through making a wide variety of stimulus-response associations.

Skinner and operant conditioning

An important point about Watson's view of learning is that the child is essentially *passive* and when presented with a stimulus associates this with a particular response. However, Skinner, while accepting that it was the environment that was most important, saw learning as a more active process in which we act on or *operate* on our environments. Based on research with animals, Skinner (1953) argued that humans and animals repeat behaviours that lead to favourable outcomes and suppress those that lead to unfavourable ones. So a rat in a cage that receives food in response to pressing a bar is likely to repeat this act. The food acts as a **reinforcer** and increases the likelihood that a particular behaviour will occur again. Sometimes behaviour will lead to a negative consequence; this acts as a **punisher** and will reduce the probability of a reoccurrence of the behaviour. Applied to child development, learning can be seen as the child making the connection between certain ways of behaving and certain desirable or undesirable outcomes and this is seen to apply to all areas of development. An infant who vocalises will be reinforced by praise and attention from parents, leading to a reoccurrence of this behaviour, and as vocalisations come closer to speech, the selective patterns of reinforcement received by the infant for this behaviour lead to the development of language. A child who behaves in a friendly and considerate manner will receive praise and encouragement and this will strengthen the child's tendency to repeat this behaviour. Reinforcers and punishers can be *positive* and *negative* in nature. Positive in this context means that a stimulus is presented and negative means that it is withdrawn. Examples of a **positive reinforcer** would be praise, social approval or rewards such as being given a toy or engaging in a fun activity. A **negative reinforcer** is the removal of an unpleasant stimulus in response to a desirable behaviour, such as the relief of pain following the taking of a painkiller. An example of a **positive punisher** would be a child receiving parental disapproval for misbehaving, or receiving a burn as a result of touching a hot object. A **negative punisher** involves the removal of something pleasant, such as the removal of a toy or being 'grounded' for misbehaviour.

Skinner argued that the totality of human development could be explained in terms of the association of behaviours and their consequences, but many will see this as an oversimplification. It does not take into account personal factors such as motivation. As we will see in Chapter 9, attempts to explain language development in these terms cannot account for the speed with which children acquire language and the complexity of this achievement. However, Skinner's views are useful in practical settings such as promoting positive behaviours and form the basis for interventions for problem behaviours in children through the process of **behaviour modification** (Martin and Pear, 2007).

Bandura's social learning theory

Bandura, another learning theorist, accepted Skinner's views on the importance of **operant conditioning** in development, but also noted that children and adults acquire many new skills in the absence of rewards and punishments simply by watching and imitating the behaviour of others (Bandura, 1977). His theory therefore stresses the role of **observational learning** or **modelling** in development. Bandura's work also allows for the role of thought processes or cognition. This means that in order to imitate a behaviour, we must *attend* to the behaviour of the model, *comprehend* that behaviour and *remember* it. One of Bandura's best known experiments demonstrated that pre-school children who were exposed to an adult model engaging in acts of 'violence' against an inflatable bobo doll tended to imitate these actions in their play with the doll later, thus demonstrating the role of observational learning in aggressive behaviour (Bandura et al., 1963). Subsequent research has indicated that a variety of other behaviours such as prosocial acts and sex-roles can also be acquired in this manner. Bandura's later work (1989) has focused on the development of a sense of **self-efficacy**, or beliefs about one's ability to succeed in everyday situations, such as learning in school. He argues that a sense of self-efficacy is also learned by observing the behaviour and attitudes of a model. Children whose role models demonstrate positive qualities, such as persistence when faced with difficult tasks, are more likely to develop a strong sense of self-efficacy than children whose models who demonstrate less positive qualities, such as giving up easily in response to minor setbacks.

Can you think of any learning experiences from your own life that would be examples of classical or operant conditioning, or observational learning?

Cognitive-developmental theories

For learning theorists, the emphasis is placed on observable aspects of behaviour and the environmental factors that influence it, and the child's thought processes or cognition are largely irrelevant. An alternative view is that development is driven by the way a child thinks about the world and changes in the patterns of thinking are of prime importance. There are three influential cognitive-developmental theories – the stage theory of Piaget, Vygotsky's sociocultural theory and, more recently, information-processing theories. These will be covered in more detail in Chapter 4, but a brief summary is provided here.

Piaget's theory

Piaget's interest in child development originated when he worked in the laboratory of Alfred Binet who was interested in measuring intelligence in children. While administering various tasks to the children, Piaget became interested in the incorrect responses they gave and noted that children of the same age often gave similar incorrect answers. He concluded that it was not the case that the children lacked intelligence, but that their thinking was *qualitatively* different to those of adults. This led to his own detailed observations of children over many years and his influential theory of cognitive development. Piaget was influenced by the biological notion of **adaptation** – just as our bodies are adapted to fit with our environments, our minds also adapt to help us to function in our worlds. Essentially human intelligence was an adaptation that enhanced our chances of survival (Piaget, 1950). Piaget noted that children's thinking was often at odds with the nature of the world and that they could not think beyond their own perspective. Their view of the world was often **egocentric** (Piaget and Inhelder, 1956), in other words, they were unable to see situations from any other viewpoint but their own, and **animistic** (Piaget, 1929), meaning that they often saw inanimate objects as having thoughts and feelings just like they did. For Piaget development was a process of change in which children, as a result of exploring their worlds, revise their knowledge so that it corresponds more closely with reality, and in so doing they achieve a state of *equilibrium* between their knowledge and the nature of the physical and social world.

Piaget saw development as passing through a series of distinct stages which he termed the *sensorimotor, preoperational, concrete operational* and *formal operational* stages. The sensorimotor stage spans the period from birth to around the age of 2, during which time infants gain a basic understanding of the world through use of their sensory and motor capabilities. The next stage of development, the preoperational stage, lasts until the child is about 7 years old, by which time they can now use basic mental representations such as images and language to represent the world, but their ability to think is very much limited to their own point of view. At around the age of 7, children move to the concrete operational stage of development wherein their thinking becomes increasingly logical. This stage lasts until they are between 11 and 12 years old. At this age, the child reaches the formal operational stage in which they gain the ability to think in more abstract and hypothetical ways and thinking is no longer tied to concrete reality.

Piaget's theory has strongly influenced the way we think about child development, and has also been applied in educational contexts. However, there have also been criticisms and in particular a tendency to underestimate the capabilities of the child. These issues will be considered in Chapter 4.

Vygotsky's sociocultural theory

Vygotsky shared Piaget's view of the child as an active explorer of their environment, but while Piaget saw children as lone explorers making discoveries on their own, Vygotsky (1978) saw development as a socially transmitted process in which children acquired knowledge and skills through their dialogues with more skilled and experienced members of their society. Vygotsky also noted that while children are unable to do many tasks on their own, they are able to do them with help and support from an adult. Vygotsky referred to this difference between the child's existing capabilities and what they can achieve with help from others as their **zone of proximal development**. Vygotsky also saw development as following a continous pattern in which the child moved from being able to do things with help from others to being able to do things on their own, in other words, development moved from the **social plane** to the **psychological plane**.

Information-processing accounts

A more recent approach to cognitive development is based on making an analogy between the human mind and the digital computer. Like computers, the human mind is seen as processing information based on a limited set of rules. Thought is seen as the flow of information through a system. We receive input from our senses, perform a series of operations on this input and transform it into some useful output, such as the answer to a question, the ability to recall a memory or the transformation of sound waves into meaningful speech. There are a variety of different **information-processing** models describing different aspects of cognition, for example memory (Atkinson and Shiffrin, 1968) and recognising printed words (Stuart, 2003). In general information-processing models see development as a continuous process in which basic abilities gradually improve as we mature. An example is the capacity of children's short-term memory (see Chapter 4) which gradually improves over the course of childhood so that by the age of around 10 it is the same as an adult's (Gathercole and Baddeley, 1993).

Ethology and evolutionary psychology

Ethology is concerned with ways in which behaviour can promote the survival of a species. It has its roots in the work of Charles Darwin, but modern ethology arose from the work of the zoologists Conrad Lorenz and Nico Tinbergen, whose observations of animal behaviour provided some important insights into the adaptive nature of some behaviours. The basic assumptions of ethology are that members of all animal species are born with a set of *biologically programmed* behaviours that are products of evolution and contribute to survival (Lorenz, 1981; Tinbergen, 1973). One of the best-known patterns of such behaviour that promotes survival is **imprinting**, an instinctual following response in birds that keeps the young close to the mother in order to be protected and fed. In birds this imprinting occurs during a restricted period of development called a **critical period**. This refers to a particular time when an animal is biologically prepared to acquire a certain pattern of behaviour. In studying geese, Lorenz noted that if the mother was not present during this period but an object resembling her features was, the baby geese would imprint on this object instead.

Ethological perspectives have been applied to various aspects of human behaviour. An example is **attachment**, or the formation of an affectionate, caring bond between the infant and primary caregiver. Bowlby (1969) argued that human infants are born with a set of behaviours that will lead them to seek close physical proximity to the mother who will in turn nurture and protect the infant from danger, and this tendency is a product of our evolutionary history. This issue will be considered further in Chapter 8.

An important issue when applying ethological perspectives to human development is the applicability of the notion of a critical period. Bornstein (1987) suggests that in the case of humans, the term **sensitive period** is more accurate. A sensitive period is a point in development when the child is particularly 'ready' to acquire a new skill. An example is the case of learning a language, where there does appear to be a sensitive period in childhood (see Chapter 9). Learning a language appears to be relatively easy for children, but beyond childhood, language learning is more difficult, though not impossible. However, given that language learning is possible beyond childhood, even if it is more difficult, the notion of a sensitive rather than a critical period seems more applicable.

Darwin's theory of evolution has influenced psychology as well and recent years have seen the development of the discipline of **evolutionary psychology**, which makes the assumption that '*the human mind is the product of evolution just like any other bodily organ, and that we can better understand the mind by examining evolutionary pressures that shaped it*' (Workman and Reader, 2007: 1). In this way, the development of various psychological attributes can be seen in terms of how they may have promoted survival in our evolutionary past. Such explanations have been applied to various aspects of development such as being able to understand other people's mental states (having a 'theory of mind', see Chapter 8), the different types of play engaged in by boys and girls to name just two. Indeed the length of time it takes a human child to reach physical and psychological maturity (compared to other animals) can in itself be seen as an evolutionary adaptation. Given the complexity of human societies, a lengthy period of development during which the child is protected by relatives ensures that the child has time to acquire the physical and psychological skills needed to function in society (Bjorklund, 1997; Shaffer and Kipp, 2010).

The bioecological model

When psychologists study child development, they often conduct their studies in the context of the immediate surroundings of the children, such as the family and school environment. However, the American psychologist Bronfenbrenner (1979) advocated an approach to development that saw the environment in broader terms, in a way that extends beyond the child's immediate surroundings. He saw the environment as consisting of a series of interacting systems with the child at the centre. This approach has become known as the **bioecological model**.

The innermost layer of Bronfenbrenner's system is the **microsystem** and refers to the immediate surroundings of the child, such as the home or school. Children are influenced by people in the microsystem, such as parents, teachers or peers, and the children's own biological and social characteristics (such as their personalities and physical abilities) also have a bearing on development, influencing how they interact with others. The interactions between other people in the microsystem may also affect the child, such as a child being adversely affected by marital conflict between parents.

The **mesosystem** is Bronfenbrenner's term for the second layer of the model; it pertains to relationships between the different microsystems, such as between home and school. An example would be the way in which the quality of a child's home life may affect performance at school or peer relationships.

The third layer is referred to as the **exosystem** and this relates to contexts or settings in which the child does not directly participate but which nevertheless can have an influence on them. An example of such an influence could be the work environment of the parent(s). Long working hours may restrict the parent's availability to the child, or a stressful working environment may have implications for the way in which the parent behaves towards them in the home environment.

At the outer layer of the model is the **macrosystem**. This refers to the broader social, cultural and political climate in which the child develops. Such influences can include broader attitudes to child-rearing, government policies, and so on.

Bronfenbrenner also included a temporal system called the **chronosystem** because he recognised that changes in the individual or the environment over time can also influence development. These can include historical events such as the effects of growing up during a time of conflict or economic difficulty, but can also apply to events having an effect related to the time of the child's life in which they occur. For example, the way in which a child reacts to parental divorce may depend on the age of the child at the time of the separation of the parents.

The bioecological model certainly provides a much broader definition of the environment that will make sense to many people and it allows us to consider how changes in one system can influence the others – for example, legislation requiring employers to pay a minimum wage (macrosystem influence) will cause changes in the parent's working life (more pay). In other words, it will affect the exosystem and improved financial circumstances may have an effect on the child's home life (the microsystem).

 Can you think of any examples from your own life that might reflect the interactions of the various systems as set out in Bronfenbrenner's model?

Chapter summary

- Development can be seen as the ways in which an individual changes over the lifespan.
- Different domains of development can be defined including biological, cognitive, social and emotional. It is important, however, to recognise that development is a holistic process in which the different domains influence and are influenced by each other.

(Continued)

(Continued)

- Researchers in child development differ over the role of nature and nurture in development.
- Some researchers argue that development proceeds in a continuous manner marked by quantitative changes in functioning. Other researchers argue that development proceeds as a series of abrupt changes in a stage-like manner, with each new stage showing qualitative differences in functioning.
- There are different theoretical approaches to development including psycho-analytic, learning theory, cognitive-developmental, ethological and evolutionary psychology, and bioecological approaches.

Further reading

Crain, W. (2010) *Theories of Development: Concepts and Applications* (6th edn). New York: Pearson.

A detailed account of theories of child development.

Workman, L. and Reader, W. (2007) *Evolutionary Psychology*. Cambridge: Cambridge University Press.

A comprehensive but very readable introduction to this field and includes evolutionary perspectives on various aspects of development.

References

Atkinson, R.C. and Shiffrin, R.M. (1968) 'Human memory: A proposed system and its control processes', in K.W. Spence and J.T. Spence (eds), *Advances in the Psychology of Learning and Motivation*, Vol.2. New York: Academic Press. pp. 90–195.

Bandura, A. (1977*) Social Learning Theory*. Englewood Cliffs, NJ: Prentice-Hall.

Bandura, A. (1989) 'Social cognitive theory', in R. Vasta (ed.), *Annals of Child Development: Vol. 6 Six Theories of Child Development*. Greenwich, CT: Jai Press. pp. 45–103.

Bandura, A., Ross, D. and Ross, S.A. (1963) 'Imitation of film-mediated aggressive models', *Journal of Abnormal and Social Psychology*, 66(1): 3–11.

Bjorkland, D.F. (1997) 'The role of immaturity in human development', *Psychological Bulletin*, 122(2): 153–169.

Bornstein, M.H. (1987) *Sensitive Periods in Development: Interdisciplinary Perspectives*. Hillsdale, NJ: Erlbaum.

Bowlby, J. (1969) *Attachment and Loss: Vol. 1 Attachment*. New York: Basic Books.

Bronfenbrenner, U. (1979) *The Ecology of Human Development*. Cambridge, MA: Harvard University Press.

Erikson, E.H. (1963) *Childhood and Society* (2nd edn). New York: Norton.

Freud, S. (1917) *Lines of Advance in Psychoanalytic Therapy*, Vol. SE xvii. London: Hogarth Press and The Institute of Psychoanalysis.

Gathercole, S.E. and Baddeley, A.D. (1993) *Working Memory and Language*. Hove: Erlbaum.

Hall, G.S. (1883) 'The content of children's minds', *Princeton Review*, 2: 249–72.

Lorenz, K.Z. (1981) *The Foundations of Ethology*. New York: Springer-Verlag.

Martin, G.L. and Pear, J. (2007) *Behavior Modification: What It Is and How to Do It* (8th edn). Upper Saddle River, NJ: Prentice-Hall.

Piaget, J. (1929) *The Child's Conception of the World*. London: Routledge and Kegan Paul.

Piaget, J. (1950) *The Psychology of Intelligence*. San Diego, CA: Harcourt Brace Jovanovich.

Piaget, J. and Inhelder, B. (1956) *The Child's Conception of Space*. London: Routledge & Kegan Paul.

Shaffer, D.R. and Kipp, K. (2010) *Developmental Psychology: Childhood and Adolescence*. Belmont, CA: Wadsworth.

Skinner, B.F. (1953) *Science and Human Behaviour*. New York: Macmillan.

Stuart, M. (2003) 'Using the dual-route cascade model as a framework for understanding reading development', in R. Stainthorp and P. Tomlinson (eds), *Learning and Teaching Reading, British Journal of Educational Psychology Monograph Series II: Psychological Aspects of Education – Current Trends*. Leicester: British Psychological Society. pp. 45–60.

Thomas, A. and Chess, S. (1986) 'The New York Longitudinal Study: From infancy to adult life', in R. Plomin and J. Dunn (eds), *The Study of Temperament: Changes, Continuities and Challenges*. Hillsdale, NJ: Erlbaum.

Tinbergen, N. (1973) *The Animal in its World: Explorations of an Ethologist, 1932–1972*, Vols 1 and 2. Cambridge, MA: Harvard University Press.

Vygotsky, L.S. (1978) *Mind in Society: The Development of Higher Mental Processes*. Cambridge, MA: Harvard University Press.

Waddington, C.H. (1975) *The Evolution of an Evolutionist*. Ithaca, NY: Cornell University Press.

Watson, J.B. (1930) *Behaviourism*. New York: Norton.

Watson, J.B. and Raynor, R.R. (1920) 'Conditioned emotional reactions', *Journal of Experimental Psychology*, 3 (1): 1–14.

Workman, L. and Reader, W. (2007) *Evolutionary Psychology*. Cambridge: Cambridge University Press.

Policy and Early Years Practice

2

 Why you should read this chapter

Much research in child development focuses on children developing in the immediate contexts of their families, schools, communities and peer groups. However, it is important to recognise that children also grow up within a wider social, political and cultural context and often these can influence the children's family, schooling and other experiences. This aspect of development was recognised in Bronfenbrenner's bioecological theory (1979), with such influences forming the macrosystem of his model. An important influence here can be the various policies pursued by governments in relation to children and young people. These can affect diverse aspects of a child's life, for example financial and social supports available to their parents and families, access to childcare, and the manner in which they are taught at school. Such policies also have an effect on the day-to-day lives of adults who work with children. An understanding of factors that influence policy development and of some current major policies and practices in the early years is therefore useful for any individual interested in the field of child development.

By the end of this chapter you should

- have an understanding of some of the broad influences on policy development including social and cultural factors, political agendas, government bodies/stakeholders, significant events and international developments

- be aware of the impact of devolution – the establishment of regional governments in the UK – on early years policy and practices

- have a basic awareness of a number of policy initiatives including the *Every Child Matters* Green Paper, the Child Workforce Development Council, and the Sure Start and Flying Start early intervention programmes

- have a basic awareness of the early years curricula in operation in England, Wales, Scotland and Northern Ireland.

Influences on early years policy

Early years policies are not created in a vacuum but develop within a broad social, cultural and political context. In their book *Understanding Early Years Policy*, Baldock et al. (2013) identify a number of specific influences including social and cultural contexts, political agendas, government bodies and stakeholders, significant events and international policy.

Social and cultural contexts

An important influence is the broad social and cultural contexts in which policies are made as changes in these over time can shape attitudes to how children and families should behave and be supported. An example of this is the provision of childcare (Baldock et al., 2013). For many decades, the predominant view was that children were best cared for by their mothers until school age. From time to time, national priorities changed this view. During the Second World War, with many men drafted into the armed forces, there arose a demand for female labour to work in the factories and on the land, and hence this gave rise to a need for provision of childcare. As a result, local authorities set up day nurseries for this purpose. However, this was seen as a temporary measure during a time of national emergency and the assumption was that once hostilities had ceased women would resume their 'traditional' roles within the home, and indeed most of the nurseries established during this period closed down after the war. There was an expansion in nursery education following the Plowden Report (DES, 1967), but even this stated that only part-time nursery places should be offered because they discouraged women from working (Baldock et al., 2013); it was still very much the view that children needed to be with their mothers for part of the day. However, this view began to be challenged from the 1970s onwards with the increasing participation of women in the workforce. This was in part because of the need for individual families to increase their income and also because of wider changes in attitudes to gender roles driven by the women's movement during the 1970s and 1980s. Recent years have continued to see a steady rise in the numbers of women who not only go out to work but also have dependent children. Moreover, due to increased geographical mobility, fewer parents can rely on family members to help with childcare. Initially the demand for extra childcare was filled by private providers but this only met the needs of better-paid parents. This combination of factors has therefore brought provision of preschool childcare to the fore as an important issue in recent years.

Political agendas

Baldock et al. (2013) have also pointed out that since 1997, early years policy has been part of a broader political agenda concerned with tackling social exclusion. Specific aims here include raising educational standards and improving basic skills (especially in socially disadvantaged children), increasing employability in school leavers, providing childcare so that parents and especially mothers can go to work or into further education or training, reducing long-term welfare dependency, improving health and wellbeing in children and reducing crime and antisocial behaviour. Immediately, one can see how early years policy will impinge on these priorities. Better educational standards and provision mean that right from the start children should have a positive journey through the educational system, reducing problems such as truancy or early drop out from education, improved basic skills and higher levels of educational qualifications will increase the employability of school leavers, and affordable levels of childcare will facilitate parents to come off welfare and seek employment. Clark and Waller (2007) point out that concerns with reducing welfare dependency mean placing the needs of children second, but others may take the view that the consequent reduction in child poverty means that children are at the centre of policy. Overall, however, early years policy cannot be viewed in isolation from the wider political priorities predominating at the time it is made.

Government bodies and other stakeholders

The role of government departments can be seen in the example provided by Baldock et al. (2013) of the transfer in 1998 of responsibility for early years policy from the Department of Health to the then Department for Education and Employment. This was followed in 2001 by the transfer of responsibility for regulation and standards from local authority directors of social care to Ofsted's Early Years Directorate, demonstrating a clear intention that future early years policies would be influenced by educationalists.

A number of non-governmental organisations (NGOs) have had an input into early years policy, too. An example is *Childcare and Education – Investing in All Our Futures* (DfES/LGA, 2001), a set of guidelines for local authorities to develop early years provision written by Daycare Trust for the Local Government Association, within the auspices of the DfES.

There has also been input into the development of early years policy from academic research. A particularly influential project here has been the *Effective Provision of Pre-school Education (EPPE) Project* (see for example Sylva et al., 2003, 2004). This is an ongoing research project which commenced in 1997 and looks at the long-term out-comes of attendance at various forms of preschool care including playgroups, day-care nurseries and nursery schools. The study is tracking the progress of 3000 children who entered various forms of early years education in 1997 and explores the effects on their development. The project seeks to identify successful examples of early years provision and the particular features they display.

Significant events

Sometimes an event occurs that exposes shortcomings in current early years provision. Often these can be tragic events such as cases of child abuse or murder. An example is the case of Victoria Climbié, an 8-year-old girl who was abused and murdered by her aunt and her aunt's boyfriend in 2001. The circumstances leading to the murder were the subject of an enquiry led by Lord Laming and his subsequent report (Laming, 2003) highlighted a variety of deficiencies in the legislation and guidelines for protect-ing children at the time. These included flaws in the management of child welfare, poor communication between the key responsible agencies and poor-quality training of staff involved in child protection. The publication of the Laming Report was influ-ential in the development of *Every Child Matters* (DfES, 2003), a policy document that will be discussed later in this chapter. While the immediate context of this document was the aftermath of the murder of Victoria Climbié, Baldock et al. (2013) point out that the report also encompassed existing developments and plans within the govern-ment and that there is not a simple linear relationship between these two events.

International influences

The United Kingdom is a signatory to *The United Nations Convention on the Rights of the Child* (UNCRC) (United Nations, 1989). This is an international treaty aiming to protect the civil, political, economic, social, health and cultural rights of children. Among the rights advocated for the child are the right to life, to be raised by their own families, to have a relationship with both parents in the event of a separation, to be consulted and heard on matters relating to their lives and to be protected from abuse and exploitation. As a signatory, the UK is required to reflect this treaty in its laws and policies relating to children. Examples of the influence of this treaty at national level include the measures in the Children Act 2004 regarding the safeguarding of children, and the emphasis on the responsibilities of adults to act in the best interests of the children in their care. The appointment of Children's Commissioners in England, Wales, Scotland and Northern Ireland can be seen as a step towards delivering the requirement to consult children in matters affecting their lives. The UNCRC is also reflected in the children and young people's policies adopted by the regional governments in the UK. An example is the Welsh Assembly Government's *Seven Core Aims for Children and Young People* (2009), which makes explicit reference to the UNCRC.

Devolution

Since 1999, regional governments have been established in Wales (The Welsh Assembly Government) and Scotland (The Scottish Executive). There has also been a regional government in Northern Ireland (The Northern Ireland Assembly) since 2007 (there have been various attempts to establish devolved administrations prior to this but due to political disagreements, the province has alternated between periods of devolved rule and direct administration from London). Each regional government has responsibility for a wide range of domestic affairs, including all matters relating to children and young people. Consequently, each province has its own separate policies and practices, and an example of this is in early years education and childcare. The next section will consider the separate policies that are in place.

Some influential policies

There have been a number of policy initiatives that have had a significant influence on early years practices in recent years. The specific initiatives examined in this section will be the Green Paper *Every Child Matters*, the Children's Workforce Development Council, the Sure Start and Flying Start early intervention programmes and the Early Years curriculum. The latter is not a single policy and there are different curricula in existence in England, Wales, Scotland and Northern Ireland, each of which will be looked at separately.

Every Child Matters

As mentioned above, *Every Child Matters* (ECM) was published in 2003 in the aftermath of the Laming report but also incorporated some other government plans in existence at the time. The initial document was followed by two further publications: *Every Child Matters: Next Steps* (DfES, 2004a) and *Every Child Matters: Change for Children* (DfES, 2004b), and ultimately led to the Children Act 2004. Five outcomes for all children plus a detailed framework for achieving these were identified. Carter (2009: 64) provides a summary of the ECM outcomes framework:

- **Be healthy**: physically, mentally and emotionally, healthy lifestyles, sexually healthy, choose not to take illegal drugs. Eating and learning to eat well, being happy, learning profitably, being sensibly cautious of danger.
- **Stay safe**: from maltreatment, neglect, violence, and sexual exploitation, from accidental injury and death, bullying and discrimination, crime and antisocial behaviour and have security, stability, and are cared for, avoiding dangers, lack of abuse, harm, or exposure to danger.
- **Enjoy and achieve**: ready to learn, attend and enjoy the setting, achieve appropriate capabilities for age, personal and social development and enjoy recreation and increasing capabilities.
- **Make a positive contribution**: begin to make choices, enjoy routines and positive behaviour, develop positive relationships and begin to understand others, develop self-confidence and successfully deal with significant challenges.
- **Achieve economic well-being**: live in decent homes and sustainable communities, have access to transport and material goods, live in households free from low income, start to communicate with others and begin the process of gaining basic skills.

The aim of ECM was to improve the way that the various agencies involved with children communicated and worked together and achieve a greater partnership between childcare providers, schools, social services, health services, police and probation services.

In the past it was argued that many children and families received poor treatment because of a failure of the various agencies to work together and share information effectively. An example was children with disabilities who relied on health services, the education system, the voluntary sector and social services in order to improve their lives but were often subject to multiple assessments and uncoordinated services (Baldock et al., 2013). One way in which ECM aimed to make this situation better was by improving the way in which information between the various agencies was shared. Specific steps taken included the **Common Assessment Framework (CAF)**, which was an assessment that could be used by any front-line professional working with a child or family with additional needs, the introduction of the role of the **Lead Professional (LP)** who would coordinate the delivery of interagency services, and the **ContactPoint** database to facilitate the sharing of information between agencies. The ContactPoint database contained information such as the agencies involved with the child and family, the lead professional involved and if a CAF had been completed. The creation of this database generated some controversy from groups concerned about privacy and risks of unauthorised access. The database was implemented, but was discontinued following a change of government in 2010.

Other ways in which ECM influenced work with children included the appointment of Children's Commissioners for England and Wales who are responsible for promoting the views and interests of children inside and outside Parliament, the appointment of a minister for young people, children and families, the establishment of the roles of Director of Children's Services and lead council member for children in every local authority. ECM also influenced the ongoing development of the SureStart early intervention programme and developments in education and training of childcare workers.

The Children's Workforce Development Council

In her overview of early years policy and practices in England, McGillivray (2007) points out that there are many different occupations involved in education and childcare settings, including nursery nurses, childminders, classroom assistants and nursery assistants. The workforce is predominantly female and the pay and status of such jobs has tended to be low. The recognition of the need to raise the status of such work can be seen in policy documents like the *National Childcare Strategy* (DfEE, 1998) and in the research findings from the EPPE project (Sylva et al., 2003) which indicated that effective childcare settings were often led by graduates. Such concerns led to the establishment of the **Children's Workforce Development Council (CWDC)** in 2005. One of the first initiatives launched by the CWDC was the establishment of training pathways for graduates working in childcare settings in England to achieve **Early Years Professional Status (EYPS)**. Such professionals would take a lead role in the provision of high-quality care. EYPS was intended to be broadly comparable with Qualified Teacher Status for professionals working with children aged 0–5 in the private, voluntary and independent sectors. By 2011, there were 8372 such professionals working in early years settings in England (Hadfield and Jopling, 2012). However, since April 2013, the CWDC has ceased to exist and its functions have been taken over by the newly established **Teaching Agency** and from September 2013, the EYPS role will be replaced by that of **Early Years Teacher**.

Sure Start

It is widely accepted that the poorest families suffer from inadequate housing, lack of training and employment opportunities, and a greater vulnerability to illness and mental health problems. The stresses associated with these conditions may also contribute to family breakdown or poor parenting. The resulting negative consequences for children may impact on their emotional, social and cognitive development making them more likely to suffer the same problems as their parents in later life, thus creating a cycle of disadvantage in families. However, there is evidence that early intervention programmes can improve the outcomes for such children. An example from the USA is Project Health Start which was launched in the 1960s to improve the school achievement of children from deprived families. The aim was to implement early interventions to boost the cognitive and linguistic development of the children and prepare them for entry to infant school by giving them the skills that they would not receive at home (Smith et al., 2011). This programme appeared to be a success and a study by Weikart (1996) which followed up on children from one such programme who were now in their twenties showed higher levels of literacy, school achievement and income and lower levels of criminality compared to a control group who had not experienced the intervention.

In England, an early intervention programme called **Sure Start** which aimed to end child poverty by providing a variety of services to children in deprived areas and their families was launched in 1998. A network of 250 **Sure Start Local Partnerships (SSLPs)** were set up in areas with the highest concentrations of 4-year-olds living in poverty. Services provided by SSLPs included playgroups, toy libraries, postnatal support for mothers, health education, and childcare to allow parents to attend adult education and training courses. Decisions about the specific services to be provided were made by the local programmes in consultation with the parents and organisations involved in delivery.

Following the publication of *Every Child Matters* (DfES, 2003) SSLPs became **Sure Start Children's Centres**. These centres are controlled by local authorities and provide services such as childcare, parenting skills support and health and employment advice.

The effectiveness of the programme was monitored through a research project run by the National Evaluation of Sure Start, and the first report (Tunstill et al., 2005) indicated that the programme was not having as much success as hoped for. Various practical problems in implementing Sure Start were noted, including tensions between local and national provision and a lack of engagement by some parents who distrusted professionals and did not wish to allow them or volunteers into their homes. However, more recently evidence of a number of positive impacts of Sure Start have been noted (NESS, 2010). These include positive health outcomes for children in Sure Start programmes, for example better physical health and lower BMIs. Mothers participating in the programmes reported providing a more stimulating and less chaotic home life for their children, less use of harsh discipline, fewer depressive symptoms and greater life satisfaction.

Flying Start

This is an early intervention programme launched in Wales by the Welsh Assembly Government (WAG) in 2005. As with Sure Start in England, it aims to improve the long-term prospects for children in deprived areas. The project is funded by the WAG but delivered by local authorities. **Flying Start** is targeted at areas where over 45 per cent of children in local schools are entitled to free school meals (Wyn Siencyn and Thomas, 2007). In these areas, the services are delivered via **Integrated Children's Centres**, some of which are attached to local primary schools. Services provided include free childcare for children aged 2–3 years, parenting support programmes, and programmes to develop early language and literacy skills through activities such as language and playgroups and 'books for babies' initiatives. There are also dedicated health visitors who provide intensive support to Flying Start children and their families and seek to identify needs for intervention at an early stage. In 2012, the WAG announced additional funding for the Flying Start programme with the aim of doubling the number of families benefiting (WAG, 2012a), indicating that this programme is likely to be a major part of the strategy to tackle child poverty for years to come.

The early years curriculum

Following the advent of devolution, responsibility for early years education in Wales, Scotland and Northern Ireland has been transferred to the respective regional administrations. The Department for Education (DfE) continues to oversee provision for England. As a result there are now separate early years curricula for England, Wales, Scotland and Northern Ireland. A brief overview of these curricula follows.

England

Prior to 2008, there were two policy documents covering early years education in England. *Birth to Three Matters* (Sure Start, 2003) set out a framework for practitioners working with infants and preschool children while *Curriculum Guidance for the Foundation Stage* (QCA, 2000) covered the curriculum for children starting school. However, in 2008, these two documents were merged to become the **Early Years Foundation Stage** (EYFS) (DCFS, 2008). The aim was to create a single framework for the care and education of children under the age of 5. The EYFS therefore removes the distinction between early childcare and education, and applies to all early years settings including childminders, nurseries and schools. The revised EYFS came into force in September 2012; it aims to promote school readiness and specifies seven areas of learning that must shape all learning experiences in early years settings. These are divided into three prime areas:

- communication and language
- physical development
- personal, social and emotional development

and four specific areas:

- literacy
- mathematics
- understanding the world
- expressive arts and design.

Within each of these areas of learning, there are specified **early learning goals** which are used to identify the skills children should have gained by the end of their reception year. Initially there were 69 learning goals but this has been reduced to 17 in the current version of the EYPS (DfE, 2012). Examples of early learning goals include listening and understanding (communication and language development), reading and writing (literacy), and managing feelings and behaviour (personal, social and emotional development).

The curriculum is taught through a mix of adult-led and child-initiated activities, the balance of these to be decided by the adult. The EYFS also makes the assumption that play is an important means by which children learn and develop and stresses the importance of implementing activities *'through planned, purposeful play'* (DfE, 2012: 6). The balance of adult-led and child-initiated activities is left for practitioners and settings to decide but there is an assumption that the balance will shift to more adult-led activities as the child gets older.

The progress of the child is determined by ongoing observations by the practitioners. There are two statutory assessment requirements. First is a progress check at the age of 2 in which practitioners must provide parents with a short written summary of their child's progress in the prime areas of learning, identifying any strengths or areas where progress is less than expected. Where any concerns are identified, there is an expectation that a targeted plan is put in place to support the child's learning and development involving other professionals such as the provider's Special Educational Needs Coordinator. The second formal assessment is the **Early Years Foundation Stage Profile (EYFSP)** which is completed in the final term of the year in which the child reaches the age of 5. Each child's level of development is assessed against the early learning goals and practitioners are required to indicate if the child is meeting the expected levels of development, if they are exceeding these levels or not yet meeting the expected levels. In addition to being provided to the parents, a copy of the child's EYFSP is also provided to the Year 1 teacher who can then use it to help the child make the transition to Year 1.

Wales

Prior to the establishment of the WAG, there were some differences between the school curriculum in Wales and England, in particular regarding the provision of education in Welsh. Since 1990, Welsh has been a compulsory subject in all Welsh schools and is taught as a first language in Welsh-medium schools and as a second language in English-medium schools. However, more recently, concerns were expressed about the nature of learning experiences in the early years in Wales including children spending too much time doing tasks at tables and having insufficient opportunities to develop language skills by talking about their activities. Concerns were also expressed about a lack of focus on children's creative expression and cultural awareness and cultural understanding, and the introduction of formal reading and writing before children were ready (Wyn Siencyn and Thomas, 2007). Such concerns led to the proposal for a new **Early Years Foundation Phase** for children aged 3–7 being set out in a document *The Learning Country* (WAG, 2003). This is a curriculum that spans both preschool settings and the initial years of primary education, and the current framework for this phase (WAG, 2012b) specifies seven areas of learning:

- Personal and social development, wellbeing and cultural diversity.
- Language literacy and communication skills.

- Mathematical development.
- Welsh language development.
- Knowledge and understanding of the world.
- Physical development.
- Creative development.

The foundation phase was piloted in 41 settings between 2005 and 2008, and the implementation was monitored by the *Monitoring and Evaluation of the Effective Implementation of the Foundation Phase (MEEIFP) Project Across Wales* (Siraj-Blatchford et al., 2006). The EYFS was fully implemented in all schools and care settings from 2008 onwards and continues to form the basis for early years education in Wales.

Play assumes a central role in the delivery of the EYFS curriculum and the framework document states *'children learn through first-hand activities with the serious business of "play" providing the vehicle. Through their play, children practice and consolidate their learning, play with ideas, experiment, take risks, solve problems, and make decisions, individually, in small and in large groups'* (WAG, 2012b: 4). The EYFS curriculum is also influenced by what are seen as successful early years programmes such as that employed in the Italian city of Reggio Emilia and the Te Whariki curriculum in New Zealand in which children are encouraged to be active and are consulted in decisions about their learning (WAG, 2003).

At the end of the **foundation stage**, practitioners are required to complete an 'Early Years Foundation Stage Profile' (WAG, 2012b) for each child which summarises the child's attainments in the seven areas of learning, and three **learning characteristics** (playing and exploring, active learning and creating and thinking critically). There are 17 specific **learning goals** related to the main areas of learning and for each goal the practitioner is required to judge whether the child is meeting the expected level of development, exceeding the expected level of development or not yet reaching this level. These judgements are also accompanied with a short narrative describing the child's three learning characteristics. Information from the profile is shared with the child's Year 1 teacher and is used to aid the transition of the child from the foundation stage to Year 1 of primary education.

Scotland

In August 2010, a new curriculum, the **Curriculum for Excellence (CfE)**, was introduced in Scotland with the aim of providing a more developmentally appropriate curriculum. Proposals for this curriculum had been set out previously in a document of the same name by the Scottish Exececutive (2005). This curriculum is not just for early years, but in fact aims to provide 'a coherent and enriched curriculum from 3 to 18' (Education Scotland, 2013). The CfE consists of five levels:

- **Early level**, covering the preschool years and primary 1 (P1).
- **First level**, covering primary years 2–4 (P22, P3 and P4).

- **Second level**, covering primary years 5–7 (P5, P6 and P7).
- **Third/fourth level**, covering the first to third years of secondary education (S1, S2 and S3).
- **Senior phase**, covering the fourth to sixth years of secondary education (S4, S5 and S6).

The early level of the CfE, like the EYFS in Wales is very much based on play and active learning. Similarly, in *A Curriculum for Excellence: Building the Curriculum 2*, the Scottish Executive states:

> *Active learning is learning which engages and challenges children's thinking using real-life and imaginary situations. It takes full advantage of the opportunities for learning presented by: [spontaneous play; planned, purposeful play; investigating and exploring; events and life experiences; focused learning and teaching.]* (Scottish Executive, 2007: 5)

An important point about the levels in the CfE is that children may move up at different times and are not required to progress to the next level until they are ready to do so, and there is an explicit recognition that some children will start learning at the different levels earlier and others later depending on their individual needs and aptitudes.

The CfE aims to develop four **capacities** in children enabling them to become successful learners, confident individuals, responsible citizens and effective contributors. It consists of three **core subject areas** – health and wellbeing, literacy, and numeracy – and eight **curriculum areas** – expressive arts, health and wellbeing, languages, mathematics, religious and moral education, sciences, social studies, and technologies. Teachers and practitioners are required to ensure that the core subject areas are represented in lessons in the specific curriculum areas and in this way the aim is to provide a holistic, joined-up curriculum.

Information about children's progress through the CfE is provided by means of report cards and parent–teacher consultations, and during the final year of primary education (P7) a profile for each child is produced detailing their achievements, with the aim of helping their transition to secondary school.

Northern Ireland

Since 2007, a foundation stage has been implemented in schools in Northern Ireland which covers the first two years of primary education, the proposals for which were first set out in two documents by the Northern Ireland Council for the Curriculum, Examinations and Assessment (CCEA, 2004, 2005). These in turn were based on findings from an intervention called the **Enriched Curriculum** which had been piloted in 120 schools in Northern Ireland from 1999 (CCEA, 1999). The aim of the enriched curriculum was to provide a less formal and more developmentally appropriate approach to early primary education with a greater involvement for play-based and child-led activities. Initial evaluations of this approach indicated its effectiveness; for example, despite a later introduction of reading and writing in the enriched curriculum, children exposed to it were performing at the same level at Year 4 as children exposed to the traditional, formal curriculum. There was also a generally positive reaction to the quality of the learning experience from both teachers and parents (Walsh, 2007).

The current foundation phase consists of seven areas of learning (CCEA, 2006):

- Language and literacy.
- Mathematics and numeracy.
- The arts.
- The world around us.
- Personal development and mutual understanding.
- Physical development and movement.
- Religious education.

Like the foundation stage in Wales, play is given an important role in the delivery of the curriculum: *'Children should have opportunities to experience much of their learning through well-planned and challenging play. Self-initiated play helps children to understand and learn about themselves and their surroundings'* (CCEA, 2006: 6). The guidelines for the foundation phase also set out a variety of other requirements for effective delivery such as working in partnership with parents and involving children in planning, reviewing, and reflecting on their learning. Ongoing assessment of progress is based on teacher observations, and at the end of each year of the foundation phase there is a requirement to produce a pupil profile detailing the child's learning and attainment and any issues that have been noted.

Chapter summary

- Policies and practices in relation to the early years do not occur in a vacuum, there are a variety of factors that influence their development such as the wider social and cultural climate of a society and political agendas of governments.
- Policies can also be influenced by significant events that may highlight shortcomings in current provision and practices in relation to children and young people, and by the need to satisfy the requirements of international treaties such as *The United Nations Convention on the Rights of the Child*.
- *Every Child Matters* was a government initiative to improve the provision of services for children and get the various agencies working with children to work in a more coordinated manner.

- There has also been an interest in raising the status, training and pay of individuals working with children and an example of this was the establishment in England of the Children's Workforce Development Council.
- Sure Start and Flying Start are examples of early intervention programmes whose aim is to improve the life prospects of children from deprived families.
- There are separate early years curricula in operation in England, Wales, Scotland and Northern Ireland, but all share a number of common features including a move away from more formal approaches to teaching and learning, a more interactive and child-centred approach to teaching, and incorporating child-led as well as adult-led activities in the classroom.

Further reading

Baldock, P., Fitzgerald, D. and Kay, J. (2013) *Understanding Early Years Policy* (3rd edn). London: Sage.
A good summary of the nature of early years policy, how policies are developed and implemented, and their implications for the work of practitioners.

Useful websites

http://www.education.gov.uk/
The website for the UK Department for Education which has responsibility for all aspects of early years policy in England.

http://wales.gov.uk/?lang=en
The website for the Welsh Assembly Government, from which information can be obtained about the various policies in relation to children and young people in Wales.

http://www.educationscotland.gov.uk/
The website for Education Scotland, the Scottish government agency responsible for policy on preschool and school education in Scotland.

http://www.ccea.org.uk/
The website of the Council for the Curriculum, Examinations and Assessment (CCEA), the government body responsible for overseeing the school curriculum in Northern Ireland.

References

Baldock, P., Fitzgerald, D. and Kay, J. (2013) *Understanding Early Years Policy* (3rd edn). London: Sage.
Bronfenbrenner, U. (1979) *The Ecology of Human Development*. Cambridge, MA: Harvard University Press.

Carter, M. (2009) 'Managing legislation and policy', in H. Fabian and C. Mould (eds), *Development and Learning for Very Young Children*. London: Sage. pp. 59–75.

Clark, M. and Waller, T. (eds) (2007) *Early Childhood Education and Care: Policy and Practice*. London: Sage.

Council for the Curriculum, Examinations and Assessment (CCEA) (1999) *Developing the Northern Ireland Curriculum to Meet the Needs of Young People, Society and the Economy for the 21st Century*. Belfast: CCEA.

Council for the Curriculum, Examinations and Assessment (CCEA) (2004) *Planning for the Foundation Stage*. Belfast: DENI.

Council for the Curriculum, Examinations and Assessment (CCEA) (2005) *Update on the Proposed Foundation Stage*. Belfast: CCEA.

Council for the Curriculum, Examinations and Assessment (CCEA) (2006) *Understanding the Foundation Stage*. Belfast: CCEA.

Department for Children, Schools and Families (DCSF) (2008) *Statutory Framework for the Early Years Foundation Stage*. London: DCFS.

Department for Education (DfE) (2012) *Statutory Framework for the Early Years Foundation Stage*. London: DfE.

Department for Education and Employment (DfEE) (1998) *Meeting the Childcare Challenge*. London: HMSO.

Department for Education and Skills (DfES) (2003) *Every Child Matters* (Green Paper). London: HMSO.

Department for Education and Skills (DfES) (2004a) *Every Child Matters: Next Steps*. London: DfES.

Department for Education and Skills (DfES) (2004b) *Every Child Matters: Change for Children*. London: DfES.

Department for Education and Skills/ Local Government Association (DfES/LGA) (2001) *Childcare and Early Education – Investing in All Our Futures*. London: DfES.

Department of Education and Science (DES) (1967) *Children and Their Primary Schools* (Plowden Report). London: HMSO.

Education Scotland (2013) 'What is Curriculum for Excellence?' Available at: http://www.education scotland.gov.uk/thecurriculum/whatiscurriculumforexcellence/index.asp (accessed 15 March 2013).

Hadfield, M. and Jopling, M. (2012) *Second National Survey of Practitioners with Early Years Professional Status* (Research Report DFE-RR239a). London: DfES.

Laming, Lord H. (2003) *The Victoria Climbié Inquiry: Report of an Inquiry by Lord Laming*. London: HMSO.

McGillivray, G. (2007) 'England', in M. Clark and T. Waller (eds), *Early Childhood Education and Care: Policy and Practice*. London: Sage. pp. 19–50.

National Evaluation of Sure Start (NESS) (2010) *The Impact of Sure Start Local Programmes on Five Year Olds and Their Families* (Research Brief DFE-RR067). London: DfE.

Qualifications and Curriculum Authority (QCA) (2000) *Curriculum Guidance for the Foundation Stage*. London: QCA.

Scottish Executive (2005) *A Curriculum for Excellence*. Edinburgh: Scottish Executive.

Scottish Executive (2007) *A Curriculum for Excellence: Building the Curriculum 2. Active Learning in the Early Years*. Edinburgh: Scottish Executive.

Siraj-Blatchford, I., Sylva, K., Laugharne, J., Milton, E. and Frances, C. (2006) *Monitoring and Evaluation of the Effective Implementation of the Foundation Phase (MEEIFP) Project Across Wales*. Cardiff: WAG.

Smith, P.K., Cowie, H. and Blades, M. (2011) *Understanding Children's Development* (5th edn). Chichester: Wiley.

Sure Start (2003) *Birth to Three Matters: A Framework to Support Children in Their Earliest Years*. London: DfES/SureStart.

Sylva, K., Melhuish, E., Sammons, P., Siraj-Blatchford, I. and Taggart, B. (2004) *The Effective Provision of Pre-School Education (EPPE) Project: Findings from Pre-School to End of Key Stage 1*. London: Sure Start.

Sylva, K., Melhuish, E., Sammons, P., Siraj-Blatchford, I., Taggart, B. and Elliot, K. (2003) *The Effective Provision of Pre-School Education (EPPE) Project: Findings from the Pre-School Period* (Research Report Brief 2503). London: DfES.

Tunstill, J., Allnock, D., Akhurst, S. and Garbers, C. (2005) 'Sure Start local programmes: Implications of case-study data from the National Evaluation of Sure Start', *Children and Society*, 19 (2): 158–71.

United Nations (1989) *The United Nations Convention on the Rights of the Child*. Geneva: United Nations.

Walsh, G. (2007) 'Northern Ireland', in M. Clark and T. Waller (eds), *Early Childhood Education and Care: Policy and Practice*. London: Sage. pp. 51–82.

Weikart, D. (1996) 'High quality preschool programs found to improve adult status', *Childhood*, 3 (1): 117–20.

Welsh Assembly Government (WAG) (2003) *The Learning Country: Foundation Phase 3–7 Years*. Cardiff: WAG.

Welsh Assembly Government (WAG) (2009) *Seven Core Aims for Children and Young People*. Available at: http://wales.gov.uk/topics/childrenyoungpeople/rights/sevencoreaims/?lang=en (accessed 15 March 2013).

Welsh Assembly Government (WAG) (2012a) *Flying Start*. Available at: http://wales.gov.uk/topics/childrenyoungpeople/parenting/help/flyingstart/?lang=en (accessed 15 March 2013).

Welsh Assembly Government (WAG) (2012b) *Framework for Children's Learning for 3 to 7-Year Olds in Wales*. Cardiff: WAG.

Wyn Siencyn, S. and Thomas, S. (2007) 'Wales', in M. Clark and T. Waller (eds), *Early Childhood Education and Care: Policy and Practice*. London: Sage. pp. 135–66.

Researching Child Development

Why you should read this chapter

Progress in any field of child development is crucially dependent on research. However, designing a research study in any area of child development is not a task to be taken lightly. There are many different types of research method available, and for each one there are various factors that must be taken into account in order to produce a piece of research that makes a useful contribution. This chapter aims to introduce you to the overall approach taken to the study of child development, and also give you an overview of the methods and ethical issues involved.

By the end of this chapter you should

- appreciate the specific ethical issues related to conducting research with children
- be familiar with the overall features of the scientific approach
- understand some general research concepts
- be aware of the various methods available to study child development and their strengths and limitations.

Ethics in research with children

Before examining approaches to researching child development, it is important to consider the issue of ethics. An important consideration in conducting any research study with human participants is a concern for their wellbeing during and after the study. This may seem an obvious point, but in fact such concerns have not always been high on researchers' lists of priorities. For example, a famous and controversial experiment on obedience to authority was conducted by Milgram in 1963 wherein he deceived adult participants into thinking they had given electric shocks to an individual in response to commands from the experimenter. While the research was very informative about the issue of obedience to an authority figure, there were concerns about the welfare of several of the participants in the study (who had become very distressed during the experiment) and such concerns resulted in ethical issues receiving a higher priority in the planning and conduct of research studies.

Today, any research study with human participants has to go through a process of ethical approval (such as scrutiny by a university or health authority ethics panel), and various professional bodies, such as the British Psychological Society and the British Educational Research Association, have explicit codes of ethics. Many of the ethical considerations for doing research with adults also apply to children, but with them there are additional considerations to take into account.

Informed consent is an important principle. This means that the participant is aware of the purpose of the study and what will be required of the individual. Participants also need to be aware of their right to withdraw from a study if they become uncomfortable with taking part. With older children, it is not too difficult to obtain such consent, but what about younger children? Young children may not fully understand their rights in a situation, or any information they are given about the study. In these cases, we rely on parents to provide this consent, and we must make all of the relevant information available to them.

Another important principle is to **do no harm**. While no researcher would intentionally set out to cause harm or distress to a child, the possibility of such effects must always be considered. Some studies may involve a child being restrained in a particular manner (e.g. if any physiological measures are being taken). Some procedures may cause distress to the child, even if only for short periods (e.g. studies in which children are briefly separated from their caregivers). Even some seemingly innocuous tasks may cause distress (e.g. a child unable to solve a puzzle provided by the experimenter and becoming upset and frustrated). A researcher must always take such possibilities into account and have steps in place to deal with any negative effects. In some cases, this may involve following up participants for a period after the study has ended. Ethics panels also have to consider the trade-off between any short-term distress to the participants and any long-term practical or theoretical gains that may come about as a result of a study.

Issues of **confidentiality** and *data security* are also important. Sometimes when assembling a participant group, the researcher may collect basic personal details such as home addresses, educational records, and so on. It is vital that access to such information is restricted only to the researcher and other appropriate individuals (such as their research supervisor), and such information should be stored in a secure manner and destroyed when it is no longer needed. It is also important to protect the anonymity of participants. When research is published, the findings must not be reported in a way that may allow an individual child to be identified. Sometimes with qualitative research, the researcher may wish to use direct quotes from participants when writing their report and if this approach is being used, then permission to use the information provided in this manner should be obtained from the children or parents beforehand. Often, the researcher may be asked to provide a report of the study for parents or teachers, and again this should be written in a manner that is easy to understand, but should mainly provide an overall summary of the research and findings and not focus on individual children.

Another issue relates to giving advice to parents or teachers. Many child development researchers are academics or students rather than *practitioners* such as educational or clinical psychologists. Occasionally a researcher may be asked by a worried parent if they think their child has a particular problem such as dyslexia, ADHD, or some other disorder. It is important to remember that being able to diagnose learning, emotional and behavioural problems is a specialised skill that cannot be undertaken without the relevant professional training. It is therefore important that a researcher does not attempt to make diagnoses of problems based on the performance of a child in their research study and instead refers the parent to more appropriate sources of information if they are concerned about their child.

The scientific approach

Understanding child development is not a concern that is unique to developmental psychologists, and indeed it is of crucial importance to many individuals, including teachers, health professionals and other professionals, who work with children, and, of course, to parents. There are many sources of information on child development. One popular source comes from what might be called 'common sense'. For example, most of us are aware of the advice 'spare the rod and spoil the child'. Our common-sense understanding of the world is full of such sayings that can be used to guide our understanding of children.

It could be argued that common sense is good enough. After all, adults have successfully raised and educated children for many years before the formal establishment of child development as a field of study. To a certain extent this cannot be argued with, but we also have to be aware of the limitations of common sense:

- Many contradictions: for example, if a parent is facing a period of separation from his or her children and is concerned about the effects on the parent–child relationship. What does common sense have to say? On the one hand, it may be beneficial ('absence makes the heart grow fonder'), whereas on the other, it may be detrimental ('out of sight, out of mind'). Which is the best advice? We simply do not know on the basis of these statements alone.
- Some common sense is plain wrong! Stanovich (2004) gives the example of bullying. For a number of years there was a notion in the media that bullies suffered from low self-esteem and this explained their behaviour towards others. However, more detailed research has shown that it is often the opposite that is true: bullying and aggression tend to be associated with high self-esteem.
- Some areas are not open to common-sense speculation. For example, how can we explain the problems encountered by autistic children? What are the causes of developmental dyslexia?

There are many other problems with common-sense approaches (see Stanovich, 2004). For these reasons, developmental psychologists (and indeed other professionals who work with children) will adopt a scientific approach when studying child development. The next section will outline some basic concepts related to this approach.

Researching child development: Basic concepts and terminology

Research using the scientific approach aims to formulate theories and test hypotheses about child development. This is done through the use of carefully designed studies and these should be reported in such a manner that the methodology and findings are clear and they can be replicated by other researchers. This section introduces some of the concepts and terminology relating to the scientific approach.

Hypothetico-deductive research

This is an approach to research that follows a number of stages. First, the scope of the problem is defined, and there is a broad assembly of all of the relevant information related to the topic. Sources of information can include past research as well as informal observations from parents, teachers or the researcher's own experience. Once the information is gathered, the researcher can formulate a **theory**: a general explanation about why a given behaviour occurs. From the theory, the researcher can deduce a **hypothesis**: a specific prediction about what will happen in a given situation. The hypothesis can then be tested in a research study, and the theory supported or amended accordingly.

For example, a researcher may be interested in understanding the causes of aggressive behaviour in children. Assembling all of the available observations may lead to the theory that aggression is a learned behaviour. This may then suggest a testable hypothesis: children exposed to violent cartoons will exhibit more aggressive acts in their subsequent play compared to children exposed to non-violent cartoons.

Inductive research

When there is a lack of detailed information on a topic, this is the initial gathering of facts that will allow the formation of a theory which can then be tested using the hypothetico-deductive approach.

Samples and populations

When we research an aspect of development in, say, 4-year-old children, we are unable to study the entire **population** of 4-year-olds. At any given time we can only test a limited number of such children, and this is our **sample**. However, most of the time, we hope our research will not just tell us something about the specific children in our study, but will be generally applicable to the wider population of 4-year-olds. We therefore need to consider how we can make our sample as representative as possible of the target population.

There are many ways of obtaining a sample, and the 'gold' standard for sampling is to obtain a **random sample**. This is where every member of the target population has the same chance or *probability* of being selected for inclusion in the study. Usually this approach involves compiling a list or database of all the members of the target population, and drawing a sample using a 'lottery'-style selection process. Such samples are very difficult to obtain in practice. Some researchers will have access to databases that allow such a random sample to be obtained (e.g. recent census data, child benefit lists, etc.). However, most researchers are restricted to using **convenience samples**: we use the children who are available to us and are willing to participate. Nevertheless, there are some steps that can be taken to improve on the quality of such samples.

Even within a convenience sample, you can use random selection. For example, you may have access to 40 children but won't have time to study all of them and you need to select 20. One approach might simply be to ask for 20 volunteers. However, a problem with this approach is that the type of child who volunteers to participate in a study might be *qualitatively* different from the child not willing to volunteer (e.g. they may be more confident, more motivated, etc.). A better approach would be to use a random, lottery-style selection process: all of the children's names are placed in a container, shuffled and the first 20 names selected will form your sample. The idea is that this will reduce any **bias** (such as the sample containing a disproportionate number of highly motivated or confident children).

Other sampling approaches include **stratified random samples** (the population is divided into different groups or **strata** that are relevant to the study, such as socio-economic status, and children are selected randomly from each stratum); **purposive samples** (children who satisfy a particular criterion are targeted, for example children from single-parent households); **snowballing** (can be used for difficult to reach samples. The researcher starts off with a participant who is known to them, and the participant or their family then helps to recruit other participants. For example, a researcher wants to study the development of children with a rare genetic disorder, and may know a family with such a child who is willing to participate. This family in turn attends a local support group where it may be able to recruit further participants, who in turn may recruit others, creating a 'snowball' effect).

Operational definitions

When we study an aspect of children's behaviour or development, it is important to provide a clear statement of what constitutes the behaviour in question. For example, we may be interested in the development of memory in childhood. What do we mean by memory for the purposes of our study? Memory can encompass many skills: remembering to do things in future (prospective memory) remembering events or lists of words, recognising faces, etc. Any study will therefore have to provide a clear statement about what aspects of memory are being studied.

Quantitative and qualitative research

Ultimately, the end product of any such research will be a large body of information about the child's responses or behaviour in the study. In some cases, this information will be in the form of numerical data. For example, we may record how many words a child can read, how many items they can recall in a memory task, how long it took them to solve a problem, and so on. When we record our data in numerical format, we are conducting **quantitative** research, and will aim to subject our data to a statistical analysis.

In other investigations, however, we are not interested in measuring behaviour in numerical terms, we are more interested in the content of children's responses. What is of interest to us is what the children have to say about a particular topic (e.g. what do they understand by friendship?) or we are interested in other materials that they have produced (such as characteristics of drawings used to represent the children and their families). Research using this approach is referred to as **qualitative research**. Because of its focus on the subjective experience of the individual, research taking a qualitative approach tends to be less concerned with issues of objectivity and replicability compared to quantitative research.

Statistical significance

As mentioned above, when we conduct research in child development we are typically involving only a sample from the wider population. However, an important consideration is the extent to which the results observed in our sample generalise to the wider population. This is a central concern of quantitative research. If, for example, we compared the reading performance of two groups of children exposed to different methods of reading instruction, we may find that one group has higher reading scores. Can this difference be attributed to the different teaching methods? Or might it have nothing to do with the method of teaching used? It may simply be the case that when the reading skills of two groups of children are tested, then two different averages will be obtained anyway, and one group will obtain higher scores by chance alone. We decide between such possibilities by means of **statistical inference**. This involves a number of procedures called **statistical tests** that we apply to the data and they allow us to work out the exact probability that the results in our study were obtained by chance alone. If we can show that this is very low, then we can conclude that the result is **statistically significant**: the findings of a study are likely to apply to the wider population. In terms of the reading example, a significant difference would indicate that the difference between the two groups is most likely a result of the different methods of teaching reading (assuming, of course, that the study was designed properly and takes into account other factors that may influence reading development), and if the study was replicated on another sample from the same population, the result is likely to be repeated. How low does the probability have to be for us to conclude that a result is statistically significant? The convention is that we accept a result as being statistically significant if there is less than a 5% or 1% probability that it occurred by chance. The 5% (or 0.05) and 1% (or 0.01) criteria are known as **significance levels**. There are a number of different statistical tests that allow us to investigate the significance of the results of a quantitative research study.

Methods of data collection

An important feature of the scientific approach is that it involves the active collection of information or data. We don't simply rely on 'common sense', personal opinions, media reports or personal anecdotes to inform our accounts of child development. When we conduct research on child development, there are a variety of approaches at our disposal. Some methods are purely quantitative in nature, others purely qualitative, but others can involve the collection of both quantitative and qualitative data. It must also be said that many topics are amenable to several different methods of investigation. For example, an experimental study may be followed up by a more open-ended interview study in which the researcher may seek to further understand the reasons behind the children's responses in the experimental study.

Interviews

If we want to find out something about children, then an obvious approach is simply to ask the children themselves, and indeed such approaches are common. Interviews can be used to collect quantitative or qualitative data, and there are a number of approaches.

Clinical interviews are designed to be open-ended and allow the participants to answer in a flexible way, the aim being to gather a rich body of information that is not constrained by the researcher's knowledge of the topic. The interviewer should try to use a conversational style when interacting with children and the direction of the interview will very much depend on the responses given. And interviews may diverge widely according to who the interviewees are. Participants are encouraged to give detailed accounts of their thoughts and feelings on an issue. Piaget (1926) made use of this technique to investigate children's understanding of their worlds.

Such interviews do have the benefit of providing rich information about children's views, but this can also be a problem: organising the information and analysing it can be a lengthy and laborious process. Interviews have to be transcribed, and then a method of organising and coding the information needs to be developed. A number of useful qualitative techniques are available (see the section on qualitative approaches below), but the task of making sense of such interviews is not one to be underestimated.

An alternative approach is to use a **structured interview**, which means that all participants will be asked the same questions, using the same wording and in the same order. Such standardisation means that (at least in theory) all children are treated in the same way by the researcher, and is useful when time is limited, or where children tend to be reticent about talking to the researcher. Questions can be open-ended, or can require 'tick box' type answers (e.g. have you ever been bullied?), or **rating scales** (e.g. how much do you enjoy reading?). Responses from these interviews are easier to code and analyse, but they will not provide the depth of information that can be obtained using a clinical interview.

Some general points need to be taken into account when using interview studies. First of all, it may sometimes be difficult to gain accurate information from children, for example asking children about past events may place demands on their memory skills. The researcher also has to be aware that some children may respond in **socially desirable** rather than accurate ways. Interviews also require a good deal of language ability in the child so that they can understand the questions, and express their answers in a clear manner. With younger children it is important that the interviewer is able to express questions in child-friendly language.

Sometimes when working with young children a degree of creativity may be needed to overcome limitations in language or reluctance to talk. A good example of this can be seen in the work of Howard and colleagues (Howard, 2002; Howard et al., 2006) who were interested in the factors or 'cues' that children use to distinguish 'play' from 'not play' situations. Rather than use a conventional interview approach, they used a photograph sorting task. Children were presented with photographs of a variety of classroom activities and were asked to sort them into two piles: 'play' and 'not play'. Examining the photographs assigned to each pile then gave some idea of the children's view of play. Photographs classified as play typically involved activities on the floor rather than on the table; activities that they chose to do rather than were told to do were usually those in which adults had a peripheral rather than a central role.

Sometimes interviews can be delivered 'in disguise' through the use of a game format. For example, Jäger and Ryan (2007) were interested in the experiences of children who were in therapy and used a number of play-based methods in their research. One technique was the 'expert show' in which children played the role of a therapy expert on a radio phone-in show who was taking calls from children who were about to experience therapy. The researcher played the role of the children phoning the 'expert' for advice and in this way was able to investigate the experience of therapy including positive and negative aspects. In effect, a clinical interview was used but in a child-friendly format and the information gained was useful in helping the therapists to adapt and refine their therapeutic approach.

Observations

Observations can be a powerful method of collecting data on child development. As with interviews, they can be used to collect qualitative or quantitative data. They can also be conducted in naturalistic settings (such as the classroom or a playground) or in laboratory settings in which the researcher has more control over the environment.

There are a number of criteria for a good observational study. First of all, there is a need for a clear **operational definition** of the behaviour(s) to be observed. These should be phrased in terms of specific, observable acts (things that the observer can see or hear). The amount of time used for the observation also needs to be considered. The researcher should be able to observe a **representative sample** of the behaviour so the observation period may last from a period of minutes, to hours, depending on the behaviour to be analysed. For example, studies of social skills in children may need to be conducted over a long period of time, while situations where a behaviour occurs frequently (such as disruptive behaviour in a classroom) may require short periods.

When conducting observations, the researcher needs to be aware of the problem of **reactivity**: changes in behaviour as a result of being observed. The presence in a classroom of one or more observers with notebooks or video cameras is bound to have an effect on the children, and researchers need to consider ways of making the observation as unobtrusive as possible. It is often a good idea to visit and spend time in the environment in which the observation will take place so that you will become a familiar part of the children's everyday lives. They are then more likely to behave in their usual manner. Also, consideration needs to be given to how the researcher will behave in the observation setting, for example not making it obvious that notes are being taken.

In conducting the observation, there are a number of ways of recording behaviours. The researcher may just take **detailed descriptive notes** which would yield qualitative data. If the researcher is interested in a wide variety of behaviours and has decided on these in advance, they may create a **checklist** in which the behaviours of interest are listed and can be checked as they occur. If, on the other hand, the researcher is interested in specific behaviours, they may opt for **event sampling** wherein they record the circumstances in which a particular behaviour occurs (such as aggressive behaviour). Another data collection approach is **time sampling**. In this approach, the observation period is divided into a number of smaller intervals (such as dividing a 60-minute period into 12 sections of 5 minutes each) and the number of times a given behaviour occurs in each interval is recorded.

Sometimes a researcher may wish to not only standardise the conditions of the observational study but also control aspects such as the environmental conditions or the amount of exposure to a particular type of event. A good example is the use of the '**strange situation**' task for studying attachment in infants (Ainsworth et al., 1978). Here, the infant is exposed in controlled conditions to a stranger with and without the parents present and the infant's reaction is observed.

Experimental research

In an experiment, the aim is to make statements of cause and effect between behaviour and factors that are thought to influence behaviour. Experiments can take place in a laboratory, or in naturalistic settings such as a school or playgroup where they are referred to as **field experiments**.

The basic approach of any experiment is firstly to identify the factor that is thought to influence the behaviour of interest. This factor is known in experiments as the **independent variable**. The experimenter manipulates this variable, and as it is manipulated, the target behaviour is recorded to see if the manipulation has caused any changes to take place. This target behaviour is referred to as the **dependent variable**. However, the researcher is always conscious of the fact that there may be other variables that may also affect the dependent variable, and therefore in setting up the experiment, the researcher will aim to **control** for these.

For example, a researcher may be interested in comparing the effects of two different methods of teaching reading such as *phonics* versus *whole word* approaches (see Chapter 8) on reading achievement. The independent variable in this study is therefore the method of teaching reading and is manipulated under two **conditions**: children being taught via a phonics approach and children being taught via a whole word approach. The dependent variable here is children's reading achievement, and this is typically measured using a standardised reading test in which children have to identify a series of individual words graded in difficulty. However, the researcher also needs to be aware that many other factors can influence reading development, and will try to standardise these across the study (e.g. ideally all of the children in the study should be from similar socio-economic backgrounds, be of the same general intelligence and have similar levels of spoken language skills and reading skills to begin with). In manipulating the independent variable, the researcher should also ensure that factors such as the amount of time used for reading instruction and maybe even the age, sex and experience of the teacher are also standardised across the two conditions. Finally, children should be allocated to the phonics or whole word groups using **random allocation** to minimise the likelihood of bias (e.g. one group being allocated a disproportionate number of highly motivated children). If at the end of the school year, having taken into account all of these factors, there is still a consistent difference between the two groups, then the researcher is able to make statements of cause and effect on the relationship between the two variables.

There are a few other points to make about experiments. The experiment described in the previous section involved children being divided into two separate groups, and this is referred to as an **unrelated experimental design**. Some experimental studies may involve just one group of children tested on several occasions or tasks (e.g. being compared on the ability to solve concrete or abstract versions of a problem-solving task). This type of approach is known as a **related** or **repeated measures** design. Such designs have the advantage of reducing the effects of individual differences between the children because the same children are used in each condition (in the reading study example above the researcher also tried to do this by careful selection of children based on various criteria). However, the experimenter needs to be aware of **order effects** (a child's responses in one condition affected by their responses in a previous condition) or **practice effects** (if the same task is used repeatedly, improvements in performance may simply reflect a child just getting used to doing this task). This can be reduced using **counterbalancing** – varying the order of a task (e.g. half the children get task 'a' followed by task 'b'), and vice versa for the other children.

There are some situations where it is not possible to manipulate an independent variable directly or randomly assign children to different groups. This is often the case when the comparison of interest is between naturally occurring groups, such as 'normal' versus 'dyslexic' readers. In these situations, the researcher may conduct a **quasi-experiment** in which the group serves as a type of independent variable and the researcher will aim to introduce a degree of control by attempting to make sure the children are as similar as possible in other relevant variables.

Supposing a researcher wished to conduct an experiment to investigate if the accuracy of children's memories changes over time. Shortly after returning from a school trip she asked the children a series of questions about events that happened during the trip and noted the number of correct answers from each child. After a week, she asked the same set of questions to the same children and again noted the number of correct answers provided by each child. She was then able to compare the number of correct answers provided on each occasion.

a Would this experiment be a related or an unrelated design?
b What would be the independent variable?
c What would be the dependent variable?
d Can you think of any variables that the researcher would have to control for?

Experiments are the only research method that can allow researchers to make statements of cause and effect. However, this approach is not without its critics. Some researchers argue that the process of isolating an independent variable and then manipulating it while controlling all other relevant factors means that we are changing the natural situation in which behaviour occurs into something completely different – in other words experiments lack **ecological validity**. There is no doubt that some experiments, particularly laboratory experiments, do involve the use of contrived tasks (such as memorising lists of unrelated words). In some cases this is reasonable. For example, in researching aspects of cognition (for instance memory), a degree of experimental control can be used to shed light on the underlying mechanisms. However, more complex social phenomena (such as aggression), are probably less suitable for experimental research.

Correlational studies

Some research questions are not concerned with the effects of an independent variable on a dependent variable, but simply if there is a consistent relationship between two. For example, a researcher may be interested in the relationship between a child's spoken language and reading skills – is it the case that children with good spoken language skills also learn to read more easily? The study then involves the administration of a test of spoken language ability (e.g. a vocabulary test) and a test of reading ability to the children, and we can then investigate if there is a consistent relationship between the two. It may be that there is a **positive correlation** between the two (children with good spoken language scores also achieve good reading scores) or a **negative correlation** (children with good spoken language scores get lower reading scores). In order to determine the extent of this relationship, a measure of association called a **correlation coefficient** is calculated. This varies in value from −1 (perfect negative) through 0 (no relationship) to +1 (perfect positive relationship). The closer the value comes to −1, the stronger the relationship in a negative direction, the closer to +1, the stronger the relationship in a positive direction. So, for example, a correlation coefficient of 0.853 would indicate a strong positive correlation, a correlation coefficient of −0.355 would indicate a moderate negative correlation.

An important limitation is that a strong correlation does not imply a cause-and-effect relationship between the two variables. Supposing, for example, we found a strong positive correlation between children's spoken language and reading skills, what could this mean? It may be tempting to conclude that a child with a well-developed vocabulary has a good mental store of words onto which they can map newly encountered written words and hence there is a causal relationship. While this is not an implausible argument, the reason for the relationship could be in the opposite direction: children who are good at reading will read more books, exposing them to more language and vocabulary, and hence it is reading that influences spoken language development. On the other hand, it could be that there is no specific relationship between the two: it may be the case that intelligent children tend to acquire spoken language easily, and because they are intelligent they also tend to be good at reading and this is the reason for the correlation. The important point is that you cannot rule any of these explanations in or out purely on the basis of a correlation alone. A correlation tells us that a relationship exists in the first place, and further, more detailed research will be needed to uncover the reasons.

Case studies

A **case study** may focus on a specific child, family, group or organisation (such as a school or childcare setting). In fact a case can be defined as 'any single unit or entity, however large or small, with clear boundaries' (Greig et al., 2013: 189). There are no specific methodologies for case studies and researchers may use a variety of approaches for collecting data, including questionnaires, interviews, observations or official documents, depending on the specific issue. An early example of a case study is Leopold (1954), who observed and documented his daughter's acquisition of the English language when the family moved from Germany to the United States.

Qualitative approaches

There are many research approaches that are designed for the collection of qualitative data. Usually the actual data collection procedures may involve interviews and observations as described above, but with the collection of qualitative data. Other data collection approaches include participants keeping a diary or children being asked to produce drawings. This section will briefly outline thematic analysis, grounded theory, ethnography and the analysis of children's drawings.

Thematic analysis is a method of analysing qualitative data that allows for hypotheses to be tested. For example, a researcher may conduct an interview study of children's perceptions of play with the aim of understanding the factors that may influence those perceptions. Previous studies (see, for example, Howard, 2002) suggest that children use features such as the location of an activity (table/floor, indoors/outdoors), choice (voluntary/compulsory) and adult presence (present/absent) to distinguish play from non-play activities. In analysing the interview transcripts, the researcher may search for evidence of themes such as *location, choice* and *adult presence* in the children's responses to questions relating to the issue of what is play and can illustrate these themes using direct quotes from the children.

Grounded theory, like thematic analysis, involves the extractions of themes from the data, but unlike a thematic analysis there is no hypothesis to be tested, the idea being that the theory is located in or *grounded* in the data (Glaser and Strauss, 1967). Data is collected using techniques such as interviews, observations or diary keeping. The raw material therefore will be the interview transcripts, observation notes or diary contents. The first stage of the analysis is to extract specific themes or categories from the data. Related themes are then linked together and this process continues until the point of **saturation**, when no more themes emerge.

Ethnographic approaches focus on the description of a cultural or social group or system. An example is Whiting's study of child-rearing practices in different countries (1963) or Leavitt's study of emotional cultures in day-care settings (1996). A wide variety of methods can be used to collect information, including observation, interviews, analysis of artistic materials, stories or autobiographies. Often such studies require the researcher to become close to and even part of the group being studied, an approach known as **participant observation**.

Children's drawings can often be used to gain insights into their understanding of the world or their social and emotional development and wellbeing. There are a number of ways in which drawings can be analysed. Coolican (2006) suggests that these can include size or inclusion of various family members, parts of the body increases or the size of significant objects. Greig et al. (2013) have suggested that problems like anxiety can also be indicated in drawings through features such as intensity of line pressure, excessive shading, or figures being drawn excessively small. While drawings can be useful data-gathering tools, a number of points must be kept in mind. First of all the researcher needs to interpret the drawings according to the age and drawing ability of the child. Children are known to pass through a number of stages of drawing development (see, for example, Lowenfeld and Brittan, 1982) and therefore it is worth bearing in mind that such basic stages of development may also influence what is produced rather than other factors such as emotional influences. When using children's drawings as indicators of emotional problems or trauma, it is important to be aware of the possibilities of making false interpretations and ideally other sources of information should also be used here.

Methods for studying development

An important issue for developmental psychologists is the study of development over time and there are a variety of approaches for doing this. Two of the most commonly used are **cross-sectional designs** and **longitudinal studies**.

Cross-sectional designs

A cross-sectional design involves the study of children of different ages at the same point in time, for example comparing conceptions of friendship in children of different ages (see, for example, Damon, 1977). Cross-sectional designs provide a convenient method of comparing children of different ages but they do have limitations. One such limitation is that it is not possible to gain information about how an individual child changes over time, because cross-sectional designs only allow the study of group differences. As a result, how a child's performance at one age may influence their performance at a later stage cannot be assessed. Another limitation of cross-sectional designs is the issue of **cohort effects**. This is where differences in performance are not necessarily age-related, but may in fact be related to wider historical or social factors. For example, a study comparing British children born in 1992 and 1998 may need to bear in mind that children born in these years would have spent their first five years under different governments. As different governments will have different social, educational and economic policies, these may impact on children's family and schooling experiences which may in turn affect their performance or responses in a study. Consequently, differences may reflect wider social and historical factors rather than real developmental differences.

Longitudinal studies

Longitudinal studies involve the collection of information from a group of children over a period of time and each child is observed or tested repeatedly at various time points over the course of the study.

Some longitudinal studies can involve a large-scale investigation of diverse factors affecting child development. An example is the **Millennium Cohort Study** conducted in the UK from 2000 onwards (see, for example, Dex and Joshi, 2004) which is following the development and progress of 19,517 children born between 2000 and 2002 and sampled from child benefit records. The study looks at the influence of diverse factors on child development such as parenting, cognitive ability, health factors, housing, childcare, parental employment, and so on. Information has been collected at regular intervals, and so far the children have been followed up at the ages of 9 months, 3 years, 5 years and 7 years. The plan is to keep tracking the children up to adulthood (Centre for Longitudinal Studies, 2013).

Other longitudinal studies focus on specific aspects of development. For example, a number of such studies have been carried out on children's reading development (see, for example, Bryant et al., 1990; Wagner et al., 1994). These studies were particularly interested in cognitive skills that are predictive of later reading – in particular the role of phonological awareness (see Chapter 8). Children were first assessed in these skills before learning to read and then retested after one and two years of schooling. The children's reading was also tested after one and two years of schooling and researchers were able to look at the ability of a number of early phonological awareness measures to predict later reading achievement. Wagner et al. (1994) were also able to use their study to investigate the influence of reading on later phonological skills.

Longitudinal studies can be very informative about development; however, they can be resource-intensive and take a long time to complete. As with cross-sectional designs, there is also the possibility of cohort effects. And if children are assessed on the same task or measure repeatedly, there is the possibility of **practice effects** whereby improvements in performance do not necessarily reflect real developmental changes but that children simply got used to doing the test. There is also the problem of **attrition**: over time children may drop out of the study. This can sometimes be due to natural issues such as children moving away or changing schools. However, if a certain type of participant is more likely to drop out of a study (for example children from poor backgrounds), this may affect the representativeness of a sample and researchers may need to monitor the characteristics of those participants to see if there are any discernable patterns.

Consider the following examples of possible research studies. What method (experimental, correlational, observational, qualitative, etc.) would you adopt for each? Could the topic be investigated by more than one method?

a You wish to compare the effectiveness of two different types of therapeutic intervention on problem behaviours in children.
b You want to investigate how children cope with having a chronic illness.
c You want to see if children from larger families have better problem-solving abilities.
d You want to investigate if boys engage in more 'rough-and-tumble' play than girls.

Chapter summary

- In setting up a research study ethical considerations are just as important as the soundness of the methodology.
- Researchers in the field of child development aim to approach the topic using a scientific approach.
- There are a wide variety of methods available to study child development, and each method has its strengths and limitations.
- Studies on child development can result in the collection of quantitative or qualitative data.

Further reading

Greig, A., Taylor, J. and MacKay, T. (2013) *Doing Research with Children* (3rd edn). London: Sage.
An accessible text looking at the various research methods used in doing research with children as well as practical and ethical issues in conducting research.

Mercer, J. (2010) *Child Development: Myths and Misunderstandings.* Los Angeles, CA: Sage.
A useful book that sets out various 'common-sense' statements about child development and what research findings have to say about the validity of these statements.

Useful websites

http://www.bera.ac.uk/
The website of the British Educational Research Association (BERA) which aims to promote research in the field of education.

http://www.bps.org.uk/what-we-do/ethics-standards/ethics-standards
The section of the British Psychological Society's website dealing with professional and research ethics, including a link to access their code of ethics and conduct, an essential tool for all researchers in the field of child development.

References

Ainsworth, M.D., Blehar, M., Waters, E. and Wall, S. (1978) *Patterns of Attachment.* Hillsdale, NJ: Erlbaum.

Bryant, P.E., MacLean, M., Bradley, L. and Crossland, J. (1990) 'Rhyme and alliteration, phoneme detection and learning to read', *Developmental Psychology*, 26 (3): 429–38.

Centre for Longitudinal Studies (2013) *Welcome to the Millennium Cohort Study.* Available at: http://www.cls.ioe.ac.uk/page.aspx?&sitesectionid=851&sitesectiontitle=Welcome+to+the+Millennium+Cohort+Study (accessed 15 April 2013).

Coolican, H. (2006) *Introduction to Research Methods in Psychology*. London: Hodder Arnold.

Damon, W. (1977) *The Social World of the Child*. San Francisco, CA: Jossey-Bass.

Dex, S. and Joshi, H. (2004) *Millennium Cohort Study First Survey: A User's Guide to Initial Findings*. London: Centre for Longitudinal Studies, Institute of Education.

Glaser, B.G. and Strauss, A.L. (1967) *The Discovery of Grounded Theory*. New York: Aldine.

Greig, A., Taylor, J. and MacKay, T. (2013) *Doing Research with Children* (3rd edn). London: Sage.

Howard, J. (2002) 'Eliciting young children's perceptions of play, work and learning using the Activity Apperception Story Procedure', *Early Child Development and Care*, 172 (5): 489–502.

Howard, J., Jenvey, V. and Hill, C. (2006) 'Children's categorisation of play and learning based on social context', *Early Child Development and Care*, 176 (3&4): 379–93.

Jäger, J. and Ryan, V. (2007) 'Evaluating clinical practice: Using play-based techniques to elicit children's views of therapy', *Clinical Child Psychology and Psychiatry*, 12 (3): 437–50.

Leavitt, R.L. (1996) 'The emotional culture of infant-toddler daycare', in J.A. Hatch (ed.), *Qualitative Research in Early Childhood Settings*. Westport, CT: Praeger. pp. 1–19.

Leopold, W. (1954) 'A child's learning of two languages', in *Fifth Annual Georgetown University Round Table on Language and Linguistics*. Washington, DC: Georgetown University Press. pp. 19–30.

Lowenfeld, V. and Brittan, W.L. (1982) *Creative and Mental Growth* (7th edn). New York: Macmillan.

Milgram, S. (1963) 'Behavioral study of obedience', *Journal of Abnormal and Social Psychology*, 67 (4): 371–8.

Piaget, J. (1926) *The Language and Thought of the Child*. New York: Harcourt, Brace and World.

Stanovich, K.A. (2004) *How to Think Straight about Psychology*. Boston, MA: Allyn and Bacon, Pearson Education.

Wagner, R.K., Torgesen, J.K. and Rashotte, C.A. (1994) 'Development of reading-related phonological processing abilities: New evidence of bidirectional causality from a latent variable longitudinal study', *Developmental Psychology*, 30 (1): 73–87.

Whiting, B. (1963) *Six Cultures: Studies of Child Rearing*. New York: Wiley.

Cognition and Memory

4

Why you should read this chapter

Cognition refers to the systematic study of thinking and mental skills that allow us to process and use the information we acquire. It covers a variety of different skills including memory, attention, language, thinking and reasoning. Understanding the development of a child's thinking is important for a number of practical reasons. First of all, it is important to know the cognitive skills of a child at a given age. What type of problem-solving and reasoning tasks are they capable of? What is their understanding of the physical world? How can parents or teachers help to extend a child's understanding? This has important practical implications in education because a child's readiness to learn will be directly influenced by their level of cognitive development. Also, understanding the course of typical mental development can help us to comprehend the problems experienced by children with learning difficulties and can help to tailor appropriate support for them. However, there is also the issue that cognitive development is interesting in its own right. In a relatively short period of time, a baby develops from an infant of largely reflexive behaviours to a child capable of thinking about their world and interacting appropriately with it. Explaining this progress is an important task for developmental psychologists.

This chapter will focus on the two most influential theories of cognitive development: those of Piaget and Vygotsky. Both theories aim to provide very broad explanations of the development of a child's understanding and are meant to apply across a wide variety of tasks and situations, such as acquiring new information, problem solving and understanding the physical world. The other approach to understanding cognitive development is to look in detail at specific areas of cognition such as memory, attention, problem solving, and so on. Following the consideration of Piaget's and Vygotsky's theories, the structure of the human information-processing system will be outlined. Given the importance of memory in this account and the general importance of memory in everyday life, the development of this aspect of cognition will be examined in more detail.

By the end of this chapter you should:

- have a broad understanding of the theories of development proposed by Piaget and Vygotsky
- understand key Piagetian concepts, such as assimilation and accommodation
- understand key Vygotskian concepts, such as zone of proximal development
- appreciate the strengths and weaknesses of both theories
- be aware of practical applications in education
- be able to describe the basic structure of the human information-processing system
- understand key distinctions about memory, such as short-term (working) memory and long-term memory
- be aware of the factors that are associated with developmental increases in a child's memory ability.

Piaget's theory

Jean Piaget produced a theory of cognitive development that is still today regarded as the starting point for understanding the development of the child's mind. His theory was constructed through detailed and careful observation of his own children and by giving them various problem-solving tasks and noting their responses. Piaget saw children as active explorers of their environment who as they interact with it construct mental structures that allow them to process their worlds. This section will outline the main features of Piaget's theory, drawing on the accounts provided by Berk (2008) and Keenan and Evans (2009), followed by an evaluation of his views.

Basic concepts

Piaget referred to the mental structures that children construct as **schemas**. These are essentially ways of making sense of experience, and they change with age. Schemas change through the processes of **adaptation** and **organisation**.

Adaptation refers to the building of schemas as a result of interaction with the environment, and takes place through the processes of **assimilation** and **accommodation**. Assimilation refers to the use of existing schemas to make sense of the world. For example, an infant may discover that shaking a rattle causes it to make a noise and then applies this action to other toys so that they also make a noise. The child is assimilating other toys into his 'shaking' schema. Accommodation involves the creation of new schemas or the adjustment of old ones and occurs when current schemas do not fit with the environment. For example, the infant finds that shaking a toy does not produce a noise, but squeezing it does produce the desired outcome. A new schema is then created for interacting with objects. Piaget saw the balance between assimilation and accommodation as varying over time, and when there isn't very much change, children tend to assimilate more, a state he referred to as cognitive **equilibrium**. However, during periods of cognitive change, children are in a state of **disequilibrium** – they realise their existing schemas cannot deal with new information and they have to rely more on accommodation. After a period of modifying their schemas, children move back to equilibrium again, with assimilation as the dominant process.

Schemas also change through **organisation**. This is a mental process whereby the child organises the different schemas and links them to other schemas to create an interconnected system. So, for example, the child may relate 'shaking' to 'squeezing' to their understanding of different ways of interacting with objects.

Piaget saw the organisation of schemas as proceeding in a series of **stages**. A stage occurs when the schemas are qualitatively similar. He saw stages as occurring in a fixed order and as universal – they occur in all children, regardless of culture.

Stages of development

Piaget identified four stages of development: The **sensorimotor** period, the **preoperational** stage, the **concrete operations** stage and the **formal operations** stage. See Table 4.1 for a summary of these stages.

The sensorimotor period

This stage covers the first two years of the infant's life, and over this period infants move from simple reflexive behaviour to ultimately acquiring mental representations that allow then to think about their environment. The major development in this period is that the infant acquires a sense of **object permanence** – the realisation that objects continue to exist even when they cannot be seen. Given the amount of development over the first two years of life, Piaget (1953) divided this stage into a number of substages.

In the first month of life, infant behaviour consists in the main of practising and gaining control over basic reflexes such as sucking and grasping. This substage is referred to as **reflexive schemas**. At around 1 month, infants enter the substage of **primary circular reactions**. Infants are now gaining voluntary control over their actions and start to repeat chance actions that led to satisfying results, such as sucking their thumbs. By the end of this substage they can also adapt their behaviours to different features in the world, such as opening their mouths differently to a spoon than to a bottle.

From 4 to 8 months, infants move to the **secondary circular reactions** substage. Infants are now able to sit up and are more oriented to objects and events outside their own bodies. They use their secondary circular reactions to repeat interesting events caused by their own actions, such as hitting or kicking a mobile over their cot to make it move. However, Piaget did not see these behaviours as intentional; it was simple repetition of a newly acquired action with respect to a given object.

The next substage, **coordination of secondary circular reactions**, sees the beginnings of goal-directed or intentional behaviour. Infants aged 8 to 12 months are able to combine schemas into new and more complex action sequences and can use these to solve simple problems. This is illustrated by Piaget's object-hiding task in which he showed the infant an attractive toy which was then hidden under a cloth or beneath a cup. In this substage, he found that infants can find the toy by coordinating two schemas: 'pushing' away the obstacle and 'grasping' the toy. Piaget saw this means-end behaviour as the first example of intelligent behaviour and the foundation for all problem solving. The fact that infants can also find a hidden toy is seen as the beginning of a sense of object permanence; however, this is limited. Piaget observed that if an object is moved from one hiding place (A) to another (B), infants still looked for it in the first location, a tendency known as the A-not-B search error. Another development in this substage is the tendency to imitate the behaviours of others, for example stirring with a spoon.

Between the ages of 12 and 18 months, infants display **tertiary circular reactions**. Here they repeat and vary new actions. Infants can now solve the A-not-B task. Through approaching the world in a deliberately exploratory way, they become better at problem solving, for example pushing a shape through a hole by twisting and turning it until it falls through. They can also imitate more complex behaviours such as stacking blocks and making funny faces.

The final sensorimotor substage is called **invention of new means through mental combinations** and lasts from around the ages of 18 to 24 months. The child has now acquired the ability to think about their world using mental representations such as images (pictures in the mind) As a result, they can 'think' before they 'act'. Piaget observed that children at this stage often solve problems suddenly rather than engaging in trial-and-error behaviours and inferred that they are in effect mentally experimenting with actions demonstrating the ability to represent experiences internally. As a result of acquiring these mental representations, infants can now engage in **deferred imitation** – the imitation of past behaviours of others – and they can solve a more advanced version of the A-not-B task called invisible displacement (finding a toy that was moved while they were out of sight). Finally, infants can engage in pretend play wherein they act out imaginary situations.

The preoperational stage

This stage spans the period from 2 to 7 years of age and is characterised by a growth in representational ability. By the end of this stage, children are able to use language, numbers, visual and spatial representations and can engage in pretend play.

However, Piaget also noted that during this stage, children experience a number of limitations to their abilities. A major feature of children's thinking in this stage is **egocentrism**: they can only see situations from their own perspectives and are unable to consider other viewpoints. Piaget and Inhelder (1956) demonstrated this through the 'three mountains task'. In this task the child is seated at one side of a table and presented with a model landscape consisting of a number of mountains and landmarks. Some landmarks can only be seen from certain perspectives and the child is given the opportunity to see this by walking around the table. The child then returns to one side of the table and a doll is placed on the opposite side. The child is then presented with a set of photographs and asked to select the photograph that describes what the doll can see. Almost all preoperational children have difficulty with this task and select the photograph that shows their own vantage point.

Related to egocentrism is **animism** (Piaget, 1929), the belief that inanimate objects have lifelike qualities such as thoughts and feelings. Piaget argued that because children cannot think beyond their own perspective, they assume that flowers, rocks, etc. have human characteristics just as they do.

Another characteristic of preoperational thinking is an **inability to conserve**. This means that preoperational children fail to understand that certain aspects of an object or substance can remain the same despite changes in physical appearance. Piaget demonstrated this limitation in the thinking of preoperational children through the use of a number of different conservation tasks. A classic example of such a task involves liquid. Children are presented with two identical tall, thin glasses of water and asked if they contain the same amount. Once the child agrees that both glasses contain equal amounts of water, the water from one glass is then poured into a short, wide glass and the child is asked which glass has more, less or equal water. Preoperational children typically answer that the tall, thin glass has more water. There are three aspects of preoperational thought that contribute to the inability to conserve. Firstly their thinking is characterised by **centration**: they are influenced by visual appearances and can only focus on one aspect of the problem, in this case the height of the water in the glass. Secondly they fail to understand the notion of **compensation**, that the width of the shorter glass *compensates* for its lack of height. Thirdly, they fail to under-stand the principle of **reversibility**, the fact that the water in the short wide glass could be poured back into the tall, thin glass restoring the original state. They treat the initial and final states of the water as unrelated events, ignoring the event in between (the pouring of the water).

The concrete operational stage

This stage extends from 7 to 11 years of age. Children's thinking is now more logical and organised than in the earlier stages of development and they can think using mental operations. They are now able to solve the liquid conservation problem as described in the previous section. Children also develop the mental skills of **hierar-chical classification** and **seriation** (Inhelder and Piaget, 1964). Hierarchical classifi-cation refers to the ability to divide objects into meaningful classes and subclasses and this can be seen in children's hobbies at this stage – collections (e.g. stamps, sports cards, rocks) become common in middle childhood and children become skilled at sorting them in many different ways: such as sorting sports cards by team, player posi-tions, and so on (Berk, 2008). This is also demonstrated in Piaget's class inclusion problem. Here, children are presented with a picture of a bunch of flowers consisting of a number of roses and a larger number of tulips. They are then asked 'are there more tulips or more flowers?' Concrete operational children will correctly answer 'more flowers', indicating that they are now aware of the fact that tulips as well as being a class in their own right can also belong to the broader class of 'flowers' and therefore there must be more flowers than tulips. Seriation refers to the ability to order objects along a quantitative dimension, such as ordering a set of sticks from shortest to longest. This skill also allows children to solve **transitive inference** problems – for example, given the information John is older than James and James is older than Robert, they can correctly make the inference that John is older than Robert.

The formal operational stage

This is regarded by Piaget as the end point of cognitive development and occurs at around 11 years of age. It is the stage where children acquire the capacity to think in more abstract, systematic and hypothetical terms. Two major achievements here are **hypothetico-deductive reasoning** and **propositional thought**.

Hypothetico-deductive reasoning involves children solving a complex problem by firstly coming up with a 'theory' which describes all of the dimensions of a problem and possible factors that might affect the outcome. From the theory they can deduce testable 'hypotheses', which are predictions about factors that might affect the out-come. They will then test these hypotheses to ascertain whether the theory is supported or needs amending. Piaget demonstrated this using a pendulum problem (Inhelder and Piaget, 1958). Here, children and adolescents are presented with pieces of string of different lengths, a set of weights to attach to the strings and a bar from which to hang the strings. They are then asked to work out what influences the speed with which the pendulum swings through the arc. There are at the end of the string four factors: the length of the string, the weight, the height from which it is hung and how forcefully it is pushed. It has been found that formal operational children consider the possible factors in a systematic manner. They carry out experiments in which one factor at a time is manipulated while holding the other factors constant and they also test the variables in combination. Eventually they discover that the length of the string is the critical factor. This can be contrasted with the performance of concrete operational children who will test for one variable without holding others constant (for example testing the effects of string length but setting up a comparison involving a short string with a light object against a long string with a heavy object). They also fail to notice factors that are beyond the immediate, concrete materials provided such as the height of the pendulum or how forcefully it is pushed.

Table 4.1   Piaget's stages of cognitive development

Stage	Ages	Description
Sensorimotor	0 to 2 years	
• Reflexive schemes	0–1 months	Infants practise and gain control over basic reflexes
• Primary circular reactions	1–4 months	Repeat behaviours that lead to satisfying events
• Secondary circular reactions	4–8 months	Repeat interesting events caused by their own actions
• Coordination of secondary circular reactions	8–12 months	Beginning of goal-directed behaviour; combination of schemas into larger action sequences
• Tertiary circular reactions	12–18 months	Repeat and vary actions in an exploratory manner; Acquisition of sense of object permanence
• Invention of new means through mental combinations	18–24 months	Ability to think using representations such as mental images Beginnings of pretend play
Preoperational	2–7 years	Thinking is largely egocentric and animistic Lack of understanding of conservation, compensation and reversibility Centration: the ability to focus on only one aspect of a problem
Concrete operational	7–11 years	Child can now think using mental operations, able to solve conservation problems Able to construct classification hierarchies such as grouping objects into classes Able to order objects according to quantitative dimensions such as size Able to solve transitive inference problems
Formal operational	11+ years	End point of cognitive development, able to think in more abstract and logical manner Able to use hypothetico-deductive reasoning Ability to engage in propositional thought

Adapted from tables in Keenan and Evans (2009)

Propositional thought refers to the ability to make judgements about the validity of a statement (or proposition) based on logic alone, without referring to real-world circumstances. This type of reasoning was demonstrated in a study by Osherson and Markman (1974–75) who presented a pile of coloured poker chips to a group of concrete operational children and adolescents. The experimenter then hid a chip in her hand and asked them to judge the truth of a series of statements such as 'either the chip in my hand is green or not green' or 'the chip in my hand is green and it is not green'. With the chip hidden from view, only the adolescents were able to make the correct true/false responses. They were able to understand that on logical grounds alone, an 'either-or' statement will always be true while an 'and' statement would always be false, regardless of the colour of the chips. On the other hand, concrete operational children could only judge the statements if they could see the chips. Propositional thought is part of a wider change in cognitive ability that allows formal operational children to think in more mature and abstract ways without reference to concrete examples or situations. They can now think about their own thoughts, and about hypothetical events and situations. They can think on a more sophisticated level about issues such as religion, politics and personal identity and this ability can also have wider implications for other aspects of development during this time of life.

Evaluation of Piaget's theory

There is no doubting the influence of Piaget's theory. His view of children as active explorers of their worlds is widely accepted and his theory integrates a wide variety of facts about children's thinking into a single theory. Moreover, his theory has also stimulated much research on children's cognitive development. However, the results of much subsequent research have questioned the conclusions reached by Piaget about the abilities of children at each stage. In particular, a consistent finding to emerge is that he underestimated the abilities of children. There are many studies but this section will illustrate this with reference to recent findings on object permanence, egocentrism and conservation.

Piaget believed that that object permanence does not become established until the ages of 12–18 months. However, a study by Baillargeon and DeVos (1991) found evidence of object permanence in 3.5-month-old infants. In this study the infants watched two carrots move along a track, then travel behind a screen at the centre of the track before reappearing on the opposite side. One carrot was tall, one was short. The screen had a window cut out so that the tall carrot would be visible as it moved behind the screen, but the short carrot would not be visible. The infants were then presented with two types of event: a possible one in which the short carrot moved behind the screen and emerged on the other side as before, and an impossible one in which the tall carrot did not appear behind the screen (even though it was tall enough to appear in the window) but still emerged on the other side. Baillargeon and DeVos measured the amount of time the infants spent looking at the possible and impossible events and found that they spent longer looking at the impossible one, indicating that it was in some way surprising to them. It was inferred that the infants expected the carrot to appear in the window behind the screen while moving and their expectations were violated by the impossible event. The fact that babies seemed to regard this as odd suggests that they did indeed have a sense of object permanence, that the tall carrot continued to exist while obscured by the screen and therefore should have appeared in the window. Several other studies have replicated the finding of young babies looking longer at unexpected events involving hidden objects (see, for example, Baillargeon, 2004; Baillargeon et al., 1989). The results of these studies suggest that findings on object permanence in infants may be dependent on the methods used. In Piaget's A-not-B task, the infant has to actively search for the hidden object, but when alternative methods of testing are used, such as the 'violation of expectation' paradigm used by Baillargeon and colleagues, infants show evidence of a sense of object permanence at an earlier age than Piaget thought possible.

Children may also acquire the ability to conserve earlier than Piaget estimated. This was demonstrated in a study by Light et al. (1979) who presented a modified version of a Piagetian conservation task to a group of 6-year-olds. For half the group, a standard Piagetian task was used – the children were presented with two identical beakers filled with pasta shells. When the children agreed that both beakers contained the same amount of pasta, the contents of one beaker were poured into a short but wider one. At this stage most of the children gave the expected response with only 5 per cent responding that the quantities were still the same. However, a different procedure was used for the other half of the group. The researcher told them that the pasta shells would be used in a competitive game. After the children had agreed that the two identical beakers contained the same amount of pasta, the researcher 'noticed' that one of the beakers was badly chipped around the rim and therefore he had to find another container. He then poured the contents into a larger beaker, and asked the children before they started their game if they had the same amount of shells each. When the conservation task was presented in this 'disguised' manner, 70 per cent responded that the quantities were equal.

A similar finding exists with regard to the issues of egocentrism when a modified version of the three mountains task is presented. Hughes and Donaldson (reported by Donaldson, 1978) presented such a task to a group of children aged between 3 and 5. It consisted of two walls that intersected to form a cross. In the first stage of the study, the children were asked if a 'policeman' doll could see a 'boy' doll from various positions. A child from the group was then asked to 'hide the doll so the policeman can't see him', with the policeman at a given position. Then a second policeman doll was introduced and the child was asked to hide the doll from both policemen. This required that the child had to take into account two points of view to work out the most effective hiding place. Over 90 per cent of the children were able to do this, indicating good perspective-taking skills in these preoperational children. Evidence of perspective taking in preoperational children can also be seen in their conversations, with the observation that even 4-year-old children can adjust their speech according to whether they are talking to younger children, peers or adults (Shatz and Gelman, 1973).

The important point about the versions of the conservation and perspective-taking tasks as described above was that they were embedded in everyday situations – in the conservation task, a 'good' reason was provided for pouring the pasta shells into a different beaker and also the issue of 'fair shares' for the purpose of a competitive game was introduced. The perspective-taking task was presented as a hiding game. This task was also spatially simpler than Piaget's three mountains task, but Donaldson (1978) argues that it is the embedding of conservation and perspective-taking tasks in familiar contexts that is crucial. She regarded the poor performance on standard Piagetian tasks, not as examples of egocentrism or lack of conservation, but simply the inability of children to *disembed* reasoning from everyday life.

In general, it has been found that when Piagetian tasks are presented in a simplified form or rely less on verbal reports, children appear to be able to solve various problems earlier than would be predicted by Piaget's theory. Bryant and Trabasso (1971) found that 4- and 5-year-old children could solve transitive inference problems which made less of a demand on memory. This can also be seen in the case of hypothetico-deductive reasoning. When a simplified problem-solving task was presented to 6-year-olds, Ruffman et al. (1993) found evidence of such reasoning in these children.

Other criticisms of Piaget include his view of development occurring in distinct stages (Brainerd, 1978) and his proposal that the sequence of stages is universal, with other researchers arguing that social and cultural factors can also play a part (Rogoff, 2003).

Overall, Piaget has made a major contribution to the understanding of cognitive development and his theory provides a framework for researching this topic. However, his findings do appear to be influenced as much by the methods that he used rather than the cognitive abilities of children at a given stage of development. When his tasks are presented in a simplified or more socially intelligible manner, it is found that children are capable of forms of thinking much earlier than predicted by their stage of development.

Practical applications of Piaget's theory

Berk (2008) has identified a number of ways in which Piaget's theories can be applied in the early years classroom. These include the use of *discovery learning* wherein children are encouraged to make discoveries for themselves through interaction with their environment. The emphasis is on the provision of a rich and stimulating environment with activities such as art, games, building blocks, etc. that are designed to promote exploration and discovery. Secondly, the notion of *readiness to learn* is important: provision of activities that are appropriate to a child's stage of development that will challenge them but will not attempt to speed up development by imposing tasks for which they are not ready. There is also an emphasis on *individual differences*. While Piagetian theory views all children as passing through the same sequence of development, there is a recognition that within each stage there can be differences in rates of development. The practical implication of this is the need for teachers to plan activities for individual children and small groups rather than the whole class, and evaluate progress in relation to the individual child's starting point rather than in relation to peers.

Piagets's concept of the schema can also be applied to early years education and childcare. This basic idea has been further developed by Athey (2007) and Atherton and Nutbrown (2013) into **schema theory**. Here, schemas can be defined as '*persistent patterns which underlie children's spontaneous behaviours*' (Atherton and Nutbrown, 2013: 13). It is argued that through careful observation of young children in school or care settings, schemas can be identified that underpin several behaviours that would otherwise appear unconnected, but when seen through the lens of schema theory, they inform about a child's thinking and understanding. When schemas are identified, the early years practitioner can then work with the child to provide further experiences that help to support and extend the child's schema. So, for example, a young child in a nursery who engages in behaviours such as putting crayons in a box, rolling themselves up in a blanket or putting spoons into a teacup is not just simply flitting from one activity to another. Instead these behaviours can be seen as them using an 'enveloping and containing' schema, a particular way of thinking about the world that informs their actions. Once this schema has been identified, the child can be offered further experiences related to this schema, such as being given sheets of paper and envelopes, and in this way the child's understanding can be enhanced by encountering other ways in which the schema can be used to interact with the environment.

However, Piagetian approaches have also met with trenchant criticism, and in particular the emphasis on discovery learning rather than active transmission of knowledge through teaching has been controversial (see, for example, Phillips, 1998).

Vygotsky's sociocultural theory of cognitive development

Like Piaget, Vygotsky (1978, 1981) saw children as active explorers of their worlds. However, while Piaget stressed the importance of the child constructing their knowledge on their own, Vygotsky stressed the importance of social interaction for development. Given the emphasis on culture and the social environment, Vygotsky's theory is referred to as a **sociocultural** theory.

Vygostsky saw the end point of development as the ability to think and reason for ourselves, and acquiring this ability is a fundamentally social process. Infants and children are social beings able to engage with others but can do little by themselves. Vygotsky characterised development as moving from a stage in which children can do things with others to a final stage when they can do things by themselves. This move from what he referred to as the **social plane** to the **psychological plane** is referred to as **internalisation**. Vygotsky argued that children do bring **elementary mental functions**, such as memory, perception and attention, to the task of development. These elementary mental functions initially develop on their own, but when the child acquires language they are able to interact with others and this becomes the driving force for development, leading the child to acquire **higher mental functions**. Vygotsky's theory places a great emphasis on language as a mediator in the process of development.

Zone of proximal development

Vygostsky saw development not so much in term of what children could achieve on their own but in terms of what they could achieve with help from others. Central to this is his notion of the zone of proximal development, which refers to the ways in which interactions between children and older more experienced members of their culture could facilitate development. This could be done by working with the child at a level slightly beyond the child's own capabilities. Vygotsky did not specify how adults and children work together within this zone of proximal development, but other researchers have developed this notion. For example Bruner (1974–75, 1983) studied interactions between mothers and their infants over a six-month period and came up with the notion of **scaffolding**. This is a process whereby adults continuously adjust the support provided to the child. They may highlight important features of the task or those that are more manageable. They may recast their instructions if the child is having difficulty understanding or use more direct interventions to help the child. As the child begins to acquire the skill, the amount of instruction is reduced. An analogy is made between development and the construction of a building. Eventually the scaffolding is removed when construction is complete, and similarly in development the aim is for the child to achieve 'stand-alone' competence in the task or skill to be mastered.

Private speech

A familiar aspect of young children's behaviour is that they talk to themselves while engaging in problem-solving behaviours and everyday tasks. For example, when playing with Lego®, children can be heard saying things like 'I need a red piece', 'Put these two together'. Piaget noted this tendency, too, and referred to it as **egocentric**

speech, reflecting his view that because children cannot take the perspective of others they express speech regardless of whether a listener can hear. However, Vygotsky (1987) saw this type of speech as a powerful tool for regulating behaviour. Language allows children to reflect on their situation, organise their behaviour and select courses of action. For Vygotsky, such speech provides self-guidance for children and as they get older and more skilled at tasks it becomes internalised and declines. Modern research is supportive of Vygotsky's view of private, self-directed speech rather than Piaget's views of egocentric speech (Berk, 1992). Children do use more private speech when presented with a task that is challenging, but within their zone of proximal development. A study by Fernyhough and Fradley (2005) studied the relationship between the amount of private speech used by 5- and 6-year-old children and task difficulty and found that private speech increased as researchers made a problem-solving task more difficult but decreased as the task became very difficult (i.e. outside their zone of proximal development). As children get older private speech becomes more covert, indicated by whispers and lip movements (Patrick and Abravanel, 2000). Children who use private speech in a challenging task are more attentive and show better task performance than children who use less speech (Fernyhough and Fradely, 2005).

Pretend play

Vygotsky was also interested in the developmental potential of children's make-believe, or pretend, play and pointed out that when they engage in such play children often engage in a variety of adult roles and activities, such as parents looking after a baby, or a shopkeeper running a shop. When they engage in such play they are essentially operating in a zone of proximal development in which they can try out a variety of different tasks that are beyond their current capabilities (such as 'buying' and 'selling'), they can learn about appropriate behaviour and social norms (such as obeying commands by 'mummy' to go to sleep), and exercise their imagination by using objects creatively, for example using a cardboard cylinder as a 'telescope'.

Evaluation of Vygotsky's theory

As with Piaget, Vygotsky's views have been very influential and have inspired much research on the role social interaction plays in human development. Vygostsky's theory also has a number of practical applications in the classroom. One weakness, however, is that it has little to say about the role of basic cognitive skills in development. He does mention the role of elementary mental functions but does not specify how these may contribute to the development of socially mediated aspects of cognition.

Vygotsky's recognition of the role of culture in human development is an important insight and this notion has been developed further by Rogoff (1998, 2003), who has pointed out that in many cultures children do not learn by going to school or receiving formal instruction. Instead they are included in the daily activities of their society, such as childcare and hunting, from an early age. Instead of receiving formal instruction, these children learn through **guided participation**: they actively participate in culturally relevant activities alongside more experienced and skilled partners who provide the necessary assistance and encouragement. Rogoff (2003) provides various examples of children from non-western cultures who have capabilities that would not be expected in western children of similar ages. These include 3-year-old children from the Kwara'ae of Oceania who are skilled caregivers for their younger siblings, or infants from the Efe of the Democratic Republic of the Congo who can use machetes safely. Rogoff is critical of the approach of developmental psychology to identifying universal principles of development based primarily on European and North American children, and for her, development must be understood as a cultural process and not simply a biological or psychological one.

Practical applications of Vygotsky's theory

Vygotsky's emphasis on social interaction with more experienced others as the driving force for development has implications for education and has inspired various teaching methods. One such approach based on Vygotskian principles is **reciprocal teaching** (Palinscar, 1986; Palinscar and Brown, 1984). This was originally designed to improve the reading comprehension skills of children identified as having difficulties in this area, but it has since been applied to helping all children learn in a range of subject areas. In reciprocal teaching, a teacher and a small group of children take turns in leading dialogues on the content of a passage of text which aim to foster a group effort between the teacher and children toward understanding the text. This is achieved through the use of four strategies: *questioning* wherein the dialogue leader (initially the teacher, but later a child) begins by asking questions about the content of the passage; *summarising* in which the leader identifies the most important information in the text; *clarifying* in which the group discusses the summary and children are given the opportunity to resolve any difficulties through asking for help or re-reading parts of the passage; and finally, *predicting* wherein the children attempt to predict the upcoming content based on the understanding they have acquired. The aim of reciprocal teaching is to create a zone of proximal development in which the children are scaffolded, initially by the teacher and then by each other, in the task of understanding the text.

Given the prominent role of play in the early years curriculum (see Chapter 2), Vygotskyian approaches can also inform how play opportunities are implemented (Berk, 2008). These include the provision of a wide variety of play materials that will encourage children to act out everyday roles in the culture, for example realistic toys such as trucks, dolls, tea-sets, dressing-up clothes, etc. However, materials without a clear function such as blocks, cardboard cylinders and sand are also useful because they will inspire even more imaginative play as children will assign roles to them. Also important is the opportunity to participate in real-world activities with adults, for example field trips, as these will provide knowledge and experience which children can further integrate into their imaginative play.

Information-processing accounts

While Piaget and Vygotsky aimed to provide a single, broad-based theory of cognitive development, information-processing approaches focus more on specific aspects of cognition such as attention, memory and problem solving. An analogy is made between a computer and the human mind: like computers, we receive information from the outside world, we then store, organise and manipulate it through a variety of operations, and finally we use this information to produce a useful output such as the solution to a problem or the recall of a series of facts.

Most information-processing theories (see, for example, Atkinson and Shiffrin, 1968) propose that information flows through three stores – the **sensory register**, **short-term or working memory** and **long-term memory**. As information passes through the system, there are various processes that we can use that help us retain information and use it effectively.

Information first enters the sensory register and this allows us to store sensory details such as visual images or sounds for very brief periods that last only milliseconds. For example, when we look around our environments we are constantly blinking; yet we do not have a sense of living in a constantly flickering world. This is because the sensory register preserves the basic sensory information when our eyes close and holds it until we open our eyes again, by which time it is refreshed.

If we consciously attend to the information in the sensory register, it can enter short-term or working memory (Baddeley, 1986). This acts as a sort of mental workspace that allows us to retain information for brief periods while we operate on it. For example, when we are doing mental arithmetic we need to keep the numbers in mind while we perform the required mathematical operation such as addition, multiplication, etc. An important feature of this store is that it is of a limited capacity which for most adults is approximately seven units of information (Miller, 1956). This capacity can be increased by **chunking** – for example, the letters BBC can be stored as one unit of information instead of three letters. Another constraint is that information only lasts in working memory for a period of seconds. However, we can increase the duration of storage by strategies such as rehearsal (repeating the information using overt or covert speech).

The longer we hold information in working memory, the more likely it will enter long-term memory. This is our permanent knowledge base and does not appear to have any limits in terms of its capacity or duration. Information in long-term memory is highly organised and thought to form an associative network in which related units of information are stored together. We can retrieve information by applying various **memory strategies**, and these will be looked at in more detail in the next section. Sometimes we have to *recall* information – that is, retrieve the information in response to a question or query without any 'hints' or *cues* to help us – while at other times we retrieve information through the process of *recognition* – such as being able to pick out the information that we have previously encountered from a list.

In terms of cognitive development, the actual structures of the information-processing system do not change but the *processes* that we use to operate on this information develop. There is also an increase in general **processing efficiency** as children get older (Case et al., 1982). While the total capacity of the information-processing system is seen as fixed, this can be divided between *storage space* and *operating space*. It is argued that for young children, tasks such as identifying items are more effortful and therefore take up more operating space. However, as children's knowledge develops, they become more efficient at identifying items and therefore devote less resources to processing and freeing up storage resources. This explanation has been applied to increases in short-term memory capacity, although, as will be seen shortly, it does not provide a full account. We can also use a variety of *strategies* to help us learn and memorise information, and as children develop they learn to use these strategies effectively. Another important process is *automatisation*. Cognitive psychologists distinguish between **controlled** and **automatic** processes (Shiffrin and Schneider, 1977). Controlled processes require conscious attention, consume more working memory resources and are used for new tasks that we have not yet become proficient at doing. However, with enough practices many processes can become automatic – they do not require conscious attention and can be performed quickly, and indeed sometimes are beyond our voluntary control. If we take the case of reading words, initially for a child this is effortful and will involve recognising the word either by remembering it as a visual pattern, or by trying to use letter-sound rules for identification. However, with practice reading most words eventually become automatised and we can recognise the word and its meaning instantly from the visual stimulus. This can also be seen in a task called the Stroop effect (Stroop, 1935) in which participants are presented with a series of colour words, but are asked to report not what the word says, but the colour in which it is printed. However, the word and its print colour do not always match (e.g. the word 'red' printed in blue ink). In this situation participants tend to be predisposed to respond 'red' rather than the correct response 'blue'; they cannot suppress the tendency to read the word even though both pieces of information they have are dealing with colour. Thus the automatic process of reading interferes with the colour-naming task.

Consider how the approaches of Piaget, Vygotsky and information processing might inform approaches to teaching arithmetic skills to young children.

The development of memory

Memory is central to information-processing views of development, and, of course, is an essential skill for everyday life; hence it is worth considering the development of memory in more detail. The first part of this section will look at the development of memory in infancy and will conclude by considering memory development in childhood.

Development in infancy

Studying infant memory does present a challenge to researchers as infants cannot report what they can remember. Indeed the question can be asked: do infants have a memory? We know as adults that we cannot remember events from when we were babies, the phenomenon known as **infantile amnesia**. However, a number of techniques have been developed to study infant memory and it is clear that infants are able to retain information during this period of the lifespan. These techniques include the **habituation-dishabituation paradigm**, the **conjugate-reinforcement paradigm** and deferred imitation.

The habituation-dishabituation paradigm involves presenting a novel stimulus such as a visual image to the infant. Normally when a new stimulus is presented, the infant will react in some way, such as directing his or her gaze towards it. The stimulus is then repeated until the infant shows no further reactions. At this stage, the infant is said to have **habituated** to the stimulus, it is no longer new and interesting to them. After a period of time, a changed stimulus is presented to the infant and the reaction is noted. If they react to this novel stimulus, this is referred to as **dishabituation** and the assumption is that the infant has recognised that the stimulus has changed from the earlier presentations. Friedman (1972) used this technique to study memory in very young infants (aged 1–4 days old). He presented them with a chequerboard pattern (consisting of either 4 or 144 squares) until the infants showed evidence of habituation (the amount of time spent looking at the pattern declined). He then presented the chequerboard again. For some infants it was the same pattern, but for others it was changed (e.g. infants who initially saw the 4 squares pattern were presented with the 144 squares pattern). Infants who were shown the same pattern as before continued to show habituation, but those presented with a changed pattern increased their looking time significantly. Overall, research using this approach has established that memory for visual objects and events is present early in infancy and develops rapidly in the first 6 to 12 months of life.

The conjugate reinforcement paradigm (Rovee-Collier, 1999) is used to study recall skills in infants. It involves teaching them to make a mobile suspended over their crib move by kicking a foot tied to the mobile with a long chord. Infants enjoy making the mobile move and stare intently at it and vocalise as it moves. There are three phases to the procedure. Firstly, the **baseline phase** in which the infant is placed in the crib with the mobile suspended above. At this stage the infant's foot is not attached to the mobile so kicking will not make the mobile move. Most infants will kick their feet anyway and this phase allows a baseline measure of kicking to be obtained. There then follows an **acquisition phase** in which the infant's foot is attached to the mobile so that kicking will make the mobile move. Typically in this phase there is a dramatic increase in the rate of kicking. This is followed by the **immediate retention phase** in which the mobile is disconnected from the infant's foot and the rate of kicking is measured. If the rate of kicking stays the same as during the acquisition phase, the infant is regarded as recalling that kicking their foot makes the mobile move. Their memory can then be tested over varying intervals to see if they can retain this information. It has been found that infants aged 2–3 months can still remember how to activate the mobile up to one week after training, and by the age of 6 months, this increases to two weeks (Rovee-Collier, 1999). In cases where the infant appears to forget how to activate the mobile, a brief reminder is effective: all the adult has to do is shake the mobile to reinstate the infant's response (Hildreth and Rovee-Collier, 2002). This task has also revealed a similarity between infant and adult memory – infants, like adults are subject to **context effects**. If infants are not tested in the same physical environment in which they learned to move the mobile, they remember poorly (Boller et al., 1995). However, from the age of 9 months the importance of context declines.

Another approach to study recall in infants is through **deferred imitation** (Meltzoff, 1985, 1988). In this approach the infant is exposed to an action performed on an object (squeezing a toy to make a noise). The object is then removed without the infant being allowed to touch it. After a delay, the object is then presented to the infant to see if they will repeat the action witnessed earlier. If the infant shows deferred imitation, then they must have committed that action to memory. It cannot be due to a memorised motor response as the infant was not allowed to handle the object in the initial presentation. The other explanation, that the infant might have performed the action by chance alone, is controlled for by comparison with a group of infants who did not witness the action. If there is a higher rate of reproducing the action compared to the control group, then this is taken as evidence of deferred imitation.

According to Piaget's theory, infants are capable of deferred imitation in the final phase of the sensorimotor period, but many research studies have found evidence of this in younger infants. Meltzoff and Moore (1994) found deferred imitation in 6-week-old infants who were exposed to an unfamiliar adult's facial expression and then imitated it when exposed to adults the next day. As motor skills improve, infants acquire the capacity to imitate actions on objects and from 6 to 9 months of age increase the amount of novel behaviours they imitate (Collie and Hayne, 1999).

Another interesting topic is the predictive value of measures of infant memory – do they predict later cognitive abilities? A number of studies have indicated that recognition memory (as evidenced by the habituation-dishabituation paradigm) and deferred imitation are predictive of later ability. Habituation has been found to be a good predictor of intelligence in childhood (Kavšek, 2004). Deferred imitation at 9 months of age has also been found to be a predictor of non-verbal communication skills at 14 months (Heimann et al., 2006). Strid et al. (2006) found that 9-month-old infants who showed poor performance in a deferred imitation task also obtained lower scores on a test of cognitive ability at 4 years of age.

Memory in childhood

Several factors underpin the development of memory in childhood. These include increases in memory span, the development of memory strategies, the increasing knowledge base and an increase in understanding of how their own memories work (**metamemory**). These factors will be looked at in turn.

Increases in memory span

Memory span is a measure of the capacity of short-term memory and is typically measured using a **digit span** task in which a child has to repeat a sequence of digits. With each correct repetition, the sequence length is increased by one digit until the child cannot successfully repeat any more sequences. Digit span is therefore the maximum sequence length that the child can repeat. As mentioned earlier the typical adult memory span is approximately seven items. The average 4-year-old child will have a digit span of two-to-three digits and will achieve adult capacity by the age of ten (Gathercole and Baddeley, 1993). A number of explanations have been proposed for this increase. One relates to increases in processing efficiency (Case et al., 1982) which argues that as children become quicker at processing information, less processing resources are required and these can be redeployed to storage. As evidence of this, item identification times (a common measure of processing efficiency) increase with age and this parallels the age-related increase in digit span. However, Henry and Millar (1991) conducted a study comparing the memory spans of 5- and 7-year-olds. They tested memory span using sequences of words rather than digits, but more importantly, the words used for each group were matched for identification times: the words used for the 5-year-olds were identified as easily as the words used for the 7-year-olds. If processing efficiency was the main factor in the developmental increase in memory span, then equalising the processing times for the words should have eliminated the developmental difference. However, the older children still out-performed the younger children. In a subsequent review of the literature, Henry and Millar (1993) identified two factors that are reliably related to the increase in memory span. Firstly, children's speech rates increase with age. As their speech rates increase, younger children are able to recall more words or digits before they fade from short-term memory and hence their memory span increases. In older children, quicker rates of speech mean that they can rehearse information more efficiently and further increase their digit spans. Secondly, long-term memory also plays a part – as children get older, their knowledge base increases and they can use their long-term memories to support performance in a memory span task. The argument is that information in short-term memory fades rapidly and that a child's familiarity with an item can help not only to compensate for this but also to boost short-term memory performance.

Why is a simple measure of short-term memory of so much developmental interest? The answer is that an efficient short-term memory is essential for normal everyday functioning and crucial for learning new information. Before information can enter long-term memory, it has to be processed in short-term memory, and any limitations here can have an adverse effect on learning. Children with developmental problems such as dyslexia or specific language impairment have consistently lower memory spans than normally developing peers (see, for example, Jorm, 1983). Short-term memory is also crucial for learning in typically developing children (Gathercole and Alloway, 2008). In reading, short-term memory is thought to play a role in helping a child to learn letter-sound rules (Gathercole and Baddeley, 1993). Memory span is also related to vocabulary acquisition in spoken language (Gathercole and Baddeley, 1993) and to arithmetic skills (Hitch, 1978). The importance of memory span means that often when a psychologist assesses a child's cognitive ability, they will include a memory span task as part of the battery of assessments.

> The next section describes the development of some strategies that are known to help memory performance. Before reading on, think about your own memory skills, what strategies do you use to help your memory for everyday tasks such as memorising a shopping list? Do they match any of the strategies listed below?

Memory strategies

A major factor underlying memory performance in adults is the ability to employ a variety of strategies to help us learn and remember information. We may continuously repeat or rehearse the information to be learnt, we may organise it by grouping similar

Table 4.2   Development of memory strategies

Phase	Description
No strategy	No spontaneous use of a strategy Unable to train use of strategy
Production deficiency	Ability to use strategy present but not used spontaneously Child can be instructed in use of strategy When used, strategy has positive effects on performance
Utilization deficiency	Ability to use strategy spontaneously No positive effect of strategy use on performance
Strategy inefficiency	Attempt to apply strategy spontaneously but in an inefficient and inconsistent manner
Mature strategy	Memory strategy used spontaneously Strategy applied to a variety of tasks and situations Use of strategy yields positive results on performance

Based on Flavell, Miller and Miller (1993), Miller (1994), Waters (2000)

items together, or we may elaborate on the information, for example linking a list together in a sentence or constructing a mental image linking the items. Children gradually acquire these strategies of **rehearsal**, **organisation** and **elaboration** during childhood.

Researchers have found some evidence of basic strategic behaviour even in very young children when presented with a memory task. DeLoache et al. (1985) conducted a study in which children aged 18–24 months watched an experimenter hide a 'Big Bird' soft toy. The children were told to remember where the toy was placed so that they could find it later. They were then distracted by being presented with more toys for four minutes. However, while they were being presented with these toys, they constantly interrupted their activities to talk about 'Big Bird', point to its location or stay near the hiding place. These appeared to be attempts to help them remember the location rather than just incidental interruptions because the frequency of occurrence was higher than that of a control group who were not told to remember where the toy was.

In general the development of memory strategies seems to follow a consistent pattern (Flavell et al., 1993) and this is summarised in Table 4.2.

Firstly, the child does not appear to have a strategy available to help them. They then go through a phase called **production deficiency** – they have the capacity to use a strategy but do not use it spontaneously; they can, however, be instructed to use it with positive effects. Miller (1994) has also suggested that some children go through a **utilisation deficiency** phase in which they spontaneously use a strategy but to no positive effect. This may be because applying the strategy in certain situations may itself be effortful and consume resources that are themselves needed for learning. Some children also show evidence of a **strategy inefficiency** wherein they attempt to apply a strategy but do so in an inefficient and inconsistent manner (Waters,

2000). Finally, children fully acquire a **mature strategy**, use it spontaneously and apply it to a variety of tasks, which yields positive results.

Rehearsal

Rehearsal – saying a list of items to yourself repeatedly in order to learn them – is a widely used memory strategy. It appears to be a skill that is acquired later in childhood, but younger children can be trained to use this approach. A study by Keeney et al. (1967) presented a memory task to children aged 5–6 years of age and used lip-reading (indicating subvocal speech) as evidence of rehearsal. Some, but not all, of the children used rehearsal, and children who did spontaneously use it showed better memory performance than non-rehearsers. However, when children who did not use rehearsal were instructed in its use, their memory performance improved in a subsequent memory task. But when provided with further memory tasks, these children did not continue to use the newly acquired strategy and reverted to their previous status as non-rehearsers. This is a good example of a production deficiency in the use of a strategy – ability to use a strategy but lack of spontaneous use, positive effects when used, but lack of persistence in use. Reasons for the lack of persistence may include a lack of insight into the general usefulness of this approach or children may simply have their own preferred idiosyncratic approaches to learning. Although some of the children in the Keeney et al. study (1967) did use rehearsal spontaneously, the evidence is that this strategy does not become widely used until about the age of 7 (Gathercole and Alloway, 2008). It has been suggested that experiences such as learning to read may influence the use of rehearsal: as children become used to subvocally saying the words they are trying to read, over time they transfer this approach to the task of memorising items (Henry and Millar, 1993).

Organisation

Grouping items by category has been shown to be an effective strategy for adults (Bousfield, 1953). There is also some evidence of organisation in memory tasks by very young children. DeLoache and Todd (1988) found that preschool children could organise objects when categories were spatial rather than meaning-based. In their study, a group of 5-year-olds watched an experimenter hide either pegs or candles in a number of opaque containers and asked the children to remember which containers held the candles. The children took each container as it was handed to them and placed it on a table. Most of the children arranged the containers into two separate groups according to whether the container held a peg or a candle. When the boxes containing the pegs and candles were made even more visually distinctive, children aged 2–4 showed evidence of spontaneous organisation. However, grouping items by meaning-based categories (e.g. 'animals', 'things you can eat', etc.) is a skill that emerges later in childhood. A longitudinal study reported by Schlagmüller and Schneider (2002) indicates that initially young children do not appear to have a strategy for organising the materials to be learned, and when organisation is used they show evidence of a utilisation deficiency. But between the ages of 8 and 10, there is a 'sudden' change in their approach: children realise that organisation is a useful strategy and they begin to use it spontaneously and consistently across tasks resulting in positive effects on their memory performance.

Elaboration

This refers to the ability to create a shared, meaningful link between two or more items and is the basis of many mnemonic strategies used by older children and adults. An example of such a strategy is remembering the colours of the rainbow (red, orange, yellow, green, blue, indigo, violet) by forming the first letters of each colour into the sentence 'Richard of York gave battle in vain'). Other strategies include forming mental images linking two items (e.g. learning the word pair 'fish' and 'bicycle' by forming the [bizarre] image of a fish riding a bicycle). Elaboration tends to be acquired later in childhood and only older children are more likely to use it spontaneously, show positive effects of using this strategy, and apply it across different tasks (Flavell et al., 1993). This is likely to be the case because generating meaningful links is itself effortful and consumes working memory resources, and the more efficient working memory skills of older children make use of such a strategy more viable.

The increasing knowledge base

By the time of middle childhood children's long-term knowledge base grows larger and highly organised. Knowledge of a domain or topic can be a powerful aid to memory, and indeed in cases where children acquire detailed knowledge of a particular area they can sometimes outperform adults in memory tests. Chi (1978) compared memory for chess positions in a group of adults and children (average age 10.5 years). The important point about the groups was that the children were 'expert' chess players and the adults were novices, and as predicted, the 'expert' children performed better than the 'novice' adults. However, the children's superiority was confined to this domain. When the two groups were given other memory tasks (such as digit span), the normal age differences in performance were observed. In general, highly knowledgeable children organise new material with little or no effort and show a more organised approach to recalling information as well (Schneider and Bjorklund, 1992).

Metamemory

This concerns children's ability to estimate their own memory capabilities, as well as their own insights into 'how memory works'. It has been observed that young children are poor at estimating their own memory abilities and have a tendency to overestimate (Barry, 2006). However, it has been suggested by Bjorklund and Green

(1992) that this is actually a positive attribute, as it encourages children to keep trying and working with their limited capacities to eventually improve their performance. But with increasing age, predicted and actual abilities are closer together (Flavell et al., 1993).

Even young children seem to have some basic insights about how memory works. An interview study conducted by Kreutzer et al. (1975) found a surprising level of knowledge even in children aged 4–6. In their study, children were provided with a number of hypothetical scenarios involving memory tasks and asked to provide a response. An example of such a scenario is as follows:

> Jim and Bill are in grade __ (S's own grade). The teacher wanted them to learn the names of all the kinds of birds they might find in their city. Jim had learned them last year and then forgot them. Bill had never learned them before. Do you think one of these boys would find it easier to learn the names of all the birds? Which one? Why? (Kreutzer et al., 1975: 8)

Most children were able to correctly respond that Jim would find the task easier and were able to justify their answers (e.g. '*because as soon as he heard the names they would probably all come back to him*') (Kreutzer et al., 1975: 9). Such responses show awareness of a memory phenomenon known as *savings during relearning* (easier to learn a list if it has been learned before but forgotten). These children were also aware of other phenomena such as the effects of *memory load* (long lists are more difficult to learn than short ones) and the effects of a delay on memory (remembering is more difficult after a period of time has passed). Children's insights into memory develop further with age and this can help memory performance in a number of ways. Firstly, they become aware of the value of using strategies such as rehearsal, elaboration and organisation on the material to be learned and will begin to apply these spontaneously and across different tasks and situations. They will also learn to approach memory tasks in a more efficient manner. For example, in some everyday learning situations, it is necessary to focus on some rather than all of the information available and such selectivity is not always present in young children. This was demonstrated in a series of studies by Flavell (reported by Flavell et al., 1993). In these studies children were presented with 12 items, each item hidden behind a small door. Behind the doors six household items and six toy animals were hidden, and the child was told to remember what animals were hidden behind the doors. Doors concealing an animal were indicated with an animal symbol and doors concealing a household item were indicated by a house. Therefore only six items were relevant, and the most efficient way to approach the task would be to open only the doors with an animal symbol. However, Flavell found that preschoolers were not selective and just followed the spatial arrangement of the doors, opening the first row followed by the second row, and so on. However, older children were able to focus on the relevant doors during the learning phase.

Chapter summary

- Piaget and Vygotsky both proposed broad theories of cognitive development.
- Piaget emphasised the process of children acquiring new knowledge on an individual basis through interacting with their environments. Development passes through a sequence of stages and all children follow these stages, regardless of environment and culture.
- Vygotsky emphasised the role of social interaction in driving development and in particular the ways in which adults could assist the development of children's understanding.
- An alternative approach is to look at cognition as an information-processing system. This consists of a sensory store, a short-term memory store and a long-term memory store.
- The structures of the information-processing system do not change, and development comes about by changes in the processes by which we deal with information, such as increases in processing efficiency and automatisation of tasks.
- Recall and recognition memory skills are present from infancy, as evidenced by performance on habituation-dishabituation, conjugate-reinforcement and deferred imitation tasks.
- Memory ability in childhood improves as the result of increases in memory span, the acquisition of memory strategies, the increasing knowledge base and growing metamemory skills.

Further reading

Atherton, F. and Nutbrown, C. (2013) *Understanding Schemas and Young Children*. London: Sage.

This book focuses on how schema theory can be used to understand young children's learning and behaviour.

Gathercole, S.E. and Alloway, T. (2008) *Working Memory and Learning: A Practical Guide for Teachers*. London: Sage.

A practical account of how research on short-term (working) memory can be applied to the issue of learning in school.

Barry, E.S. (2006) 'Children's memory: A primer for understanding behavior', *Early Childhood Education Journal*, 33 (6): 405–11.

This article provides a clear and useful summary of how findings on children's memory development can be used to understand behaviour in settings such as the classroom.

References

Atherton, F. and Nutbrown, C. (2013) *Understanding Schemas and Young Children*. London: Sage.

Athey, C. (2007) *Extending Thought in Young Children* (2nd edn). London: Paul Chapman Publishing.

Atkinson, R.C. and Shiffrin, R.M. (1968) 'Human memory: A proposed system and its control processes', in K.W. Spence and J.T. Spence (eds), *Advances in the Psychology of Learning and Motivation*, Vol. 2. New York: Academic Press. pp. 90–195.

Baddeley, A.D. (1986) *Working Memory*. Oxford: Clarendon.

Baillargeon, R. (2004) 'Infants' reasoning about hidden objects: Evidence for event-general and event-specific expectations', *Developmental Science*, 7 (4): 391–424.

Baillargeon, R. and DeVos, J. (1991) 'Object permanence in young infants: Further evidence', *Child Development*, 62 (6): 1227-46.

Baillargeon, R., Devos J. and Graber, M. (1989) 'Location memory in 8-month-old infants in a nonsearch AB task', *Cognitive Development*, 4 (4): 345–67.

Barry, E.S. (2006) 'Children's memory: A primer for understanding behaviour', *Early Childhood Education Journal*, 33 (6): 405–11.

Berk, L.E. (1992) 'Children's private speech: An overview of theory and the status of research', in R.M Diaz and L.E. Berk (eds), *Private Speech: From Social Interaction to Self-regulation*. Hillsdale, NJ: Erlbaum. pp. 17–54.

Berk, L.E. (2008) *Infants, Children and Adolescents* (6th edn). Boston, MA: Pearson.

Bjorklund, D.F. and Green, B.L. (1992) 'The adaptive nature of cognitive immaturity', *American Psychologist*, 47 (1): 46–54.

Boller, K., Grabelle, M. and Rovee-Collier, C. (1995) 'Effects of postevent information on infants' memory for a central target', *Journal of Experimental Child Psychology*, 59 (3): 372–96.

Bousfield, W. (1953) 'The occurrence of clustering in the recall of randomly arranged associates', *Journal of General Psychology*, 49 (2): 229–40.

Brainerd, C.J. (1978) 'The stage question in cognitive-developmental theory', *Behavioral and Brain Sciences*, 1 (2): 173–213.

Bruner, J. (1974–75) 'From communication to language – a psychological perspective', *Cognition*, 3 (3): 255–87.

Bruner, J. (1983) *Child's Talk: Learning to Use Language*. Oxford: Oxford University Press.

Bryant, P.E. and Trabasso, T. (1971) 'Transitive inferences and memory in young children', *Nature*, 232 (5311): 456–58.

Case, R., Kurland, D.M. and Goldberg, J. (1982) 'Operational efficiency and the growth of short-term memory span', *Journal of Experimental Child Psychology*, 33 (3): 386–404.

Chi, M.T.H. (1978) 'Knowledge structure and memory development', in R. Siegler (ed.), *Children's Thinking: What Develops?* Hillsdale, NJ: Erlbaum. pp. 73–96.

Collie, R. and Hayne, H. (1999) 'Deferred imitation by 6- and 9-month-old infants: More evidence for declarative memory', *Developmental Psychobiology*, 35 (2): 83–90.

DeLoache, J.S. and Todd, C.M. (1988) 'Young children's use of spatial organisation as a mnemonic strategy', *Journal of Experimental Child Psychology*, 46 (1): 1–10.

DeLoache, J.S., Cassidy, D.J. and Brown, A.L. (1985) 'Precursors of mnemonic strategies in very young children's memory', *Child Development*, 56 (1): 125–37.

Donaldson, M. (1978) *Children's Minds*. New York: Norton.

Fernyhough, C. and Fradley, E. (2005) 'Private speech on an executive task: Relations with task difficulty and task performance', *Cognitive Development*, 20 (1): 103–20.

Flavell, J.H., Miller, P.H. and Miller, S.A. (1993) *Cognitive Development*. Englewood Cliffs, NJ: Prentice-Hall.

Friedman, S. (1972) 'Habituation and recovery of visual response in the alert human newborn', *Journal of Experimental Child Psychology*, 13 (2): 339–49.

Gathercole, S.E. and Alloway, T. (2008) *Working Memory and Learning: A Practical Guide for Teachers*. London: Sage.

Gathercole, S.E. and Baddeley, A.D. (1993) *Working Memory and Language*. Hove: Erlbaum.

Heimann, M., Strid, K., Smith, L., Tjus, T., Ulvund, S.E. and Meltzoff, A.N. (2006) 'Exploring the relation between memory, gestural communication, and the emergence of language in infancy: A longitudinal study', *Infant and Child Development*, 15 (3): 233–49.

Henry, L.A. and Millar, S. (1991) 'Memory span increase with age: A test of two hypotheses', *Journal of Experimental Child Psychology*, 51 (3): 459–84.

Henry, L.A. and Millar, S. (1993) 'Why does memory span improve with age? A review of the evidence for two current hypotheses', *European Journal of Cognitive Psychology*, 5 (3): 241–87.

Hildreth, K. and Rovee-Collier, C. (2002) 'Forgetting functions of reactivated memories over the first year of life', *Developmental Psychobiology*, 41 (3): 277–88.

Hitch, G.J. (1978) 'The role of short-term memory in mental arithmetic', *Cognitive Psychology*, 10 (3): 302–23.

Inhelder, B. and Piaget, J. (1958) *The Growth of Logical Thinking from Childhood to Adolescence*. London: Routledge and Kegan Paul.

Inhelder, B. and Piaget, J. (1964) *The Early Growth of Logic in the Child: Classification and Seriation*. London: Routledge and Kegan Paul.

Jorm, A. (1983) 'Specific reading retardation and working memory: A review', *British Journal of Psychology*, 74 (3): 311–42.

Kail, R. (1990) *The Development of Memory in Children* (3rd edn). New York: Freeman.

Kavšek, M. (2004) 'Predicting later IQ from infant visual habituation and dishabituation: A meta-analysis', *Journal of Applied Developmental Psychology*, 25 (3): 369–93.

Keenan, T. and Evans, S. (2009) *An Introduction to Child Development* (2nd edn). London: SAGE.

Keeney, T.J., Cannizzo, S.R. and Flavell, John H. (1967) 'Spontaneous and induced verbal rehearsal in a recall task', *Child Development*, 38 (4): 953–66.

Kreutzer, M.A., Leonard, C. and Flavell, J.H. (1975) 'An interview study of children's knowledge about memory', *Monographs of the Society for Research in Child Development*, (Serial No. 159), 40 (1): 1–60.

Light, P., Buckingham, M. and Robbins, A.H. (1979) 'The conservation task as an interactional setting', *British Journal of Educational Psychology*, 49 (3): 304–10.

Meltzoff, A.N. (1985) 'Immediate and deferred imitation in fourteen- and twenty-four-month-old infants', *Child Development*, 56 (1): 62–72.

Meltzoff, A.N. (1988) 'Infant imitation after a 1-week delay: Long-term memory for novel acts and multiple stimuli', *Developmental Psychology*, 24 (4): 470–6.

Meltzoff, A.N. and Moore, M.K. (1994) 'Persons and representation: Why infant imitation is important for theories of human development', in J. Nadel and G. Butterworth (eds), *Imitation in Infancy*. Cambridge: Cambridge University Press. pp. 9–35.

Miller, G.A. (1956) 'The magical number seven, plus or minus two: Some limits on our capacity for processing information', *Psychological Review*, 63 (2): 81–97.

Miller, P.H. (1994) 'Individual differences in children's strategic behaviour: Utilization deficiencies,', *Learning and Individual Differences*, 6 (3): 285–307.

Osherson. D. and Markman, E. (1974–75) 'Language and the ability to evaluate contradictions and tautologies', *Cognition*, 3 (3): 213–26.

Palinscar, A.S. (1986) The role of dialogue in providing scaffolded instruction', *Educational Psychologist*, 21 (1–2): 73–98.

Palinscar A.S. and Brown, A.L. (1984) 'Reciprocal teaching of comprehension-fostering and comprehension-monitoring activities', *Cognition and Instruction*, 1 (2): 117–75.

Patrick, E. and Abravanel, E. (2000) 'The self-regulatory nature of preschool children's private speech in a naturalistic setting', *Applied Psycholinguistics*, 21 (01): 45–61.

Phillips, M. (1998) *All Must Have Prizes*. London: Time Warner.

Piaget, J. (1929) *The Child's Conception of the World*. London: Routledge and Kegan Paul.

Piaget, J. (1953) *The Origins of Intelligence in Children*. London: Routledge and Kegan Paul.

Piaget, J. and Inhelder, B. (1956) *The Child's Conception of Space*. London: Routledge and Kegan Paul.

Rogoff, B. (1998) 'Cognition as a collaborative process', in W. Damon, D. Kuhn and R.S. Siegler (eds), *Handbook of Child Psychology: Vol. 5 Cognition, Perception and Language*. New York: Wiley. pp. 679–744.

Rogoff, B. (2003) *The Cultural Nature of Human Development*. New York: Oxford University Press.

Rovee-Collier, C. (1999) 'The development of infant memory', *Current Directions in Psychological Science*, 8 (3): 80–5.

Ruffman, T., Perner, J., Olson, D.R. and Doherty, M. (1993) 'Reflecting on scientific thinking: Children's understanding of the hypothesis-evidence relation', *Child Development*, 64 (6): 1617–36.

Schlagmüller, M. and Schneider, W. (2002) 'The development of organizational strategies in children: Evidence from a microgenetic longitudinal study', *Journal of Experimental Child Psychology*, 81 (3): 298–319.

Schneider, W. and Bjorklund, D.E. (1992) 'Expertise, aptitude, and strategic remembering', *Child Development*, 63 (2): 461–73.

Shatz, M. and Gelman, R. (1973) 'The development of communication skills: Modifications in the speech of young children as a function of listener', *Monographs of the Society for Research in Child Development*, (Serial No. 152), 38 (5): 1–38.

Shiffrin, R.M. and Schneider, W. (1977) 'Controlled and automatic human information processing: II. Perceptual learning, automatic attending, and a general theory', *Psychological Review*, 84 (2): 127–90.

Strid, K., Tjus, T., Smith, L., Meltzoff, A.N. and Heiman, M. (2006) 'Infant recall memory and communication predicts later cognitive development', *Infant Behavior and Development*, 29 (4) 545–53.

Stroop, John Ridley (1935) 'Studies of interference in serial verbal reactions', *Journal of Experimental Psychology*, 18 (6): 643–62.

Vygotsky, L.S. (1978) *Mind in Society: The Development of Higher Mental Processes*. Cambridge, MA: Harvard University Press.

Vygotsky, L.S. (1981) 'The genesis of higher mental functions', in J.V. Wertsch (ed.), *The Concept of Activity in Soviet Psychology*. Armonk, NY: Sharpe. pp. 144–88.

Vygotsky, L.S. (1987) 'Thinking and speech', in R.W. Rieber, A.S. Carton (eds), and N. Minick (trans.), *The Collected Works of L.S. Vygotsky: Vol. 1, Problems of General Psychology*. New York: Plenum. pp. 37–285.

Waters, H.S. (2000) 'Memory strategy development: Do we need yet another deficiency? *Child Development*, 71 (4): 1004–12.

Biology and Development

Why you should read this chapter

A great many physical changes take place over the course of childhood. It is tempting to think of physical growth and brain development as a process that happens naturally if a few basic conditions are met, such as being provided with adequate nutrition. There is undoubtedly a pre-programmed element to biological development; however, as you will see from this chapter, the development of the brain and even physical growth itself are affected significantly by the child's experience as well and require more than just satisfying certain conditions. The provision of a stimulating and emotionally caring environment also plays a crucial role in biological development in childhood.

By the end of this chapter you should

- have a basic understanding of prenatal development

- have a basic understanding of the physical changes that take place during childhood and be familiar with factors related to those changes

- understand the distinction between fine and gross motor skills and be aware of how these skills develop

(Continued)

> *(Continued)*
>
> - be familiar with the basic structure of the brain and understand some of the key concepts and terminology related to brain development
> - understand how the environment in which the child is raised plays a crucial role in physical growth and the development of the brain.

Prenatal development

The nine-month period between conception and birth is divided into three stages: the **germinal stage**, which covers the first two weeks after conception; the **embryonic stage**, which lasts from the third to the eighth week; and the **fetal stage**, which lasts from nine weeks to birth. The following sections summarise some of the main developments at each stage, based on the accounts of prenatal development provided by Berk (2008) and Moore and Persaud (2003).

The germinal stage

Conception occurs when the egg and sperm unite to form a single cell called a **zygote**. The zygote then journeys from the fallopian tubes to the uterus and the process of *cell division* begins: the zygote divides into two cells, then into four cells, sixteen cells, and so on. By about the fourth day, the zygote is now a hollow, fluid-filled ball called a **blastocyst**. The cells on the inside of the blastocyst form the **embryonic disk** that will become the new organism. The outer layer of the blastocyst is called the **trophoblast** and this will combine with cells in the uterus to form the structures that will protect and nourish the developing organism. Between the seventh and ninth days, the blastocyst begins to implant in the wall of the uterus. The trophoblast starts to multiply rapidly and first forms a protective membrane called the **amnion**, which encloses the organism in **amniotic fluid**. This fluid maintains a stable temperature and also acts as a cushion again jolts caused by the mother's movements. A **yolk sac** also develops that produces blood cells. In the second week of this state the cells of the trophoblast form a second protective layer called the **chorion**. From the chorion, finger-like structures called **villi** emerge which burrow deep into the uterine wall and lead to the development of the **placenta**, which brings the mother and embryo's blood supply close together allowing food and oxygen to transfer to the organism and waste products to be carried away. The placenta is linked to the developing child by the **umbilical cord**, which will grow to about three feet during pregnancy. After about two weeks the process of implantation is complete and the developing organism is now called the **embryo**.

The embryonic stage

This stage lasts from the third to the eighth week of gestation and sees the formation of the body structures and internal organs. The embryonic disk forms into three layers: the **ectoderm**, which will become the skin and nervous system; the **mesoderm**, which will become the skeletal and muscle systems; and the **endoderm**, which will form into the digestive and respiratory systems. The ectoderm folds over to form the **neural tube**, which eventually develops into the spinal cord. After about three weeks the top of the neural tube swells to form the brain and production of neurons begins within the neural tube leading to the development of the brain and nervous system. During this stage, the heart begins to pump blood and the backbone, ribs, muscles and digestive tract start to appear. This is followed by the development of the eyes, ears, nose, jaw, neck and limbs. Later in this stage there is further development of the internal organs, such as the heart forming four chambers and the liver and spleen taking over the production of blood from the yolk sac. At the end of this stage the embryo has all of the basic organs and body parts other than the sex organs. It can move, and respond to touch; however, these responses and movements cannot yet be felt by the mother.

The fetal stage

This stage lasts from the ninth week to birth. The brain, muscles and organs continue to develop and the fetus is capable of actions such as arm movements, opening its mouth and sucking its tongue. By the twelfth week, the sex organs have formed. From the seventeenth week on the fetus is big enough for the mother to be able to feel its movements. Eyebrows and head hair are visible by the twentieth week. At around 21 weeks the fetus reacts to sounds and the sense of sight also begins to emerge. Between 22 and 25 weeks it enters the **age of viability**, meaning that if born prematurely and given intensive care, the baby has a chance of survival. In the final three months of pregnancy, the fetus alternates between periods of sleep and wakefulness, and becomes even more responsive to external stimulation. In the final weeks the fetus has grown to a size that fills the entire womb and there is a corresponding reduction in movement. Most fetuses assume an upside-down position. Growth slows and the fetus is ready for birth.

Environmental influences on prenatal development

Although the process of prenatal development is strongly predetermined and follows a set of genetic instructions, environmental factors can also play a part. This can be seen through the effects of a number of factors that can have an adverse effect on the development of the unborn child. These factors are called **teratogens**.

From your own general knowledge, can you think of some possible teratogens?

Teratogens can include the health and wellbeing of the mother and exposure to environmental pollutants, drugs or alcohol, and they can affect the growth of the fetus, or they can result in physical abnormalities that are present from birth, or they may result in cognitive, emotional and behavioural difficulties in childhood. Other teratogenic effects may be expressed in the vulnerablility of children to certain health problems. However, the extent to which a teratogen will affect the child can depend on a number of different factors. These include:

- **Dose**: Large doses over a long period of time have more negative effects.
- **Heredity**: The genetic make-up of the mother and developing organism also plays a role as some individuals are less vulnerable to teratogens.
- **Combinations**: Poor living conditions and nutrition can exacerbate the effect of a teratogen.
- **Age**: The period of pregnancy in which exposure to the teratogen takes place, with certain growth periods more sensitive to teratogens.

There are a wide variety of teratogens: the following sections look at some of them and their effects.

Prescription and non-prescription drugs: Perhaps the most well-known example of damage caused by prescription drugs is the case of thalidomide. This was a drug prescribed to expectant mothers in the 1950s for the treatment of morning sickness. When taken in the early weeks of pregnancy, thalidomide resulted in serious physical abnormalities such as missing or malformed limbs and, less commonly, facial deformities and heart and kidney defects (Moore and Persaud, 2003). Another example of a medication with harmful effects was diethylstilbestrol (DES) which was used to prevent miscarriages. The daughters of mothers prescribed this drug were found to have a greater risk of developing cervical cancer, while their sons were at a higher risk of genital abnormalities (Mittendorf, 1995; Wilcox et al., 1995). Over the counter drugs can also have teratogenic effects. It has been found that regular use of aspirin in pregnancy is associated with problems such as lower intelligence and attention spans in childhood (Streissguth et al., 1987). In general, however, it is difficult to state for definite that such drugs cause problems. Often expectant mothers take more than one drug and if there is damage to the fetus, it is difficult to say which drug was the cause. There may also be individual differences in susceptibility to damage from these drugs. In general, it is recommended that pregnant women if possible avoid such drugs.

Illegal drugs: Babies born to users of cocaine are at risk from a variety of problems including prematurity low birth weight and physiological regulation difficulties (Richardson et al., 1999; Schuetze and Eiden, 2006). Such babies may also be born experiencing drug withdrawal resulting in feverishness, irritability and sleep difficulties. These difficulties can also have a negative effect on the mother–infant bond (Eiden, 2001). Marijuana is another widely used illegal drug and there is some evidence of a link with later problems with attention and memory (Fried, 1993; Fried and Watkinson, 2001). However, a problem with identifying the effects of specific drugs here is that some drug users may use more than one drug, or drug use may be accompanied by heavy smoking or alcohol consumption, and moreover, some drug users may also neglect their physical health and nutrition. Thus all of these factors may have an effect on the health of the unborn child and subsequent developmental outcomes. This can be seen in a review of studies of the long-term effects of prenatal cocaine exposure reported by Frank et al. (2001), who found that adverse developmental outcomes that were thought to be specific to the effects of cocaine were in fact correlated with other factors such as prenatal exposure to alcohol, tobacco, marijuana and the quality of the child's environment.

Alcohol, tobacco and caffeine: The negative effects of smoking during pregnancy are well documented. Nicotine, the addictive substance in tobacco, has the effect of reducing blood flow to the uterus and this in turn has a negative effect on the transfer of nutrients to the fetus, which will affect growth. Babies of mothers who smoke tend to have lower birth weights and are also at greater risk of experiencing impaired heart rate and breathing during sleep and developing respiratory problems later (Jaakola and Gissler, 2004; Schuetze and Zeskind, 2001). Furthermore, such babies can also be unresponsive and restless, which may in turn have a negative impact on the mother–child bond. There is also some evidence that prenatally exposed children have problems with attention and memory (Fried and Watkinson, 2001). Excessive alcohol consumption during pregnancy can result in an infant being born with fetal alcohol spectrum disorder (FASD). Characteristics of babies with this disorder include slow growth, facial deformities and brain injury leading to a variety of cognitive and behavioural problems (Loock et al., 2005). Unfortunately, the damage associated with FASD is irreversible. Even in the case of women who drink moderately during pregnancy, there is an increased risk of babies having reduced head size and body growth (Day et al., 2002) and some evidence of lower IQ scores at aged 8 (Lewis et al., 2012). Currently in the UK, the advice to pregnant women is to avoid all alcohol in the first three months of pregnancy, and if they wish to drink, to limit their consumption to 1–2 units per week (National Institute for Health and Clinical Excellence, 2008). There are also risks associated with high caffeine intake. These include low birth weight and newborn withdrawal symptoms such as vomiting and irritability (Klebanoff et al., 2002).

Infectious disease: Some bacterial and viral infections during pregnancy can harm the developing fetus. Perhaps the best known of these is the rubella (German measles) virus. The damage is greatest if a mother contracts this virus during the first trimester of pregnancy, with infants exposed during this period showing problems such as eye cataracts, deafness, heart defects and mental impairment (Moore and Persaud, 2003). An example of a harmful bacterial infection is toxoplasmosis caused by a parasite found in many animals, the main source of exposure to which is through eating raw or undercooked meat. If the woman is exposed to the illness in the first three months of pregnancy there is a risk of eye or brain damage to the fetus. Infection during the second trimester leads to a risk of mild visual and cognitive impairments. However, many children who were exposed prenatally to this illness do not suffer any damage or adverse long-term consequences. A longitudinal study reported by Freeman et al. (2005) found no evidence of a higher incidence of behaviour or developmental impairments in a group of children aged 3 who had been exposed to the disease prenatally when compared to a group of 3-year-olds who had not been prenatally exposed.

Maternal factors: The wellbeing of the fetus can also be affected by factors such as the age of the mother, maternal nutrition and the mother's emotional wellbeing. Older mothers are more at risk of having a child with a chromosomal disorder such as Down's syndrome (Hook and Cross, 1981). Infants born to teenage mothers also appear to have a higher incidence of problems, but these are not related to the age of the mother. Rather, teenage mothers are at a greater risk of poverty and social exclusion; however, the negative outcomes that these may bring can be avoided with appropriate care and support (Duncan et al., 2010). Malnutrition during pregnancy can result in physical and neural defects. Prolonged emotional stress during pregnancy can also affect the fetus and is linked with stunted fetal growth, low birth weight and premature delivery (Lobel, 1994). There are a variety of ways in which stress may adversely affect the fetus. The mother's stress hormones (which prepare the body to respond to a stressor) may divert nutrients away from the fetus, or the stressed mother may fail to eat properly or she may be drinking alcohol or using drugs, which as mentioned above can have a negative impact on a pregnancy (DiPietro, 2004).

Physical development in infancy and childhood

Physical growth follows two distinct patterns: the **cephalocaudal trend** and the **proximodistal trend**. The cephalocaudal trend refers to growth proceeding in a head-to-toe direction. At birth, the head takes up a relatively large proportion of the total body length, but by the age of 2 the ratio has declined as the lower parts of the body catch up. The proximodistal trend refers to growth proceeding from the centre of the body outward. This can be seen in the prenatal period where the head, chest and trunk grow first, followed by the arms and legs, and finally the hands and feet. This trend continues in childhood where the arms and legs continue to develop ahead of the hands and feet (Berk, 2008).

Changes in body size and appearance

The most obvious signs of physical growth are changes in height and weight, with very rapid changes observed during infancy. By the end of the first year, the infant's height has gained about 50 per cent on their birth size. By two years it is 75 per cent greater (Berk, 2008). In the case of weight, at five months, birth weight has doubled, by one year it has tripled and by two years it has quadrupled. Overall, physical growth follows the **general growth curve**: rapid growth during infancy, a slow but steady pace in childhood followed by a rapid growth spurt in adolescence (Malina and Bouchard, 1991; Tanner, 1990). There are some exceptions to this pattern. The genitals develop slowly from birth to childhood but grow rapidly in adolescence. In contrast the lymph glands (which help fight infection) grow rapidly in infancy and childhood followed by a slight decline in adolescence.

By the middle of their first year, infants take on a plump and rounded appearance with an increase in 'baby fat' which peaks by the end of the first year. In the second year, toddlers slim down and this trend continues during early childhood. By the age of 5, the typical child has a slimmer appearance with body proportions similar to an adult. This leads to improvements in posture and balance which also assist in the development of motor skills (Adolph and Berger, 2005).

Influences on physical growth

It is not surprising that physical growth is influenced by genetic factors and environmental factors such as nutrition. However, emotional wellbeing can also influence it.

Heredity: The influence of heredity can be seen in the observation that children's physical size and growth rates are related to those of their parents (Bogin, 2001). Further evidence of the role of heredity can be seen from studies of identical and fraternal twins. It has been found that the growth curves for height of identical twins are closer to each other and more similar in shape than those of fraternal twins (Hauspie et al., 1994).

Genes influence growth through the production of hormones. In particular the pituitary gland releases two hormones that induce growth. The first of these is **growth hormone (GH)**, which is necessary for the development of all body tissues except the central nervous system and the genitals. Children who lack GH fail to reach their expected height, but if treated early with GH injections, show catch-up growth and then grow at a normal rate (Vance and Mauras, 1999). The other hormone released by the pituitary gland is **thyroid-stimulating hormone (TSH)**, which prompts the thyroid gland in the neck to release thyroxine a substance necessary for brain development, and for GH to have its full impact on body size. Some infants are born with a thyroxine deficiency, and without prompt, early treatment will suffer from severe mental impairment.

Nutrition: Unsurprisingly, physical growth is also affected by nutritional intake. Infants do not simply require food, but the right kind of food. In early infancy, breast milk is the ideal source of nutrition. It contains the ideal balance of fat and proteins, and also provides antibodies to fight disease. Formula milk attempts to mimic the characteristics of breast milk. Overall, however, evidence indicates that breast milk is best, and the benefits extend beyond physical growth. Kramer (2010) has reported on a large-scale study comparing the long-term outcomes of breastfeeding versus formula milk which found that breastfed babies tended to have higher IQ scores and generally better cognitive abilities in later life. On the other hand, with regard to emotional adjustment, there do not appear to be any long-term differences between children who breastfeed and those who are bottle-fed (Fergusson and Woodward, 2002). The importance of nutrition continues through childhood. From the ages of 1–5, the steady pace of growth means that children require proportionately more energy-rich foods than older children and adults, but from the age of 5, children can follow the same healthy eating guidelines appropriate for adults (Albon and Mukherji, 2008).

Emotional wellbeing: While it is unsurprising that factors such as heredity and nutrition have a crucial effect on physical growth, emotional wellbeing may be a less obvious factor. However, the evidence does suggest that being raised in a loving and stimulating environment is as important for physical growth as food. Some infants suffer from **nonorganic failure to thrive**, a growth disorder resulting from a lack of parental love (Black et al., 1994). This disorder is present by the time the child is 18 months old. Infants suffering from this disorder stop growing and have similar symptoms to marasmus (a wasting condition of the body caused by malnutrition) despite provision of adequate food and no other illnesses. Emotional wellbeing continues to be important for growth in childhood and extreme emotional deprivation can interfere with the production of growth hormone and lead to a condition called **psychosocial dwarfism** (see for example, Mouridsen and Nielsen, 1990). Typical characteristics include shortness of stature, immature skeletal age and cognitive and behavioural problems, and these characteristics can be used to differentiate the condition from normal short stature (Voss et al., 1998). However, in cases of nonorganic failure to thrive and psychosocial dwarfism, appropriate interventions, such as removing the child from an abusive environment, result in infants and children showing evidence of catch-up growth (Brockington, 1996; Mouridsen and Nielsen, 1990).

The development of motor skills

In addition to physical growth, children's control over their body movements is another skill that develops rapidly in infancy and early childhood, progressing from a very limited range of motor skills at birth to the ability to walk independently at around 12 months. As with physical growth, motor development also follows the cephalocaudal and proximodistal trends. Babies learn to hold their head upright before gaining control of the arms and trunk. Head, trunk and arm control precedes control of the hands and fingers. In the study of motor development, a distinction can be made between **gross** and **fine motor skills**. Gross motor skills refer to actions that help a child to get around their environment, such as walking and crawling. Fine motor skills refer to smaller sequences of movement, such as reaching and grasping.

The acquisition of motor skills also has an impact on other areas of development. The ability to move around one's environment is also considered to facilitate the development of spatial skills and infants make fewer errors when searching for hidden objects once they have started crawling (Campos and Bertenthal, 1989). The development of reaching and grasping can also have a substantial impact on cognitive development because by grasping, exploring and manipulating objects children can learn a great deal about how these objects look, sound and feel.

Gross motor skills

Bayley (2005) has produced a set of infant development scales indicating the average age at which infants and toddlers acquire a variety of gross and fine motor skills, and also the age range at which 90 per cent of toddlers and infants acquire these skills.

Gross motor skills emerge as follows in infancy: typically, at the age of 6 weeks infants can hold their head upright, and by the time they are 2 months old they can roll from side to back. At around 7 months of age they can sit up alone and begin to crawl. At the age of 11 months they can stand alone and shortly after this they start to walk unaided. Within the various milestones, however, there is also considerable individual variation. So while the 'average' infant will crawl at 7 months, some infants will start crawling before this age and other infants will not start crawling until they are 11 months. Indeed, according to Bayley's scales, while the average age of crawling is 7 months, 90 per cent of infants will start crawling sometime between the ages of 5 and 11 months. It is therefore important to remember that individual variation in acquiring motor skills is normal and early or lack of progress is not a good predictor of the final outcome.

Motor skills develop further throughout childhood. Once a child is able to walk, locomotor skills progress rapidly and by the time they are 4 years old they can walk like an adult, descend a flight of stairs without holding a support, run, jump and hop on one foot (Adolph and Berger, 2005; Malina and Bouchard, 1991). As time passes, children can run faster and further and jump higher. This in part is due to muscular development, but also because children are practising and refining their motor techniques. For example, young children will execute a long jump 'vertically' but older children will angle their bodies and coordinate their knee, hip and arm movements to put more momentum into the jump (Malina and Bouchard, 1991).Hence older children's gross motor skills reflect not just physical development but also the more efficient use of their basic physical capabilities. Another feature of motor skills during childhood is a tendency for children to overestimate their physical abilities (Plumert and Schwebel, 1997; Schwebel and Plumert, 1999). While this may be beneficial as it will motivate them to extend their physical skills further, it can also mean that children are more prone to accidental injuries.

Fine motor skills

Newborn infants will make clumsy, poorly coordinated attempts to reach for objects placed in front of them, a behaviour referred to as **prereaching**. However, as their hand and arm control is not well developed, prereaching is rarely successful and declines at around 2 months of age (von Hofsten, 1984). From 3 months infants will attempt **directed reaching** (Thelen et al., 1993), which is more coordinated and efficient, and coincides with increased eye, head and shoulder control, and reaching gradually improves in accuracy (Bhat et al., 2005). Infants, however, do not appear to depend on vision to help guide their reaching behaviour. Research by Clifton et al. (1994) has shown that even if a light is switched off during reaching, infants will still continue to reach for the object, indicating that they also make use of **proprioception**, a sense of movement and location arising from bodily sensations such as muscle contractions.

When infants start to reach for objects, they will also make attempts at grasping them. Initially this consists of the **palmar** or **ulnar grasp**, a clumsy grasping action in which the fingers close against the palm. Gradually, they start to adjust their grasp to the physical characteristics of an object, allowing them to grasp it more effectively (Butterworth et al., 1997). Towards the end of their first year, infants will start to use the **pincer grasp** (Halverson, 1931) wherein they use their thumb and index finger to lift and explore objects. This allows for more detailed exploration of objects as well as performing specific actions such as turning a knob or a dial. During the second year, they become more proficient with their hands and by the end of this period they can perform various actions such as scribbling with a crayon or building a tower of blocks (Bayley, 2005).

Fine motor skills develop further during early childhood. This can be seen in areas such as drawing, which progresses from scribbling to clear attempts to represent reality (Lowenfeld and Brittan, 1982). This skill, of course, also depends on developments in perception and cognition but increases in the ability to hold and control pens and crayons are also an important factor. Fine motor skills contribute to a variety of self-help skills as well. Children become more proficient at using knives and forks leading to greater self-sufficiency in feeding, and they are able to do and undo buttons and zips, which means they are capable of dressing and undressing themselves on their own.

Maturation versus experience in motor skill development

The existence of cephalomodal and proximodistal trends in motor development would suggest that motor development follows a biologically predetermined pattern. This was very much the view of Gessell and Thompson (1929) who conducted a study of identical twins learning a motor task. One twin was given extra opportunities to practise the task while the other was not given any extra training. However, a subsequent test in which both twins performed the task resulted in them both performing it to a similar level; the twin who received the extra training did not appear to have an advantage. Thus Gessell and Thompson concluded that maturation rather than experience was the prime factor in the acquisition of motor skills.

While it is widely accepted that maturation is a major factor in the development of motor skills, most researchers argue that experience also plays an important role. This can be seen in cases where children have not had sufficient opportunities to practice their motor skills. Morison et al. (1995) reported on the development of Romanian orphans who had been adopted by Canadian families. As infants, they had been reared in extremely deprived conditions in Romanian orphanages and by the time they arrived in Canada, the majority exhibited severe delays in their gross and fine motor skills. The role of experience can also be seen in cross-cultural studies of infant development. The Kipsigi tribe of Kenya aim to promote motor skills in their infants from early on; for example, adults hold infants by their armpits in order to encourage them to practise walking. Super (1976) found that Kipsigi infants are able to walk unaided about a month earlier than western infants. Zelazo et al. (1993) also conducted a series of experiments with North American infants and found that holding them in an upright position and encouraging them to practise their stepping reflex resulted in them walking earlier than a control group of infants who did not receive this intervention.

More recently, instead of just looking at motor skills in terms of maturation or experience, **dynamic systems theory** has been used to characterise their development. This approach does not see motor skills as simply occurring due to maturation and the opportunity to practise skills, but sees the infant as an active participant in this process. Essentially, motor skills develop as the infant reorganises existing skills into more complex patterns of action. Another important aspect of dynamic systems theory for looking at motor development is the recognition that infants are motivated to develop skills that allow them to become interested in objects or achieve other goals (Thelen, 1995). Shaffer and Kipp (2010) give the example of the development of crawling to illustrate this, based on research by Goldfield (1989) who found that before infants learned to crawl, they began to turn their heads towards interesting features of their environment, then to reach towards stimuli and finally to thrust their leg opposite to the outstretched arm. Crawling was therefore preceded by a visual orientation towards objects of interest, an orientation of the body in the direction of the object and a propelling of the body forward through kicking. Thus crawling can be seen as the reorganisation and coordination of existing capabilities into a new skill that allows the infant to achieve a desired goal.

Brain development

At birth, the brain is close to its adult size and develops rapidly throughout childhood. The following sections will look at the structure of the brain and various aspects of brain development.

The structure of the brain

There are various ways of characterising the structure of the brain, but one influential approach proposed by MacLean (1990) is to divide the brain into three regions: The **brain stem**, the **limbic system** and the **cerebrum**. The brain stem controls basic physiological processes such as relexes, respiration and digestion. The limbic system consists of a number of structures that are involved in emotional responses and memory. The cerebrum is responsible for conscious awareness and consists of two cerebal **hemispheres**, a left and a right. The two hemispheres control different functions (which will be considered later) and are connected by a set of nerve fibres called the **corpus callosum**. The hemispheres are surrounded by an outer layer called the **cerebral cortex**. This is the '*grey matter*' that gives the brain its distinctive 'wrinkled' look. Each hemisphere is divided into four lobes: the **frontal lobe**, which is concerned with higher mental functions such as planning and organisation; the **temporal lobe**, which deals with language, hearing and smell; the **parietal lobe**, which is where the processing of bodily sensations takes place; and the **occipital lobe**, which is involved in visual processing.

Neurons and glial cells

The basic unit of the brain and nervous system is a cell called the **neuron**. Neurons receive and transmit electrical signals (neural impulses) which allow information to be sent to and from various parts of the brain and nervous system. As we saw earlier in the chapter, production of neurons begins during the embryonic period when they are produced in the neural tube, from which they migrate to form the various areas of the brain. Once neurons complete this neuronal migration they become **differentiated** according to the site to which they have migrated and assume specific functions, such as processing visual or auditory information. There are approximately 100 to 200 billion neurons in the human brain, the majority of which will have formed by the end of the second trimester of pregnancy (Kolb and Fantie, 1989). There are tiny gaps between the neurons called **synapses**. This is where the neuronal fibres come close together but do not meet. Information is transmitted between the neurons through the production of **neurotransmitters,** substances which can cross the synapses.

Given that production of neurons is almost complete before birth, what accounts for the growth of the brain during infancy and childhood? This is largely due to the development of a second type of cell called the **glial cell**. These cells are responsible for nourishing the neurons and also for a process called **myelination** in which the neurons are covered with an insulating layer of a fatty substance called myelin. This substance helps to improve the efficient transmission of neural impulses. At birth, the neural pathways between the brain and sense organs are fairly well myelinated giving the newborn good sensory abilities. The process of myelination continues rapidly during the first few years of life; however, some areas of the brain do not become fully myelinated until early adulthood (Kalat, 2004). Improvements in neural transmission due to myelination are also thought to contribute to cognitive growth during childhood.

Hemispheric specialisation

Although the two hemispheres of the cerebrum look identical it has been established that they serve different functions and control different areas of the body. This specialisation of the hemispheres is referred to as **cerebral lateralisation**. The left hemisphere controls movement and sensation in the right side of the body and the right controls movement and sensation in the left side. For most people the left hemisphere is specialised for language processing while the right is specialised for processing visuospatial information and non-speech sounds (Kalat, 2004). Both hemispheres (as well as the limbic system) are involved in the processing of emotions, but the left appears to be specialised for dealing with positive (in the sense of approaching the environment) emotions such as joy, anger and interest while the right appears to be specialised for dealing with negative (withdrawal from the environment) emotions such as fear, distress and disgust (Workman et al., 2000).

It is thought that the process of lateralisation may begin prenatally and continues after birth. One suggestion is that most fetuses end up positioned in the womb with their right ear facing outward and this may lead to a right ear (and thus left hemisphere) advantage for language processing (Previc, 1991). Most newborns appear to have a preference for turning to their right when lying on their back and also have a tendency to use the right sides of their bodies in their reflex reactions (Rönnqvist and Hopkins, 1998). Also, a right ear (left hemisphere) advantage for speech sounds has been observed in newborns (Bertoncini et al., 1989). In general, with increasing age the brain becomes more lateralised. By the age of 18 months, most toddlers show a clear preference for one hand over the other (Fagard and Marks, 2000) and a right ear advantage for speech is clearly apparent from 3 years of age (Ingram, 1975).

However, while the process of cerebral lateralisation may be well under way at birth, it is far from complete and it has been observed that children who suffer from traumatic brain injuries to the left hemisphere can still develop language normally (Bates and Roe, 2001). This demonstrates another quality of the brain known as **plasticity** which will be considered in the next section.

Brain development and plasticity

You will recall (see above) that neurons are the basic unit for transmitting information in the brain and nervous system and production of neurons is more or less complete by the end of the second trimester of pregnancy. Another notable feature of neuronal development is that more neurons are produced than are necessary, and the average infant has more neurons and synaptic connections than an adult (Elkind, 2001). It is this overproduction of neurons that can allow rapid recovery from brain injury in infants because other neural circuits assume the roles of those that have died. This overproduction ensures plasticity, which refers to the fact that in the early stages many areas of the brain are not yet committed to a specific function and the brain therefore is receptive to the effects of learning. Plasticity also means that if an area of the brain is damaged, then other areas can take on the functions of those that are damaged.

While there is initially an overproduction of neurons and synapses, this eventually ceases through the processes of **neuronal death**, wherein neurons that connect with each other crowd out the remaining ones which then die, and **synaptic pruning**, in which the brain disposes of the synaptic connections of neurons that are not regularly stimulated. The phrase '*neurons that fire together, wire together*' is often used to describe this process. This indicates that stimulation from the outside environment is also essential for brain development, and two types of plasticity have been noted: **experience-expectant plasticity** and **experience-dependent plasticity** (Bruer and Greenhough, 2001).

Experience-expectant plasticity refers to the development of synapses which respond to experiences that are expected and common in the human species. It appears that as a result of millions of years of evolution, the newborn brain 'expects' to encounter certain experiences, such as patterned light, sounds, language, opportunities to explore and manipulate objects, and responsive caregivers (Twardosz, 2012). If these experiences happen, the existing synapses will continue and will not be pruned. Experience-expectant plasticity is also associated with the concept of *sensitive periods*, times when certain areas of the brain require and are especially receptive to stimulation from specific experiences. It is well established from research with animals that development of the visual system is dependent on certain forms of light stimulation, and animals raised in circumstances of limited visual stimulation experienced permanent and irreversible changes to the visual cortex of the brain (Hubel and Wiesel, 1970). There is also some evidence from studying children who received abnormal visual input (due to problems such as cataracts) that exposure to normal visual experiences is necessary for the development of various aspects of vision, such as visual acuity and peripheral vision (Lewis and Maurer, 2005).

However, it is not just basic processes such as vision and hearing that appear to be experience-expectant; this may also apply to other areas of development related to psychological wellbeing. One such aspect is the ability to regulate and manage emotional experiences (a topic that will be covered in Chapter 8). Young infants have not developed the capacity to regulate their emotions and impulses, are unable to obtain their own gratification and require help in learning to plan their actions. The development of these skills depends on the maturation of the frontal lobes and the limbic system. It is therefore likely that the development of these areas is also dependent on sensitive interaction with a caregiver (Glaser, 2000; Joseph, 1999). Stressful experiences related to poor caregiving and maltreatment can also lead to heightened levels of the stress hormone cortisol in the infant. While this hormone is necessary for preparing the body to deal with stressful situations, in infants it can interfere with processes such as the formation of neurons, synaptic overproduction and pruning, and myelination of the developing brain. Therefore it is generally accepted that a lack of care as well as child abuse and neglect can have a negative effect on brain development, particularly in areas that are involved in buffering the effects of stressful experiences (Tarullo and Gunnar, 2006; Twardosz and Lutzker, 2010).

The other form of plasticity is experience-dependent plasticity. Unlike experience-expectant brain development, which will occur naturally providing the infant receives appropriate care, experience-dependent plasticity refers to the modification of synapses or the generation of new ones on the basis of specific experiences. These experiences can include reading and writing, and acquiring specific types of expertise. This type of plasticity is present throughout life and is not associated with sensitive periods.

 Would learning music be an example of experience-expectant or experience-dependent development?

The notion of plasticity has given rise to a number of misinterpretations, especially in relation to its role in early education and development. Twardosz (2012) and Zambo (2008) point out that there has been much public interest in neuroscience since the 1990s, which they refer to as 'the decade of the brain', and specifically, interest in the role of early experiences for producing later favourable outcomes. In particular there has been a focus on the importance of the first three years of life, which were seen as a limited window of opportunity for influencing brain development. Findings on plasticity have been misinterpreted so that parents and teachers became convinced that they were in a race against time to stop synapses from being lost. This also has led to the publication of many books on the theme of brain development, for example *125 Brain Games for Baby: Simple Games to Promote Early Brain Development* (Siberg, 2001) and encouraged toy manufacturers to produce 'brain stimulating' toys and educational materials. The problem here is confusion between experience-dependent and experience-expectant plasticity and a general lack of understanding that experience-dependent plasticity takes place *throughout life*, and a failure to understand that synaptic pruning is, far from being a bad thing, a normal process of brain development. This also indicates the importance of educating parents and childcare workers about the nature of brain development and indeed in her study of American childcare workers Zambo (2008) found a lack of knowledge of brain development, suggesting that it is important for this to be incorporated in the training they receive.

Chapter summary

- Prenatal development is divided into three stages: the germinal stage, the embryonic stage and the fetal stage.
- While prenatal development follows a predetermined process, it can also be affected by environmental factors and there are a variety of teratogens that can have a negative effect on development.
- Physical growth in infancy and childhood follows a cephalocaudal and a proximodistal trend, and is influenced by a number of factors including heredity, nutrition and emotional wellbeing.
- In addition to changes in physical size, control over body movements also increases during infancy and childhood. A distinction can be made between gross and fine motor skills.
- Motor skills appear to develop through a combination of maturation and experience as well as the motivation of the infant to explore the environment.
- The brain is made up of neurons, most of which have developed during the prenatal period, and glial cells.
- The brain also overproduces neurons and synaptic connections between them, but this process is eventually curtailed through neuronal death and synaptic pruning. These are normal processes of development.
- The developing brain also exhibits considerable plasticity, meaning that if an area of the brain is damaged, other areas can assume the functions of those that are damaged.
- Development of the brain is affected by experience and two forms have been noted: experience-expectant plasticity and experience-dependent plasticity.
- Experience-expectant plasticity means that the brain expects to encounter certain experiences that are common to humans, such as exposure to language, patterned light and appropriate caregiving. There appears to be a sensitive period when the brain expects and is receptive to stimulation from such experiences.
- Experience-dependent plasticity means that certain non-standard learning experiences can also affect brain development, such as the acquisition of various skills.
- There has been confusion about the nature of experience-dependent plasticity, with many parents and teachers believing, erroneously, that they are in a race against time for children to acquire certain skills. However, there is no evidence of a sensitive period for experience-dependent plasticity.

Further reading

Twardosz, S. and Bell, M.A. (eds) (2012) *Early Education and Development*, Special Issue: Neuroscience Perspectives on Early Development and Education, 23 (1): i–137.

A special edition of the academic journal *Early Education and Development* focusing on recent findings in the field of brain development and their implications for child development and education.

References

Adolph, K.E. and Berger, S.E. (2005) 'Physical and motor development', in M.H. Bornstein and M.E. Lamb (eds), *Developmental Science: An Advanced Textbook* (5th edn). Mahwah, NJ: Erlbaum. pp. 223–81.

Albon, D. and Mukherji, P. (2008) *Food and Health in Early Childhood*. London: Sage.

Bates, E. and Roe, K. (2001) 'Language development in children with unilateral brain injury', in C.A. Nelson and M. Luciana (eds), *Handbook of Developmental Cognitive Neuroscience*. Cambridge MA: MIT. pp. 281–307.

Bayley, N. (2005) *Bayley Scales of Infant and Toddler Development* (3rd edn). San Antonio, TX: Harcourt Assessment.

Berk, L.E. (2008) *Infants, Children and Adolescents* (Sixth edn). Boston, MA: Pearson.

Bertoncini, J., Morais, J., Bijeljac-Bebic, R., McAdams, S., Peretz, I. and Mehler, J. (1989) 'Dichotic perception and laterality in neonates', *Brain and Language*, 37 (4): 591–605.

Black, M.M., Hutcheson, J.J., Dubowitz, H. and Berenson-Howard, J. (1994) 'Parenting style and developmental status among children with nonorganic failure to thrive', *Journal of Pediatric Psychology*, 19 (6): 689–707.

Bogin, B. (2001) *The Growth of Humanity*. New York: Wiley-Liss.

Bhat, A., Heathcock, J. and Galloway, J.C. (2005) 'Toy-oriented changes in hand and joint kinematics during the emergence of purposeful reaching', *Infant Behaviour and Development*, 28 (4): 445–65.

Brockington, I. (1996) *Motherhood and Mental Health*. Oxford: Oxford University Press.

Bruer, J.T. and Greenhough, W.T. (2001) 'The subtle science of how experience affects the brain', in D.B. Bailey Jr., J.T. Bruer, F.J. Symons and J.W. Lichtman (eds), *Critical Thinking about Critical Periods*. Baltimore, MD: Brookes. pp. 209–32.

Butterworth, G., Verweij, E. and Hopkins, B. (1997) 'The development of prehension in infants: Halverson revisited', *British Journal of Developmental Psychology*, 15 (2): 223–36.

Campos, J.J. and Bertenthal, B.I. (1989) 'Locomotion and psychological development in infancy', in F. Morrison, C. Lord and D. Keating (eds), *Applied Developmental Psychology*, Vol. 3. New York: Academic Press. pp. 229–58.

Clifton, R.K., Rochat, P., Robin, D. and Berthier, N.E. (1994) 'Multimodal perception in the control of infant reaching', *Journal of Experimental Psychology: Human Perception and Performance*, 20 (4): 876–86.

Day, N.L., Leach, S.L., Richardson, G.A., Cornelius, M.D., Robles, N. and Larkby, C. (2002) 'Prenatal alcohol exposure predicts continued deficits in offspring size at 14 years of age', *Alcoholism: Clinical and Experimental Research*, 26 (10): 1584–91.

DiPietro, J. (2004) 'The role of prenatal maternal stress in child development', *Current Directions in Psychological Science*, 13 (2): 71–4.

Duncan, S., Edwards, R. and Alexander, C. (2010) *Teenage Parenthood: What's the Problem?* London: The Tufnell Press.

Eiden, R.D. (2001) 'Maternal substance abuse and mother-infant feeding interactions', *Infant Mental Health Journal*, 22 (4), 497–511.

Elkind, D. (2001) 'Authority of the brain', *Pediatrics*, 107 (Suppl. 1): 964–66.

Fagard, J. and Marks, A. (2000) 'Unimanual and bimanual tasks and the assessment of handedness in toddlers', *Developmental Science*, 3 (2): 137–47.

Fergusson, D.M. and Woodward, L.J. (2002) 'Breast feeding and later psychosocial adjustment', *Paediatric and Perinatal Epidemiology*, 13 (2): 144–57.

Frank, D.A., Augustyn, M., Knight, W.G., Pell, T. and Zuckerman, B. (2001) 'Growth, development, and behavior in early childhood following prenatal cocaine exposure: A systematic review', *Journal of the American Medical Association*, 285 (12): 1613–25.

Freeman, K., Salt A., Prusa, A., Malm, G., Ferret, N., Buffolano, W., Schmidt, D., Tan, H.K., Gilbert, R.E. and The European Multicentre Study on Congenital Toxoplasmosis (EMSCOT) (2005) 'Association between congenital toxoplasmosis and parent-reported developmental outcomes, concerns, and impairments in 3 year old children', *BMC Pediatrics*, 5 (23). Available at: http://www.biomedcentral.com/1471-2431/5/23/ (accessed 15 July 2013).

Fried, P.A. (1993) 'Prenatal exposure to tobacco and marijuana: Effects during pregnancy, infancy, and early childhood', *Clinical Obstetrics and Gynecology*, 36 (2): 319–37.

Fried, P.A. and Watkinson, B. (2001) 'Differential effects on facets of attention in adolescents prenatally exposed to cigarettes and marijuana', *Neurotoxicology and Teratology*, 23 (5): 421–30.

Gessell, A.L. and Thompson, H. (1929) 'Learning and growth in identical infant twins: An experimental study by the method of co-twin control', *Genetic Psychology Monographs*, 6 (1): 1–124.

Glaser, D. (2000) 'Child abuse and neglect and the brain – a review', *Journal of Child Psychology and Psychiatry*, 41 (1): 97–116.

Goldfield, E.C. (1989) 'Transition from rocking to crawling: Postural constraints on infant movement', *Developmental Psychology*, 25 (6): 913–19.

Halverson, H.M. (1931) 'An experimental study of prehension in infants by means of systematic cinema records', *Genetic Psychology Monographs*, 10: 107–286.

Hauspie, R.C., Bergman, T., Bielicki, T. and Susanne, C. (1994) 'Genetic variance in the pattern of the growth curve for height: A longitudinal analysis of male twins', *Annals of Human Biology*, 21 (4): 347–62.

Hook, E.B. and Cross, P.K. (1981) 'Temporal increase in the rate of Down syndrome livebirths to older mothers in New York State', *Journal of Medical Genetics*, 18 (1): 29–30.

Hubel, D.H. and Wiesel, T.N. (1970) 'The period of susceptibility to the physiological effects of unilateral eye closure in kittens', *Journal of Physiology*, 206 (2): 419–36.

Ingram, D. (1975) 'Cerebral speech lateralization in young children', *Neuropsychologia*, 13 (1): 103–5.

Jaakola, J.J. and Gissler, M. (2004) 'Maternal smoking in pregnancy, fetal development, and childhood asthma', *American Journal of Public Health*, 94 (1): 136–40.

Joseph, R. (1999) 'Environmental influences on neural plasticity, the limbic system, emotional development and attachment: A review', *Child Psychiatry and Human Development*, 29 (3): 189–208.

Kalat, J.W. (2004) *Biological Psychology* (8th edn). Belmont, CA: Thomson.

Klebanoff, M.A., Levine, R.J., Clemens, J.D. and Wilkins, D. (2002) 'Maternal serum caffeine metabolites and small-for-gestational age birth', *American Journal of Epidemiology*, 155 (1): 32–7.

Kolb, B. and Fantie, B. (1989) 'Development of the child's brain and behaviour', in C.R. Reynolds and E. Fletcher-Jansen (eds), *Handbook of Clinical Child Neuropsychology*. New York: Plenum Press. pp. 17–39.

Kramer, M.S. (2010) 'Breast is best: The evidence', *Early Human Development*, 86: 729–32.

Lewis, S.J., Zuccolo, L., Davey Smith, G., Macleod, J., Rodriguez, S., Draper, E.S., Barrow, M., Alati, R., Sayal, K., Ring, S., Golding, J. and Gray, R. (2012) 'Fetal alcohol exposure and IQ at age 8: Evidence from a population-based birth-cohort study', *Plos One*. Available at: http://www.plosone.org/article/info%3Adoi%2F10.1371%2Fjournal.pone.0049407 (accessed 4 March 2013).

Lewis, T.L. and Maurer, D. (2005) 'Multiple sensitive periods in human visual development: Evidence from visually deprived children', *Developmental Psychobiology*, 46 (3): 163–83.

Lobel, M. (1994) 'Conceptualizations, measurement, and effects of prenatal maternal stress on birth outcomes', *Journal of Behavioral Medicine*, 17 (3): 225–72.

Loock, C., Conry, J., Cook, J.L., Chudley, A.E. and Rosales, T. (2005) 'Identifying fetal alcohol spectrum disorder in primary care', *Canadian Medical Association Journal*, 172 (5): 628–30.

Lowenfeld, V. and Brittan, W.L. (1982) *Creative and Mental Growth* (7th edn). New York: Macmillan.

MacLean, P.D. (1990) *The Triune Brain in Evolution: Role in Paleocerebral Functions*. New York: Plenum Press.

Malina, R.M. and Bouchard, C. (1991) *Growth, Maturation and Physical Activity*. Champaign, IL: Human Kinetics.

Mittendorf, R. (1995) 'Teratogen update: Carcinogenesis and teratogenesis associated with exposure to diethylstilbestrol in utero', *Teratology, 51* (6): 434–45.

Moore, K.L. and Persaud, T.V.N. (2003) *Before We are Born: Essentials of Embryology and Birth Defects* (6th edn). Philadelphia, PA: Saunders.

Morison, S.J., Ames, E.W. and Chisholm, K. (1995) 'The development of children adopted from Romanian orphanages', *Merrill-Palmer Quarterly, 41* (4): 411–30.

Mouridsen, S.E. and Nielsen, S. (1990) 'Reversible somatotropin deficiency (psychosocial dwarfism) presenting as conduct disorder and growth hormone deficiency', *Developmental Medicine and Child Neurology*, 32 (12): 1093–98.

National Institute for Health and Clinical Excellence (2008) 'Antenatal care', *NICE Clinical Guideline CG62*.

Plumert, J.M. and Schwebel, D.C. (1997) 'Social and temperamental influences on children's overestimation of their physical abilities: Links to accidental injuries', *Journal of Experimental Child Psychology*, 67 (3): 317–37.

Previc, F.H. (1991) 'A general theory concerning the prenatal origins of cerebral lateralization in humans', *Psychological Review*, 98 (3): 299–334.

Richardson, G.A., Hamel, S.C., Goldschmidt, L. and Day, N. (1999) 'Growth of infants prenatally exposed to crack/cocaine: Comparison of a prenatal care and a no prenatal care sample', *Pediatrics*, 104 (2): e18. Available at: www.pediatricsdigest.mobi/content/104/2/e18.full (accessed 15 July 2013).

Rönnqvist, L. and Hopkins, B. (1998) 'Lateral biases in head-turning and the moro response in the human newborn: Are they both vestibular in origin?', *Developmental Psychobiology, 33* (4): 339–49.

Schuetze, P. and Eiden, R.D. (2006) 'The association between maternal cocaine use during pregnancy and physiological regulation in 4- to 8-week-old infants: An examination of possible mediators and moderators', *Journal of Pediatric Psychology*, 31 (1): 15–26.

Schuetze, P. and Zeskind, P.S. (2001) 'Relation between maternal cigarette smoking during pregnancy and behavioral and physiological measures of autonomic regulation in neonates', *Infancy*, 2 (3): 371–83.

Schwebel, D.C. and Plumert, J.M. (1999) 'Longitudinal and concurrent relations among temperament, ability estimation, and injury proneness', *Child Development*, 70 (3): 700–12.

Shaffer, D.R. and Kipp, K. (2010) *Developmental Psychology: Childhood and Adolescence*. Belmont, CA: Wadsworth.

Siberg, J. (2001) *125 Brain Games for Baby: Simple Games to Promote Early Brain Development*. New York: MJF Books.

Streissguth, A.P., Treder, R.P., Barr, H.M., Shepard, T.H., Bleyer, W.A., Sampson, P.D. and Martin, D.C. (1987) 'Aspirin and acetaminophen use by pregnant women and subsequent child IQ and attention decrements', *Teratology*, 35 (2): 211–19.

Super, C.M. (1976) 'Enviromental effects on motor development: The case of "African infant precocity"', *Developmental Medicine and Child Neurology*, 18 (5): 561–7.

Tanner, J.M. (1990) *Foetus into Man* (2nd edn). Cambridge, MA: Harvard University Press.

Tarullo, A.R. and Gunnar, R. (2006) 'Child maltreatment and the developing HPA axis', *Hormones and Behaviour*, 50 (4): 632–9.

Thelen, E. (1995) 'Motor development: A new synthesis', *American Psychologist*, 50 (2): 79–95.

Thelen, E., Corbetta, D., Kamm, K. Spencer, J.P., Schneider, K. and Zernicke, R.F. (1993) 'The transition to reaching: Mapping intention and intrinsic dynamics', *Child Development*, 64 (4): 1058–98.

Twardosz, S. (2012) 'Effects of experience on the brain: The role of neuroscience in early development and education', *Early Education and Development*, 23 (1): 96–119.

Twardosz, S. and Lutzker, J. (2010) 'Child maltreatment and the developing brain: A review of neuroscience perspectives', *Aggression and Violent Behavior*, 15 (1): 59–68.

Vance, M.L. and Mauras, N. (1999) 'Growth hormone therapy in adults and children', *New England Journal of Medicine*, 341: 1206–16.

von Hofsten, C. (1984) 'Developmental changes in the organisation of prereaching movements', *Developmental Psychology*, 20 (3): 378–88.

Voss, L.D., Mulligan, J. and Betts, P.R. (1998) 'Short stature at school entry – an index of social deprivation? (The Wessex Growth Study)', *Child Care, Health and Development*, 24 (2): 145–56.

Wilcox, A.J., Baird, D.D., Weinberg, C.R., Hornsby, P.P. and Herbst, A.L. (1995) 'Fertility in men exposed prenatally to diethylstilbestrol', *New England Journal of Medicine*, 332: 1411–16.

Workman, L., Peters, S. and Taylor, S. (2000) 'Lateralisation of perceptual processing of pro- and anti-social emotions displayed in chimeric faces', *Laterality*, 5 (3): 237–49.

Zambo, D. (2008) 'Childcare workers' knowledge about the brain and developmentally appropriate practice', *Early Childhood Education Journal*, 35 (6): 571–7.

Zelazo, N.A., Zelazo, P.R., Cohen, K.M. and Zelazo, P.D. (1993) 'Specificity of practice effects in elementary neuromotor patterns', *Developmental Psychology*, 29 (4): 686–91.

Disorders and Development

6

 Why you should read this chapter

During the course of growing up, some children will encounter adverse circumstances that may lead to the development of a psychological or behavioural problem. According to the charity Young Minds (2013), 850,000 children in the UK have a mental health problem. There are a variety of problems that can be suffered including the following: **internalising problems** (such as anxiety and depression); **externalising problems** (such as aggression and conduct); **pervasive developmental disorders** (in which a wide variety of functioning is adversely affected); **elimination disorders** (such as bed-wetting [enuresis] or problems with uncontrolled bowel movements [encopresis]); or **'tic' disorders** involving involuntary movements or speech acts (such as Tourette's syndrome). Understanding the causes of such problems, and finding ways to treat or, preferably, prevent them is an important concern for child psychologists. This chapter will look at an approach to this called **developmental psychopathology** and how this has informed the study of mental health and behavioural problems in childhood.

(Continued)

(Continued)

By the end of this chapter you should

- be aware of the approach of developmental psychopathology and understand basic concepts such as developmental pathways, equifinality and multifinality
- be aware of some of the techniques used to diagnose psychopathology
- have a basic understanding of a number of childhood disorders including depression, anxiety, conduct disorder, attention deficit hyperactivity disorder and autism
- understand what is meant by the terms risk and resilience and how research in this area informs us about the prevention of childhood disorders.

Developmental psychopathology

Wenar and Kerig (2006: 16) define developmental psychopathology as '*the study of developmental processes that contribute to, or protect against, psychopathology*'. An important feature of developmental psychopathology is that it does not adhere to a single theory that can account for all disorders (Cicchetti, 2006; Rutter and Sroufe, 2000). Rather, the emphasis is on looking at a range of factors that may be related to psychological problems including biological, psychological, social and cultural factors.

Table 6.1   Ways in which development can be disrupted

Disruption	Description	Example
Developmental delay	Development proceeds at a slower pace than normal	A 3-year-old child who has not learned to talk
Regression	Child falls off course of normal development or loss of developmental achievements	Return to bed-wetting in late childhood
Asynchrony	Different aspects of development proceed out of step with one another	A child whose language development follows the same course as peers but behind in social development
Precocity	An accelerated rate of development that may be linked to psychopathology	A young child who worries excessively about 'grown-up' matters
Developmental deviation	Behaviours that are qualitatively different from normal development	Echolalia in children with autism (tendency to repeat back people's speech with no purpose)

Another important feature of developmental psychopathology is the assumption that there is a *continuum* between normal and abnormal development. Whether a child follows a healthy or maladaptive life course, the same developmental principles apply and therefore it is important to understand normal development in order to understand how development may go awry (Wenar and Kerig, 2006). In general there are a number of ways in which development can deviate from a normal, adaptive course. Wenar and Kerig (2006) describe five ways in which development may be disrupted and these are summarised in Table 6.1.

Four of these – *developmental delay, asynchrony, regression and precocity* – can be seen as **quantitative departures from normal development** (e.g. less language skills, more worry and anxiety). *Developmental deviation* can be seen as a **qualitative departure from normal development** wherein behaviours that would not be expected in normal development are apparent.

Taking a developmental approach to psychopathology allows psychologists to examine the different **developmental pathways** that may lead to the emergence of psychopathology. It is recognised that there are potentially many factors that can contribute to the development of disorders and their relative contribution will vary among individuals (Cicchetti, 1993). Related to this are the principles of **equifinality** and **multifinality** (Cicchetti and Rogosch, 1996). Equifinality refers to the observation that there are different pathways which can lead to the same outcome, for example aggressive behaviour in one child may be the result of physical abuse and for another it may be as a result of neglect. Multifinality refers to an adverse event resulting in different outcomes, depending on the individual, for example one child reacting to a bereavement by becoming angry and aggressive, while for another the end result may be withdrawal or depression.

Some children may carry on experiencing psychological problems in adolescence and into adulthood, while for other children they may cease. The factors that promote or prevent the reoccurrence of psychological disorders in childhood and beyond are another area of interest to developmental psychopathologists, who look for patterns of **continuity** and **discontinuity**.

The assessment of psychopathology

A number of different classification systems have been developed for the assessment and diagnosis of psychopathology. These systems usually focus on specific behaviours that are dangerous or cause distress, and aim to organise the various descriptors and observations into meaningful units that will facilitate diagnosis (Wenar and Kerig, 2006). This section will focus on three such systems, the *Diagnostic and Statistical Manual of Mental Disorders* (DSM), the Child Behaviour Checklist (CBCL) and the Strengths and Difficulties Questionnaire (SDQ).

The **Diagnostic and Statistical Manual of Mental Disorders** is a long-established and well-known system for the diagnosis of psychopathology and is now in its fourth edition (DSM-IV) (APA, 2000). A clinician will observe the patient and use the DSM-IV to determine whether the symptoms presented by the patient match a particular mental disorder. The emphasis in its use is the classification of disorders, not individuals. The manual does not refer to a schizophrenic or an alcoholic, but will use phrases such as 'a child with schizophrenia' or 'an adult with alcohol dependency' (Wenar and Kerig, 2006).

DSM-IV uses five dimensions or axes in assessing a child. The first axis concerns the diagnosis of specific disorders, such as depression. The second is concerned with personality disorders and mental retardation, as these can affect functioning in a pervasive manner. The third axis concerns any medical conditions in the patient that may be relevant to understanding the disorder, such as injuries or physical illnesses. The fourth examines the individual's psychosocial and environmental problems and focuses on negative life events or environmental stressors that provide the wider context in which problems occur, such as inadequate social support, or family problems. The final axis is a global assessment of functioning and is based on the clinician's overall judgement of the individual's level of functioning. This judgement is made on a scale ranging from 1 (lowest, persistent inability to maintain personal hygiene) to 100 (highest, superior functioning).

Although DSM-IV is a comprehensive system for the diagnosis of psychopathology, it has its limitations when used with children. In particular, it does not address the issue of the developmental dimension (Wenar and Kerig, 2006). In general, it assumes that the diagnostic criteria remain the same across development; however, research has shown that this is not the case. For example, in the case of depression (which will be covered in the section on childhood disorders), the symptoms can vary with the age of the child.

DSM-IV takes a *categorical* approach to diagnosis, classifying children into whether or not a child has a disorder. An alternative dimensional approach is taken by the **Child Behaviour Checklist (CBCL)**, developed by Achenbach (1991). This involves the child being rated on the extent to which he or she shows a disorder. This approach is more in keeping with the notion of normality and abnormality lying on a continuum. There are three different forms of the CBCL – a self-report, a parent report and a teacher report. The CBCL consists of 118 items which can be used to create a profile of the child based on eight 'narrow-band' and two 'wide-band' factors. The narrow-band factors include withdrawn/depressed, somatic (physical) disorders, social problems, attention problems, and aggressive behaviour. The wide-band factors are the internalising and externalising scales. Internalising disorders refer to an inwardly directed suffering such as anxiety and depression whereas externalising refers to problems such as expressing aggression or antisocial behaviour. It is important to note that internalising and externalising behaviours are not mutually exclusive and a child may demonstrate elements of both, for example a child may be sad and aggressive. There are norms by age and gender available for the CBCL and an individual child's scores can be compared against the relevant norms, allowing a clinician to determine the extent to which aspects of a child's behaviour falls within the normal range and which falls outside. For example, a child may be within the normal limits for the internalising scales but exceeding the norm for the externalising scales.

A number of limitations have been identified with the CBCL. It does not include some major childhood disorders, such as autism, and where such disorders are suspected, the DSM-IV is more appropriate. Other issues relate to discrepancies between the different forms of the checklist. Teachers and parents tend to provide more accurate accounts of externalising behaviours while children provide more accurate accounts of their internalising behaviours (Rey et al., 1992). It has been found that parent characteristics can also affect how the child is viewed, for example a depressed mother may have a more negative view of her child's behaviour (Webster-Stratton and Hammond, 1988).

The **Strengths and Difficulties Questionnaire (SDQ)** was developed by Goodman (1997) and is a brief behavioural screening questionnaire for use with children and adolescents. It consists of 25 items, divided into 5 scales: emotional problems, conduct problems, hyperactivity/inattention, peer problems and prosocial behaviour. Scores on the first four scales can be added together to provide a total 'difficulties' score and the final scale provides a 'strengths' score. Like the CBCL, the SDQ is a dimensional measure, and there are self-report versions (for use with adolescents) and informant versions which are completed by the parents or teachers of young children. One advantage of the SDQ over the CBCL is its brevity and quickness of administration and these qualities do not affect its reliability and validity. A study by Goodman and Scott (1999) found that the SDQ was as accurate as the longer CBCL in detecting externalising and internalising problems, and better at detecting inattention and hyperactivity. However, like the CBCL, the SDQ does not include disorders such as pervasive developmental disorders. Also, there can be differences in perceptions between different informants. Davé et al. (2008) found that when the parent form was used, there were some differences between reports supplied by mothers and fathers, with fathers tending to report more abnormal behaviours than mothers, and it is recommended that perspectives of both parents are taken into account in clinical settings using this questionnaire.

Some childhood disorders

There are many different childhood disorders and a comprehensive review is not possible here. This section will look at five common ones. Two internalising disorders will be examined: depression and anxiety. This will be followed by two externalising ones: conduct disorder and attention deficit hyperactivity disorder. Finally, the pervasive developmental disorder of autism will be considered. For each disorder, we will look at the main characteristics, long-term outcomes associated with the disorder, proposed causes, and treatment.

Depression

Feeling depressed is a common experience for most people and we all go through periods of feeling down and in low spirits every now and then. However, for a diagnosis of clinical depression to be made, the normal depressive symptoms such as sadness and tiredness are marked and severe to the extent that they can impair everyday functioning.

For many years it was thought that children did not suffer from clinical depression as it was assumed that they did not have the cognitive complexity to exhibit the symptoms. Based on observations of their reactions to traumatic losses, it was suggested that children were masking out their depression with somatic complaints or acting-out behaviours (Kovacs and Devlin, 1998). However, more recently, this view of **masked depression** has been rejected. When asked directly, distressed children are able to report the symptoms of depression (Kovacs and Devlin, 1998), and the behaviour problems previously thought to mask depression actually accompany it (Hammen and Compas, 1994). Based on a number of different studies of childhood depression Wenar and Kerig (2006) have identified some developmental differences in the symptoms of depression. In infants and toddlers, depression is characterised by a sad face, loss of developmental accomplishments (such as toilet-training), sleep disturbances, self-harming behaviours (such as head banging) or self-soothing behaviours (such as tongue sucking). In preschool children, symptoms can include a sad face, loss of cognitive and language skills, somatic complaints and a lack of interest in pleasurable activities. Older children are better able to verbalise their distress and more adult-like symptoms are present including low self-esteem, self-criticism and guilt. Loss of motivation is also a problem which may affect the child's participation in social activities and they may also engage in disruptive or aggressive behaviour. Eating and sleep disorders may also be present.

Regarding the long-term effects of depression, there is much evidence to suggest that depression may continue over a number of years. Children can be prone to depressive symptoms for up to two years after the initial onset of depression (Nolen-Hoeksema et al., 1992). Even when children do recover from a depressive episode, relapse rates appear to be high, with 40 per cent of children experiencing another episode over the next three to five years. Evidence also suggests that there is a greater likelihood of early onset depression (depression prior to puberty) developing into adult depression (Wenar and Kerig, 2006).

Various factors have been implicated in the onset of depression. These include biological factors such as a genetic predisposition to depression, and children who have close relatives who are sufferers are at an increased risk of developing it themselves (Rutter et al., 1999). Deficiencies in the neurotransmitter serotonin have also been related to depression, particularly in adults, but there is some uncertainty about its role in childhood depression as the seratonergic systems in children may not yet be mature (Bylund and Reed, 2007). A variety of psychological theories have been proposed.

One is the role of negative thoughts and cognitions such as feeling worthless ('I'm no good'), helpless ('there's nothing I can do about this') and hopeless ('it will always be like this'). Such cognitions are characteristic of adult depression (Beck, 2002) and some studies have identified these cognitive aspects to mood in children (see, for example, Gladstone and Kaslow, 1995). Another cognitive perspective is related to attachment theory, which suggests that insecure attachment in infancy leads to depression in childhood and adolescence (Cicchetti and Toth, 1998). It is argued that insecure attachment leads to the acquisition of a negative internal working model (see Chapter 8) which leads the individual to feel unlovable and that other people are unreliable and these feelings in turn make the individual more vulnerable to depression. Other viewpoints stress the role of poor social support and peer rejection in childhood and the effects of negative and traumatic life events (Wenar and Kerig, 2006).

There are a variety of treatments for depression. In adults the use of antidepressant medications is popular; however, the efficacy of their use in children is less clear. A number of studies have been conducted which have shown the beneficial effects of various medications, but a review by Wagner and Ambrosini (2001) has identified a number of methodological flaws in these studies, such as inconsistent criteria for identifying depression and problems with the measures used. Also concern has been expressed about the side effects of such medications in children, for example restlessness, irritability and gastrointestinal discomfort (Jain et al., 1992). In the United Kingdom the general guidance is only to use antidepressant medications in severe cases of childhood depression, and their use should be accompanied by close monitoring of the child (National Institute of Health and Clinical Excellence, 2005). Psychological therapies for depression include psychodynamic therapies which focus on personality problems arising from negative childhood experiences. In the case of young children, therapists will often use play as the medium to explore such issues. Cognitive-behavioural therapy can be used with older children and the aim of this therapy is to focus on the negative cognitions such as hopelessness, worthlessness and helplessness that go with depression and try to change them.

Anxiety

Fear is a normal response to a threatening situation and has survival value, and being fearful, like depression, is familiar to most of us. However, sometimes feelings of fear become so severe that normal functioning is adversely affected and in these circumstances, fear becomes an anxiety disorder. The DSM-IV lists a variety of anxiety disorders including specific phobias, separation anxiety disorder, obsessive compulsive disorder and social anxiety disorder, to name but a few.

There are variations in the developmental course of the anxiety disorders. Adults diagnosed with general anxiety disorder (GAD) report that they have been fearful all their lives (APA, 2000). Separation anxiety disorder is common in the preschool years, with 5- to 8-year-olds showing excessive worry about harm befalling an attachment figure and nightmares involving separation from that figure, whereas 9- to 12-year-olds are distressed by separation itself (Wenar and Kerig, 2006). In general, for all anxiety disorders, anxiety increases with age. One possible reason for this is, paradoxically, normal cognitive development. Put simply, as children get older, their capacity for worry increases (Kertz and Woodruff-Borden, 2011). Children have an increased ability to think about the future, and for anxious children this can mean worrying about what might happen, and children can also use *counterfactual thinking* (what could have happened) and these cognitive skills, which are a normal part of cognitive development, can contribute to their levels of fearfulness.

Both biological and environmental factors have been implicated in anxiety disorders. There is some evidence of a genetic predisposition to develop anxiety disorders in general but not specific anxieties (Eaves et al., 1997). Genetic factors may cause a child to be born with an emotional style or temperament that biases them towards being upset by unfamiliar experiences and a desire to withdraw from them, or what Kagan (2003) referred to as a **behaviourally inhibited temperament**. However, it is not temperament alone that will lead to the development of an anxiety disorder, the parenting such a child receives may also play a part. Some parents of infants with a low toleration for novelty will protect the child from minor stresses, but such overprotective parenting may make it more difficult in the long run for a child to overcome an urge to retreat.

Treatments for anxiety will depend on the specific disorder. Specific phobias can be treated using **systematic desensitisation**, which aims to substitute a fear response with relaxation through gradual exposure to the feared object or situation. Other anxiety disorders can be treated using cognitive approaches which aim to counter the negative thoughts associated with fear with more adaptive ways of thinking (King et al., 2005). An example is the 'coping cat' programme (Kendall, 1994) in which children with anxiety disorders were first given training in coping and relaxation skills, and were then gradually exposed to an anxiety-provoking situation involving the use of these coping skills. Such approaches have been found to be successful in treating anxiety disorders in children.

Conduct disorder

Conduct disorder is a form of childhood psychopathology that leads the child to engage in serious antisocial behaviour. DSM-IV defines conduct disorder as *'a repetitive and persistent pattern of behaviour in which the basic rights of others or major age-appropriate societal norms or rules are violated'* (APA, 2000: 93). While behaviours such as lying, stealing and fighting are common in childhood, conduct disorder involves extremes of these behaviours and can have a serious effect on many aspects of an individual's life.

Two forms of conduct disorder have been identified: **childhood onset conduct disorder** in which conduct problems are present from the preschool years onwards and their problem behaviours tend to increase in frequency and severity through the course of childhood and on into adolescence (Lahey and Loeber, 1997); and **adolescent onset conduct disorder** where there are no significant behavioural problems in childhood and delinquent and antisocial behaviour emerges at the onset of adolescence (Hinshaw et al., 1993).

Of the two forms of the disorder, childhood onset conduct disorder appears to be the more serious form and appears to show high levels of continuity into adolescence and adulthood (Frick and Loney, 1999). Indeed one of the criteria for making a diagnosis of adult antisocial personality disorder using DSM-IV is the presence of conduct disorder in childhood (APA, 2000). Many studies have demonstrated a link between childhood onset CD and criminality in adolescence and adulthood (Farrington et al., 1988; Moffitt et al., 2002).

By contrast, for most individuals the adolescent form of the disorder appears to be a more transitory form of antisocial behaviour which does not persist beyond adolescence (Moffitt, 1993a). However, while this behaviour shows signs of discontinuity, there can still be long-term negative consequences including a vulnerability to develop internalising disorders (Aguilar et al., 2000). Nevertheless, the long-term difficulties are generally a consequence of their adolescent antisocial behaviour, which may have led to substance misuse, dropping out of school or gaining a criminal record, rather than being related to ongoing, continuous antisocial behaviour (Moffitt and Caspi, 2001).

While the distinction between childhood and adolescent onset conduct disorder is widely accepted, recently it has been found that there appear to be two distinct groups of children with childhood onset conduct disorder (Frick, 2004; Frick and Viding, 2009). One group of children is characterised by what has been termed a **callous-unemotional (CU)** interpersonal style, meaning that they are lacking in guilt and empathy, they use people in a callous manner to achieve their own aims, and they show high levels of aggression that is both reactive and proactive in nature (Enebrink et al., 2005). The other group are low in CU traits and their aggression tends to be reactive in nature, in response to real or perceived provocation by others (Frick et al., 2003). Another important characteristic of this group is difficulties in emotional regulation which can result in impulsive and unplanned aggressive acts for which the child is remorseful afterwards but will still have difficulty controlling in the future (Pardini et al., 2003).

Differing explanations have been put forward for childhood and adolescent onset forms of the disorder. Moffitt (1993a, 2004) has argued that the adolescent onset form can be seen as an exaggeration of normal teenage rebelliousness. All teenagers show some level of rebelliousness to parents and authority figures. However in the case of some teenagers, this follows a maladaptive course, usually through association with a delinquent peer group and mimicking their peers' acts of antisocial behaviour in a misguided attempt to achieve a sense of maturity and adult status. However, there are no fundamental vulnerabilities involved and the behaviour is unlikely to last beyond adolescence.

In the case of childhood onset conduct disorders, there appears to be a complex interplay between biological, cognitive, social and environmental factors. This form of conduct disorder does appear to have some genetic roots, for example studies of the criminal records of adopted boys are more similar to the records of their biological rather than their adoptive fathers (Mednick et al., 1984). It has also been suggested that there are neurological deficits underlying this disorder, particularly in relation to the frontal lobes which are involved in the planning and regulating of behaviour (Moffit, 1993b) and one source of these deficits may be antenatal exposure to teratogens or exposure to environmental pollutants during the preschool years (Loeber, 1990). These deficits may lead to problems in temperament which may be exacerbated by poor parenting. It is well established that conduct disorder is linked with low socioeconomic status, maternal depression, paternal delinquency and dysfunctional family relationships (Frick, 1994; Loeber, 1990; Robins, 1991). These in turn can lead to problems such as dysfunctional emotional regulation, and faulty social information processing leading to a tendency to interpret other people's behaviours as hostile (Crick and Dodge, 1994) which leads to acts of aggression against peers. Aggressive interactions with peers can lead to retaliation and this can lead to a cycle of interactions which maintains aggressive and antisocial behaviours.

Treatments of children with conduct disorder will often seek to address the impulsivity and biased social information processing that accompany the disorder through the use of cognitive-behavioural techniques. Nolen-Hoeksema (2001) describes how such an intervention might proceed. The children will be thought to recognise situations that trigger anger and aggressive behaviours. The children are encouraged to analyse their thoughts in these situations and consider alternative responses. They are given strategies to help them deal with such situations such as the use of 'self-talk' to help calm themselves. Adaptive problem-solving skills are also taught by discussing real and hypothetical situations and getting the children to think of positive solutions to the problems and role play may be used. For example, the therapist and child may discuss how to respond when another child engages in queue jumping. The therapist might model an assertive (rather than aggressive) response ('please wait your turn'). Role play can be used to practise these types of response and sometimes the child may be encouraged to take the role of the offending child in an attempt to gain some perspective on why the offender might do this. Sometimes the therapy may also involve the parents who are taught to reinforce positive behaviours and discourage aggressive and antisocial behaviour. They may also be provided with strategies for managing their own anger and the use of non-violent discipline and in this way provide a more positive model for their child. Studies of the use of cognitive-behavioural techniques for conduct disorder have indicated positive results, with a reduction in aggressive and impulsive behaviour and in general, the earlier that a child receives such an intervention the more likely it will have a long-term positive effect (Webster-Stratton and Reid, 2010).

Attention deficit hyperactivity disorder

Behaviours such as inattention, fidgeting and an inability to sit still or stay quiet are common and expected in young children, and an important developmental task for them is to learn to pay attention and control their impulses and behaviour in order to achieve long-term goals. However, for some children, this presents serious difficulties and they display levels of hyperactivity, inattention and impulsivity that go well beyond developmentally appropriate levels, to the extent that their schooling and interpersonal and home lives are adversely affected. Children showing these behaviours may be diagnosed with attention deficit hyperactivity disorder (ADHD). This disorder is thought to affect about 8–12 per cent of children worldwide (Biederman and Faraone, 2005). However, it has been suggested that the incidence in the UK is under-reported and British clinicians are less likely to diagnose ADHD compared to their counterparts in other countries (Sayal et al., 2010). The disorder appears to affect boys more than girls; however, it has been suggested that the incidence in girls is also under-reported and they are less likely to be referred for treatment (Biederman and Faraone, 2005).

Children with ADHD have poor peer relationships and in interacting with other children they are disruptive, want to play by their own rules and may become violent when they don't get their own way (Henker and Whalen, 1989). Unsurprisingly, children with ADHD frequently experience peer rejection (Hoza, 2007). The behavioural problems of some children are so severe that they are often diagnosed with conduct disorder as well and in general there is a high degree of **co-morbidity** between the two disorders (Beauchaine et al., 2010).

The long-term outcomes for children with ADHD are mixed. Approximately 30 to 50 per cent of children with the disorder will continue to have it as adults. Nevertheless, Faraone et al. (2006) have noted that for many children, the symptoms of ADHD decline with age so that by the time they reach adulthood they do not meet the criteria for a diagnosis. However, in the same study they argue that further research is necessary to determine if this reflects ADHD going into remission in adulthood, or if it reflects developmental insensitivity in the diagnostic criteria for the disorder. Children diagnosed for ADHD still experience a higher incidence of problems in adulthood such as substance abuse, marital problems and frequent job changes (Mannuza et al., 1998), and those whose ADHD coincides with a diagnosis of conduct disorder have the worst outcomes in terms of antisocial behaviour and adjustment problems in later life (Moffitt, 1990).

An early hypothesis about the cause of ADHD was that it was a result of mild brain damage, but this view is no longer accepted as neurological studies have revealed no history of brain damage in the vast majority of children with the disorder (Barkley, 1990). However, more recent studies have indicated that there are abnormalities of electrical activity and blood flow in certain areas of the brain, in particular the frontal lobes which, as mentioned in Chapter 5, are thought to have a role in planning and regulating behaviour (Spencer et al., 2002). There also appears to be a genetic basis to the disorder, and family, twin and adoption studies have indicated a high degree of heritability of the disorder (Coghill and Banaschewski, 2009; Khan and Faraone, 2006). Environmental factors have also been implicated in ADHD including long-term exposure to prenatal teratogens such as alcohol, illegal drugs, tobacco, and birth complications (Milberger et al., 1997). Children diagnosed with ADHD are also more likely to come from families characterised by high levels of conflict and stress (Biederman et al., 1995). However, rather than directly causing ADHD, family and home factors are more likely to exacerbate any underlying problem.

ADHD is usually treated using a mix of medication and behavioural therapies. The most commonly used drug to treat the disorder is the stimulant drug methylphenidate (better known by its trade name, Ritalin). It may seem counter-intuitive to administer a stimulant drug to a hyperactive child; however, neurological studies of children with ADHD indicate lower levels of blood flow and electrical activity in the frontal lobes and other areas of the brain related to attention (Spencer et al., 2002). Hence the fundamental problem of these children is one of *under-arousal* making it very difficult for such children to focus and pay attention and hence the hyperactive behaviour. Most children respond to these drugs by becoming less disruptive and more compliant in their behaviour, as well as showing improvements in mood and in interactions with their peers (Gadow, 1992; Whalen et al., 1989).

But treatments using drugs alone produce only short-term improvements and better long-term outcomes are obtained if drug treatments are combined with behavioural therapies (Smith et al., 2006). These latter therapies focus on reinforcing attentive, goal-directed and prosocial behaviour. An example would be the use of what is called a **token economy**. In this type of intervention, a child may be given a token such as a sticker to place on a chart each time in the week they engage in a desired behaviour, for example sitting quietly at a table during mealtimes. If the child does not engage in the desired behaviour, they lose tokens, and if they become aggressive, they are sent to their room for a 'time out'. Once a certain number of tokens have been achieved, they can be exchanged for a 'reward' such as a toy or being allowed to engage in a fun activity. Such techniques are more likely to improve parent-child relationships and also encourage the children to anticipate the consequences of their behaviour and make less impulsive choices (Nolen-Hoeksema, 2001).

Autism

Autism belongs to the category of psychopathology referred to as pervasive developmental disorders and is a severe and lasting disorder that affects many areas of functioning. The disorder was first identified by Kanner (1943).

The deficits exhibited by autistic children can be grouped into three categories (Nolen-Hoeksema, 2001; Wenar and Kerig, 2006). The first is deficits in social interactions.

Kanner (1943) described autistic children as existing in a state of 'autistic aloneness' characterised by an extreme lack of interest in other people. As infants they are not responsive to attention and affection from their caregivers. They tend to avoid eye contact. This lack of interest in social interaction continues into childhood with autistic children preferring to remain in solitary play rather than engaging with peers.

The second category of deficits relates to communication. Approximately 50 per cent of autistic children fail to develop useful speech (Gillberg, 1991) and children who do develop language use it in different ways to their typically developing peers. Some children engage in **echolalia**, a tendency to repeat back what has been said to them but with no attempt to comprehend the meaning. They often have difficulty with pronouns such as using 'you' when they mean 'I'. Often their speech has a very stilted and formal manner, as if they were using rote-learned phrases from a foreign language (Wenar and Kerig, 2006). They also have severe difficulties with the pragmatic aspects of language. Their speech lacks the rhythms and intonations (known as **prosody**) of normal speech and they fail to use these types of signals in speech to understand the meaning intended by the speaker. As an example, on a wet and windy day, an individual might remark 'what lovely weather'. A typically developing child will use the manner in which these words are spoken to identify that this was intended sarcastically, but to an autistic child, this remark will seem odd. Related to this is the observation that their speech is very literal, they assume that the literal remark was the intended meaning, as in the previous example. Frith (2003) provides another example of a girl becoming distressed when asked by a nurse to 'give me your hand'; she literally thought that the nurse wanted to remove her hand! This extreme literality and inability to attend to prosodic features of speech means that children with autism have serious difficulties in the communicative use of language.

The third category of deficits relates to the types of activities and interests of affected children, and in particular their desire for sameness. Routines and rituals are often very important and can be seen in the child insisting on having the same food from the same plate and with the same utensils, or having the furniture arranged in a particular way. They will often become very distressed if their normal daily routine is disrupted, such as their mother making an unplanned stop at the shop on the way to school. They may also engage in repetitive behaviours, for example rocking backwards and forwards for long periods of time, flapping their hands or banging their heads. When playing with toys, they may just focus on one aspect of the toy, such as repeatedly twirling a wheel on a toy truck.

Other features associated with autism include under- or oversensitivity to stimulation. They may be hypersensitive to touch or to sounds or to visual stimuli, or lacking in sensitivity to cold or pain. Deficits in intellectual functioning can also be present, and there appears to be a high incidence of these in children with autism (Matson and Shoemaker, 2009). Cases have also been noted of autistic savants, individuals who despite their autism have unusually high levels of ability in specific domains, such as in music, mathematical ability or extraordinary feats of memory. However, while such cases have been documented in the literature (see for example, Obler and Fein, 1988), they remain a rarity in the wider population of individuals with autism.

Regarding the long-term consequences of autism, approximately 60 per cent of those affected will continue to be severely affected by their condition throughout adulthood and will remain dependent on their families or institutions for care (Nordin and Gilberg, 1998). However, a small proportion do appear to improve in their functioning and manage to lead relatively normal adult lives (Gillberg, 1991). The remaining individuals function somewhere in between, achieving a degree of independence but perhaps living in residential facilities with other autistic individuals and being looked after by carers and relying on rules they have learned about acceptable behaviours to function in everyday life.

A number of explanations have been advanced for the causes of autism. Initially, Kanner (1943) speculated that it was of biological origin, but later changed to the view that it was caused by poor parenting, particularly on the part of the mother. This view was also advanced by the psychiatrist Bettelheim (1967) in his book *The Empty Fortress*. They argued that the parents of autistic children were cold, distant and uncaring – the term 'refrigerator mother' became common – and autistic symptoms were the result of the child retreating into their own worlds in response to their parents' unavailability. However, this view has been discredited and many studies of parents of autistic children show them to be no different to others in their parenting skills or attitudes to their children, and in many cases they show great skill in adapting their own behaviour to engage socially with their offspring (Siller and Sigman, 2002). Unfortunately, the views of Kanner and Bettelheim were influential in their time and for many years the parents of autistic children were burdened not just with the demands of raising a profoundly disabled child, but also with feelings of guilt that they may have in some way caused their child's condition.

Another controversial explanation for the causes of autism linked the condition to the use of the measles, mumps and rubella (MMR) vaccine. This emanated from a paper published in 1998 in the medical journal *The Lancet* by Dr Andrew Wakefield and other colleagues wherein they reported a number of cases of autism and chronic bowel disease linked to the MMR vaccine. However, the results of this work are no longer accepted and the paper has now been retracted by *The Lancet*. A review by DeStefano (2007) concluded that there is no strong evidence of an association between the MMR vaccine and the development of autism. Nevertheless, the publicity surrounding Wakefield's work did lead to a reduction in parents availing of this vaccination for their children and a subsequent increase in cases of these diseases.

A widely accepted view today is that the communication and interaction problems exhibited by individuals with autism are caused by the absence of a theory of mind (the development of a theory of mind is considered in more detail in Chapter 8). A theory of mind begins to emerge during the preschool years. Initially, children understand that other people have desires, followed by an understanding that people have beliefs as well as desires, and by the age of 4 they understand that people's beliefs do not always correspond to actual situations. This skill is regarded as crucial for normal social interaction and being able to understand why people act as they do. However, there is a wealth of evidence that this skill is lacking in autistic children. Baron-Cohen et al. (1985) provided one of the first demonstrations of this by administering a false-belief task (see Chapter 8) to three groups of 4-year-old children: a group with autism; a group with Down's syndrome, and a group of typically developing children. They found that while over 80 per cent of the typically developing and Down's syndrome children could succeeded in the task, only 20 per cent of the autistic children were successful. They argued that the performance of the autistic children could be explained by a specific deficit in a theory of mind rather than a general intellectual deficit, as children with Down's syndrome could perform the task as easily as typically developing children. These findings have been supported by the results of numerous other studies which have shown that children with autism fail various tasks requiring an understanding of other's mental states, such as ordering a set of pictures depicting a story in which a protagonist has a false belief or predicting responses to deception (Frith, 2003). The weight of evidence for the lack a of theory of mind appears to be very strong; in spite of this, Smith et al. (2011) have pointed out that in all of these types of study, a small proportion of children with autism succeed in these tasks. It appears that the ability of such children to succeed on these tasks may be related to their age and verbal ability (Happé, 1995). However, it has been found that autistic individuals who do succeed on first-order false-belief tasks rarely succeed on second-order false-belief tasks (Baron-Cohen, 1989). But Smith et al. (2011) also point out that the lack of a theory of mind may not explain other characteristics of autism, such as echolalia. More recently the suggestion has been made that there may be several different types of autism, and each may require a different explanation (Happé et al., 2006).

While the ultimate cause of autism is not known, it is likely to have a biological basis. Family and twin studies have indicated that genetics play a role, with siblings of autistic children being 50 times more likely to have the disorder (Rutter et al., 1990), and there is a high level of co-occurrence of the disorder in identical twins (Bailey et al., 1995). Neurological abnormalities have also been noted in children with autism (Frith, 2003). These may have a genetic origin, but it has also been noted that there is a higher than average incidence of prenatal and birth complications in children with autism (Brimacombe et al., 2007) and there is the possibility that these may also have resulted in neurological problems.

While autism cannot be cured, there are therapies which aim to improve the overall level of functioning of children with autism and these can include behavioural techniques and specially adapted educational approaches (Nolen-Hoeksema, 2001; Wenar and Kerig, 2006). Behavioural techniques such as modelling and reinforcement are used to teach children to speak, reduce inappropriate behaviours, and how to interact socially with others. Education of children with autism will take place in highly structured environments and often employ specially adapted teaching materials (such as books that do not have bright colours) to avoid the problems of hypersensitivity to sensory stimulation. Parents may also be taught behavioural techniques to use in the home, and in general, improvements in cognitive and behavioural skills have been observed through the use of such techniques in both home and school settings (Bregman and Gerdtz, 1997). Play therapy has also been employed with autistic children, with the therapist using play as a means of improving social interaction and communication skills, and some success has been reported from the use of this approach (Josefi and Ryan, 2004).

 Think back to the concepts of equifinality/multifinality and continuity/discontinuity mentioned at the start of the chapter. Can you see any examples of these concepts in the account just provided of the various disorders?

Risk and resilience

So far, the emphasis has been on children who develop some form of psychopathology. However, as was mentioned earlier in the chapter, another issue of interest in developmental psychopathology is why some children, despite exposure to extremely stressful and harmful experiences, do not go on to develop behavioural or mental health problems. Consequently, the issues of risk and resilience are also important topics in this field of study.

A risk is any factor that increases the likelihood of a child developing psychopathology. Various **risk factors** have been suggested and there is no universally agreed list (Wenar and Kerig, 2006). Some factors that have been suggested include biological factors such as birth defects or poor nutrition, individual factors such as low intelligence or low self-esteem, family factors such as parental conflict, parental psychopathology or domestic abuse and neglect, and broader social factors such as poverty, poor living conditions or poor peer relations. In addition to risk factors, there are also **vulnerability factors**, which are factors that increase the likelihood that a child will succumb to a risk factor. These can include sex: while boys and girls are adversely affected by stress, boys are more likely to react with behavioural problems; and temperament: an infant with a difficult temperament may be more vulnerable to the negative effects of poor parenting (Wenar and Kerig, 2006). Often, risk and vulnerability factors may have an *additive effect*, i.e. the more that are present, the greater the likelihood of psychopathology (Appleyard et al., 2005; Webster-Stratton, 1999).

Resilience refers to the ability of an individual to function competently and successfully despite encountering stressful and adverse circumstances. **Protective factors** are those factors that act as a buffer against the development of problems when faced with the various risk factors. The role of such factors is illustrated in a 40-year longitudinal study following the progress of a large sample of individuals from infancy to adulthood on the Hawaiian island of Kauai, reported by Werner (1993, 1995). This study examined the long-term outcomes of perinatal problems, poverty, parental psychopathology and discord. Of particular interest here were a group of individuals who, despite being identified as high risk on the basis of the number of risk factors present in infancy and early childhood, grew into competent and caring adults with no significant problems. Werner identified three types of protective factor that were related to positive outcomes. The first was *personal characteristics* such as an easy temperament that elicited positive responses from family members and other adults. The second was *effective and caring parental substitutes* such as older siblings and grandparents. The third was an *external support system* provided by schools, churches or youth groups.

However, rather than just identify a list of protective factors, Rutter (1987) has argued that what is needed is an understanding of why a given set of factors protect against psychopathology, and based on the existing research he has identified four **protective mechanisms**. The first he termed **reduction of risk impact**, meaning that some factors act as a buffer for the child exposed to a risk factor. An example would be the various support measures for disadvantaged families provided by schemes such as Sure Start, as described in Chapter 2. The second protective mechanism he called **reduction of negative chain reactions**. An example would be a temperamentally easy child who is less likely to be a target of parental anger, so in turn is less likely to develop behavioural problems, which in turn lessens parental stress and anger, thus avoiding a vicious circle of parent–child conflict. The third mechanism is **factors that promote self-esteem and self-efficacy** which help children to feel that they can deal with their problems. Achievements in school or sports, which can foster self-confidence, would be an example of a specific factor here. The final factor is **opening of opportunities**, whereby there are turning points in a child's life that offer a chance to reduce the impact of risk factors, and a resilient child will take advantage of these when they are presented. An example would be a decision to stay at school and obtain qualifications that will lead to more opportunities later on in life.

 Do you think that children who appear to be resilient in the face of adversity may still suffer from the consequences of their situation? In what ways might this suffering show itself?

There is much evidence of the resilience of children in the face of adversity. However, it is important to be aware of the possibility that resilient children may still suffer negative consequences of their situation, despite an outward appearance of success and competence. It has been observed that children who appear to be coping well with difficulty often internalise their stress in the form of depression and anxiety (D'lmperio et al., 2000). Similarly, results from the Hawaiian longitudinal study indicated that many resilient children suffered from stress-related health problems in adulthood (Werner, 1993). Therefore, the provision of support is as necessary for resilient children as it is for children who go on to develop psychopathology. Overall, however, research on risk and resilience is important, as the identification of protective factors and mechanisms may be used to develop early interventions for the prevention of psychopathology.

Chapter summary

- Developmental psychopathology is an approach to childhood disorders that does not rely on any one theoretical approach, and views the distinction between normality and abnormality as a continuum with the aim being to judge the point at which behaviours move from being aspects of normal development to indicating a problem.
- A number of approaches to diagnosing psychopathology have been developed including the *Diagnostic and Statistical Manual of Mental Disorders*, the Child Behaviour Checklist and the Strengths and Difficulties Questionnaire.
- Some childhood disorders can be seen as extremes of normal behaviour (such as feeling depressed or fearful) which have a negative effect on other areas of functioning, for example home and school life and family and peer relations.
- Various factors have been identified in the development of childhood disorders, including genetic, cognitive and environmental factors. Often, there is a complex interplay between these factors leading to a disorder.
- Not all children exposed to adverse circumstances will develop a disorder and the factors that promote such resilience, as well as the factors that make other children more vulnerable, have been the subject of much research.

Further reading

Bailey, S. and Shooter, M. (eds) (2009) *The Young Mind*. London: Transworld Publishers/Royal College of Psychiatrists.

A practical and accessibly written guide to mental health issues in children and young people written specifically with concerned parents, teachers and young people as the audience.

Wenar, C. and Kerig, P. (2006) *Developmental Psychopathology: From Infancy Through Adolescence*. New York: McGraw Hill.

A comprehensive account of the various childhood psychological disorders from a developmental psychopathology perspective, aimed at an audience with a specialist interest in this field.

Useful website

http://www.youngminds.org.uk/
The website of the charity Young Minds, which is concerned with promoting the emotional wellbeing and mental health of children and young people. Contains links to resources for parents, children and young people as well as professionals working with children.

References

Achenbach, T.M. (1991) Integrative Guide for the 1991 CBCL/4-18, YSR, and TRF Profiles. Burlington, VT: University of Vermont Department of Psychiatry.

Aguilar, B., Sroufe, L., Egeland, B. and Carlson, E. (2000) 'Distinguishing the early-onset/persistent and adolescent-onset antisocial behavior types: From birth to 16 years', *Developmental Psychopathology*, 12 (2): 109–32.

American Psychiatric Association (APA) (2000) *Diagnostic and Statistical Manual of Mental Disorders DSM-IV-TR* (4th edn). Washington, DC: American Psychiatric Association.

Appleyard, K., Egeland, B., van Dulmen, M.H.M. and Sroufe, L.A. (2005) 'When more isn't better: The role of cumulative risk in child behaviour outcomes', *The Journal of Child Psychology and Psychiatry*, 46 (3): 235–4.

Bailey, A., Le Couteur, A., Gottesman, I., Bolton, P., Sominoff, E.,Yuzda, E. and Rutter, M. (1995) 'Autism as a strongly genetic disorder: Evidence from a British twin study', *Psychological Medicine*, 25 (01): 63–77.

Barkley, R.A. (1990) *Attention-deficit Hyperactivity Disorder: A Handbook for Diagnosis and Treatment*. New York: Guilford Press.

Baron-Cohen, S. (1989) 'The autistic child's theory of mind: A case of specific developmental delay', *Journal of Child Psychology and Psychiatry*, 30 (2): 285–97.

Baron-Cohen, S., Leslie, A. and Frith, U. (1985) 'Does the autistic child have a "theory of mind"?', *Cognition*, 21 (1): 37–46.

Beauchaine, T.P., Hinshaw, S.P. and Lang, K.L. (2010) 'Comorbidity of attention- deficit/hyperactivity disorder and early-onset conduct disorder: Biological, environmental, and developmental mechanisms', *Clinical Psychology: Science and Practice*, 17 (4): 327–36.

Beck, A.T. (2002) 'Cognitive models of depression', in R.L. Leahy and T.E. Dowd (eds), *Clinical Advances in Cognitive Psychotherapy: Theory and Application*. New York: Springer. pp. 29–61.

Bettelheim, B. (1967) *The Empty Fortress: Infantile Autism and the Birth of the Self*. New York: Free Press.

Biederman, J. and Faraone, S.V. (2005) 'Attention-deficit hyperactivity disorder', *The Lancet*, 366 (9481): 237–48.

Biederman, M.D., Milberger, S., Faraone, S.V., Kiely, K., Guite, J., Mick, E., Abion, S., Warburton, R. and Reed, E. (1995) 'Family-environment risk factors for attention-deficit hyperactivity disorder: A test of Rutter's indicators of adversity', *Archives of General Psychiatry*, 52 (6): 464–70.

Bregman, J.D. and Gerdtz, J. (1997) 'Behavioral interventions', in D.J. Cohen and F.R. Volkmar (eds), *Handbook of Autism and Pervasive Developmental Disorders*. Toronto: Wiley. pp. 606–30.

Brimacombe, M., Ming, X. and Lamendola, M. (2007) 'Prenatal and birth complications in autism', *Maternal and Child Health*, 11 (1): 73–79.

Bylund, D.B. and Reed, A.L. (2007) 'Childhood and adolescent depression: Why do children and adults respond differently to antidepressant drugs?', *Neurochemistry International*, 51 (5): 246–53.

Cicchetti, D. (1993) 'Developmental psychopathology: Reactions, reflections, projections', *Developmental Review*, 13 (4): 471–502.

Cicchetti, D. (2006) 'Development and psychopathology', in D. Cicchetti and D.J. Cohen (eds), *Developmental Psychopathology*, Vol. 1 (2nd edn). New York: Wiley. pp. 1–23.

Cicchetti, D. and Rogosch, F. (1996) 'Equifinality and multifinality in developmental psychopathology', *Development and Psychopathology*, 8 (04): 597–600.

Cicchetti, D. and Toth, S.L. (1998) 'The development of depression in children and adolescents', *American Psychologist*, 53 (2): 221–41.

Coghill, D. and Banaschewski, T. (2009) 'The genetics of attention-deficit/hyperactivity disorder', *Expert Review of Neurotherapeutics*, 9 (10): 1547–65.

Crick, N.R. and Dodge, K.A. (1994) 'A review and reformulation of social information-processing mechanisms in children's social adjustment', *Psychological Bulletin*, 115 (1): 74–101.

Davé, S., Nazareth, I., Senior, R. and Sherr, L. (2008) 'A comparison of father and mother report of child behaviour on the Strengths and Difficulties Questionnaire', *Child Psychiatry and Human Development*, 39 (4): 399–413.

DeStefano, F. (2007) 'Vaccines and autism: Evidence does not support a causal association', *Clinical Pharmacology and Therapeutics*, 82 (6): 756–9.

D'Imperio, R.L., Dubow, E.F. and Ippolito, M.F. (2000) 'Resilient and stress-affected adolescents in an urban setting', *Journal of Clinical Child Psychology*, 29 (1): 129–42.

Eaves, L.J., Silberg, J.L., Meyer, J.M., Maes, H.H., Simonoff, E., Pickles, A., Rutter, M., Reynolds, C.A., Heath, A.C., Truett, K.R., Neale, M.C., Erikson, M.T., Loeber, R. and Hewitt, J.K. (1997) 'Genetics and developmental psychopathology: 2. The main effects of genes and environment on behavioral problems in the Virginia Twin Study of Adolescent Behavioral Development', *Journal of Child Psychology and Psychiatry*, 38 (8): 965–80.

Enebrink, P., Anderson, H. and Langstrom, N. (2005) 'Callous-unemotional traits are associated with clinical severity in referred boys with conduct problems', *Nordic Journal of Psychiatry*, 59 (6): 431–40.

Faraone, S.V., Biederman, J. and Mick, E. (2006) 'The age-dependent decline of attention deficit hyperactivity disorder: A meta-analysis of follow-up studies', *Psychological Medicine*, 36 (2): 159–65.

Frick, P.J. (1994) 'Family dysfunction and the disruptive behaviour disorders: A review of recent empirical findings,' in T.H. Ollendick and R.J. Prinz (eds), *Advances in Clinical Child Psychology*, Volume 16. New York: Springer. pp. 203–26.

Farrington, D.P., Gallagher, B., Morley, L., St. Ledger, R.J. and West, D. (1988) 'Are there any successful men from criminogenic backgrounds?', *Psychiatry: Interpersonal and Biological Processes*, 51 (2): 116–30.

Frick, P.J. (2004) 'Developmental pathways to conduct disorder: Implications for serving youth who show severe aggression and antisocial behavior', *Psychology in the Schools*, 41 (8): 823–34.

Frick, P.J. and Loney, B.R. (1999) 'Outcomes of children and adolescents with conduct disorder and oppositional defiant disorder', in H.C. Quay and A. Hogan (eds), *Handbook of Disruptive Behavior Disorders*. New York: Plenum. pp. 507–24.

Frick, P.J. and Viding, E. (2009) 'Antisocial behavior from a developmental psychopathology perspective', *Development and Psychopathology*, 21 (Special Issue 04): 1111–31.

Frick, P.J., Cornell, A.H., Bodin, S.D., Dane, H.A., Barry,C.T. and Loney, B.R. (2003) 'Callous-unemotional traits and developmental pathways to severe conduct problems', *Developmental Psychology*, 39 (2): 246–60.

Frith, U. (2003) *Autism: Explaining the Enigma*. Oxford: Blackwell.

Gadow, K.D. (1992) 'Pediatric psychopharmacotherapy: A review of recent research', *Journal of Child Psychology and Psychiatry*, 33 (1): 153–95.

Gillberg, C. (1991) 'Outcome in autism and autistic-like conditions', *Journal of the American Academy of Child and Adolescent Psychiatry*, 30 (3): 375–82.

Gladstone, T.R.G. and Kaslow, N.J. (1995). 'Depression and attributions in children and adolescents: A meta-analytic review', *Journal of Abnormal Child Psychology*, 23 (5): 597–606.

Goodman, R. (1997) 'The Strengths and Difficulties Questionnaire: A research note', *Journal of Child Psychology and Psychiatry*, 38 (5): 581–6.

Goodman, R. and Scott, S. (1999) 'Comparing the Strengths and Difficulties Questionnaire and the Child Behavior Checklist: Is small beautiful?', *Journal of Abnormal Child Psychology*, 27 (1): 17–24.

Hammen, C. and Compas, B.E. (1994) 'Unmasking unmasked depression in children and adolescents: The problem of comorbidity', *Clinical Psychology Review*, 14 (6): 585–603.

Happé , F. (1995) 'The role of age and verbal ability in the theory of mind task performance of subjects with autism', *Child Development*, 66 (3): 843–55.

Happé, F., Ronald, A. and Plomin, R. (2006) 'Time to give up on a single explanation for autism', *Nature Neuroscience*, 9: 1218–20.

Henker, B. and Whalen, C.K. (1989) 'Hyperactivity and attention deficits,' *American Psychologist*, 44 (2): 216–223.

Hinshaw, S.P. (1994) *Attention Deficits and Hyperactivity in Children*. Thousand Oaks, CA: Sage.

Hinshaw, S.P., Lahey, B.B. and Hart, E.L. (1993) 'Issues of taxonomy and comorbidity in the development of conduct disorder', *Development and Psychopathology*, 5 (1–2): 31–49.

Hoza, B. (2007) 'Peer functioning in children with ADHD', *Journal of Pediatric Psychology*, 32 (6): 655–63.

Jain, U., Birmaher, B., Garcia, M., Al-Shabbout, M. and Ryan, N. (1992) 'Fluoxetine in children and adolescents with mood disorders: A chart review of efficacy and adverse effects', *Journal of Child and Adolescent Psychopharmacology*, 2 (4): 259–65.

Josefi, O. and Ryan, V. (2004) 'Non-directive play therapy for young children with autism: A case study', *Clinical Child Psychology and Psychiatry*, 9 (4): 533–51.

Kagan, J. (2003) 'Behavioural inhibition as a temperamental category', in R.J. Davidson, K.R. Scherer and H.H. Goldsmith (eds), *Handbook of Affective Sciences*. New York: Oxford University Press. pp. 177–236.

Kanner, L. (1943) 'Autistic disturbances of affective contact', *Nervous Child*, 2: 217–50.

Kendall, P.C. (1994) 'Treating anxiety disorders in children: Results of a randomized clinical trial', *Journal of Consulting and Clinical Psychology*, 62 (1): 100–10.

Kertz, S.J. and Woodruff-Borden, J. (2011) 'The developmental psychopathology of worry', *Clinical Child and Family Psychology Review*, 14 (2): 174–97.

Khan, S. and Faraone, S.V. (2006) 'The genetics of ADHD: A literature review of 2005', *Current Psychiatry Reports*, 8: 393–7.

King, N.J., Heyne, D. and Ollendick. T.H. (2005) 'Cognitive-behavioral treatments for anxiety and phobic disorders in children: A review', *Behavioral Disorders*, 30 (3): 241–57.

Kovacs, M. and Devlin, B. (1998) 'Internalizing disorders in childhood', *Journal of Child Psychology and Psychiatry*, 39 (01): 47–63.

Lahey, B.B. and Loeber, R. (1997) 'Attention-deficit/hyperactivity disorder, oppositional-defiant disorder, conduct disorder and adult antisocial behavior: A lifespan perspective', in D.M. Stoff, J. Breiling and J.D. Maser (eds), *Handbook of Antisocial Personality Disorder*. New York: Wiley. pp. 51–9.

Loeber, R. (1990) 'Developmental and risk factors of juvenile antisocial behavior and delinquency', *Clinical Psychology Review*, 10 (1): 1–41.

Matson, J.L. and Shoemaker, M. (2009) 'Intellectual disability and its relationship to autism spectrum disorders', *Research in Developmental Disabilities*, *30* (6): 1107–14.

Mannuza, S., Klein, R.G., Bessler, A., Malloy, P. and LaPadula, M. (1998) 'Adult psychiatric status of hyperactive boys grown up,' *American Journal of Psychiatry*, 155 (4): 493–98.

Mednick,. S.A., Gabrielli, W.F. and Hutchings, B. (1984) 'Genetic influences on criminal convictions: evidence from an adoption cohort', *Science*, 224 (4651): 891–94.

Milberger, S., Biederman, J., Faraone, S.V., Guite, J. and Tsuang, M.T. (1997) 'Pregnancy, delivery and infancy complications and attention deficit hyperactivity disorder: Issues of gene-environment interaction', *Biological Psychiatry*, 41 (1): 65–75.

Moffitt, T.E. (1990) 'Juvenile delinquency and attention deficit disorder: Boys' developmental trajectories from age 3 to age 15', *Child Development*, 61 (3): 893–910.

Moffitt, T.E. (1993a) 'Adolescence-limited and life-course-persistent antisocial behavior: A developmental taxonomy', *Psychological Review*, 100 (4): 674–701.

Moffit, T.E. (1993b) 'The neuropsychology of conduct disorder', *Development and Psychopathology*, 5 (1–2): 135–51.

Moffit, T.E. (2004) 'Adolescence limited and life course persistent offending: A complementary pair of development theories', in T.P. Thornberry (ed) *Developmental Theories of Crime and Delinquency*. New Brunsnick NJ: Transaction publishers. pp. 11–54.

Moffitt, T.E. and Caspi, A. (2001) 'Childhood predictors differentiate life-course persistent and adolescence-limited antisocial pathways in males and females', *Development and Psychopathology*, 13 (02): 355–75.

Moffitt, T.E., Caspi, A., Harrington, H. and Milne, B.J. (2002) 'Males on the life-course-persistent and adolescence-limited antisocial pathways: Follow-up at age 26 years', *Development and Psychopathology*, 14 (01): 179–207.

National Institute for Health and Clinical Excellence (2005) 'Depression in children and young people: Identification and management in primary, community and secondary care', *NICE Clinical Guidelines CG28*, September.

Nolen-Hoeksema, S. (2001) *Abnormal Psychology* (2nd edn). New York: McGraw Hill.

Nolen-Hoeksema, S., Girgus, J.S. and Seligman, M.E. (1992) 'Predictors and consequences of childhood depressive symptoms: A 5-year longitudinal study', *Journal of Abnormal Psychology*, 101 (3): 405–22.

Nordin, V. and Gilberg, C. (1998) 'The long-term course of autistic disorders: Update on follow-up studies', *Acta Psychiatrica Scandinavica*, *97* (2): 99–08.

Obler, L.K. and Fein, D. (eds) (1988) *The Exceptional Brain: Neuropsychology of Talent and Special Abilities*. New York: Guilford Press.

Pardini, D.A., Lochman, J.E. and Frick, P.J. (2003) 'Callous/unemotional traits and social-cognitive processes in adjudicated youths', *Journal of the American Academy of Child & Adolescent Psychiatry*, 42 (3): 364–71.

Rey, J.M., Schrader, E. and Morris Yates, A. (1992) 'Parent-child agreement on children's behaviours reported by the child behaviour checklist (CBCL)', *Journal of Adolescence*, 15 (3): 219–30.

Robins, L.N. (1991) 'Conduct disorder', *Journal of Child Psychology and Psychiatry*, 32: (1) 193–212.

Rutter, M. (1987) 'Psychosocial resilience and protective mechanisms', *American Journal of Orthopsychiatry,* 24 (3): 316–31.

Rutter, M. and Sroufe, L.A. (2000) 'Developmental psychopathology: Concepts and challenges', *Development and Psychopathology*, 12 (3): 265–96.

Rutter, M., Bolton, P., Harrington, R., Le Couteur, A., Macdonald, H. and Simonoff, E. (1990) 'Genetic factors in child psychiatric disorders – I. A review of research strategies', *Journal of Child Psychology and Psychiatry*, 31 (1): 3–37.

Rutter, M., Silberg, J., O'Connor, T. and Siminoff, E. (1999) 'Genetics and child psychiatry: II Empirical research findings', *Journal of Child Psychology and Psychiatry*, 40 (1): 19–55.

Sayal, K., Ford, T. and Goodman, R. (2010) 'Trends in recognition of and service use for attention-deficit hyperactivity disorder in Britain, 1999–2004', *Psychiatric Services*, 61 (8): 803–10.

Siller M. and Sigman, M. (2002) 'The behaviors of parents of children with autism predict the subsequent development of their children's communication', *Journal of Autism and Developmental Disorders*, 32 (2): 77–89.

Smith, B.H., Barkley, R.A. and Shapiro, C.J. (2006) 'Attention-deficit hyperactivity disorder', in E.J. Mash and R.A. Barkley (eds), *Treatment of Childhood Disorders* (3rd edn). New York: Guilford. pp. 65–136.

Smith, P.K., Cowie, H. and Blades, M. (2011) *Understanding Children's Development* (5th edn). Chichester: Wiley.

Spencer, T.J., Biederman, M.D., Wilens, T.E. and Faraone, S.V. (2002) 'Overview and neurobiology of attention-deficit/hyperactivity disorder', *Journal of Clinical Psychiatry, 63* (suppl 12): 3–9.

Wagner, K.D. and Ambrosini, P.J. (2001) 'Childhood depression: Pharmacological therapy/ treatment (pharmacotherapy of childhood depression)', *Journal of Clinical Child Psychology*, 30 (1): 88–97.

Webster-Stratton, C. (1999) *How to Promote Children's Social and Emotional Competence.* London: Paul Chapman.

Webster-Stratton, C. and Hammond, M. (1988) 'Maternal depression and its relationship to life stress, perceptions of child behavior problems, parenting behaviors, and child conduct problems', *Journal of Abnormal Child Psychology*, 16 (3): 299–315.

Webster-Stratton, C. and Reid, M.J. (2010) 'The Incredible Years parents, teachers and children training series: A multifaceted treatment approach for young children with conduct disorders', in J. R. Weisz and Kazdin, A.E. (eds), *Evidence-Based Psychotherapies for Children and Adolescents* (2nd edn). New York: Guilford Press. pp. 194–210.

Wenar, C. and Kerig, P. (2006) *Developmental Psychopathology: From Infancy Through Adolescence.* New York: McGraw Hill.

Werner, E.E. (1993) 'Risk, resilience and recovery: perspectives from the Kauai Longitudinal Study, *Development and Psychopathology, 5*: 503–15.

Werner, E.E. (1995) 'Resilience in development', *Current Directions in Psychological Science, 4* (3): 81–85.

Whalen, C.K., Henker, B., Buhrmester, D., Hinshaw, S.P. , Huber, A. and Laski, K. (1989) 'Does stimulant medication improve the peer status of hyperactive children?', *Journal of Consulting and Clinical Psychology, 57* (4): 545–9.

Young Minds (2013) *What's the problem?* Available at: http://www.youngminds.org.uk/about/whats_the_problem (accessed 11 February 2013).

Health and Development

 Why you should read this chapter

Ensuring the health and wellbeing of children is a priority for both parents and professionals. Taking steps to ensure and improve health and wellbeing are also policy priorities, and being safe and healthy are explicit outcomes mentioned in the *Every Child Matters* Green Paper. While modern developments in medicine, such as immunisations against infectious disease and better medical diagnosis and treatment, have improved the health prospects for children in the western world, children will still suffer from illness and accidents at some points in their lives and these are relevant concerns in the study of child development. Health outcomes related to birth can have long-term developmental consequences. Illness in childhood is not just a medical issue, children need to learn about their own health and factors that can influence it, such as diet and personal hygiene. When children experience illness, they require explanations of what is happening to them and what they need to do in order to recover. Children who suffer from long-term illnesses also need to learn to make certain adjustments to their lives to help them manage their condition. Children also need to be aware of the risk of accidental

(Continued)

(Continued)

injury as do parents and professionals. These are all issues related to the developmental status of children and will be looked at in this chapter.

By the end of this chapter you should

- be aware of the developmental outcomes related to prematurity and low birth weight
- have an understanding of how children define health and illness
- understand how aspects of children's knowledge of illness develops, including their concepts of the causes of illness and their knowledge of various illnesses
- be aware of the psychosocial effects of chronic illness on children and their families
- be aware of the factors that are related to risk of accidental death and injury in childhood, and the different types of strategies to reduce such risks.

The health of the infant

Immediately after birth, the health of the infant is assessed by the midwife using the **Apgar scale** (Apgar, 1953). The infant's heart rate, breathing, reflexes, skin colour and muscle tone are examined and given a score from 0–2. The test is administered twice, the first at one minute after birth and the second after five minutes. A combined Apgar score of 7 or above indicates that the baby is in good physical condition. A score of 4–6 indicates that the baby will require some assistance in breathing and other vital signs. A score of below 3 indicates that the baby is in serious danger and requires emergency medical intervention.

Another important check in the early days after birth are blood tests to check for two rare but serious disorders of metabolism: **phenylketonuria (PKU)** and **hypothyroidism** (Young and McConway, 2004). Phenylketonuria is the inability of the body to process a particular type of amino acid (a building block for proteins) and if undetected can result in brain damage and learning difficulties. Hypothyroidism was mentioned in Chapter 5 and is a deficiency in the production of the thyroid hormone which can cause poor growth and mental impairment. Early detection of these conditions can lead to remedial action to reduce their effects. Children with PKU can be put on a special diet and children with hypothyroidism can be given supplements of the thyroid hormone.

Birth complications and development

Although the vast majority of childbirths proceed without any problems, occasionally complications do occur. There are three birth complications that can have an adverse effect on the baby's development: **anoxia**, **prematurity** and a **low birth weight**.

Anoxia

Sometimes during birth, the supply of oxygen to the infant is interrupted. This is known as anoxia (oxygen deprivation) and can occur for a number of reasons including:

- The umbilical cord becomes twisted or squeezed during childbirth: Babies in a **breech position** (who are born feet or buttocks first) are at risk from this complication and will often be delivered by Caesarean section.
- **Placental abruption**: The placenta becomes detached from the wall of the uterus leading to an interruption of the blood supply to the infant.
- The infant swallows mucus during childbirth and this becomes lodged in the infant's throat.

Newborns are able to tolerate oxygen deprivation for longer than older children and adults; they can reduce their metabolic rate and conserve the limited oxygen that is available (Fewell, 2005). However, prolonged oxygen deprivation may lead to permanent brain damage.

The long-term effects of anoxia will depend on the severity of the oxygen deprivation, and unsurprisingly, severe oxygen deprivation is associated with cognitive, motor and behavioural problems in early and middle childhood (Marlow et al., 2005; van Handel et al., 2007). In cases of mild anoxia, there is a tendency for children to obtain lower than average scores on tests of motor and cognitive development in the first three years, but in general the long-term developmental outcomes for these children are positive (Bass et al., 2004; van Handel et al., 2007).

Prematurity and low birth weight

An infant is classed as *premature* if born before a full 38 weeks of gestation. Recent years have seen great advances in the care of premature infants, with babies born as early as 24 weeks surviving (Young and McConway, 2004). Nevertheless, infants who survive a premature birth are still at a greater risk of experiencing a variety of health and developmental problems. Infants born more than six weeks early will often have serious respiratory problems as their lungs are not yet mature enough to allow them to breathe unaided. Often in cases where there is a risk of premature delivery, a mother to be will be given injections of steroid drugs in order to boost the development of the fetus's lungs. Premature infants also have difficulties in regulating their body temperature. Because of their vulnerabilities to a variety of health problems, premature infants are often cared for in a special type of bed called an **isolette**. The temperature within the isolette is carefully controlled and in order to protect the baby from infection, air is filtered before entry. The infant is fed through a nasal tube and is helped to breathe with the aid of a respirator, and is cleaned and changed through a small hole.

Prematurity can have short-term consequences for caregiving. An infant reared in an isolette cannot be held and cared for in the normal way by parents. When removed from the isolette, they are often irritable and less responsive to attention from their caregivers. These factors can increase the risk of the baby forming a less secure bond with the parents (Goldberg, 1977). The lack of responsiveness of premature babies sometimes results in parents resorting to behaviours such as poking to gain a response (Barrat et al., 1996) and there is also a greater risk of such babies becoming victims of abuse (Brockington, 1996).

It used to be the practice to minimise contact between parents and premature babies, as doctors felt that such contact and stimulation could be harmful, but this concern has changed in recent years. Parents are now encouraged to visit their child and to gently touch and caress their infant through the hole in the isolette. These actions will help to facilitate the development of the bond between the infant and parents, but such interventions are also known to have beneficial physical effects and a number of studies have shown actions such as gentle rocking, stroking and massaging are linked with weight gain, mental and motor development (Field, 2001; Schanberg and Field, 1987).

Birth weight is a major predictor of health and developmental outcomes in infants. Researchers make a distinction between two categories of low birth-weight infants. **Preterm infants** are born several weeks before their due date but are of a normal size and weight based on the time they have spent in the uterus. **Small for date babies** are below their expected weight taking into account the length of the pregnancy. Some of these are full-term babies but below their expected birth weight, others are seriously underweight premature babies. These are babies who experienced low growth during the antenatal period and may have been exposed to some of the teratogens as discussed in Chapter 5.

All underweight babies are vulnerable to a variety of problems, but small for date babies have the greatest risk for serious complications. They are more likely to die, catch infections and show signs of brain damage during the first year of life. There are also a number of negative long-term developmental outcomes associated with low birth weight. As children they are more likely to have low scores in intelligence and cognitive ability (Shenkin et al., 2004), impaired motor skills (Gidley Larson et al., 2011), as well as higher incidences of behavioural problems (Taylor et al., 2000).

Despite their vulnerability to a variety of long-term problems, there is much evidence that positive environmental factors can mitigate the disadvantages suffered by low birth-weight children. In one Canadian study, researchers tracked the progress of a group of low birth-weight babies and found that by adulthood they had similar educational and social achievements to normal birth-weight peers (Saigal et al., 2006).

However, the authors point out that most of the children in this study were from stable, middle-class families with good social resources. On the other hand, low birth-weight children from less stable and/or socio-economically disadvantaged families are likely to experience more emotional, behavioural and intellectual difficulties (Hack et al., 1995). However, the outcomes for children from such families can be improved if parents receive support and advice about promoting healthy development. A study reported by Eickmann et al. (2003) found that such an intervention resulted in improved cognitive and motor development in a sample of low birth-weight children from deprived communities in north-east Brazil.

Health and illness in childhood

All children will experience illness at various times in childhood. This can include **acute illness**, which is characterised by a rapid onset and a short duration, and **chronic illness**, which is characterised by a slow onset and a long duration. Examples of chronic illnesses include respiratory problems such as asthma, metabolic diseases such as diabetes, genetic diseases such as cystic fibrosis, as well as serious illness such as cancer. Typically there is no cure for such illnesses and they have to be managed over the course of the lifespan through the use of medication, and changes to lifestyle in terms of diet and physical activity.

Achieving an understanding of health and illness is important for children. An understanding of the causes of illness is important so that children can adopt healthy lifestyles in terms of diet and physical activity, as well as essential steps such as personal hygiene. This will require a basic understanding of mechanisms of disease transmission such as **contamination**, in which an object becomes negatively affected through contact with another, and **contagion**, in which contamination is spread between individuals. When children become ill, it is important that they receive age-appropriate explanations so that they can understand what is happening to them and understand what needs to be done in terms of treating the illness. For example, children who suffer from illnesses that necessitate them avoiding certain types of food or activities. Consequently, the issue of children's understanding of health and illness has received attention from researchers.

The next section will look at how children define health and illness. Before reading on, consider your own views of what constitutes these states. What are the characteristics of being healthy and ill? Do your characteristics match any of those identified by children in the studies listed below?

Children's definitions of health and illness

One issue of interest is how children define states of health and illness. This was examined in a study by Myant and Williams (2005) as part of a larger study examining children's knowledge of illness. Children aged from 4–12 years were asked for their views of what it meant to be ill or healthy. Myant and Williams examined the responses of the children and found that definitions of health and illness could be coded into four types of response. In the case of illness, this could be defined in terms of symptoms or *physical aspects* ('be sick'), *behavioural aspects* ('you have to stay off school'), *psychological aspects* ('be sad') or by the response *'don't know'*. Similarly, health was defined in terms of absence of symptoms ('you're fit and able to run and stuff'), behavioural aspects ('means you eat a lot of healthy stuff like fruit and vegetables'), psychological aspects ('to be happy and run around without having to worry'), as well as some don't know responses. The incidence of explanations across the different age groups was then examined. They found that in relation to definitions of illness, symptom-related responses were the most popular in all of the age groups, with the proportion of such responses increasing with the age of the children, while behavioural and psychological aspects were less popular. When it came to defining health, however, there was a difference in the pattern of responses. The majority of children aged 4–5 mainly tended to give don't know responses, with behavioural aspects being the next most favoured. Children aged 7–8 and 11–12 tended to describe health mainly in behavioural terms, while 9- to 10- year-olds focused mainly on the absence of symptoms. In general these results indicate that children distinguish between these two states and for the majority of the children health is separate from illness, and is not just defined in terms of the absence of illness.

The development of children's concepts of illness

The results of Myant and Williams (2005) show that children do have concepts of what it means to be ill and healthy. Another area of interest has focused on children's concepts of illness and how these develop through childhood. A number of researchers have applied a cognitive-developmental approach to this issue and have used Piaget's stages of development as a framework for understanding children's concepts of illness.

This approach was pioneered by Bibace and Walsh (1980, 1981) who asked children aged from 4–11 a series of questions about the causes of illness in general as well as more specific illness such as the common cold, cancer, measles and heart attacks. Based on their ages the children were classed as being 'prelogical' (preoperational) (4-year-olds), concrete operational (7-year-olds) and formal operational (11-year-olds). From examining the responses of the children, they identified six stages of development in the understanding of illness which they mapped on to Piaget's stages of cognitive development. These stages and their corresponding Piagetian stages are summarised in Table 7.1.

Table 7.1   Development of children's concepts of illness

Stage	Description	Corresponding Piagetian stage
Phenomenism	Illness linked with external events co-occurring with the illness but remote from the child, child unable to explain cause of the illness Some use of immanent justice to explain illness	Preoperational
Contagion	Illness caused by people or objects proximate to but not touching the child Link between cause and illness explained by proximity or 'magic' Contagion overextended to problems such as injuries and toothache	Preoperational
Contamination	Illness caused by physical contact with an individual or object with a quality that is 'bad' or 'harmful' to the body	Concrete operational
Internalisation	Cause of illness is still seen to be external to the child, but child becomes ill through processes such as inhalation or swallowing	Concrete operational
Physiologic	Illnesses have an external cause but internal physiological processes give rise to symptoms	Formal operational
Psychophysiologic	Illnesses described in terms of physiological processes, but child is also aware that psychological processes, such as thoughts and feelings, can affect the body	Formal operational

Sources: Bibace and Walsh, 1980, 1981

The first stage they called **phenominism** where the causes of illness are explained in relation to spatially or temporally remote external events that co-occurred with the illness. For example, in response to the question '*how do people get colds?*', one child replied '*from the sun*'. When asked how the sun can cause a cold the child replied '*it just does, that's all*' (Bibace and Walsh, 1980: 914). In some cases, children attributed illness to **immanent justice** (Piaget, 1932), the notion that illness is a consequence of misbehaviour. This is probably unsurprising and it was pointed out many years ago by Langford (1948) that parents often predict disaster if their child is naughty ('you'll get sick if you go outside without wearing warm clothes'). Phenominism is followed by **contagion**, wherein children believe that they can get sick through physical proximity to other people but not through touching them. Some children in this stage will overextend contagion to other problems including injuries and toothache. The link between the illness and its cause is explained in terms of 'magic' (people get colds '*when someone gets near them*'). The next stage of development is **contamination**, in which illness is caused by physical contact with an individual or object that is 'bad' or 'harmful' to the body, such as catching a cold from touching the hands of a person with a cold who had just sneezed on them. This stage is followed by **internalisation**: here children still consider the cause of illness to be external but the mechanism of transmission is ingesting 'germs' through inhalation and swallowing. The next stage is **physiologic**. In this stage, children realise that while illnesses have external causes, it is internal, physiological processes that give rise to the symptoms. They can identify the sequence of events that describe the illness, such as a virus entering the bloodstream and having an effect on the cells of the body. The final stage in Bibace and Walsh's model is **psychophysiologic**. Children in this stage continue to think of illness in terms of internal physiological processes but are also now aware that there may be psychological causes of illness as well, and thoughts and feelings can influence what goes on in the body, such as stress causing a heart attack.

In terms of mapping these stages to Piaget's developmental stages, Bibace and Walsh suggest that phenomenism and contagion overlap with the preoperational stage of development, contamination and internalisation with the concrete operational stage and their physiological and psychophysiological stages with the formal operational stage.

This research has led to suggestions for communicating medical information to sick children. Bibace and Walsh suggest that for children younger than 7, explanations should be limited to perceptual aspects such as descriptions of medicine, medical equipment, and so on. In the case of children aged 7–10, it has been suggested that explanations should be related to everyday aspects of children's experience. Whitt et al. (1979) suggest the use of metaphors, such as explaining epilepsy by making an analogy between the brain and a telephone system, with a fit being like a crossed wire or wrong number. In the case of older children and adolescents, simple medical explanations would be adequate.

Various studies (reviewed by Burbach and Peterson, 1986) have been supportive of the notion of a stage-like progression in children's understanding of illness broadly consistent with Piagetian notions of cognitive development. However, more recently there have been some criticisms of this approach. You will recall from Chapter 4 that one general criticism of Piagetian approaches is that they tend to underestimate the abilities of children. This same criticism has been made of studies that view a stage-like progression as a basis for children's understanding of illness.

According to views such as those of Bibace and Walsh, young, preoperational children would not understand contamination as a factor in illness. However, a study by Siegal and Share (1990) found evidence of contamination sensitivity in children as young as 3. In one experiment, children were presented with a number of scenarios in which a glass of juice had been contaminated through contact with a cockroach. The cockroach had then been removed and the children were asked to indicate whether or not the juice was safe to drink. In one scenario the children were asked directly when presented with the contaminated juice if it was safe to drink, in another scenario they were asked to evaluate the correctness of another child's response that the juice was safe or not safe to drink, in a third scenario the children were required to decide how to prevent another child from becoming ill (by offering an alternative to the contaminated drink even if the child desired the contaminated drink), and finally, they had to select the correct face (happy or sad) that should be used to warn children of the consequences of ingesting the contaminated drink. In each case the majority of the children were able to respond correctly. In a second experiment, children were able to reject a piece of mouldy bread as inedible, even after the mould was obscured by a breakfast spread. For Siegal and Share, the results of the study demonstrated contamination sensitivity in young children, but there was also the possibility that children's understanding of contaminants might reflect parental reinforcement. However, Siegal and Share (1990) argue that the children in their study were also able to evaluate the answers of others and infer necessary preventative action, which indicated that they were displaying more than just a rote understanding and had a rudimentary ability to detect causal relations between contamination and illness.

Other studies have also indicated a more mature understanding of illness in young children, in particular in relation to the role of contamination and germs in the causation of illness (Kalish, 1996; Springer and Ruckel, 1992). In reviewing some of these studies, Raman and Winer (2002) have noted that they often make use of multiple-choice questions and these can be contrasted with the open-ended interviews used by the Piagetian-based cognitive-developmental studies. In studies where children (and adults) are given forced-choice or multiple-choice questions, there is a tendency to provide answers showing more advanced conceptions of illness.

Factors other than stage of development have also been implicated in children's concepts of illness. One factor is *experience of illness* and it might be supposed that experiencing illness might have a positive effect on children's understanding but in fact the evidence here is mixed. Some studies have indicated less cognitive maturity in children who have been hospitalised (Cook, 1975, cited in Burbach and Peterson, 1986), other studies have found no difference between hospitalised and healthy children (Brewster, 1982), and other studies suggest a greater level of cognitive maturity in ill children (Williams, 1979). Various factors have proposed to account for the discrepant findings such as differences in methodologies and sampling procedures across the studies. Burbach and Peterson (1986) suggest that the nature and severity of the illness prior may also be a factor. One possibility is that children whose illness prevents them from interacting with their environment may have lower levels of cognitive development and less sophisticated concepts of illness due to a lack of real-world experience.

Myant and Williams (2005) in their study of 4- to 12-year-old children also found that children's concepts of illness varied across specific illnesses. Children of all ages tended to believe that colds were caused by cold weather rather than by contagion. On the other hand, children as young as 4 years of age understood the role of contagion in chickenpox. This indicates that young children's misconceptions of colds are not caused by a general lack of understanding contagion. When questioned about the nature of toothache children aged 11–12 were able to give sophisticated accounts of the decay processes associated with it, but even younger children were able to give behavioural factors that would contribute to toothache, such as not brushing their teeth. Children of all age groups showed a good understanding of injuries such as a bruise and a broken leg. All were able to give physical causes for injuries, although more detailed and causal accounts were given by older children.

There is also evidence that children can benefit from interventions to increase their knowledge and understanding of illness. Williams and Binnie (2002) tested a group of 4- and 7-year-old children on their understanding of contagious illnesses (chickenpox and common cold), non-contagious illnesses (asthma and cancer) and injuries (scraped knee and broken arm). As expected, the older children had a more sophisticated knowledge of illness than the younger children. Some of the children from both age groups were then allocated to interventions designed to increase their understanding of illness, such as being presented with factual stories about having an illness or injury and recovering and taking part in structured group discussions in which an interviewer asked the group questions about the nature, cause and recovery from illness. The discussions involved the interviewer highlighting similarities and differences between individual responses, discussing as a group their responses to the questions and arriving at a group consensus regarding answers to the questions. Then the children were tested again on their knowledge of illnesses one week after the intervention and their performance compared with a control group. Williams and Binnie found that while the intervention made little difference to understanding injuries, this was because most children in each age group already had a good understanding of them. However, in the case illnesses there were significant improvements in understanding in the intervention group, in particular in the 4-year-olds.

A feature of the Piagetian-based stage approaches to children's concepts of illness is that when children proceed to a new stage, the style of thinking in the new stage 'replaces' the style of thinking in the previous stage. Thus as children develop, they will move away from less mature concepts of illness towards more mature biological and psychological ways of thinking about illness. However, Raman and Winer (2002) have suggested that in fact it is possible for 'naive' as well as 'sophisticated' views of illness to coexist within the individual and this applies to children and adults. In their study of concepts of illness in children and adults, they did find a general move in the direction of adopting biological and psychological explanations that coincided with increased age. However, even in their adult participants, they were still able to identify instances of folkloric views of illness coinciding with biological views, for example understanding that colds are caused by viruses but still believing that they are also related to factors such as going outside with wet hair. Moreover, they also identified instances where adults adopted imminent justice concepts to explain illness, particularly when presented with accounts of a bad person developing a serious illness, to which one individual responded with the maxim 'what goes around comes around' even though their responses to other questions indicated a sophisticated, biological/psychological understanding of illness.

Coping with chronic illness

A chronic illness in a child can be defined as

any physical, emotional or mental condition that prevented him or her from attending school regularly, doing regular school work, or doing usual childhood activities or that required frequent attention or treatment from a doctor or other health professional, regular use of medication or use of special equipment. (Van Cleave et al., 2010: 624)

Chronic illnesses are characterised by a prolonged duration, the absence of a spontaneous resolution and they are rarely cured completely (Stanton et al., 2007).

From the definition above, chronic illness can cover a wide variety of conditions, both psychological and physical. As psychological disorders have been covered in Chapter 6 this section will look at chronic physical conditions and their psychosocial impact. Many children suffer from chronic illnesses. Respiratory complaints are a common chronic illness of which asthma is one. According to the charity Asthma UK (2013), the condition affects over 1.1 million children in the UK, a prevalence rate of 1 in 11 children. Another common condition is diabetes. In diabetes sufferers the body is unable to produce insulin leading to dangerous levels of glucose in the bloodstream. There are an estimated 29,000 children in the UK affected by the condition (Diabetes UK, 2012).

The diagnosis of a chronic condition provides many challenges to children and their parents. In addition to the normal challenges of growing up, the child must learn to manage their condition and comply with the medical treatment. Often the diagnosis of a chronic condition is unexpected. Compas et al. (2012) give the example of a child brought to the doctor with a suspected bladder infection after waking up several times a night to urinate who is diagnosed with type 1 diabetes. The diagnosis of this condition will lead to a lifetime of monitoring blood glucose levels, administration of insulin injections, restrictions on diet and excercise and the possibility of other physical complications, such as sight problems. The diagnosis of a chronic illness therefore produces the acute stress of the diagnosis, and following a period of adaptation, the long-term stress of the illness itself.

Chronic illness in children is related to a variety of psychological difficulties. An extensive review of studies of children with chronic illnesses by Boekaerts and Röder (1999) indicated that such children have higher levels of behavioural problems compared to their healthy peers, but less than children diagnosed with behavioural disorders. They also noted a higher level of internalising problems such as depression and anxiety. Some researchers have suggested that children with chronic conditions are also at risk from social isolation and poor peer relations (see, for example, Miller and Wood, 1991). Peers may fear that the illness is contagious and avoid the child, or the child may feel different from their peers. Spirito et al. (1991) have found that in general, such children do not experience poorer peer relations than other schoolchildren. However, the effect of chronic illness on peer relations did appear to vary with different illnesses. Eiser et al. (1992) found that children with asthma and epilepsy were more adversely affected socially than children with diabetes, leukaemia, and cardiac conditions. Another issue of concern is the effect of the illness on school performance given that such illnesses can frequently disrupt school attendance. However, in their review, Boekaerts and Röder (1999) found that despite a higher frequency of school absences compared to their healthy peers, chronically ill children did not show lower school performances, except in the case of children with epilepsy. Nevertheless, there is the possibility of adverse effects on intellectual functioning due to the treatment they are receiving. A study by Eiser (1980) found that in a group of children receiving treatment for leukaemia, treatment involving irradiation of the central nervous system had an adverse effect on intellectual functioning.

Given that chronic illnesses can impose stress and difficulties on children in a number of ways, how do they cope with their conditions? A review by Compas et al. (2012) has identified three coping strategies used by these children. One approach is called **primary control or active coping** and involves attempts to change the source of stress or one's response to the stressor. Strategies used here include seeking social support and taking active steps to deal with the symptoms. A second strategy identified was **secondary coping** in which the child seeks to adapt to their situation through acceptance, cognitive restructuring and positive thinking. Some children engage in **disengagement coping** through the use of strategies such as avoidance and denial. Overall, Compas et al. concluded that secondary coping was associated most strongly with successful adjustment to chronic illness, disengagement was associated with poorer adjustment and mixed outcome in the case of children who engaged in primary control-based coping. The results of these studies will have clear implications for psychological interventions with children suffering from chronic illnesses.

Chronic illness and family functioning

The diagnosis of a chronic illness does not just affect the child; it will also have implications for the child's parents and siblings. Quite apart from the worry of having a sick child, the diagnosis of the illness will have many practical implications for the parents as they have to take into account the specific requirements of their child's illness. Boekaerts and Roder (1999) list just some of the practical effects. Parents of children with asthma may need to clean their home more frequently and take care that their child avoids certain allergens and takes the necessary medication on time. They will also spend more time taking their child to see doctors and other health professionals. There are other emotional factors, too, such as parents having to come to terms with the knowledge that their child may not achieve as much as hoped for. Some parents may feel resentful of the burden of the disease. Siblings may be affected adversely as well. The demands of caring for the chronically sick child may mean that parents have less time to spend in social and recreational activities with the siblings.

Cohen (1999) conducted an extensive review of the effects of chronic illness on the family and noted that chronic illness can have a negative effect on parental mental health and that these difficulties were related in most cases to the behavioural demands of coping with the illness rather than the severity of the illness itself. Mothers of children are more likely to experience higher levels of distress related to the severity of illness in the child while fathers are more likely to report stress in relation to finances and emotional attachment to the child. Greater risks of marital discord were also noted, with parents reporting spending personal time in caring for the child and fewer positive spousal interactions. Siblings of chronically ill children were noted for being at risk of developing behavioural problems. These findings indicate that the effects on family functioning also need to be kept in mind in interventions with a chronically sick child.

Accidents and injuries in childhood

Accidents are another major threat to the health and wellbeing of children, and indeed in the UK, accidents are the main cause of death in children under the age of 15 (Green, 2004). For every child that is killed many more are injured and in some cases the injuries sustained may result in permanent disabilities. The term 'accident' might suggest that such occurrences are merely 'bad luck' and cannot be prevented. However, the evidence suggests that accidents are not randomly distributed, and factors such as *age, sex, social class* and *individual characteristics* of children are all related to the occurrence of accidents.

Age

The major causes of accidental injury and death change as children get older (see for example Roberts et al., 1998). For children aged under 5, the majority of accidents occur in the home, the major causes of death being fires, suffocation, drowning, poisoning and falls. As children get older, road traffic accidents become a major cause. There are also different environmental risks associated with specific types of accident that vary with age. An example is drowning. An American study reported by Quan et al. (1989) found that in infants, the majority of drowning and near-drowning incidents occurred in bathtubs; in pre-schoolers, they occurred mostly in swimming pools; and in adolescents, the most frequent locations were rivers and lakes. It is unsurprising that the nature of accident risks varies with age, as increasing age results in increasing mobility and the probability of venturing further from home, thus changing exposure to the various risks.

Sex

At all ages, boys are more likely to die from accidents than girls. Green (2004) points out that this discrepancy has not been fully explained but may be due to effects of socialisation and expectations regarding gender roles. Girls may be encouraged to be more aware of physical risks, while boys are expected to engage in more 'rough-and-tumble' play which may inevitably expose them to a higher risk of accidental injury. Morrongiello and Rennie (1998) found that boys tend to judge risky play activities as less likely to result in injury and they pay less attention to injury risk cues such as wary facial expressions in peers. A study by Morrongiello and Dawber (2000) also provides some evidence for the notion of different treatment of sexes with regard to accident risks. They found, for example, that mothers of daughters intervened more frequently and quickly in cases of risky behaviour than mothers of sons.

Social class

Accident statistics indicate that the relationship between social class and risk of accidental death and injury is stronger than the relationship for any other factors and children from deprived backgrounds have a heightened risk of accidental injury and death. According to the Child Accident Prevention Trust (2013), children from the poorest families in the UK are 13 times more likely to die from accidents, and are also more likely to be admitted to hospital with accidental injuries.

Various factors have been suggested to explain the relation between social class and accident risk. According to Green (2004), the view has sometimes been expressed that working-class parents might be more 'fatalistic' about accidents and as a result may not engage in many preventative actions; however, there is little evidence to support this view. In fact a study by Roberts et al. (1992, 1993) on accidents in a deprived area of Glasgow found that parents were very aware of the risks to their children, in particular of various environmental hazards, and took considerable steps both as individuals and as campaigners to keep their children safe. Furthermore, Roberts et al. found that these parents were often more knowledgeable about local risks than professionals who proposed that these parents needed education in accident prevention! The various environmental risks noted by Roberts et al. included the presence of main roads nearby, broken glass in play areas and road and building works. There were also hazards in the home caused by bad design, such as gaps in balconies big enough for toddlers to crawl through, inadequate window fastenings and electric sockets with no 'off' switches. They also noted a basic practical problem faced by parents on low incomes: they simply were unable to afford the costs of making their homes safe. Similar findings were reported in a study by Colver et al. (1982) who also noted that disadvantaged families were well aware of the preventability of childhood accidents and did not display ignorance or apathy about hazards but faced practical problems in converting their concerns into action.

While there is not much evidence to support the notion of fatalistic attitudes to accidents among poorer parents, nevertheless such parents are more likely to suffer from stresses related to adverse life events. Brown and Davidson (1978) found that children of working-class mothers with a psychiatric disorder had an accident rate of

19.6 per 100, compared to a rate of 9.6 accidents per 100 for children of a working-class mother without a psychiatric disorder. The association between maternal psychopathology and increased risk of child injury has also been observed in other studies (see, for example, Bradbury et al., 1999; Russell, 1998). It may be the case that in such families, the stresses suffered by parents result in less supervision of their children and monitoring of their safety. Indeed a study by Oyserman et al. (2005) found that mothers with mental health problems tended to adopt a permissive parenting style (see Chapter 11), in which little attempt is made to control or regulate children's behaviour.

Individual characteristics of the child

As we have already seen in Chapter 5 with regard to the development of motor skills, children have a tendency to overestimate their abilities, for example how far they can reach or jump, and this can pose a risk of accidental injury. There is also evidence that this tendency to overestimate physical abilities is more pronounced in some children. Studies by Plumert and Schwebel (1997) and Schwebel and Plumert (1999) gave children aged 6–8 a number of physical tasks (such as removing a toy from a high shelf while standing on their toes) which were graded in the ability of the children to perform them. It was found that children with more extraverted and impulsive personalities were more likely to overestimate their abilities to perform these tasks. They also found the relationship between personality and ability estimation to be linked with susceptibility to accidental injury. Children who were high on extraversion and low in inhibitory control as toddlers tended to overestimate their abilities and have higher rates of injury at age 6. On the other hand, children who were more introverted and had higher levels of inhibitory control as toddlers tended to underestimate their abilities and had lower rates of injury at age 6. It is likely that more extraverted and impulsive children will seek out experiences that put them at risk of accidental injury and the risk of such injury is compounded by their tendency to overestimate their abilities. In some cases, risk taking in children may also be related to parenting. A research review by Tuchfarber et al. (1997) found that by middle childhood, the biggest risk takers tend to be those that have parents who do not act as safety-conscious models, supervise their children's activities or use punitive and inconsistent discipline to enforce rules. Also, it has been found that parents who lack confidence in their ability to control their children's risky behaviour have children who are more susceptible to accidental injury (Damashek et al., 2005).

Preventing accidents

Green (2004) identifies three levels at which attempts can be made to reduce the impact of accidents. These are **primary accident prevention**, which aims to prevent accidents happening at all, **secondary accident prevention**, which aims to minimise the effect of an accident if it does happen, and **tertiary accident prevention**, which minimises the outcome of the injury resulting from the accident. The strategies for prevention at the various levels can be divided into the **'three E's' of accident prevention**: **education** to raise awareness of accident risks and ways to avoid them; **engineering** to make the environment safer; and **enforcement**, which involves applying legal sanctions against risk-taking behaviour. Providing first aid training to parents and teachers would be an example of an education strategy at the tertiary level of accident prevention, placing covers on electrical sockets would be an example of an engineering strategy at the primary level, and laws requiring parents to use child safety seats in cars would be an example of an enforcement strategy at the secondary level of accident prevention.

Educational approaches have been popular strategies to reduce accidents, a good example being road safety. You can probably recall the various television adverts regarding crossing the road safely. However, Green (2004) reminds us that providing safety information to young children can be difficult. Recall from our consideration of illness concepts in children that often young children use 'magical' or 'immanent justice' concepts to explain illness. There is also the possibility that children use such concepts to explain accidents. Adults may wish to explain to children about finding a safe place to cross the road, but as Green points out, such places may be seen as 'magical' and the children are safe whatever they do. The message that roads are dangerous may itself be translated into dangerous behaviours, for example running across the road to minimise the amount of time spent in a dangerous area. Moreover, giving children messages such as 'don't run across the road because it's dangerous' may result in children seeing the injury as arising from their own disobedience rather than from the risk of being run over.

Given that some children have a tendency to be impulsive and take risks researchers such as Schwebel and Plumert (1999) argue that engineering strategies at the primary level are most effective. They give the example of railway crossings – it is not enough to just provide flashing lights warning of the approach of a train, it is better to prevent risky behaviour in the first place by the use of barriers to prevent attempts at crossing.

It may be that employing a mix of strategies for accident prevention might be most effective. An example of such a successful strategy is a programme called 'Children can't fly' which was implemented in New York in the 1970s (Spiegel and Lindaman, 1977). This was a project to reduce the number of deaths caused by falls from heights which accounted for 12 per cent of all accidental deaths in New York city and it involved both education and engineering strategies. Education strategies included a media campaign to highlight the dangers of open, unguarded windows and visits by outreach workers who provided practical safety advice to parents. The engineering aspects involved the distribution of free and easy-to-install window guards to families with preschool children who were living in high-rise buildings. The project appears to have been a success. Following the intervention, a 50 per cent reduction in falls from windows was observed and no falls were reported from windows with guards installed.

Can you think of some more educational, engineering and enforcement strategies that might be employed across the various levels of accident prevention?

Chapter summary

- The first health check received by the infant is an assessment using the Apgar scale to check heart rate, breathing, reflexes, skin colour and muscle tone. In the first few days, blood tests are also taken to check for PKU and hypothyroidism.
- Children appear to make distinctions between states of health and illness. Illness tends to be described in terms of symptoms whereas health is predominantly described in behavioural terms of what the child can do.
- It has been proposed that children pass through a series of stages in their understanding of the causes of illness and that these stages overlap with Piaget's stages of cognitive development. Children move from immature, 'magical' explanations of illness to ultimately a more sophisticated understanding involving an awareness of both biological and psychological causes.
- Children's understanding of illness can also be affected by the nature of the illness and their experience of illness.
- Chronic illnesses are those which last over the course of the lifespan and require compliance with medical treatment to manage the symptoms as well as lifestyle changes such as avoiding certain types of foods, environments and activities.
- Children suffering from chronic illnesses are at risk from a variety of psychological problems, but effective forms of coping strategies have been identified.
- Chronic illnesses can also have a negative effect on the families of the sufferers.
- Susceptibility to accidental death and injury in childhood is not random. It is influenced by age, sex, social class and personality characteristics.
- Attempts at accident prevention take place at the primary, secondary and tertiary levels, and within each level there are a variety of educational, engineering and enforcement strategies.

Further reading

Davey, B. (ed.) (2004) *Birth to Old Age: Health in Transition*. Milton Keynes: Open University Press. An interdisciplinary book taking a lifespan perspective on health, illness and wellbeing. Includes a number of useful chapters relating to health and wellbeing in children and young people.

Useful websites

http://www.asthma.org.uk/
http://www.diabetes.org.uk/

There are various organisations aiming to support individuals suffering from chronic illnesses. The two examples above are the websites for Asthma UK and Diabetes UK and they contain a variety of resources for suffers and their families. The websites have dedicated sections related to child sufferers of these conditions.

http://makingthelink.net/

A website run by the Childhood Accident Prevention Trust aimed at supporting professionals working with children in preventing childhood accidents and injuries.

References

Apgar, V. (1953) 'A proposal for a new method of evaluation of the newborn infant', *Current Researches in Anesthesia and Analgesia*, 32 (4): 260–7.

Asthma UK (2013) *Asthma Facts and FAQs*. Available at www.asthma.org.uk/asthma-facts-and-statistics (accessed 5 September 2013).

Barrat, M.S., Roach, M.A. and Leavitt, L.A. (1996) 'The impact of low-risk prematurity on maternal behaviour and toddler outcomes', *International Journal of Behavioral Development*, 19 (3): 581–602.

Bass, J.L., Corwin, M., Gozal, D., Moore, C., Nishida, H., Parker, S., Schonwald, A., Wilker, R.E., Stehle, S. and Kinane, T.B. (2004) 'The effect of chronic or intermittent hypoxia on cognition in childhood: A review of the evidence', *Pediatrics*, 114 (3): 805–16.

Bibace, R. and Walsh, M.E. (1980) 'Development of children's concepts of illness', *Pediatrics*, 66 (6): 912–17.

Bibace, R. and Walsh, M.E. (1981) 'Children's conceptions of illness', in R. Bibace and M.E. Walsh (eds), *New Directions for Child Development: Children's Conceptions of Health, Illness and Bodily Functions*. San Francisco, CA: Jossey-Bass. pp. 34–42.

Boekaerts, M. and Röder, I. (1999) 'Stress, coping, and adjustment in children with a chronic disease: A review of the literature', *Disability and Rehabilitation*, 21 (7): 311–37.

Bradbury, K., Janicke, D.M., Riley, A.W. and Finney, J.W. (1999) 'Predictors of unintentional injuries to school-age children seen in pediatric primary care', *Journal of Pediatric Psychology*, 24 (5): 423–33.

Brewster, A. (1982) 'Chronically ill hospitalized children's concepts of their illness', *Pediatrics*, 69 (3): 355–62.

Brockington, I. (1996) *Motherhood and Mental Health*. Oxford: Oxford University Press.

Brown. G.W. and Davidson, S. (1978) 'Social class, psychiatric disorder of mother, and accidents to children', *The Lancet*, 311 (8060): 378–81.

Burbach, D.J. and Peterson, L. (1986) 'Children's concepts of physical illness: A review and critique of the cognitive-developmental literature', *Health Psychology*, 5 (3): 307–25.

Child Accident Prevention Trust (2013) *Who we are*. Available at: http://capt.org.uk/who-we-are (accessed 6 June 2013).

Cohen, M.S. (1999) 'Families coping with childhood chronic illness: A research review', *Families, Systems, and Health*, 17 (2): 149–64.

Colver, A.F., Hutchinson, P.J. and Judson, E.C. (1982) 'Promoting children's home safety', *British Medical Journal*, 285 (6349): 1177–80

Compas, B.E., Jaser, S.S., Dunn, M.J. and Rodriguez, E.M. (2012) 'Coping with chronic illness in childhood and adolescence', *Annual Review of Clinical Psychology*, 8: 455–80.

Damashek, A.L., Williams, N.A., Sher, K.J., Peterson, L., Lewis, T. and Schweinle, W. (2005) 'Risk for minor childhood injury: An investigation of maternal and child factors', *Journal of Pediatric Psychology*, 30 (6): 469–80.

Diabetes UK (2012) *Diabetes in the UK 2012: Key statistics on diabetes*. Available at: www. diabetes.org.uk/Documents/Reports/Diabetes_in_the_UK_2012.pdf (accessed 5 September 2013).

Eickmann, S.H., Lima, A.C.V., Guerra, M.Q., Lima, M.C., Lira, P.I.C., Huttly, S.R.A. and Ashworth, A. (2003) 'Improved cognitive and motor development in a community-based intervention of psychosocial stimulation in northeast Brazil', *Developmental Medicine and Child Neurology*, 45 (8): 536–41.

Eiser, C. (1980) 'Effects of chronic illness on intellectual development: A comparison of normal children with those treated for childhood leukaemia and solid tumours', *Archives of Disease in Childhood*, 55 (10): 766–70.

Eiser, C., Havermans, T., Pancer, M. and Eiser, J.R. (1992) 'Adjustment to chronic disease in relation to age and gender: Mothers' and fathers' reports of their children's behavior', *Journal of Pediatric Psychology*, 17 (3): 261–75.

Fewell, J.E. (2005) 'Protective responses of the newborn to hypoxia', *Respiratory Physiology and Neurobiology*, 149 (1–3): 243–55.

Field, T. (2001) 'Massage therapy facilitates weight gain in preterm infants', *Current Directions in Psychological Science*, 10 (2): 51–4.

Gidley Larson, J.C., Baron, I.S., Erickson, K.K., Ahronovich, M.D., Baker, R.R. and Litman, F.R. (2011) 'Neuromotor outcomes at school age after extremely low birth weight: Early detection of subtle signs', *Neuropsychology*, 25 (1): pp. 66–75.

Goldberg, S. (1977) 'Premature birth: Consequences for the parent–infant relationship', *American Scientist*, 67 (2): 214–20.

Green, J. (2004) 'Children and accidents', in B. Davey (ed.), *Birth to Old Age: Health in Transition*. Milton Keynes: Open University Press. pp. 104–23.

Hack, M.H., Klein, N.K. and Taylor, H.G. (1995) 'Long-term developmental outcomes of low birth weight infants', *The Future of Children*, 5 (1): 176–96.

Kalish, C. (1996) 'Causes and symptoms in preschoolers' conceptions of illness', *Child Development*, 67 (4): 1647–70.

Kopp, C. and Kaler, S.R. (1989) 'Risk in infancy: Origins and implications', *American Psychologist*, 44 (2): 224–30.

Langford, W.S. (1948) 'Physical illness and convalescence: Their meaning to the child', *Journal of Pediatrics*, 33 (2): 242–50.

Marlow, N., Rose, A.S., Rands, C.E. and Draper, E.S. (2005) 'Neuropsychological and educational problems at school age associated with neonatal encepalopathy', *Archives of Disease in Childhoood: Fetal and Neonatal Edition*, 90 (5): 380–87.

Miller, B.D. and Wood, B.L. (1991) 'Childhood asthma in interaction with family, school, and peer systems: A developmental model for primary care', *Journal of Asthma*, 28 (6): 405–14.

Morrongiello B.A. and Rennie, H. (1998) 'Why do boys engage in more risk taking than girls? The role of attributions, beliefs, and risk appraisals', *Journal of Pediatric Psychology*, 23 (1): 33–43.

Morrongiello, B.A. and Dawber, T. (2000) 'Mothers responses to sons and daughter's engaging in injury-risk behaviors on a playground: Implications for sex differences in injury rates', *Journal of Experimental Child Psychology*, 76 (2): 89–103.

Myant, K.A. and Williams, J.M. (2005) 'Children's concepts of health and illness: Understanding of contagious illnesses, non-contagious illnesses and injuries', *Journal of Health Psychology*, 10 (6): 805–19.

Oyserman, D., Bybee, D., Mowbray, C. and Hart-Johnson, T. (2005) 'When mothers have serious mental health problems: Parenting as a proximal mediator', *Journal of Adolescence*, 28 (4): 443–63.

Piaget, J. (1932) *The Moral Development of the Child*. Harmondsworth: Penguin.

Plumert, J.M. and Schwebel, D.C. (1997) 'Social and temperamental influences on children's overestimation of their physical abilities: Links to accidental injuries', *Journal of Experimental Child Psychology*, 67 (3): 317–37.

Quan, L., Gore, E.J., Wentz, K., Allen, J. and Novack, A.H. (1989) 'Ten-year study of pediatric drowning and near-drownings in King County, Washington: Lessons in injury prevention', *Pediatrics*, 83 (6): 1035–40.

Raman, L. and Winer, G.A. (2002) 'Children's and adults' understanding of illness: Evidence in support of a coexistence model', *Genetic, Social, and General Psychology Monographs*, 128 (4): 325–55.

Roberts, I., DiGuiseppi, C., and Ward, H. (1998) 'Childhood injuries: Extent of the problem, epidemiological trends and costs', *Injury Prevention*, 4 (suppl): S10–6.

Roberts, H., Smith, S. and Bryce, C. (1993) 'Prevention is better …', *Sociology of Health & Illness*, 15 (4): 447–63.

Roberts, H., Smith, S.J. and Lloyd, M. (1992) 'Safety as a social value: A community approach', in S. Scott, G. Williams, S. Platt and H. Thomas (eds), *Private Risks and Public Dangers*. Basingstoke: Avery Press. pp. 184–200.

Russell, K.M. (1998) 'Preschool children at risk for repeat injuries', *Journal of Community Health Nursing*, 15 (3): 179–90.

Saigal, S., Stoskopf, B., Streiner, D., Boyle, M., Pinelli, J. Paneth, N. and Goddeeris, J. (2006) 'Transition of extremely low-birth-weight infants from adolescence to young adulthood: comparison with normal birth-weight controls', *Journal of the American Medical Association*, 295 (6): 667–75.

Schanberg, S.M. and Field, T.M. (1987) 'Sensory deprivation stress and supplemental stimulation in the rat pup and preterm human neonate', *Child Development*, 58 (6): 1431–47.

Schwebel, D.C. and Plumert, J.M. (1999) 'Longitudinal and concurrent relations among temperament, ability estimation, and injury proneness', *Child Development*, 70 (3): 700–12.

Shenkin, S.D., Starr, J.M. and Deary, I.J. (2004) 'Birth weight and cognitive ability in childhood: A systematic review', *Psychological Bulletin*, 130 (6): 989–1013.

Siegal, M. and Share, D.L. (1990) 'Contamination sensitivity in young children', *Developmental Psychology*, 26 (3): 455–8.

Spiegel, C.N. and Lindaman, F.C. (1977) 'Children can't fly: A program to prevent childhood morbidity and mortality from window falls', *American Journal of Public Health*, 67 (12): 1143–7.

Spirito, A., DeLawyer, D.D. and Stark, L.J. (1991) 'Peer relations and social adjustment of chronically ill children and adolescents', *Clinical Psychology Review*, 11: 539–564.

Springer, K. and Ruckel, J. (1992) 'Early beliefs about the cause of illness: Evidence against immanent justice', *Cognitive Development*, 7 (4): 429–43.

Stanton, A.L., Revenson, T. and Tennen, H. (2007) 'Health psychology: Psychological adjustment to chronic disease', *Annual Review of Psychology*, 58: 565–92.

Taylor, H.G., Klein, N.N., Minich, N.M. and Hack, N.M. (2000) 'Middle-school-age outcomes in children with very low birthweight', *Child Development*, 71 (6): 1495–511.

Tuchfarber, B.S., Zins, J.E. and Jason, L.A. (1997) 'Prevention and control of injuries', in R. Weissberg, T.P. Gullota, R.L. Hampton, B.A. Ryan and G.R. Adams (eds), *Enhancing Children's Wellness*. Thousand Oaks, CA: Sage. pp. 250–77.

Van Cleave, J., Gortmaker, S.L. and Perrin, J.M. (2010) 'Dynamics of obesity and chronic health conditions among children and youth', *Journal of the American Medical Association*, 303 (7): 623–30.

van Handel, M., Swaab, H., de Vries, L.S. and Jongmans, M.J. (2007) 'Long-term cognitive and behavioral consequences of neonatal encapholopathy following perinatal asphyxia: A review', *European Journal of Pediatrics*, 166 (7): 645–54.

Whitt, J.K., Dykstra, W. and Taylor, C.A. (1979) 'Children's conceptions of illness and cognitive development: Implications for pediatric practitioners', *Clinical Pediatrics*, 18 (6): 327–39.

Williams, J.M. and Binnie, L.M. (2002) 'Children's concepts of illness: An intervention to improve knowledge', *British Journal of Health Psychology*, 7 (2): 129–47.

Williams, P. (1979) 'Children's concepts of illness and internal body parts', *Maternal-Child Nursing Journal*, 8 (2): 115–23.

Young, G. and McConway, K. (2004) 'Care in pregnancy and childbirth', in B. Davey (ed.), *Birth to Old Age: Health in Transition*. Milton Keynes: Open University Press. pp. 46–81.

Emotional and Social Development

Why you should read this chapter

In order to develop into a socially competent individual, a child has to acquire many emotional and social skills. Children need to learn to describe and manage their own emotional experiences and recognise emotional states in other people so that they can respond accordingly. They need to form close attachments with caregivers, and the quality of these relationships can often set the scene for future interpersonal ones. Participation in the social world also requires that the child understand other people's beliefs and desires and this understanding is crucial to understanding why people say the things they say and do the things they do. There are a number of influences on these processes, but it will also be seen from reading this chapter that adults can play a significant part in facilitating these developments in the child. Indeed, the issue of personal, social and emotional development is recognised as a formal area of learning in the various early years curricula in the UK, so an understanding of basic social and emotional development will be important for working with young children. This chapter aims to provide you with such an understanding.

By the end of this chapter you should

- know what the basic emotions are and understand the course of their development in infancy and childhood

- be aware of the nature and development of more complex emotional states, such as self-conscious emotions and holding multiple emotions

- understand the importance of being able to regulate emotional states, and the factors related to the development of this capacity and in particular the role of caregiving and adult interactions

- understand what is meant by the term **attachment**, how attachment relationships develop, and the different types of attachment styles

- be aware of the consequence of early attachment relationships

- have an understanding of the development of peer relationships

- understand the concept of peer status and its consequences

- understand the development of social understanding in children and in particular children's understanding of other people's mental states.

 The next section lists what are referred to as basic emotions. Before reading on, can you think of any basic emotions that you would expect to see expressed by an infant?

Development of basic emotions in infancy

It is widely accepted that humans are equipped with a set of basic emotions that are universal and have an evolutionary history of promoting survival. This notion was first proposed by Darwin (1872) based on his observations of different cultures as he travelled on his expeditions. There is evidence to support this notion. Ekmen and Friesen (1971) discovered an isolated tribe in New Guinea who had no contact with other cultures. However, when shown photographs of emotional expressions from other cultures they were able to recognise the emotional states depicted. Similarly, American students shown photographs of emotional expressions on the New Guinea tribe were able to correctly identify the emotions being expressed. There has been some debate over the nature and number of basic emotions. Eckman and Friesen (1971) have proposed that there are six: surprise, anger, sadness, disgust, fear and happiness. Other researchers have proposed lists ranging from five to eight (Workman and Reader, 2007). However, these lists include the emotions identified by Eckman and Friesen indicating some consensus around these six basic emotions.

There is evidence that these basic emotions are present during infancy. Initially, the main emotional states that can be observed are contentment and distress but by 6 months most of the basic emotions will have made an appearance (Izard, 1994). Infants are unable to verbalise their emotions and therefore facial expressions are used as an indicator of an infant's emotional state.

Happiness, as evidenced by smiles, and later by laughter, makes an important contribution to development. A smiling infant will evoke similar responses from a caregiver. The resulting playful and affectionate behaviour will encourage the infant to smile more and this strengthens the bond between infant and caregiver (Malloch, 1999). In the first few weeks of life infants smile when full and when they are asleep rather than in response to external stimulation. However, by the end of the first month, they will smile in response to eye-catching events such as a bright object coming into their field of vision (Berk, 2008). The infant will attend to the caregiver's voice and facial expressions and between 1 and 2 months of age there is the appearance of the social smile, a broad grin evoked by social interactions such as smiling human faces (Anisfeld, 1982). By the age of 6 months, smiles are evoked immediately by an interesting stimulus. Laughter appears at around 3–4 months of age reflecting an increased understanding of the world and ability to perceive unusual events such as a parent talking in a funny voice (Sroufe and Wunsch, 1972). By the end of the first year, infants appear to have a number of different smiles including a broad 'cheek-raised' smile (known as a *Duchenne smile*) in response to the approach of a smiling parent, and an open-mouthed smile during play (Berk, 2008; Messinger and Fogel, 2007).

Responses to unpleasant and distressing experiences are present from birth, with infants showing distress in response to hunger, medical procedures such as injections, and over- or understimulation. Expressions of anger become more distinct and frequent from about 4–6 months of age. This was demonstrated in a study by Izard et al. (1987) who studied the facial expressions of infants aged between 2 and 8 months being given routine inoculations. Younger infants tended to react with generalised distress, whereas older infants showed distinctly angry expressions. Anger responses are also observed in response to situations such as loss of control over a pleasant stimulus or being physically restrained (Camras et al., 1992; Sullivan and Lewis, 2003). Expressions of sadness can also occur in response to these situations but are less frequent. They occur more frequently when an infant is deprived of a familiar caregiver or in cases of disruption of normal, affectionate interactions with the caregiver. This was demonstrated in a number of studies using the *still-face paradigm* (see, for example, Mesman et al., 2009; Murray and Trevarthen, 1985) in which the parent was asked to assume a still-faced, unresponsive pose or a depressed state. The infants tried to use a variety of behaviours such as facial expressions and body gestures to elicit a response from the parent and when these failed, the infants turned away and showed signs of distress. These responses are also observed in infants of depressed parents (Stanley et al., 2004).

The most noticeable manifestation of fear is the infant's response to strangers, a response called **stranger anxiety**. This emerges around the time that the infant is starting to form attachment bonds with familiar caregivers. Young infants will smile indiscriminately at parents and strangers alike but by 4 months of age there is evidence of some wariness of strangers, and from around 7 months a distinct fear reaction is evident in response to their presence including crying, whimpering and attempts at avoidance (Sroufe, 1977). This reaction usually begins to decline during the second year of life. The presence of stranger anxiety can be affected by a number of factors. These include the behaviour of the stranger (infants are less likely to be afraid of strangers who interact in a friendly, non-intrusive manner) and the age of the stranger (infants show less fear towards children than adults) (Brooks and Lewis, 1976; Sroufe, 1977). Individual differences may also play a role, with some infants being more fearful than others (DeRosnay et al., 2006). Eventually, however, this anxiety declines as further cognitive development allows toddlers to discriminate more effectively between threatening and non-threatening people and situations.

Emotional development in childhood

During the second year of life, children begin to display **self-conscious emotions** including *guilt, shame, embarrassment, envy and pride*. These emotions are related to damage or enhancement to the sense of self and coincide with the child's emerging sense of having a unique self, different from the world around them. The development of self-conscious emotions is also related to wider cognitive developments that allow children to evaluate their situation and understand that there are standards for judging conduct and behaviour. Toddlers show shame and embarrassment through reactions such as smiles accompanied by gaze aversion, lip-biting and body-touching (Barrett, 2005). Envy occurs when a child is able to compare themselves to others and is present by the age of 3 (Masciuch and Kienapple, 1993). Pride is related to a child's ability to evaluate their performance and the difficulty of a task and is also present by the age of 3: children of this age are more likely to feel pride if they solve a difficult task and shame if they fail an easy task (Lewis et al., 1992).

As they get older, children also begin to understand that people can experience **multiple emotions**. Harter and Buddin (1987) propose that this understanding develops in five stages. Initially, up to the age of 6, children can only conceive of an individual experiencing one emotion at a time ('since you only have one mind'). From 6 to 8 years of age, they can conceive of an individual experiencing two emotions of the same valence sequentially (such as happiness followed by pride). At around the age of

8–9, they will understand that two emotions of the same valence can be held simultaneously (such as being angry *and* upset). By the age of 10, children can describe opposing feelings in response to different 'targets' in the same situation (being *scared* at the dentist, but *happy* to be getting teeth fixed) and by the age of 11, they will understand that a single event can induce a mix of positive *and* negative feelings.

Emotional understanding

In addition to experiencing emotions, another important aspect of development is the ability to understand other people's emotional states. This process appears to begin in infancy and can be seen in the infant's use of **social referencing**.

Social referencing refers to the use of other people's emotional expressions to respond to situations that are uncertain and ambiguous. Adults will use this approach frequently; for example, if during a conversation an individual makes a comment and you are not sure of the appropriateness of this comment, you will use other people's reaction to it to guide your own. Social referencing appears in infants at around 12 months of age and has been demonstrated by Sorce et al. (1985) using the **visual cliff technique**. This involves setting up two tables with a small gap in between them and covering the gap with perspex. A baby is then placed on one of the tables, where they will usually appear reluctant to cross over the cliff (perspex) to the other table as there appears to be a drop. In the study by Sorce et al., the infants' mothers were placed on the opposite side of the 'cliff' and instructed to make a 'happy' or a 'frightened' expression. When mothers used a happy expression, most infants crossed the cliff and when they wore a frightened expression most infants refused to cross. Caregivers' emotional expressions have also been found to influence aspects of infant behaviour such as reactions to a stranger (De Rosnay et al., 2006) or playing with a toy (Klinnert, 1984). It is not just facial expressions that can be used for social referencing: tone of voice can also be important as this contains both emotional and verbal information and this cue alone or in combination with facial expression can be very powerful (Mumme et al., 1996; Vaish and Striano, 2004).

Emotional development continues through childhood and is influenced by gains in language and cognition as well as wider socialisation processes. Gains in language mean that the child has a wider vocabulary for talking about feelings. Growth in cognitive abilities means that children can understand the causes of emotional states and how they may affect behaviour, and this ability becomes more accurate over time. Russell (1990) found that children aged 4–5 could suggest appropriate causes and consequences of basic emotions (such as sadness caused by being taunted and a child who is scared staying in her room). Initially children are focused on external causes of emotions, but later they come to understand that feeling can also arise from internal causes such as sadness caused by thinking about a sad experience (Harris et al., 1981). Socialisation also contributes to emotional development, with parents playing an important role here. Children of parents who acknowledge their emotions and use emotional terms in their conversations with them are better able to judge other's emotions at a later stage (Denham and Kochanoff, 2002; Laible, 2004). The understanding that children gain about emotions from their interactions with adults is later transferred to other contexts and helps them in their interactions with other children. This knowledge is very important for social development generally, and in 3- to 5-year-old children knowledge of emotions is related to teacher ratings of social competence and the ability to establish positive relations with other children (Cassidy et al., 2003; Denham et al., 2003).

Emotional regulation

It is clear that emotions can have a major effect on our day-to-day functioning. Negative emotions can have a deleterious effect on our performance, for example anxiety preventing us from doing a task well. However, as Keenan and Evans (2009) point out, excessive positive emotions can also have a disruptive effect, such as excitement leading to inappropriate behaviour. An important skill we have to acquire is to manage our emotions and adjust them to a comfortable level so that we avoid extremes of emotions. The processes by which we reach this comfortable state are referred to as **emotional regulation**. As adults we engage in emotional regulation when we try to remind ourselves that a stressful situation is only temporary or when we avoid such a situation to begin with.

Emotional regulation requires the effortful and voluntary management of our emotions. Thompson (1991) also points out that it requires both *intrinsic* and *extrinsic* processes. Intrinsic processes are internal to the individual and are typically the thought processes that allow us to reflect about a stressful situation and decide how to react. Extrinsic processes are factors external to the individual such as a parent soothing a distressed child or the availability of friends with whom we can discuss our problems.

As we saw in Chapter 5, young infants have not developed the capacity to regulate their emotions and impulses, or plan their actions. The development of these skills depends on the maturation of the frontal lobes and limbic system in the brain. Only a small number of behaviours are available to them such as sucking their thumb when they are upset and they can easily become overwhelmed by an excess of stimulation. At this stage, infants are primarily reliant on extrinsic processes, for example the intervention and attention of parents and caregivers to reduce distress through actions such as holding, stoking, gentle rocking or other soothing gestures (Thompson, 1991).

As the the brain develops, so does the infant's ability to tolerate stimulation. Caregivers can build on this development by interacting with the infant appropriately and sensitively so that the infant does not become overstimulated, and this in turn leads to further development of the infant's tolerance for stimulation (Fogel, 1982; Kopp and Neufeld, 2003).

At around 4 to 6 months of age, infants have more control over their actions and impulses. However parents continue to play an important role in regulating the infant's emotions by noticing the relevant signals from their child and responding in a sympathetic and comforting manner (Crockenberg and Leerkes, 2004). We also saw in Chapter 5 that the development of brain structures involved in moderating stress is *experience-expectant* and a lack of responsive caregiving in infancy can impair the development of these structures resulting in anxiety and difficulty in regulating emotions in later childhood (Twardosz and Lutzker, 2010). By the age of 12 months, motor skills can also contribute to emotion regulation. The infant can now crawl or walk and thus is able to approach or retreat from various situations.

During childhood, increases in language ability result in an expansion of the vocabulary enabling the child to talk about feelings and make requests to the caregiver for actions that will help to manage these feelings (for example 'mummy, I want a cuddle'). As the child's language comprehension grows, caregivers can use commands to direct the child's regulatory processes ('please stop crying') and also suggest strategies to the child to help them manage their emotional states, or they can attempt to distract the child from the cause of distress (Keenan and Evans, 2009; Thompson, 1991). As a child's cognitive ability increases they can employ a variety of strategies to help them manage their feelings, such as thinking about a carer when that carer is not present, thinking about something 'nice' during a distressing experience, or thinking about a difficult situation in an entirely different way (Band and Weisz, 1988; Thompson, 1994).

Temperament

Our own informal observations of infants suggest that there are variations in their behavioural characteristics. Some babies cry, some are generally content, some tend to be very active. These individual differences have long been noted by researchers (Gessell and Ames, 1937; Shirley, 1933). An influential study on what is now referred to as **temperament** was carried out by Thomas and Chess (1977) who conducted an interview study in which they interviewed mothers of infants at three-month intervals and noted consistencies in the characteristics of infant temperament. From this study, Thomas and Chess identified nine dimensions of temperament and these are summarised in Table 8.1.

From these nine dimensions, Thomas and Chess proposed three broad categories of infant temperament: **easy infants** (who are sociable, quickly establish regular routines and adapt easily to new experiences); **difficult infants** (who have difficulty in establishing regular routines, are slow to accept new experiences and have a tendency to cry and fuss often); and **slow to warm-up infants** (who are in between the easy and difficult categories, and are slow to adapt to new experiences, but with repeated exposure will gradually 'warm up' and adapt).

It is considered that temperament has a biological, genetic component. Identical twins show a greater similarity in aspects of temperament such as activity level, attention span

Table 8.1 Dimensions of infant temperament

Dimension	Description
Activity level	The amount of physical activity
Rhythmicity	The regularity and predictability of activities such as eating, sleeping, excretion
Approach/Withdrawal	Responses to new stimuli and experiences
Adaptability	The ease with which the infant adapts to new situations
Intensity	How intense are responses such as crying, laughing or motor behaviour
Threshold	The intensity of a stimulus required to evoke a response in the infant
Attention span and persistence	How long an infant remains engaged in an activity
Distractability	The effectiveness of external stimuli in altering behaviour
Mood	The amount of pleasant, friendly behaviour and unpleasant, unfriendly behaviour throughout the day

Adapted from Thomas and Chess (1977), Keenan and Evans (2009) and Smith Cowie and Blades (2011)

and shyness/sociability (Plomin and Rowe, 1977). Some researchers have also noted stability in traits of temperament. A longitudinal study conducted by Caspi and Silva (1995) found that measures of temperament taken at 3 years of age were predictive of measures of adjustment in adult life. However, other studies have noted a lack of stability in temperament over time (see, for example, Putnam et al., 2000).

The consensus is that while there may be a genetic component to temperament, this can also be modified by environmental factors such as child-rearing. This view was taken by Thomas and Chess (1986) who proposed a **goodness of fit** model to explain how temperament and environment can act together to influence an outcome. Therefore, a difficult infant will not necessarily become a difficult child – parents who respond to a difficult infant in a sensitive and supportive manner have a greater chance of altering the infant's behaviour in a positive direction than parents who respond in a negative manner. There is evidence to support this proposition: infants and toddlers with difficult and irritable temperaments who receive patient and supportive parenting tend to decline in these negative traits over time (Lerner, 1984; Feldman et al., 1999).

The development of attachment

Attachment refers to the strong and affectionate bond between the infant and caregiver. The most influential theory of attachment is Bowlby's ethological theory of attachment (1969). Bowlby saw the infant's attachment to the caregiver as an evolved response that promotes survival – the infant is born with a set of behaviours that lead them to seek an appropriate level of closeness (in terms of physical distance) to the parent who will in turn nurture and protect the infant from danger. In our early evolutionary history, where there was likely to be a potential threat to the infant from dangers such as predators, keeping close to the caregiver increased the infant's chance of survival. Bowlby was also influenced by the psychodynamic approach which stresses the importance of early experiences and was of the view that early attachment experiences have implications for later psychological wellbeing and the capacity to form close and stable relationships. Another significant figure in the field of attachment is Ainsworth (1973) who introduced the notion of the caregiver as a safe haven and a safe base – infants will use the attachment figure as a source of comfort in times of distress, but also as a safe starting point for exploring their environment.

Development of the attachment relationship

Bowlby (1969) identified four phases over which the attachment relationship develops. The first phase he termed **orientation and signals without discrimination of figure** and this takes place over the first six to eight weeks of life. At this stage infants emit behaviours such as smiling, grasping and crying that will bring them into contact with adults who will care for them; however, they do not yet show a preference for the primary caregiver over other adults. The second phase, termed **orientation and signals directed towards one (or more) discriminated figures**, runs from approximately 2–7 months of age and marks the beginning of the infant differentiating familiar and unfamiliar people. Infants are more likely to smile at the primary caregiver and be comforted by them when distressed. From about 7 months, the infant enters the phase of **maintenance of proximity to a discriminated figure by means of locomotion as well as signals**. Infants now have a clear preference for individuals with whom they are familiar (parents, grandparents, a particular care worker) and will seek physical proximity and contact with those individuals and become upset when they leave. The final phase of attachment is the formation of a **goal-corrected partnership** with the caregiver and begins at around 3 years of age. The attachment relationship is now more reciprocal in nature and the child can take into account the needs of the caregiver. Developments in language and cognition allow the child to understand the caregiver's coming and going and predict their return.

Attachment theory has tended to stress the role of the mother as the primary attachment figure but there is also recognition that infants will form a variety of attachment relationships. Fathers are also significant attachment figures and fathers who interact with their infants in an affectionate and sensitive manner are as effective at caregiving as the mother, and will have securely attached infants (Lundy, 2003; Parke, 2002). There are also differences in the ways in which mothers and fathers play with infants. Mothers tend to engage in verbal play (such as games of 'peek-a-boo') and provide more toys (Power and Parke, 1982) whereas fathers tend to engage in more rough-and-tumble physical play (Tamis-LeMonda, 2004). It has also been argued that this latter form of play fosters 'openness to the world' (Paquette, 2004) may prepare infants to venture confidently into the surrounding world and approach unfamiliar situations with confidence. Infants also form attachment relationships with grandparents, siblings and peers (Howes and Spieker, 2008; Stewart, 1983).

Measuring the security of attachment

While infants will form an attachment to a primary caregiver, the quality of the attachment relationship can vary from child to child and will be affected by the parenting received. The importance of this has been highlighted by the work of Ainsworth et al. (1978). Sensitive parenting, where the mother is responsive to the infant's needs, will foster a **secure attachment** relationship that provides the infant with a sense of security and confidence. On the other hand, insensitive, inconsistent or neglectful parenting can lead to an insecure attachment which will fail to provide that sense of security and confidence to the infant.

Ainsworth et al. (1978) developed a laboratory-based observation technique that has come to be widely used to assess the quality of attachment in 1- to 2-year-old children. This technique is known as the **strange situation** and consists of a series of eight brief episodes in which the infant is separated from the mother, exposed to a stranger and reunited again with the mother. From observing the responses of the infants to these episodes, Ainsworth et al. (1978) identified three categories of attachment relationship. The most frequently occurring category was secure attachment. Infants who are placed in this category use the parent as a secure base for exploring the room, may or may not be upset when the parent leaves, but are happy when the parent returns and actively seek contact. If distressed during the separation, their distress is relieved upon the return of the parent. Some infants are classified as having an **insecure-avoidant attachment** style, being unresponsive to the parent and showing no overt signs of distress when the parent departs. During the reunion episodes, the infant fails to respond to the parent and often actively avoids them. The third category identified was **insecure-resistant**. Here, before separation the infant will fail to explore the room and is distressed when the parent leaves. During the reunion episodes, the infant shows an ambivalent attitude to the parent, seeking contact yet also simultaneously shows resistant behaviour such as struggling when picked up and being generally difficult to soothe. Research by Main and colleagues (Main et al., 1985; Main and Solomon, 1990) has also identified a further category of insecure attachment which they termed **insecure-disorganised**. This is regarded as the most insecure form of attachment and appears to be a combination of the avoidant and resistant attachment styles. The infant appears to be confused about whether to avoid or approach the caregiver. During the reunion episodes they may freeze, or they may begin to approach the caregiver only to move away as the caregiver draws near.

The strange situation is used for assessing attachment in infants but is less useful for assessing attachment in young children who are becoming more used to separations from the caregiver and encounters with strangers. This has led to the development of the **Attachment Q-set (AQS)** for assessing attachment in children (Waters and Deane, 1985). The AQS involves a trained observer sorting a set of 90 attachment behaviours, such as 'child greets caregiver with big smiles', into categories ranging from 'most like' to 'least like' a child's behaviour at home. This produces a profile that can be used to characterise how secure the child is with the caregiver. In general, this appears to provide a reliable assessment of attachment and it has been found that results from the AQS for infants and toddlers are usually the same as strange situation assessments (van Ijzendoorn et al., 2004).

The stability of attachment

Once an attachment relationship has been formed, is it likely to stay the same? Will a secure or insecure attachment style remain that way? The evidence on this question is mixed. Waters (1978) used the strange situation to assess attachment security in infants at 12 months of age and again at 18 months and found similarities in attachment styles on both occasions. Fraley (2000) has reviewed a number of longitudinal studies of attachment and noted a general stability of attachment security across the first nineteen years of life. However, it has been pointed out that studies reporting stability of attachment have typically used middle-class samples with stable living conditions. It has been found that life events affecting the family can produce changes in attachment and these changes can be positive (changes from insecure to secure attachment) or negative (a secure attachment becomes insecure). Vaughn et al. (1979) conducted a study of US infants whose families experienced difficult living conditions and noted cases of positive change that coincided with improvements in family circumstances and negative changes coinciding with adverse life events affecting the family. A number of other studies (see for example Bar-Heim, 2000; Belsky and Fearon, 2002) have also noted changes in quality of caregiving and attachment security between infancy and early childhood that have coincided with adverse life events affecting the mother. One attachment pattern that does appear to show long-term stability is the insecure-disorganised style (van Iljzendoorn et al., 1999; Weinfield et al., 2004). Typically, this style tends to co-occur with child maltreatment and neglect (Carlson et al., 1989; van Iljzendoorn et al., 1999), and infants with this style tend to continue to experience poor-quality caregiving from parents who often have their own histories of disorganised attachment (Hesse and Main, 2000).

The consequences of attachment relationships

Bowlby (1973, 1980) proposed that children's early experiences of attachment lead them to acquire what he called an **internal working model**. This is a mental representation of themselves, their relationship with the primary caregiver and expectations they may have of the caregiver providing comfort and support. It is argued that this model serves as a guide to future close relationships (Bretherton and Munholland, 2008). An internal working model may be *positive* (the child feels worthy of love and sees other people as kind and dependable) or *negative* (individual feels unworthy of love, other people cannot be depended on). In this way, it is argued that early attachment experiences can exert a considerable influence on future relationships and wellbeing.

Many studies have reported a link between secure and affectionate early attachments and positive developmental outcomes. Children who were securely attached as infants are better problem solvers at age 2 (Matas et al., 1978), display more pleasant emotions (Kochanska, 2001) and are more sociable toward other toddlers (Pastor, 1981). Studies conducted over longer periods confirm these findings. Waters et al., (1979) found that preschoolers who were securely attached as infants were rated by observers as being high in social competence. This trend continued into later childhood with the same children at age 11 showing more favourable relationships with peers and better social skills (Elicker et al., 1992). There is also consistent evidence of a link between an insecure-avoidant attachment style in infancy and a high incidence of internalising problems (anxiety and depression) and externalising problems (anger and aggression) during the school years (Fearon et al., 2010; Lyons-Ruth et al., 1997). Insecure-disorganised attachment in infants is also a predictor of childhood aggression and mental health problems (Fearon et al., 2010; Moss et al., 2004; van IJzendoorn et al., 1999).

There is evidence that the relationship between early attachment security and later development is also affected by the *stability* of these relationships over time: children who receive sensitive and affectionate care in infancy and throughout childhood are more likely to develop favourable outcomes. This issue was investigated by Belsky and Fearon (2002) in their analysis of data from a large-scale longitudinal study tracking children from 1 to 3 years of age. They found that children who experienced a combination of secure attachment at 15 months followed by sensitive caregiving at 24 months achieved the most favourable cognitive, social and emotional outcomes. Conversely, a combination of insecure attachment at 15 months and insensitive caregiving at 24 months was linked with negative outcomes, and children with mixed histories scored in between. Therefore, the positive long-term effects of secure early attachments are also probably related to the fact that these attachments often remain stable over time. However, the studies also indicate that infant attachment histories by no means determine the final outcome. Belsky and Fearon also found that insecurely attached infants who received sensitive caregiving at 24 months showed improved developmental outcomes.

Social development

In order to become a socially competent individual, the infant has to acquire a number of important skills. Firstly, they have to acquire a sense of self as distinct from other people and objects. The infant also has to acquire the ability to interact with peers and form friendships. Crucial to this is the development of social understanding: the ability of the infant to take the perspective of others and understand how his or her behaviour affects those others. Accordingly, the following sections will look at the differentiation of the self from others, the development of peer interactions and friendships, and the development of social understanding.

Acquiring a sense of self

Evidence that newborns have some awareness of self as distinct from others comes from a study by Dondi et al. (1999) which demonstrated that newborn infants became distressed when hearing a recording of another infant's cries but not when exposed to a recording of their own. During the early months of life, it is also likely that the infant's own movements help to develop a sense of **personal agency**, the notion that they can have an effect on their surrounding environment. Infants of this age enjoy producing sounds and moving objects when their legs are connected to a mobile (Thelen and Fisher, 1983), and studies using the conjugate reinforcement technique as discussed in Chapter 4 show that infants can retain this information over time (Rovee-Collier, 1999).

Linked to the developing sense of self is the capacity of infants to recognise their own appearance. How do infants come to recognise their own face from others? One possibility is that this arises from their early interactions with caregivers in which the caregiver plays a game with them in front of a mirror (Hidalgo, 1990). These experiences allow them to match the sensation of their own facial and body movements with that of one of the figures in the mirror and differentiate them from the other whose movements do not correspond with their own.

Lewis and Brooks-Gunn (1979) investigated the topic of self-recognition by placing infants aged 9 to 24 months in front of a mirror and noting their actions. They then asked their mothers to place a spot of rouge on their child's nose (under the pretext of wiping their face) and placed the infants in front of the mirror again. Before the rouge had been applied very few of the children had touched their noses. After the application of the rouge, Lewis and Brooks-Gunn found that hardly any of the 9- to 12-month-old infants responded to the change in their appearance, a minority of the 15- to 18-month-old children touched their noses, while the majority of children aged 20 months and above touched their noses realising that their appearance had changed.

Beyond infancy, developments in language and cognition contribute to emerging self-awareness. Infants now have a vocabulary to describe themselves and also recognise that there are ways in which other people differ, allowing them to categorise themselves on various dimensions. This leads to the development of the **categorical self** (Stipek et al., 1990), and children begin to categorise themselves on the basis of sex ('boy' or 'girl'), age ('baby', 'boy') and even goodness and badness ('I good girl').

The development of peer interactions

So far this chapter has focused on the role of caregiving adults in the social and emotional development of children. However, peers are also important in social development. Hartup (1989) has pointed out that children's relationships with peers are **horizontal** in nature, meaning that the relationships are more on an equal footing, and this could be contrasted with the **vertical** nature of their relationships with adults in which children are less powerful. Therefore it is argued that the egalitarian nature of peer relationships provide distinct learning opportunities for children. Children must *'learn to appreciate each other's perspectives, negotiate and compromise, and cooperate with each other if they hope to get along or achieve joint goals'* (Shaffer and Kipp, 2010: 614). Peer interactions may then allow children to develop social competencies that they could not acquire from their unequal interactions with adults.

Infants appear to show an interest in other babies from the first few months of life. Legerstee et al. (1998) found that 5-month-old infants who viewed videos of themselves and a same age baby spent more time looking at the peer, indicating that the peer was more interesting to them. By the age of 6 months, they will start to vocalise and gesture to other infants (Rubin and Coplan, 1992), and by 12 months, they may even imitate other infants' actions with a toy (Rubin et al., 2006). Between 12 and 24 months, more definite signs of interactions with peers emerge. Initially, these take the form of 'action/reaction'-type episodes, for example an infant may vocalise at a peer, and when this produces a reaction such as laughing, the sequence is repeated (Mueller and Lucas, 1975). Interactions between infants gradually become more coordinated and show a clear intent to communicate (Howes and Matheson, 1992; Rubin and Coplan, 1992). By the age of 2 years, increased language skills allow toddlers to describe their activities to each other or direct each other's activities.

Between the ages of 2 and 4 years, children become more peer-orientated and different types of interactions can be observed. This was first noted by Parten (1932) who observed the free play of children aged 2–4, and noted that their play could be categorised into a number of different types: **non-social solitary play** in which the child plays alone, or watches other children play but does not join in; **parallel play** wherein children play alongside each other, use the same toys but do not interact; **associative play** in which there are some basic interactions such as sharing toys and commenting on each other's activities; and **cooperative play**, which is characterised by a high level of interaction involving joint activities such as playing formal games, engaging in pretend play in which each child takes on a role or building things together. Parten found that non-social activity and parallel play declined with age and associative and cooperative play increased with age. There is a general consensus that the different types of interactions emerge in this order; however, more recent studies have indicated that the onset of one type of play is not accompanied by the demise of the previous type; all types of play continue to coexist in early childhood (Rubin et al., 2006). Nevertheless, the cognitive maturity of each type of play increases with age (Howes and Matheson, 1992).

In middle childhood, sex segregation in play becomes more apparent and from the age of 7 children show a clear preference for playing with a same-sex partner (Maccoby 1998). It has been suggested that this may be due to personality differences between boys and girls, with boys being more aggressive and engaging in more rough-and-tumble play (Hughes, 2010). Another development in peer interactions during this period is the increasing tendency for contacts to occur in **peer groups** (Rubin and Coplan, 1992), in other words, a group of children who interact frequently have a sense of membership, and have norms governing the behaviour of members.

Peer acceptance and its consequences

How well a child is liked or disliked by his or her peers and the consequences of this is another topic that has generated much research. Studies investigating the peer status of children typically use a technique called **sociometry**, in which a group of children in a setting such as a school are asked to nominate several students that they like or dislike. Examination of the number of children who are nominated can then be used to gain information about each child's peer status. An influential study using this approach was conducted by Coie et al. (1982) and identified five categories of peer status: **popular children** who receive many 'like' and few 'dislike' nominations; **rejected children** who receive many 'dislike' and few 'like' nominations; **neglected children** who receive few nominations in the 'like' or 'dislike' category and are essentially ignored by their peers; **controversial children** who are liked by many of their peers but disliked by many others; and **average children** who are not as liked as popular children but who are not as disliked as rejected children.

What factors affect the peer status of a child? Typically popular children tend to have good interpersonal skills and are low in aggression (Newcomb et al., 1993). Physical attractiveness also appears to be related to popularity, especially in the case of girls (Vaughn and Langlois, 1983). Rejected children appear to fall into one of two subgroups: **rejected-aggressive** children who, as the label implies, display high levels of aggression, are impulsive and have a poor capacity for emotional regulation; and **rejected-withdrawn** children who tend to be socially anxious, withdrawn and submissive (Asher et al., 1990). Controversial children have a mix of positive and negative characteristics. They can show high levels of aggression but also appear to have sufficient social skills to protect them from social exclusion (Newcomb et al., 1993). Neglected children tend to show low rates of social interaction, but nevertheless appear to be socially and academically skilled (Asher at al., 1990; Wentzel and Asher, 1995).

Peer status has been shown to have long-term consequences. Popular children tend to remain popular while rejected children will continue to experience rejection (Coie and Dodge, 1983). Unsurprisingly, rejected children experience a variety of negative outcomes including reduced classroom participation and feelings of loneliness (Buhs and Ladd, 2001; Parkhurst and Asher, 1992). Over a longer period, rejection is also linked with absenteeism and drop out from school (DeRosier et al., 1994), low self-esteem, antisocial behaviour and adjustment problems in later life (Dodge and Petit, 2003; Ladd and Troop-Gordon, 2003). Rejected-withdrawn children are also particularly vulnerable to bullying due to their withdrawn and submissive nature (Sandstrom and Cillessen, 2003). A surprising finding, however, is that a neglected peer status is not necessarily linked with negative outcomes. Although their rates of social interaction are low, they do not report more feelings of loneliness compared to their peers (Asher and Wheeler, 1985; Crick and Ladd, 1993). Moreover, neglected status is often temporary and some children can alter their pattern of playing alone (Ladd and Burgess, 1999) and if they move to a new school or playgroup they are likely to achieve a more favourable peer status (Coie and Dodge, 1983).

Friendship

Friends can be distinguished from peers, for example a child may interact with many other children but not have any friends. Various studies have been conducted looking at the nature of friendship, how friendships are formed and children's conceptions of friendships.

> The next section looks at the nature and development of friendships. Before reading on, take a moment to consider your own views on what constitutes 'friendship'. Are any of the characteristics you have come up with similar to the research findings outlined below?

Nature and formation of friendships

Newcomb and Bagwell (1995) reviewed a large body of research on the nature of friendship and concluded that the main features that distinguished relations between friends from relations between non-friends were *reciprocity* and *intimacy, more intense social activity* and *better conflict resolution and task performance.* The role of increased social activity, reciprocity and intimacy can be seen in studies such as Doyle et al. (1980) who found that as preschool children became more familiar with each other, they engaged more in social play and their play became more complex. Fonzi et al. (1997) established that friends were better than non-friends at using negotiation and compromise to resolve conflicts. Zajac and Hartup (1997) have noted that when school children work together in pairs, task performance is more effective if the pairs are friends than non-friends.

The issue of how children become friends was studied by Gottman (1983) who tape-recorded the interactions between pairs of children aged 3 to 9. The results of their research suggested that children moved from an initial state of parallel play in a common activity, followed by *'information exchange'* (for example commenting on each other's activities), followed by a joint activity such as pretend play. This gradual 'escalation' toward joint activities can also be seen in the results found by Doyle et al. (1980) of a shift toward more pretend play as children become more familiar with each other.

Conceptions of friendship

Children's conceptions of friendship appear to change over time. A number of studies have investigated children's knowledge and expectations of friendships. These include Bigelow and La Gaipa (1980) who asked a large sample of Scottish and Canadian children to write an essay about their expectations of best friends, and Damon (1977) who asked children a number of questions about friendship (for example 'tell me about your best friend'). Analysis of the interviews and essays revealed a number of common trends. From the ages of around 4 to 8, friends are playmates and factors such as engaging in common activities or living nearby are most prominent. From about the ages of 8 to 10, there is a shift to issues of trust and reciprocity and a concentration on the traits that the child likes in the friend. From the age of 11 onwards, friendships are conceived more in terms of mutual trust and intimacy with self-disclosure and sharing of thoughts, feelings and attitudes.

The importance of friendship

Parker and Gottman (1989) have argued that friendships are important for the development of social competence and this can be seen in studies showing higher levels of pretend play and conflict resolution in friends. It has also been suggested that in the case of rejected children, even one quality friendship can mitigate the worst aspects of their unfavourable peer status (Parkhurst and Asher, 1992).

The development of social cognition

We saw from Chapter 4 that children undergo a number of changes in their cognitive ability during childhood. A related issue of interest is if a child's developing cognitive ability is related to their ability to understand and interact with other people. There are a number of different areas of research in this field of social cognition, but an important focus for research has been on the child's ability to understand the mental states of others, an ability known as **'theory of mind'**.

Theory of mind

As adults we are aware that just as we have feelings, desires and beliefs which can influence our behaviour, so do other people, and we will try to explain other people's actions in terms of their mental states ('she walked out of the meeting because she was angry'). This ability to attribute mental states to others and use these to explain their behaviour is referred to as a theory of mind. Such ability is important for normal social interaction as it allows us to understand and predict other people's behaviour, and where necessary amend our behaviour towards that person. The acquisition of a theory of mind is therefore crucial for a child to develop into a socially competent individual.

Children's understanding of the mind

At around the age of 2, children's everyday speech will include words that refer to mental states, and in particular words relating to *desires* and *intentions* (Wellman, 1990). Young children are good at indicating what they want and according to Wellman this is the first manifestation of a theory of mind. He termed this a **desire psychology**. Children recognise that just as they have desires, so do other people, and this can be used to explain and predict behaviour in others. In a study by Wellman and Wooley (reported by Wellman, 1990) 2-year-old children were told a story about a character named Sam who wanted to find his rabbit to take to school. The rabbit was in one of two locations and the children saw Sam go to each location. After Sam had looked in one location, the children were asked if Sam would look in the other location or go to school. If Sam had found his rabbit they were able to answer correctly that he would go to school and if he failed to find the rabbit they could answer correctly that he would search the other location. These children were therefore able to predict Sam's actions from his desires.

By the age of 3, children can also incorporate beliefs into their basic theory and acquire what Wellman called a **belief-desire psychology**. Children are now able to make more sophisticated judgements about a person's actions. In another study, Bartsch and Wellman (reported by Wellman, 1990) showed a group of 3-year-old children two locations, a box and a shelf, containing books. They were then presented with a character 'Amy' who wanted some books, but believed that the books were only located on the shelf. The children, who were aware that there were books in both locations, were asked to say where Amy would look for the books and most of the children of this age correctly answered that she would look on the shelf. They understood that Amy's belief would influence where she looked for the books.

However, while children of this age realise that other people hold beliefs, they do not understand that sometimes people's beliefs can be wrong and do not correspond to actual reality. It is not until around 4 years of age that children begin to understand that a belief is a representation of reality but not reality itself. This understanding is referred to as a **representational theory of mind** (Perner, 1991). The presence of this ability is investigated using a technique called the **false belief task**, developed by Wimmer and Perner (1983). In this task the child is presented with two puppets, one of whom places an object such as a piece of chocolate in a box. The puppet then leaves the room and the second puppet removes the chocolate from the box and places it in a different coloured box. The first puppet then returns to the room and the children are asked in which box the puppet will look for the chocolate. A consistent finding from this type of study is that the majority of 3-year-old children fail this task and state that the puppet will look for the chocolate where it currently is rather than where it was left. It appears that most children of this age do not appreciate that there can be a discrepancy between an individual's belief and the actual state of the world. However, the majority of 4-year-olds correctly understood that the puppet would look for the chocolate in the place it had been put before the puppet left the room, confirming that the puppet had a false belief that conflicted with reality.

This finding – that children younger than 4 fail the false belief task – has been replicated in many studies (Wellman et al., 2001). However, a number of other studies have focused on where children look rather than what they actually say in the false belief task. These studies have found that while children may give a wrong response in terms of identifying the box where the puppet would look, they do look at the box where the puppet would believe the chocolate to be located and this pattern of appropriate looking has been observed in children as young as 1 year of age (Onishi and Baillargeon, 2005). Therefore it may be the case that children do develop an *implicit* understanding of false belief before they are able to respond verbally.

Beyond the age of 4, the main development in theory of mind is the acquisition of an understanding of what has been termed **higher order mental states** (Perner, 1988). The typical false belief task deals with **first-order beliefs** – trying to understand what another believes. However, a full understanding of the mind is also reliant on **second-order beliefs**, the notion that a person can have beliefs about a third person (for example, I think my boss thinks that my colleague is off sick today). The ability to work out these types of false belief occurs later. Sullivan et al. (1994) gave tasks involving second-order false beliefs to children aged 4 to 8 and found that only some 4-year-olds but most 5-year-olds could respond correctly.

Although it would be wrong to say that a child has acquired a mature, adult-like theory of mind at around the age of 4 to 5 years, they do make rapid strides in acquiring a theory of mind from these ages onwards. As a result they are very soon able to apply this understanding to working out second-order false beliefs, judging how people may act or react based on their false beliefs, and manipulating people's belief, for example planting a false belief in order to deceive another person.

How children acquire a theory of mind

Research has indicated a number of factors in early childhood that are related to performance on the false belief task. These include language ability, interactions with siblings, and family size.

Milligan et al. (2007) reviewed a large number of studies and concluded that the development of language was strongly related to the development of theory of mind. In general, children who were able to perform the false belief task had better language abilities compared to children who were unable to perform this task.

There is also evidence that *family interactions* and *size* are related to the acquisition of a theory of mind. McAlister and Peterson (2007) found that children with at least two child-aged siblings scored higher on theory of mind tasks than children with no child-aged siblings. Why would the presence of siblings be related to an understanding of mind? This may be due to the nature of interactions between siblings. Brown et al. (1996) compared the ways that 4-year-old children talked to their mothers, siblings and friends and found that they were more likely to talk about thoughts and beliefs when interacting with siblings and friends. This appears to tie in with what was suggested earlier in this chapter: that the horizontal nature of relationships between peers may offer the child learning experiences that they could not gain from the more unequal relationships with adults. It is probably the case that siblings and peers are more likely to engage in pretend play in which children have to discuss their thoughts with each other and that this in turn may provide experiences that facilitate the development of theory of mind. The age of the siblings appears to be a factor also, and having older siblings may be an advantage (Ruffman et al., 1998) as exposure to their more sophisticated talk about thoughts and beliefs may provide better opportunities for the acquisition of a theory of mind. Workman and Reader (2007) have also suggested that children with older siblings may be forced into situations in which they have to think about the mental states of others: '*Younger siblings are often in competition for resources such as food, toys and parental attention and the ability to get what you want by deception and other forms of manipulation is likely to be advantageous*' (Workman and Reader, 2007: 130).

While sibling (and peer) interactions may provide some unique opportunities for children to acquire a theory of mind, adults are still important. The way in which adults interact with the child, and in particular a parent's use of mental state terms (regarding desire, belief and knowledge) may also be a key factor. You will recall from the section 'Emotional development in childhood' above that parents who label emotional states tend to produce children with a better emotional understanding later in childhood. Similar findings have been found in parents' use of mental state terms. Meins et al. (1998, 2002) found that children who passed the false belief task at an early age tended to have mothers who used mental state terms in their early interactions with them. Ruffman et al. (2002) found a similar result. In their study, they asked mothers to describe a series of pictures to their 3-year-old children. It was found that mothers' use of mental state terms in their descriptions (such as references to thoughts or feelings of characters in the pictures) was predictive of their children's performance in false belief and a number of other theory of mind tasks 5 and 12 months later.

Chapter summary

- It is generally agreed that there are six basic emotions: disgust, happiness, anger, fear, sadness and surprise.
- Basic emotions are apparent from around 6 months of age, and during childhood self-conscious emotions and an understanding of multiple emotions appear. During childhood children also acquire the ability to talk about emotions, recognise emotional states in others and respond accordingly.
- The development of emotional regulation is initially dependent on the behaviour of caregivers towards the infant, but later is influenced by developments in language and cognitions.
- Children vary in their temperament and a number of different temperament styles have been identified.
- Temperament appears to have a genetic component but it can also be affected by the nature of caregiving received by the infant.
- Infants form close attachments with their caregivers, these attachments vary in their security and several different attachment styles have been identified.
- Early attachment relationships are also related to a variety of positive and negative developmental outcomes.
- There is evidence that a distinct sense of self is present from early infancy.
- With increasing age, infants and children become more peer-orientated.
- Studies using the technique of sociometry have identified a number of different types of peer status in children and that peer status can have long-term consequences.
- A favourable peer status is linked with positive outcomes in terms of both school achievement and general adjustment and wellbeing, and an unfavourable peer status is linked with negative outcomes in terms of the same conditions.
- From about the age of 2, children begin to understand that other people have desires and beliefs.
- By the age of 4, children are able to understand that people can hold beliefs that are false and show evidence of a developing theory of mind. They display this through their ability to pass false belief tasks. Initially they can pass first-order false belief tasks, but eventually acquire the ability to pass more complex second-order belief tasks.

Further reading

Dowling, M. (2009) *Young Children's Personal, Social and Emotional Development* (3rd edn). London: Paul Chapman Publishing.

A book that links research in social and emotional development to educational practices that foster this aspect of children's development.

References

Ainsworth, M.D. (1973) 'The development of infant–mother attachment', in B. Caldwell and H. Ricciuti (eds), *Review of Child Development Research: Vol. 3*. Chicago, IL: University of Chicago Press. pp.1–94.

Ainsworth, M.D., Blehar, M., Waters, E. and Wall, S. (1978) *Patterns of Attachment*. Hillsdale, NJ: Erlbaum.

Anisfeld, E. (1982) 'The onset of social smiling in preterm and full-term infants from two ethnic backgrounds', *Infant Behaviour and Development*, 5 (4): 387–95.

Asher, S.R. and Wheeler, V.A. (1985) 'Children's loneliness: A comparison of rejected and neglected peer status', *Journal of Consulting and Clinical Psychology*, 53 (4): 500–5.

Asher, S.R., Parkhurst, J.T., Hymel, S. and Williams, G.A. (1990) 'Peer rejection and loneliness in childhood', in S.R. Asher and J.D. Coie (eds), *Peer Rejection in Childhood*. New York: Cambridge University Press. pp. 253–73.

Band, E.B. and Weisz, J.R. (1988) 'How to feel better when it feels bad: Children's perspectives on coping with everyday stress', *Developmental Psychology*, 24 (2): 247–53.

Bar-Heim, Y., Sutton, D.B., Fox, N.A. and Marvin, R.S. (2000) 'Stability and change of attachment at 14, 24, and 58 months of age: Behavior, representation, and life events', *Journal of Child Psychology and Psychiatry*, 41 (3): 381–8.

Barrett, K.C. (2005) 'The origins of social emotions and self-regulation in toddlerhood: New evidence', *Cognition and Emotion*, 19 (7): 953–79.

Belsky, J. and Fearon, R.M.P. (2002) 'Early attachment security, subsequent maternal sensitivity, and later child development: Does continuity in development depend on caregiving?', *Attachment and Human Development*, 4 (3): 361–87.

Berk, L.E. (2008) *Infants, Children and Adolescents* (6th edn). Boston, MA: Pearson.

Bigelow, B.J. and La Gaipa, J.J. (1980) 'The development of friendship values and choice', in H.C. Foot, A.J. Chapman and J.R. Smith (eds), *Friendship and Social Relations in Children*. Chichester: Wiley. pp. 13–42.

Bowlby, J. (1969) *Attachment and Loss: Vol. 1 Attachment*. New York: Basic.

Bowlby, J. (1973) *Separation and Loss*. New York: Basic.

Bowlby, J. (1980) *Attachment and Loss: Vol. 3 Loss*. New York: Basic.

Bretherton, I. and Munholland, K.A. (2008) 'Internal working models in attachment relationships: Elaborating a central construct in attachment theory', in J. Cassidy and P.R. Shaver (eds), *Handbook of Attachment: Theory, Research and Clinical Applications* (2nd edn). New York: Guilford. pp. 102–30.

Brooks, J. and Lewis, M. (1976) 'Infants responses to strangers: Midget, adult and child,' *Child Development*, 47 (2): 323–32.

Brown, J.R., Donelan-McCall, N. and Dunn, J. (1996) 'Why talk about mental states? The significance of children's conversations with friends, siblings, and mothers', *Child Development*, 67 (3): 836–49.

Buhs, E.S. and Ladd, G.W. (2001) 'Peer rejection as antecedent of young children's school adjustment: An examination of mediating processes', *Developmental Psychology*, 37 (4): 550–60.

Camras, L.A., Oster, H., Campos, J.J., Miyake, K. and Bradshaw, D. (1992) 'Japanese and American infants' responses to arm restraint', *Developmental Psychology*, 28 (4): 578–83.

Carlson, V., Cicchetti, D., Barnett, D. and Braunwald, K. (1989) 'Disorganized/disoriented attachment relationships in maltreated infants', *Developmental Psychology*, 25 (4): 525–31.

Caspi, A. and Silva, P.A. (1995) 'Temperamental qualities at age three predict personality traits in young adulthood: Longitudinal evidence from a birth cohort', *Child Development*, 66 (2): 486–98.

Cassidy, K.W., Werner, R.S., Rourke, M. and Zubernis L.S. (2003) 'The relationship between psychological understanding and positive social behaviors', *Social Development*, 12 (2): 198–221.

Coie, J.D., Dodge, K.A. (1983) 'Continuities and changes in children's social status: A five-year longitudinal study', *Merrill-Palmer Quarterly*, 29 (3): 261–82.

Coie, J.D., Dodge, K.A. and Coppotelli, H. (1982) 'Dimensions and types of social status: A cross-age perspective', *Developmental Psychology*, 18: 557–570.

Crick, N.R. Ladd, G.W. (1993) 'Children's perceptions of their peer experiences: Attributions, loneliness, social anxiety, and social avoidance', *Developmental Psychology*, 29 (2): 244–54.

Crockenberg, S.C and Leerkes, E.M. (2004) 'Infant and maternal behaviors regulate infant reactivity to novelty at 6 months', *Developmental Psychology*, 40 (6): 1123–32.

Damon, W. (1977) *The Social World of the Child*. San Francisco, CA: Jossey-Bass.

Darwin, C.R. (1872) *The Expression of Emotion in Man and Animals*. London: John Murray.

Denham, S.A., Blair, K.A., DeMulder, E., Levitas, J., Sawyer, K., Auerbach-Major, S. and Queenan, P. (2003) 'Preschool emotional competence: Pathway to social competence?', *Child Development*, 74 (1): 238–56.

Denham, S. and Kochanoff, A.T. (2002) 'Parental contributions to preschoolers' understanding of emotion', *Marriage and Family Review*, 34 (3–4): 311–43.

DeRosier, M., Kupersmidt, J.B. and Patterson, C.J. (1994) 'Children's academic and behavioral adjustment as a function of the chronicity and proximity of peer rejection', *Child Development*, 65 (6): 1799–813.

DeRosnay, M., Cooper, P.J., Tsigaras, N. and Murray, L. (2006) 'Transmission of social anxiety from mother to infant: An experimental study using a social referencing paradigm', *Behaviour Research and Therapy*, 44 (8): 1165–75.

Dodge. K.A. and Petit, G.S. (2003) 'A biopsychosocial model of the development of chronic conduct problems in adolescence', *Developmental Psychology*, 39 (2): 349–71.

Dondi, M., Simion, F. and Caltran, G. (1999) 'Can newborns discriminate between their own cry and the cry of another newborn infant?', *Developmental Psychology*, 35 (2): 418–26.

Doyle, A.B., Connolly, J. and Rivest, L.P. (1980) 'The effect of playmate familiarity on the social interactions of young children', *Child Development*, 51 (1): 217–23.

Ekman, P. and Friesen, W. (1971) 'Constants across cultures in the face and emotion', *Journal of Personality and Social Psychology*, 17 (2): 124–9.

Elicker, J., Englund, M. and Sroufe, L.A. (1992) 'Predicting peer competence and peer relationships in childhood from early parent–child relationships', in R.D. Parke and G.W. Ladd (eds), *Family–Peer Relationships: Modes of Linkage*. Hillsdale, NJ: Earlbaum. pp. 77–106.

Fearon, R.P., Bakermans-Kranenburg, M.J., van Ijzendoorn, M.H., Lapsley, A.M. and Roisman, G.L. (2010) 'The significance of insecure attachment and disorganisation in the development of children's externalizing behaviour: A meta-analytic study', *Child Development*, 81 (2): 435–56.

Feldman, R., Greenbaum, C.W. and Yirmiya, N. (1999) 'Mother–infant affect synchrony as an antecedent of the emergence of self-control', *Developmental Psychology*, 35 (1): 223–31.

Fogel, A. (1982) 'Affect dynamics in early infancy: Affective tolerance', in T. Field and A. Fogel (eds), *Emotion and Early Interaction*. Hillsdale, NJ: Erlbaum. pp. 25–56.

Fonzi, A., Schneider, B.H., Tani, F. and Tomada, G. (1997) 'Predicting children's friendship status from their dyadic interaction in structured situations of potential conflict', *Child Development*, 68 (3): 496–506.

Fraley, R.C. (2002) 'Attachment stability from infancy to adulthood: Meta-analysis and dynamic modelling of developmental mechanisms', *Personality and Social Psychology Review*, 6: 123–151.

Gesell, A. and Ames, L. (1937) 'Early evidences of individuality in the human infant', *The Scientific Monthly*, 45 (3): 217–25.

Gottman, J.M. (1983) 'How children become friends', *Monographs of the Society for Research in Child Development* (Serial No. 201), 48 (3): 1–86.

Harris, P.L., Olthof, T. and Terwogt, M. (1981) 'Children's knowledge of emotion', *Journal of Child Psychology and Psychiatry*, 22 (3): 246–61.

Harter, S. and Buddin, B.J. (1987) 'Children's understanding of the simultaneity of two emotions: A five-stage developmental acquisition sequence', *Developmental Psychology*, 23 (3): 388–99.

Hartup, W. (1989) 'Social relationships and their developmental significance', *American Psychologist*, 44 (2): 120–26.

Hesse, E. and Main, M. (2000) 'Disorganized infant, child, and adult attachment: Collapse in behavioral and attentional strategies', *Journal of the American Psychoanalytic Association*, 48 (4): 1097–127.

Hidalgo, V. (1990) 'Influence of parent-infant interactions on the development of self-recognition', in L. Oppenheimer (ed.), *The Self-Concept: European Perspectives on its Development, Aspects and Applications*. Berlin: Springer-Verlag. pp. 75–85.

Howes, C. and Matheson, C.C. (1992) 'Sequences in the development of competent play with peers: Social and social pretend play', *Developmental Psychology*, 28 (5): 961–74.

Howes, C. and Spieker, S.J. (2008) 'Attachment in the context of multiple caregivers', in J. Cassidy and P.R. Shaver (eds), *Handbook of Attachment: Theory, Research and Clinical Applications* (2nd edn). New York: Guilford. pp. 317–32.

Hughes, F. (2010) *Children, Play and Development*. Los Angeles, CA: Sage.

Izard, C.E. (1994) 'Innate and universal facial expressions: Evidence from developmental and cross-cultural research', *Psychological Bulletin*, 115 (2): 288–99.

Izard, C.E., Hembree, E.A. and Huebner, R.R. (1987) 'Infants' emotion expressions to acute pain: Developmental change and stability of individual differences', *Developmental Psychology*, 23 (1): 105–13.

Keenan, T. and Evans, S. (2009) *An Introduction to Child Development*. London: Sage.

Klinnert, M.D. (1984) 'The regulation of infant behavior by maternal facial expression', *Infant Behavior and Development*, 7 (4): 447–65.

Kochanska, G. (2001) 'Emotional development in children with different attachment histories: The first three years', *Child Development*, 72 (2): 474–90.

Kopp, C.B. and Neufeld, S.J. (2003) 'Emotional development during infancy', in R.J. Davidson, K.R. Scherer and H.H. Goldsmith (eds), *Handbook of Affective Sciences*. New York: Oxford University Press. pp. 347–74.

Ladd, G.W. and Burgess, K.B. (1999) 'Charting the relationship trajectories of aggressive, withdrawn, and aggressive/withdrawn children during early grade school', *Child Development*, 70 (4): 910–29.

Ladd, G.W. and Troop-Gordon, W. (2003) 'The role of chronic peer difficulties in the development of children's psychological adjustment problems', *Child Development*, 74 (5): 1344–67.

Laible, D. (2004) 'Mother-child discourse surrounding a child's past behavior at 30 months: Links to emotional understanding and early conscience development at 36 months', *Merrill-Palmer Quarterly*, 50 (2): 159–80.

Legerstee, M., Anderson, D. and Shaffer, A. (1998) 'Five and eight-month-olds recognise their faces and voices as familiar social stimuli', *Child Development*, 69 (1): 37–50.

Lerner, J.V. (1984) 'The import of temperament for psychosocial functioning: tests of a goodness of fit model', *Merril-Palmer Quarterly*, 30 (2): 177–88.

Lewis, M., Alessandri, S.M. and Sullivan, M.W. (1992) 'Differences in shame and pride as a function of children's gender and task difficulty', *Child Development*, 63 (3): 630–8.

Lewis, M. and Brooks-Gunn, J. (1979) *Social Cognition and the Acquisition of Self*. New York: Plenum.

Lundy, B.L. (2003) 'Father– and mother–infant face-to-face interactions: Differences in mind-related comments and infant attachment?', *Infant Behavior and Development*, 26 (2): 200–12.

Lyons-Ruth, K., Easterbrooks, A. and Cibelli, C. (1997) 'Infant attachment strategies, infant mental lag, and maternal depressive symptoms: Predictors of internalizing and externalizing problems at age 7', *Developmental Psychology*, 33 (4): 681–92.

McAlister, A. and Peterson, C. (2007) 'A longitudinal study of child siblings and theory of mind development', *Cognitive Development*, 22 (2): 258–70.

Maccoby, E.E. (1998) *The Two Sexes: Growing Up Apart, Coming Together*. Cambridge, MA: Belknap/Harvard University Press.

Main, M. and Solomon, J. (1990) 'Procedures for identifying infants as disorganised/disorientated during the Ainsworth strange situation', in M.T. Greenberg, D. Cicchetti and E.M. Cummings (eds), *Attachment During the Preschool Years: Theory, Research and Intervention*. Chicago, IL: University of Chicago Press. pp. 121–60.

Main, M., Kaplan, N. and Cassidy, J. (1985) 'Security in infancy, childhood, and adulthood: A move to the level of representation', in I. Bretherton and E. Waters (eds), *Growing Points of Attachment Theory and Research*, Monographs of the Society for Research in Child Development (Serial No. 209), 50 (1–2): 66–104.

Malloch, S. (1999) 'Mothers and infants and communicative musicality', *Musicae Scientiae* (Special Issue 1999–2000), 3 (1): 29–57.

Masciuch, S and Kienapple, K. (1993) 'The emergence of jealousy in children 4 months to 7 years of age', *Journal of Social and Personal Relationships*, 10 (3): 421–35.

Matas, L., Arend, R.A. and Sroufe, A. (1978) 'Continuity of adaptation in the second year: The relationship between quality of attachment and later competence', *Child Development*, 49 (3): 547–56.

Meins, E., Fernyhough, C., Russell, J. and Clark-Carter, D. (1998) 'Security of attachment as a predictor of symbolic and mentalising abilities: A longitudinal study', *Social Development*, 7 (1): 1–24.

Meins, E., Fernyhough, C., Wainwright, R., Das Gupta, M., Fradley, E. and Tuckey, M. (2002) 'Maternal mind-mindedness and attachment security as predictors of theory of mind understanding', *Child Development*, 73 (6): 1715–26.

Mesman, J., van Ijzendoorn, M. H. and Bakermans-Kranenburg, M.J. (2009) 'The many faces of the still-face paradigm: A review and meta-analysis', *Developmental Review*, 29 (2): 120–62.

Messinger, D. and Fogel, A. (2007) 'The interactive development of social smiling', in R.V. Kail (ed.), *Advances in Child Development and Behavior: Vol. 35*. London: Elsevier. pp. 327–66.

Milligan, K., Astington, J.W. and Dack, L.A. (2007) 'Language and theory of mind: Meta-analysis of the relation between language belief and false-belief understanding', *Child Development*, 78 (2): 622–46.

Moss, E., Cyr, C. and Dubois-Comtois, K. (2004) 'Attachment at early school age and developmental risk: Examining family contexts and behavior problems of controlling-caregiving, controlling-punitive, and behaviorally disorganized children', *Developmental Psychology*, 40 (4): 519–32.

Mueller, E. and Lucas, T. (1975) 'A developmental analysis of peer interactions among toddlers', in M. Lewis and L. Rosenblum (eds), *Friendship and Peer Relations*. New York: Wiley. pp. 223–57.

Mumme, D.L., Fernald, A. and Herrera, C. (1996) 'Infants' responses to facial and vocal emotional signals in a social referencing paradigm', *Child Development*, 67 (6): 3219–37.

Murray, L. and Trevarthen, C. (1985) 'Emotional regulation of interactions between 2-month-olds and their mothers', in T.M Field and M.A. Fox (eds), *Social Perception in Infants*. Norwood, NJ: Ablex. pp. 177–97.

Newcomb, A.F. and Bagwell, C.L. (1995) 'Children's friendship relations: A meta-analytic review', *Psychological Bulletin*, 117 (2): 306–47.

Newcomb, A.F., Bukowski, W.M. and Pattee, L. (1993) 'Children's peer relations: A meta-analytic review of popular, rejected, neglected, controversial, and average sociometric status', *Psychological Bulletin*, 113 (1): 99–128.

Onishi, K.H. and Baillargeon, R. (2005) 'Do 15-month-old infants understand false beliefs?', *Science*, 308 (5719): 255–8.

Paquette, D. (2004) 'Theorizing the father-child relationship: Mechanisms and developmental outcomes', *Human Development*, 47 (4): 193–219.

Parke, R.D. (2002) 'Fatherhood and families', in M. Bornstein (ed.), *Handbook of Parenting* (2nd edn). Mahwah, NJ: Erlbaum. pp. 27–73.

Parker, J.G. and Gottman, J.M. (1989) 'Social and emotional development in a relational context: Friendship interaction from early childhood to adolescence', in T.J. Berndt and G.W. Ladd (eds), *Peer Relationships in Child Development*. New York: Wiley. pp. 95–131.

Parkhurst, J.T. and Asher, S.R. (1992) 'Peer rejection in middle school: Subgroup differences in behavior, loneliness, and interpersonal concerns', *Developmental Psychology*, 28 (2): 231–41.

Parten, M.B. (1932) 'Social participation among pre-school children', *Journal of Abnormal and Social Psychology*, 27 (3): 243–69.

Pastor, D. (1981) 'The quality of mother-infant attachment and its relationship to toddlers' initial sociability with peers', *Developmental Psychology*, 17 (3): 326–35.

Perner, J. (1988) 'Higher-order beliefs and intentions in children's understanding of social interaction', in J.W. Astington, P.L. Harris and D.R. Olson (eds), *Developing Theories of Mind*. Cambridge: Cambridge University Press. pp. 271–94.

Perner, J. (1991) *Understanding the Representational Mind*. Cambridge, MA: MIT Press.

Plomin, R and Rowe, D.C. (1977) 'A twin study of temperament in young children', *The Journal of Psychology: Interdisciplinary and Applied*, 97 (1): 107–13.

Power, T.G and Parke, R.D. (1982) 'Play as a context for early learning: Lab and home analyses', in L.M. Laosa and I.E. Sigel (eds), *Families as Learning Environments for Children*. New York: Plenum. pp. 147–78.

Putnam, S.P., Samson, A.V. and Rothbart, M.K. (2000) 'Child temperament and parenting', in V.J. Molfese and D.L. Molfese (eds), *Temperament and Personality Across the Lifespan*. Mahwah, NJ: Erlbaum. pp. 255–77.

Rovee-Collier, C. (1999) 'The development of infant memory', *Current Directions in Psychological Science*, 8 (3): 80–5.

Rubin, K.H., Bukowski, W.M. and Parker, J.G. (2006) 'Peer interactions, relations and groups', in N. Eisenberg (ed.), *Handbook of Child Psychology: Vol. 3 Social, Emotional and Personality Development* (6th edn). Hoboken, NJ: Wiley. pp. 571–645.

Rubin, K.H. and Coplan, R. (1992) 'Peer relationships in childhood', in M. Bornstein and M. Lamb (eds), *Developmental Psychology: An Advanced Textbook* (3rd edn). Hillsdale, NJ: Erlbaum. pp. 519–78.

Ruffman, T., Perner, J., Naito, M., Parkin, L. and Clements, W.A. (1998) 'Older (but not younger) siblings facilitate false belief understanding', *Developmental Psychology*, 34 (1): 161–74.

Ruffman, T., Slade, L. and Crowe, E. (2002) 'The relation between children's and mothers' mental state language and theory of mind understanding', *Child Development*, 73 (3): 734–751.

Russell, J.A. (1990) 'The preschooler's understanding of the causes and consequences of emotion', *Child Development*, 61 (6): 1872–81.

Sandstrom, M.J. and Cillessen, A.H.N. (2003) 'Sociometric status and children's peer experiences: Use of the daily diary method', *Merrill-Palmer Quarterly*, 49 (4): 427–52.

Shaffer, D.R. and Kipp, K. (2010) *Developmental Psychology: Childhood and Adolescence*. Belmont, CA: Wadsworth.

Shirley, M.M. (1933) *The First Two Years: A Study of 25 Babies*. Minneapolis, MN: University of Minnesota Press.

Smith, P. K., Cowie, H. and Blades, M. (2011) *Understanding Children's Development* (5th edn). Chichester: Wiley.

Sorce, J.F., Emde, R.N., Campos, J.J. and Klinnert, M.D. (1985) 'Maternal emotional signaling: Its effect on the visual cliff behavior of 1-year-olds', *Developmental Psychology*, 21 (1): 195–200.

Sroufe, L.A. (1977) 'Wariness of strangers and the study of infant development', *Child Development*, 48 (3): 731–46.

Sroufe, L.A. and Wunsch, J.P. (1972) 'The development of laughter in the first year of life', *Child Development*, 43 (4): 1326–44.

Stanley, C., Murray, L. and Stein, A. (2004) 'The effect of postnatal depression on mother-infant interaction, infant response to the still-face perturbation, and performance on an instrumental learning task', *Development and Psychopathology*, 16 (1): 1–18.

Stewart, R.B. (1983) 'Sibling attachment relationships: Child-infant interaction in the strange situation', *Developmental Psychology*, 19 (2): 192–99.

Stipek, D.J., Gralinski, J.H. and Kopp, C.B. (1990) 'Self-concept development in the toddler years', *Developmental Psychology*, 26 (6): 972–7.

Sullivan, K., Zaitchik, D. and Tager-Flusberg, H. (1994) 'Preschoolers can attribute second-order beliefs', *Developmental Psychology*, 30 (3): 395–402.

Sullivan, M.W. and Lewis, M. (2003) 'Contextual determinants of anger and other negative expressions in young infants', *Developmental Psychology*, 39 (4): 693–705.

Tamis-LeMonda, C.S. (2004) 'Conceptualising fathers' roles: Playmates and more', *Human Development*, 47 (4): 220–27.

Thelen, E. and Fisher, D.M. (1983) 'From spontaneous to instrumental behaviour: Kinematic analysis of movement changes during very early learning', *Child Development*, 54 (1): 129-40.

Thomas, A. and Chess, S. (1977) *Temperament and Development*. NewYork: Bruner/Mazel.

Thomas, A. and Chess, S. (1986) 'The New York Longitudinal Study: From infancy to adult life', in R. Plomin and J. Dunn (eds), *The Study of Temperament: Changes, Continuities and Challenges*. Hillsdale NJ: Erlbaum. pp. 39–52.

Thompson, R.A. (1991) 'Emotional regulation and emotional development', *Educational Psychology Review*, 3 (4): 269–307.

Thompson, R.A. (1994) 'Emotional regulation: A theme in search of definition', *Monographs of the Society for Research in Child Development*, 59 (2/3): 25–52.

Twardosz, S. and Lutzker, J. (2010) 'Child maltreatment and the developing brain: A review of neuroscience perspectives', *Aggression and Violent Behavior*, 15 (1): 59–68.

Vaish, A. and Striano, T. (2004) 'Is visual reference necessary? Contributions of facial versus vocal cues in 12-month-olds' social referencing behavior', *Developmental Science*, 7 (3): 261–9.

van Ijzendoorn, M.H., Schuengel, C. and Bakermans-Kranenburg, M.J. (1999) 'Disorganized attachment in early childhood: Meta-analysis of precursors, concomitants, and sequelae', *Development and Psychopathology*, 11 (2): 225–49.

van Ijzendoorn, M.H., Vereijken, C.M.J.L., Bakermans-Kranenburg, M.J. and Riksen-Walraven, J. (2004) 'Assessing attachment security with the attachment Q sort: Meta-analytic evidence for the validity of the observer AQS', *Child Development*, 75 (4): 1188–213.

Vaughn, B., Egeland, B., Sroufe, L.A. and Waters, E. (1979) 'Individual differences in infant-mother attachment at twelve and eighteen months: Stability and change in families under stress', *Child Development*, 50 (4): 971–5.

Vaughn, B.E. and Langlois, J.H. (1983) 'Physical attractiveness as a correlate of peer status and social competence in preschool children', *Developmental Psychology*, 19 (4): 561–7.

Waters, E. (1978) 'The reliability and stability of individual differences in infant-mother attachment', *Child Development*, 49 (2): 484–94.

Waters, E. and Deane, K. (1985) 'Defining and assessing individual differences in attachment relationships: Q-methodology and the organization of behavior in infancy and early childhood', in I. Bretherton and E. Waters (eds), *Growing Points of Attachment Theory and Research, Monographs of the Society for Research in Child Development* (Serial No. 209), 50 (1–2): 41–65.

Waters, E., Wippman, J. and Sroufe, L.A. (1979) 'Attachment, positive affect, and competence in the peer group: Two studies in construct validation', *Child Development*, 50 (3): 821–9.

Weinfield, N.S., Whaley, G.J.L. and Egeland, B. (2004) 'Continuity, discontinuity, and coherence in attachment from infancy to late adolescence: Sequelae of organization and disorganization', *Attachment and Human Development*, 6 (1): 73–97.

Wellman, H.M. (1990) *The Child's Theory of Mind*. Cambridge, MA: MIT.

Wellman, H.M., Cross, D. and Watson, J. (2001) 'Meta-analysis of theory-of-mind development: The truth about false belief', *Child Development*, 72 (3): 655–84.

Wentzel, K.R. and Asher, S.R. (1995) 'The academic lives of neglected, rejected, popular, and controversial children', *Child Development*, 66 (3): 754–63.

Wimmer, H. and Perner, J. (1983) 'Beliefs about beliefs: Representation and constraining function of wrong beliefs in young children's understanding of deception', *Cognition*, 13 (1): 103–28.

Workman, L. and Reader, W. (2007) *Evolutionary Psychology: An Introduction*. Cambridge: Cambridge University Press.

Zajac, R.J. and Hartup, W.W. (1997) 'Friends as co-workers: Research review and classroom implications', *The Elementary School Journal*, 98 (1): 3–13.

Language and Literacy

9

☀ Why you should read this chapter

The ability to communicate successfully, whether in speaking or writing, is an essential skill. Understanding the course of spoken language development informs us about what we can expect in terms of language skills in a child of a given age. This can also be important in detecting problems with language development. Unlike spoken language, which develops naturally if a child is exposed to language, reading and spelling are skills that have to be taught. Understanding the nature of literacy development can facilitate the development of effective approaches to teaching these skills and can also help to explain the underlying problems in children with **developmental dyslexia**.

By the end of this chapter you should

- be aware of the different aspects of language skill such as phonology, syntax, semantics and pragmatics

- be aware of the major milestones in a child's acquisition of language

- understand what speech errors, such as over-regularisations, tell us about language development

- understand the theoretical approaches to language development and their strengths and limitations

- have a basic understanding of sign language development, language development in children with learning difficulties, bilingual children and children with
specific language impairment
- understand the different phases of reading development in children
- have a knowledge of the nature of phonological awareness and its importance
in reading development
- see how research in language and literacy development can be used to support
early language and literacy skills in children.

The development of language

Children acquire language with amazing speed. If we look at the following example
of Eve provided by Brown (1973) we can see just how much skill develops in a very
small period of time:

Eve at 18 months: 'Right down', 'look dollie'

Eve at 27 months: 'I go get a pencil 'n' write', 'We're going to make a blue house'

It can be seen that within a period of nine months, Eve has moved from simple two-
word phrases to complete and well-formed sentences, and indeed such rapid development is commonplace in children. This rapid development is even more impressive
when we consider the different skills that a child has to master to use language. At the
most basic level, a child has to learn to produce the basic sounds that make up the
words of a language, referred to as a language's **phonology**. The child has to understand the meanings of the words, as a set of skills referred to as **semantics**. However,
while necessary, knowing the meanings of words is not sufficient to use language. The
child also has to master a set of rules relating to the correct ordering of words in sentences, for example the ordering of nouns and adjectives. This can vary from language
to language. In English, the adjective comes before the noun (e.g. 'big house') while
Spanish requires the adjective to come after the noun ('*casa grande*'). Knowledge of
the rules about correct ordering of words is referred to as **syntax**. However, knowledge
of these 'technical' aspects of language is not enough – there are a whole range of skills
that need to be acquired on top of these in order to use language to communicate with
others. The child needs to know how to communicate their intentions, take into
account the other person's perspective, understand how meaning can also be communicated through tone of voice, and understand differences between literal and intended
meanings. These skills, to go beyond the immediate words and phrases and bring in
broader skills to communicate, are referred to as **pragmatic** skills. Therefore the child
has to acquire all of these skills in a short timescale.

The course of language development

Developments in infancy

Although infants lack the capacity to speak, they nevertheless possess a number of basic perceptual and communicative skills that can been seen as important precursors of language. Firstly, infants have a preference for listening to speech over other types of sounds (deVilliers and deVilliers, 1979). Indeed, it is not just speech in general, but a form of speech known as **infant-directed speech** or **motherese** (Fernald, 1985) that seems to be of greatest interest to infants. This is the form of speech that is often used by adults to talk to a baby and has a distinct 'musical' quality characterised by use of exaggerated intonation and pitch and is used to attract a baby's attention. Fernald (1985) found that 4-month-old infants preferred to listen to tape-recorded motherese than to adult talk.

Infants also prefer their mother's voice over other speakers, and this preference has been noted within the first three days of life (DeCasper and Fifer, 1980). Given that an infant's auditory system is functional several weeks before birth, it is possible that this preference for the mother's voice may be a result of prenatal exposure. Evidence for this comes from a study by DeCasper and Spence (1986) that has become known as the 'Cat in the Hat' study. A group of pregnant women were asked to read aloud from a selected children's book (one of which was the Dr Seuss story 'The Cat in the Hat') twice a day during the final six weeks of pregnancy. Two days after they were born, the babies of these women were tested in a 'differential sucking' test: the babies were given an artificial nipple, which if sucked at a particular rate would activate a recording of their mother reading the same story as had been read during the final weeks of pregnancy. DeCasper and Spence found that babies could quickly alter their rate of sucking to access the recording of their mother's voice.

Infants also appear to be able to distinguish a variety of speech sounds (**phonemes**) from early on, and indeed perceive speech sounds in a similar manner to adults. An example of this is the phenomenon of **categorical perception** – as adults we can perceive differences between phonemes such as /b/ and /d/ but we don't notice variations within a single phoneme (which occur in everyday speech as a result of different accents or due to the positions of phonemes in words). Infants also show this capacity (Eimas, 1975).

The first sounds made by infants are crying sounds. Crying can be used to signify boredom, hunger, loneliness or pain. At around 1 month of age, infants begin **cooing**, which involves the production of soft, low vowel sounds such as 'oo'. They will often make sounds in response to others and this may provide an early opportunity to learn about taking turns in conversation (Trevarthen, 1974). At 5 to 6 months of age, they enter into the **babbling** stage. This is where they combine vowel and consonant sounds into syllables and repeat them, producing sounds such as '*babababa*'. It is generally accepted that the onset of babbling is controlled by maturational factors, rather than any real learning, because 'all' babies begin babbling at around the same age. For example, deaf babies will begin to babble even if they cannot hear themselves, and babies of deaf parents will continue to babble even in the absence of a response from their parents (Lenneberg et al., 1965). It used to be thought that babbling was a preparatory period for language in which infants practise and perfect sounds needed to make words; however, there is little evidence for this. The amount and frequency of babbling does not predict later language skills. Moreover, it has been shown that infants who have been prevented from babbling due to medical treatment (for example having had a breathing tube inserted in their throat) are still able to develop language (Hill and Singer, 1990), indicating that babbling is not necessary for language development.

Alongside early vocalisations, infants also show evidence of non-verbal communication skills. When they are between the ages 3 and 4 months, infants start to gaze in the same general direction as adults and this becomes more accurate by the time they are 10 to 11 months old. Adults also follow the infant's line of vision and comment on what the baby sees, a process known as **joint attention**, and there is evidence that attending to the same object as the caregiver who labels it can contribute to language development (Silvén, 2001). At around 4–6 months, infants also engage in give-and-take communications known as **proto-conversations** (Bruner, 1974–75). These include games such as 'peek-a-boo' and may help the infant to gain their first experiences of the rules of conversation in everyday speech, such as turn taking and responding to others. These interactions are also noted to have a 'musical' quality about them. Earlier in this section, it was mentioned that infants have a preference for a form of speech known as infant-directed speech. Infants are not just passive recipients of this form of speech, they will also seek to initiate these types of interactions with caregivers. Based on recordings of interactions between mothers and infants, Malloch (1999) and Malloch and Trevarthen (2009) have noted that such interactions display what they call **communicative musicality**. The mother's speaking voice has a distinct musical quality with clearly discernible rhythms and melodious patterns and the infant mirrors these qualities in response. In addition to facilitating the development of communicative skills, these playful interactions can also help to establish an affectionate bond between mother and infant.

Around the end of the first year, infants can also use pointing to communicate and two forms have been noted (Bates, 1976): **protodeclarative pointing**, which is when the infant uses gestures to bring an object to another's attention; and **protoimperative pointing**, which is when pointing is used to make a request, such as pointing to a toy that is out of their reach.

First words

A child's first words usually emerge between 10 and 13 months of age. First words are usually one or two syllables in length, and often consist of duplicated syllables such as 'mama' or 'dada'. Unsuprisingly, first words usually refer to important people in the child's life, as well as objects (e.g. 'ball'), actions or activities (e.g. 'give'). Children also learn greetings (e.g. 'hi'), relational words ('more'), action words ('up') and locational terms ('there'). There appears to be a remarkable similarity across cultures in the nature of children's first words (Nelson, 1973). However, there also appear to be individual differences in children's early vocabularies (Nelson, 1981). Some children have been labelled as **referential** and acquire lots of object names while other children, referred to as **expressive**, acquire many terms useful for social interaction (e.g. 'please', 'want'). At around 15–18 months of age there is a rapid acquisition of words that has been labelled the **naming explosion** (Markman, 1991). An example of this can be seen in a case study reported by Dromi (1987) in which her 15-month-old daughter learned 111 new words in three weeks.

An important feature of this phase of language development is that a child's **comprehension** exceeds **production** – children know more words than they can actually produce. Benedict (1990) studied the first 50 words comprehended and produced by each of a sample of eight infants and found that the rate of acquisition for comprehension was twice that of production.

Children's first words tend to be at an intermediate level of generality, i.e. a child will learn the word 'dog' before they will learn 'spaniel' (more specific) or 'animal' (more general). It is thought that these labels are the most useful for children in their interactions with the world. This is also possibly due to labelling practices employed by parents and caregivers, who often tend to label at this level: a parent is unlikely to point to a dog and say 'look at the spaniel' (Flavell et al., 1993).

An notable feature of early vocabulary development is that children can acquire word meanings very rapidly and it has been observed that 2-year-olds can learn a new word after only a single brief exposure, a phenomenon known as **fast mapping** (Carey, 1978). A number of explanations have been put forward for this development. One proposal is that rather than consider all the possible hypotheses about the meaning of a newly encountered word, children focus only on a limited range of possible meanings using inbuilt strategies called **constraints** (Markman, 1991). Examples of these include **whole-object constraints** (a tendency to assume that names refer to whole rather than parts of objects) and **mutual-exclusivity constraints** (the assumption that a new word applies to an object for which they do not already know a name). It has also been proposed that children pay attention to the way a word is used in a sentence to infer meaning, a process known as **syntactic bootstrapping**, and this can be used in particular to learn verbs (Gleitman, 1990).

Two other phenomena of early vocabulary development are **underextensions** and **overextensions**. Underextensions occur when a child uses a word in a very restricted way, such as using the word 'car' to refer only to the family car, and not to other cars. Overextensions occur when, for example, the word 'cat' is applied not just to cats, but also to dogs, and other four-legged animals. Overextensions are usually based on similarities of shape, size, sound, texture or movement (Clark, 1973), and are very common. It has been estimated that one-third of a child's first words are overextended

(Rescorla, 1980). Often this simply reflects limitations in the child's spoken vocabulary: a child who overgeneralises the word 'apple' can still point out the apple from a series of pictures of round objects (Thompson and Chapman, 1977). However, it is clear that children do not use overextensions randomly, and the fact that they apply overextensions to particular classes of object shows that language learning is an active process, with the child actively trying to make sense of their world, noticing similarities and differences between objects and trying to label them accordingly.

First sentences

Between the ages of 18 months and 2 years, children begin to combine words together. Initially this consists of pairs of words such as *'where daddy'*, *'give me'*, and so on. These initial two-word utterances are like simplified versions of adult sentences and consist of nouns and verbs and adjectives, and tend to omit words such as articles ('the'), prepositions (e.g. in, on), conjunctions (e.g. and) and inflections (endings to denote plurals or tenses). For this reason, such early speech is referred to as **telegraphic speech** (Brown, 1973). There is also evidence of creativity in such utterances, such as a child saying *'more up'* when he wants his father to continue lifting him up (Flavell et al., 1993). Despite the apparent simplicity of these utterances, children are able to communicate a lot of information to others – adults can generally infer what the child is trying to say from the word order used as well as from attending to the general context in which the utterance is made (deVilliers and deVilliers, 1992). The fact that children can use word order to convey meaning also shows evidence of an emerging knowledge of syntax.

From around 30 months, children begin to expand on their telegraphic utterances and begin to incorporate articles, prepositions and inflections in their speech (Bowerman, 1982). Children also begin to use negations (e.g. *'I won't do it'*) and to apply tense markings to words (e.g. *'mummy baked a cake'*). As children's sentences grow longer, evidence of syntactic development becomes clearer and a grammatical structure is evident. For example, a child's sentence *'big dog run home'* consists of a *noun phrase* (big dog) and a *verb phrase* (run home). The noun phrase precedes the verb phrase as required by the syntactic rules of English, and within the noun phrase 'big' is correctly used before 'dog' and within the verb phrase 'run' is correctly placed before 'home' (Flavell et al., 1993).

Children also demonstrate their expanding knowledge of grammatical rules in the errors they make in their speech. **Over-regularisations**, in which children treat all words as regular words, are common at this stage. For example, phrases such as *'I see two sheeps'*, *'he runned home'* are typical errors. They do, however, show that a child has noticed something about the language they are hearing – that typically adding 's' to nouns denotes a plural, and adding 'ed' to a verb forms a past tense.

The ability to understand complex sentences such as passive sentences develops gradually through childhood. Bever (1970) found that children aged 2–3 could use toys to act out the sentence '*the truck hits the car*', but when presented with the sentence '*the car is hit by the truck*', they made the car hit the truck, apparently interpreting the first noun in the sentence as the agent or actor. It appears that such passive sentences are not used by children until about the age of 6 (Horgan, 1978). Other later developments include coping with pronoun reference (understanding who the pronoun 'he' refers to in the sentence '*John told James that he liked Mary*') and improved questioning skills, such as using appropriate syntax to form a question (e.g. inverting the subject and the verb as in '*you have something to eat*' versus '*have you something to eat?*').

 Think of a young child with whom you are familiar. Have you encountered any examples of the various features of child language mentioned above (underextensions, overextensions, etc.) in that child's speech?

Development of pragmatic skills

Along with acquiring the vocabulary and grammatical rules of language, children also need to learn to use language to communicate effectively. These include turn taking in conversations, stating their messages clearly, and taking the listener's perspective – '*the ability to say the appropriate thing at the appropriate time and place to the appropriate listeners and in relation to the appropriate topics*' (Dore, 1979: 337). These skills are referred to as **pragmatics** and children show evidence of developing these skills in childhood.

The foundations of conversational skills may lie in experiences in infancy, where infants often engage in interactive games with adults such as 'peek-a-boo' and other games that involve an alternating sequence of sending and receiving. By the beginning of childhood children have basic conversational skills and are able to take turns and respond to their conversational partner's remarks (Pan and Snow, 1999). However, children are better at holding conversations in a one-to-one situation rather than in a group situation where they are more likely to interrupt other speakers (Ervin-Tripp, 1979).

By the age of 4, children are able to adjust their speech to suit their audience. A study by Shatz and Gelman (1973) observed 4-year-olds talking to 2-year-olds, fellow 4-year-olds and adults. In their interactions with the 2-year-olds, the children used simpler, shorter sentences and more attention-getting words such as 'hey', whereas conversations with peers and adults involved longer and more complex sentences.

Narrative skills also develop as childhood progresses. A young child will typically produce a narrative along the lines of '*we went to the park, we played on the swings, we had a picnic!*' By the time they are between 6 and 7 years old, children will add extra information (such as details of time, place and people) and use connectives (such as 'next' and 'then'), both of which help them to provide a more coherent story. By the ages of 8 or 9, children are able to produce lengthy, well-organised and detailed narratives (Bliss et al., 1998).

Children also gradually acquire the **say–mean distinction**, the understanding that people don't always say exactly what they mean. This is a common feature of everyday speech, for example someone making the sarcastic remark 'well-done!' to someone who has made a mistake. Ackerman (1981) found that 6-year-old children have some ability to recognise sarcastic statements as false, but were not really able to understand fully the communicative intention of the speaker until about the age of 12. Similarly Demorest et al. (1983) found that 6-year-old children often interpreted sarcastic remarks literally, while 8-year-olds recognised the incongruity of the remark but failed to recognise the

Table 9.1   Summary of the course of language development

Appoximate age	Development
Birth	Cries serve a number of communicative functions
	Preference for human voices and mother's voice in particular
1 to 6 months	Infants begin cooing followed by babbling
	Begin to engage in joint attention with caregiver
	Infants show preference for infant-directed speech
	Beginning of 'proto-conversations'
	'Communicative musicality' in infant–caregiver interactions
6 to 12 months	More accurate in engaging in joint attention
	Beginning of use of pointing to communicate
12 to 18 months	Emergence of first words
	Comprehension exceeds production
18 to 24 months	Rapid expansion of vocabulary – the naming explosion
	Telegraphic speech – first use of two-word sentences
	Ordering of words indicates beginnings of syntactic awareness
24 to 36 months	Fast mapping – children can learn new words after only a single brief exposure
	Overextensions and underextensions in use of words
	Beginning of three-word sentences
	Over-regularisations in use of verbs
36 to 48 months	Construction of more complex sentences
	Improved conversational skills
48 months onward	Children able to adjust speech to suit their audience
	Ability to understand passive sentences
	Able to produce increasingly sophisticated narratives
	Pragmatic skills gradually more sophisticated, awareness of aspects of language such as sarcasm, say–mean distinction

Adapted from Keenan and Evans (2009)

intention of the speaker. However, between the ages of 8 and 12, children's ability to deal with this type of language increases and they are able to use features such as intonation and context to identify sarcasm (Capelli et al., 1990).

It is highly likely that developments in aspects of language such as narrative skills and the 'say–mean' distinction are influenced by wider developments in cognition including improved memory and perspective-taking abilities as well as experience of social interaction. A summary of the course of language development is provided in Table 9.1.

Theories of language development

How can the acquisition of so much language skill in such a relatively short period of time be explained? There are three theoretical approaches to language development: **learning theory**, which stresses the role of reinforcement and imitation; **nativist theory**, which sees language as an innate ability; and **interactionist theories,** which see language as an innate ability but further developed by social interaction experiences.

Learning theory

Skinner (1957) outlined his theory of language in his book *Verbal Behaviour*. His basic proposal is that language, like any other form of behaviour, is acquired through a process of **operant conditioning**. When children make a vocalisation they are **reinforced** (e.g. they receive praise and attention), leading them to repeat these behaviours. The transition from babbling to producing words occurs through a process of **shaping**: parents selectively reinforce children for producing vocalisations that approach real words. When children start producing sentences, they are reinforced for producing grammatically correct sentences.

Another learning theory approach was proposed by Bandura's social learning theory (1989), which stresses the role of **observational learning** and **imitation** in children's language development. Children acquire words and phrases by listening to others and imitating their behaviours.

It is reasonable to assume that reinforcement may certainly play a role in encouraging a child to produce speech and indeed there is a role for imitation in language acquisition: at the most basic level children acquire the language they are exposed to – British children learn English, German children learn German, and imitation may help children to pick up some words and phrases. However, learning theory in general cannot provide a full account of language development and a number of criticisms can be made of this approach.

Firstly, it is argued that reinforcement alone cannot account for the speed with which a child acquires language – if this was primarily dependent on reinforcement there are potentially an infinite number of utterances that would need to be reinforced. Moreover, when a child is reinforced for producing a correct utterance, they do not receive direct feedback on what was correct about their speech, a problem referred to as **poverty of the stimulus**. Secondly, when a child is reinforced, they are often reinforced for producing speech that is true rather than grammatically correct – for example producing the sentence '*mama isn't boy, he a girl*' (Brown and Hanlon, 1970). Finally, as was mentioned earlier, a notable feature of children's language is its creativity and when children produce phrases such as 'more up' or when they over-regularise they are unlikely to be imitating utterances heard from adults. Therefore, learning theory cannot provide a full and adequate account of language development.

Nativist theory

In the same year that Skinner's book on verbal behaviour was published, the linguist Noam Chomsky published *Syntactic Structures* which proposed an account of language which took an opposite point of view to learning theory approaches to language. Chomsky (1957, 1965) argued that given the complexity of the task of language learning, the child's mind must be predisposed to process language. To this end, he argued that all children have a brain structure called a **language acquisition device (LAD)**. This is an innate system that contains a **universal grammar** – the set of features common to all languages (e.g. all languages contain concepts such as subject, object and verb). The important point about this theory is that children are not taught grammar, the LAD allows the child to infer rules of their language when they hear words and sentences. This is done through a process of **parameter setting**. Once the LAD infers a rule or parameter about the child's language, such as the basic order of words in that language, the rule becomes fixed and is used to interpret further speech.

Arguments in support of Chomsky's view include the universality of the course of language development. Regardless of the language being learnt, all children appear to progress through the sequence of babbling, one-word utterances, two-word utterances, and mastery of most grammatical rules by the time they are 4 or 5.

It has also been proposed by nativist theorists that there is a **sensitive period** (see, for example, Elliot, 1981) for language development when the brain is especially ready to process language. Informal evidence for this view can be seen in the case of adult immigrants who often find it difficult to learn the language of their adopted homeland, while their pre-adolescent children acquire their second language quickly and speak in a local accent.

There have been a number of criticisms of Chomsky's theory, in particular his notions of a language acquisition device and universal grammar. Although certain areas of the brain have been identified as specialised for language processing, no specific structure corresponding to the LAD has been identified. Linguists have also encountered difficulty in agreeing on the nature of a universal grammar. Also, despite the speed with which children acquire language, it is argued that grammar is not acquired as quickly as would be expected if so much knowledge is innate.

An alternative version of a nativist theory comes from cognitive theorists such as Piaget and Slobin. They argue against the notion of a specialised inborn mechanism for language acquisition and instead stress the role of innate cognitive and information-processing abilities. Piaget (1967) argued that language development is driven by cognitive development. It is pointed out that language does not appear until after the sensorimotor period, and language acquisition does not begin until a number of cognitive abilities such as object permanence have emerged. Slobin (1973) has argued that all children possess a number of cognitive strategies called **operating principles** and they apply these to the task of acquiring language. Examples of such principles include 'pay attention to the order of words' and 'pay attention to the ends of words'. By using these strategies to analyse the speech they hear, children gradually acquire a knowledge of the structure of language.

There is no doubt that wider cognitive developments, such as improvements in memory ability, categorisation, and perspective taking, play a role in facilitating language development. However, if language development was critically dependent on cognitive development, then one would expect problems in one to be accompanied by problems in the other. But, as will be seen shortly, studies of language development in children with learning difficulties show that this is not necessarily always the case and in general, cognitive accounts cannot fully explain language development.

Interactionist views

Interactionist theorists accept the nativist view that there is an innate component to language acquisition, but unlike nativist theorists, they also stress the role of social support that adults can provide to children in acquiring language. Bruner (1983) has argued that parents provide their children with a **language acquisition support system (LASS)** which comprises a collection of strategies used to facilitate language development in the child. One such strategy is the use of infant-directed speech. It was mentioned earlier that infants show a preference for this type of speech or normal adult speech, and it is argued that this approach helps to gain the infant's attention and help them to understand the message. Other examples of such strategies include **expansions** and **recasting** of the child's speech. For example, if a child says 'mummy eat', the mother might expand the sentence to 'yes, mummy is eating her dinner'. In this way she has expanded the child's utterance into a longer and more complex sentence, and often when parents do this they also recast the sentence providing a grammatically correct example. In this way parents can fill in the gaps and provide grammatical information which can aid the child's language development.

Interactionist views provide useful pointers to parents as to how they can assist their child's language development, but as with all theories of language development, these views also have their limitations. It has been pointed out that practices regarding communication and social interaction vary across cultures and languages and not all the practices described above are used. For example, it used to be thought that infant-directed speech was used across all cultures, but other researchers have pointed out that this is not the case (Pinker, 2007). Despite these variations in practices, children still seem to acquire language in the same manner, so language acquisition cannot be critically dependent on these.

Other topics in language development

Language development is a very broad topic and indeed numerous textbooks have been devoted to this issue alone, and it is not possible to cover all of the possible areas in a single chapter. The following sections will provide a brief overview of a few other aspects of language development that may be of interest and will look at the issues of learning disabilities and language development, sign language acquisition, bilingual language development and specific language impairment.

Learning disabilities and language development

The account of language development covered so far has focused on typically developing children, but what about cases of atypical development? Do children with learning difficulties develop language in much the same way as other children or do they encounter difficulties? This question is important both from a practical point of view in terms of highlighting areas where children may need support with their language, and from a theoretical point of view in that it can allow the question of the relationship between cognition and language development to be considered. The evidence is mixed.

One of the most common learning disabilities is *Down's syndrome*. Evidence suggests that children who have Down's syndrome experience difficulties in acquiring language. Initial indications are a delay in language, with children's language lagging behind their chronological age, but consistent with their mental age (Harley, 2001). After the age of 4, however, language also starts to lag behind mental age and problems with grammar and vocabulary are apparent (Hoff-Ginsberg, 1997). However, there is also evidence of individual variation as well. Yamada (1990) reports a case study of 'Laura' whose linguistic ability exceeded her other cognitive abilities.

Studies have also been conducted on the language development of children with *Williams syndrome*. Children suffering from this genetic disorder display physical abnormalities and have a very low IQ, typically around 50 (Bellugi et al., 1990). Despite profound intellectual disabilities, however, these children are able to produce fluent and grammatically correct speech. They also display a good ability to acquire vocabulary and their non-word repetition skills are also very good (Grant et al., 1997).

Children with *autism* have particular difficulty with pragmatic aspects of language; however, these difficulties are more likely to be a consequence of lacking a theory of mind and the resultant difficulties in perspective taking, rather than specific linguistic difficulties.

Overall, the evidence from these cases is rather mixed but does demonstrate that impressive language development can take place even in the presence of serious cognitive impairments.

Sign language acquisition

Another interesting issue relates to the acquisition of sign language. Deaf communities throughout the world have their own languages based on signs and gestures made with the hands. Sign language is more than just the words of the spoken language translated into signs. They have their own structure and grammar and different forms of sign language are used in different countries. For example, in Britain, deaf children learn British Sign Language (BSL), in the USA children learn American Sign Language (ASL). Does the acquisition of sign language follow the same course as spoken language?

There do appear to be some similarities between spoken and sign language acquisition. Just as hearing (and deaf) infants go through a 'babbling' phase, there is also evidence that if deaf infants are exposed to sign language, they appear to go through a phase of producing babble-like hand movements (Petitto et al., 2004). And just as hearing children go through one-word and two-word phases of development, there appear to be comparable 'one-sign' and 'two-sign' periods in sign language development (Marschark, 1993).

There is some evidence that first signs in deaf children appear earlier than first words in their hearing counterparts, with studies reporting the emergence of first signs between 7 and 9 months of age (McIntire, 1977; Orlansky and Bonvillian, 1985). There also appears to be an early advantage in vocabulary development in deaf children who are native signers. McIntire (1974, cited in Marschark, 1993) reported a 20-sign vocabulary in a 10-month-old child and in a subsequent study observed an 85-sign vocabulary in a 13-month-old child, which expanded to 200 signs at 21 months. This can be contrasted to the vocabulary development of hearing children in Nelson's study (1973) who typically produced 10 words at around 15.1 months and 50 words at around 19.6 months. However, the structure and content of the sign vocabularies of deaf children appear to be broadly comparable with those of hearing children (Bonvillian et al., 1983).

This early advantage of sign language may be due to the fact that manual dexterity matures earlier than the vocal apparatus (Marschark, 1993). However, this early advantage does not last and appears to disappear at the equivalent of the 'two-word' phase when syntactic and semantic factors start to exert an influence (Meier and Newport, 1990). Semantic development in deaf children appears to parallel that of hearing children (Marschark, 1993).

As is the case with spoken language, there also appears to be a sensitive period for sign language acquisition. It has been found that adults in the USA who learned ASL in adolescence or adulthood do not acquire the same level of proficiency as those acquiring ASL in early childhood (Newport 1991; Singleton and Newport, 2004).

Bilingual language development

There are many parts of the world where children have to acquire not just one but two languages. In some countries two languages are spoken in the community (for example Welsh and English in parts of Wales, French and English in parts of Canada). Moreover, many children belong to immigrant communities and learn to speak the language of their family as well as the language of the country in which they reside. In bilingualism research, a child's first language is referred to as *L1* and their second language as *L2*. Two questions are of interest here. Can children acquire full fluency in two or more languages? Are there any costs and benefits associated with bilingualism? These are discussed below.

Researchers in bilingualism distinguish between three types of bilingual individual: **simultaneous bilinguals** who learned L1 and L2 at the same time (e.g. having parents who speak different languages in the home); **early sequential bilinguals** who learned L1 first but learned L2 relatively early in childhood; and **late sequential bilinguals** who learned L2 in adolescence or later.

Overall, the consensus is that children who learn two languages simultaneously in infancy or early childhood show no problems in language development and their acquisition does not appear to be qualitatively different from monolingual acquisition (Meisel, 2008). In the case of early sequential bilingualism, the evidence suggests that preschoolers acquire good to native ability in their second language, but the degree of fluency achieved will also depend on their first language proficiency at the time of exposure to the second language and the manner in which fluency is assessed (Butler and Hakuta, 2008). Second language acquisition can also be influenced by factors such as the time of residence in the new country (Johnson and Newport, 1989), as well as personality and wider cognitive variables (Cummins, 1991).

Studies of bilingual language acquisition also provide evidence for the notion of a sensitive period in language development. Johnson and Newport (1989) conducted a study of Chinese and Korean immigrants to the USA and found a strong relationship between English language ability and age of arrival: the younger they were on arrival, the better their language ability as adults. However, there is no clear cut-off point for a decline in second language learning ability, but there appears to be a gradual decrease from childhood to adulthood (Butler and Hakuta, 2008).

Are there any costs or benefits associated with bilingualism? Generally there do not appear to be any linguistic disadvantages from learning two languages (Snow, 1993). Bilingual children do show evidence of increased **metalinguistic awareness** – an understanding of the nature of language, evidenced by skills such as identifying gram-matical errors in sentences – (Hakuta and Diaz, 1985), they score higher on tests of creativity (Ricciardelli, 1992) and they also have better reading skills (Bialystok et al., 2005), particularly if one of their languages has a consistent and regular sound-spelling pattern.

Specific language impairment

Although most children develop language with relative ease, there are some children who experience specific problems in their language development. A diagnosis of **specific language impairment (SLI)** is made when a child's language lags behind other areas of development, and does not appear to be related to wider learning dis-abilities, hearing loss, neurological problems or impoverished language environment (Bishop, 1987). Such children appear to have normal IQs and the problem appears to be specifically related to language. It is estimated that SLI has a prevalence rate of about 7 per cent (Shaywitz, 1998). There also appears to be a genetic component to SLI, and it appears to run in families (Hurst et al., 1990).

The largest group of children diagnosed with SLI tend to display problems with pho-nological aspects of language and the acquisition of grammar. There does appear to be some variation across languages: English-speaking SLI children have particular problems with inflections such as tenses (applied 'ed' to words) (while Spanish- and Italian-speaking SLI children have difficulties with articles and function words (Leonard, 2009).

There is some debate about the underlying deficits in SLI. The fact that language is specifically impaired has led some researchers to argue that the problem is a deficit in an innate language learning mechanism (see, for example, van der Lely and Ullman, 2001). However, the consensus among most researchers is that the underlying deficits relate to problems in verbal short-term memory and processing the phonological aspects of language. Children with SLI typically have poor short-term memory ability (see, for example, Laws and Bishop, 2003) and it is well established that this ability plays a significant role in vocabulary development in children (Gathercole and Baddeley, 1993). Deficiencies in processing the phonology of language can also impair acquisition of grammar – for example to acquire the past tense of a word, it is necessary to perceive the final sound of the word, and this could be impaired by dif-ficulties in segmenting the speech signal.

The development of literacy

In addition to acquiring spoken language skills, children also need to learn written language skills, i.e. reading and spelling. Unlike spoken language skills, which develop naturally, written language skills need to be taught explicitly. The topic of literacy development is itself a broad area of study and encompasses the development of many skills including word recognition, grammatical rules and comprehension skills. This section will focus on the development of word recognition skills.

The course of reading development

Models of reading development have been proposed by Ehri (1991, 1995), Frith (1985) and Marsh et al. (1980). Each of these models see children's reading skills as passing through a series of distinct developmental stages or phases. Initially, during the pre-school phase, reading tends to be visually mediated, then children start to apply their developing knowledge of the alphabetic principle to reading words, and finally, in late childhood, they are able to read in much the same way as adults, showing the ability to recognise words directly from the visual stimulus. We will concentrate on Ehri's phases of reading development to illustrate the development of reading in children.

Ehri's phase theory

According to Ehri (1991, 1995), learning to read words by sight can be seen as a connection-forming process whereby individual written words are linked to their pronunciations and meanings. Her model identifies four different phases of reading development, with different types of connections predominating at each phase. The first phase she has termed the **pre-alphabetic phase**. Children in this phase do not have the ability to decode words using letter-sound knowledge and word reading here is achieved by remembering prominent visual features of words. Children at this phase may be able to read words encountered frequently in the environment, such as *milk* or *McDonald's*. However, when environmental cues such as logos or distinctive print are removed and the word is presented by itself, children can no longer read the words (Mason, 1980). Pre-alphabetic children may also read words through use of meaningful visual cues, such as remembering *look* by the two 'eyes' in the middle (Gough et al., 1983). Children engage in pretend reading and can guess words from pictures, but all feats of reading at this phase do not involve any alphabetic knowledge (Ehri, 2003).

Children begin to use alphabetic knowledge when they progress to the **partial alphabetic** phase. In this phase they possess a very basic knowledge of the alphabetic system which they can use to make partial connections between some of the letters in a written word and the sounds in the spoken version. First and final letters are often selected as cues to be remembered, for example reading the word 'spoon' by detecting the /s/ and /n/ sounds in its spoken form and connecting these to the letters S and N in its written form, while overlooking the other letters and sounds in the word (Ehri, 1995). The availability of this strategy means that children can learn to read words by sight more effectively in this phase, but it can also cause children to confuse similarly spelled words, such as mistaking the words BOOK and BLACK for BLOCK (see, for example, Ehri and Wilce, 1987). This approach to reading has also been termed *phonetic cue reading* (Ehri and Wilce, 1985, 1987). Ehri and Wilce (1985) demonstrated the difference in reading strategies between the pre- and partial alphabetic phases. They observed that beginners in the pre-alphabetic phase found it easier to learn to read invented words that had a distinct visual form but bore no relation to sounds (e.g. WcB for 'elephant'), whereas children classed as partial alphabetic phase readers found it easier to learn to read words containing salient cues linking letters to sounds (e.g. LFT for elephant).

When children gain an extensive knowledge of letter-sound relations they enter the **full alphabetic** phase. They are now able to form full connections between the letters in the written forms of words and the phonemes in their pronunciation. Because of this, word reading becomes more accurate and full alphabetic readers are less prone to confusing similarly spelled words than partial alphabetic phase readers (Ehri and Wilce, 1987). Moreover, full alphabetic readers also gain the ability to decode words never read before, leading to a rapid expansion of their sight vocabulary.

The final phase proposed by Ehri is the **consolidated alphabetic phase**. As children in the full alphabetic phase become more proficient at reading, their sight vocabulary continues to grow. Fully connected spellings of more and more words are retained and spelling patterns that recur across different words become consolidated. This consolidation allows readers to operate with multi-letter units such as morphemes and syllables, and the use of such units facilitates word decoding accuracy and speed (Juel, 1983). The first letter sequences to become consolidated are likely to be those that occur frequently in children's texts, including morphemic suffixes such as -ING and -ED, and spelling patterns that recur in many words such

Table 9.2   Summary of Ehri's phases of reading development

Phase	Features
Pre-alphabetic	No use of alphabetic knowledge Reading visually mediated
Partial alphabetic	Beginning of use of letter-sound rules to read words Able to make connections between *some* of the letters in a word and the sounds in their spoken form
Full alphabetic	Able to form complete connections between letters and sounds in words Reading becomes more accurate
Consolidated alphabetic	Able to read like an adult Ability to use multi-letter segments such as morphemic suffixes and commonly occurring letter combinations to read words

Sources: Ehri, 1991, 1995

as -IT, -AT, -IN, -AND, -ALL (Bryant et al., 1997). There is evidence that words containing familiar letter patterns are read more accurately by children than words containing unfamiliar patterns, even when these words are constructed out of the same grapheme-phoneme correspondences (Treiman et al., 1990).

A summary of Ehri's model is provided in Table 9.2.

Phonological awareness and reading development

An important issue in reading research is the nature of the basic skills that contribute to reading development. An important point about reading is that in terms of human evolution, reading – the representation of language using visual symbols – is a relatively recently acquired skill. It is therefore agreed that unlike spoken language, which is an innate skill and has a strong biological component, we do not have any specialised brain structures that evolved for the purpose of reading and therefore, reading must involve skills that evolved for other purposes (Anderson, 1993).

In developmental models of reading development, a major step forward occurs when children begin to exploit their knowledge of the alphabetic system and form connections between the letters in the written forms of words and the sounds in their spoken form. Given the importance of this skill in early reading development, it is reasonable to assume that a child's understanding of the sound structure of spoken language will play an important role in the acquisition of literacy, and there has been much interest in children's ability to process the phonological aspects of language. In the context of reading, this skill is referred to as **phonological awareness**.

There are a number of different forms of phonological awareness, related to the differing ways in which a word can be divided into different sound segments. The largest is at the level of the **syllable** – for example the word 'robot' can be divided into two syllables. The smallest units of sound are the *phonemes*, which are the individual sounds that blended together make up a word. So, for example, the word 'cat' consists of three phonemes: /c/, /a/ and /t/. Although alphabetic letters typically represent phonemes, this is not always the case. Letters can also represent different phonemes – for example the 'i' sound in the words 'bit' and 'bite' represent two different phonemes. Phonemes can also be represented by a variety of letter combinations – for example the letter combination 'eigh' (as in 'height') can also represent the phoneme /ai/. The English language is considered to have 44 +/– phonemes, the specific number depending on the classification system used (see, for example, Denes and Pinson, 1963). In addition to syllabic and phonemic units, a word can also be divided into its **onset and rime** components. These represent units that are larger than individual phonemes, but smaller than a syllable. The onset of a syllable consists of the opening consonant or consonant cluster. The rime component contains the vowel and succeeding consonants. Thus the syllable 'string' consists of an onset 'str' and rime 'ing'.

Phonological skills in children can be assessed in different ways. Onset-rime awareness is usually tested using *rhyming oddity tasks*, for example '*which of these words – cat, mat, cot – doesn't rhyme with the others?*' Phonemic awareness can be assessed using *deletion* tests ('*say "cat" without the /c/ sound at the beginning*'), *segmentation* tests ('*what sounds can you hear in "cat"?*') or *blending* tests ('*what words do the sound /c/, /a/ and /t/ make?*'). Skills at the onset-rime level develop first, and this skill is present in children before they learn to read (Bradley and Bryant, 1983). Skills at the phonemic level emerge next and seem to be a consequence of learning to read and specifically being introduced to the alphabetic principle (Goswami and Bryant, 1990). Phonemic skills can also develop before children learn to read but only if they have some basic knowledge of the alphabet (Johnson et al., 1996).

Numerous correlational and longitudinal studies have found links between onset-rime awareness and reading (see, for example, Bradley and Bryant, 1983) and phonemic skills and reading (see, for example, Stanovich et al., 1984). What specific roles do they play in reading development?

Phonemic skills are considered to facilitate the development of **phonological recoding** whereby the child can identify the sounds represented by the letters in the printed word and blend them together to help them recognise the word.

It has been suggested that onset-rime levels may play two roles. Firstly, onset-rime skills may be a precursor to the more refined skill of phonemic awareness. A study by Bryant et al. (1990) found that a child's rhyming skills at age 4 were predictive of phonemic skills at age 5, which in turn predicted reading at age 6. So it may be that a child with good onset-rime skills will develop strong phonemic skills which in turn promote reading. A second role played by onset-rime levels of awareness is that they are related to a child learning to read new words using a strategy of **analogy**: the child comes to realise that words which sound similar also have similar spelling patterns. Hence a child who recognises the word 'hat' can learn to read 'cat' by realising the sound made by the 'at' component and just needs to add the initial sound. Research by Goswami (1986) has suggested that this is indeed a strategy used by children to read new words.

More recently there has been some debate about the best predictor of reading, and the role of the onset-rime level of phonological awareness has been questioned. Studies by Muter et al. (1998, 2004) have found that phonemic skills are better predictors than rhyming skills. One reason for this may be related to onset-rime skills and the use of analogies to read. It has been argued that the tendency of children to read using the strategy of analogy has been overestimated: it is one thing to observe a child using the strategy of analogy in a formal testing situation, but it seems that this is not something that happens widely in the everyday classroom, where children are more likely to use letter-sound rules to read new words rather than rhyme analogies (Brown and Deavers (1999).

There is also evidence of an interactive relationship between phonological awareness and reading development, in that phonological skills facilitate the development of reading, but reading itself helps to further develop a child's phonological awareness. In an American study, Wagner et al. (1994) found that phonemic skills in the kindergarten year were predictive of word recognition skills in the first grade, but knowledge of the alphabet also was predictive of phonemic skills in the second grade.

Overall, the consensus in the literature is that phonological awareness does play a causal role in reading development in that it facilitates the child in linking the letters in the printed word with the sounds in its spoken form. This also has practical implications because measuring a child's phonological skills can help to identify children at risk for reading problems.

Other topics in literacy development

As is the case with spoken language, the development of written language skills covers a wide range of issues and it is impossible to cover them all in a single chapter. This section will look in brief at two selected areas: the development of spelling and developmental dyslexia.

The development of spelling

In addition to recognising the visual forms of words, children also have to learn to be able to produce the correct spellings in order to write. There appear to be some differences between reading and spelling, despite the fact that they are both important literacy skills. It is possible for an individual to be a good reader, but a poor speller (Frith, 1985), and indeed there is some evidence of early reading and spelling developing out of step with each other. It has been found that sometimes children can read a word but not spell it, or spell a word but not read it (Bradley and Bryant, 1983). It is generally agreed that early reading is visually mediated, but there is no reliable evidence that spelling goes through a similar phase, and the consensus is that spelling is driven by phonological skills right from the start. Indeed Frith (1985) argues that children first start to apply a phonological recoding strategy to spelling and only later do they transfer this strategy to the task of reading. Thereafter, reading and spelling follow a similar developmental course, passing from an alphabetically based phase to a mature orthographic phase (Goswami and Bryant, 1990).

Developmental dyslexia

As with specific language disorder, there are children who fail to acquire reading skills despite normal cognitive development and adequate opportunities to develop them. A diagnosis of developmental dyslexia is made when a child shows specific reading problems that cannot be explained in terms of wider cognitive problems, or other obvious factors such as frequent school absences etc. (Snowling, 2000).

Some researchers have argued that there are different types of developmental dyslexia. Castles and Coltheart (1993) examined 56 children diagnosed with developmental dyslexia and argued that they could be categorised as **surface developmental dyslexics** who typically could read regular words but had great difficulty with irregular words, or **phonological dyslexics** who were poor at reading regular words or non-words. However, other researchers who have examined a large number of case studies of developmental dyslexia have questioned the validity of such a distinction (see, for example, Wilding, 1989) and have argued that the patterns of performance that appear to reflect different types of dyslexia simply result from individual strategies used by children to cope with the difficult task of reading words.

There is a wide consensus that it is problems processing the phonological aspects of language that underpin developmental dyslexia. Such children are typically poorer at tests of phonological processing than children of the same age, but also compared to **reading-age controls**, children who are younger, but have the same reading age as the dyslexic children (Snowling, 2000). Developmental dyslexics also have impaired verbal short-term memories (see, for example, Jorm, 1983) and it is widely accepted that this cognitive skill plays a role in reading development, particularly in helping a child to learn letter-sound rules (Gathercole and Baddeley, 1993). Indeed, it has also been suggested that this is a manifestation of problems at a more basic sensory level in dealing with sounds, as children with developmental dyslexia often have problems such as learning musical rhythms, discriminating between musical tones, and so on (Overy, 2000). Recent research (with adults) by Perrachione et al. (2011) has suggested that dyslexics also have problems in recognising voices and understanding speech in noisy environments (over and above the difficulties that we would expect anyone to have with this type of task). This could have important practical implications, as children with developmental dyslexia may be more affected by noisy environments compared to their peers.

 Before reading on, consider some ways in which findings from research in language and literacy development can be applied to facilitate the development of these skills in children.

Supporting language and literacy development

This chapter has covered a large body of research and theory on language and literacy development; research and theory that can also provide some pointers for supporting the development of language and literacy skills. Here are some possible suggestions, but this list is by no means meant to be exhaustive:

- Responding to infant vocalisations and engaging in proto-conversations: this encourages the infant to produce sounds and also provides them with initial experience of the rules of conversation.
- Engaging in joint attention with the infant: there is evidence that infants who experience this often have better comprehension skills and show faster vocabulary development (Silvén, 2001).
- The simple act of engaging toddlers in conversations and reading to them exposes them to many aspects of language including vocabulary and grammar and can also help to develop narrative skills.
- Nursery rhymes are enjoyed by young children and there is evidence that their knowledge of them is also predictive of later phonological awareness (Maclean et al., 1987).
- There is much debate about the most effective ways of teaching children to read and in particular the relative merits of 'whole word' approaches, in which children learn words as visual patterns, or phonics-based approaches, which encourage children to focus on the sounds that make up words and on the use of letter-sound rules. There is a general consensus that phonics-based approaches are superior (Adams, 1990) and most studies on reading development see discovery of the alphabetic principle as the key to learning to read.

Chapter summary

- In acquiring spoken language, children need to develop skills in phonology, semantics, syntax and pragmatics.
- Infants are equipped with basic perceptual and communicative skills that can be seen as precursors to language.
- There is a consistent course of language development in children – initially crying followed by cooing and babbling in infancy; a period of one-word utterances, followed by two-word and longer sentences. By the age of 5, children have mastered much of the grammar and vocabulary of their language.
- Theories of language development include learning theories, which see language as a skill that is learnt; nativist theories, which see language as innate and simply require the child to be exposed to language; and interactionist theories, which stress the role of social interaction in language development.
- Learning disabilties are sometimes accompanied by language problems, particularly in the case of children with Down's syndrome. However, other children with disorders, such as children with Williams syndrome, have good language skills despite profound cognitive impairments.

(Continued)

(Continued)

- Deaf children learning sign language follow a similar developmental course to their hearing counterparts, but do appear to have an early advantage in vocabulary development.
- Bilingual children can learn a second language easily if they are exposed to it early in childhood.
- Children with specific language impairment appear to have difficulties with processing the phonological aspects of language and this can impair the acquisition of vocabulary and grammatical skills.
- Reading passes through a number of distinct phases of development. Initially it is visually mediated, there then follows a period where children apply their developing alphabetic knowledge to the task of reading new words, and this is followed by the final phase in which their knowledge of words becomes consolidated: the child has now acquired a detailed sight vocabulary and is able to recognise most words immediately without the use of phonological recoding.
- Phonological awareness, an understanding of the sound structure of spoken words, is a critical cognitive skill for the acquisition of reading. A lack of phonological awareness is a notable characteristic of children with developmental dyslexia.

Further reading

Saxton, M. (2010) *Child Language: Acquisition and Development*. London: Sage.
A comprehensive account of research on all aspects of child language development for those with a specialist interest in this field.

Whitehead, M. (2010) *Developing Language and Literacy with Young Children 0–8* (4th edn). London: Sage.
A practical look at promoting the development of language and literacy in young children.

Useful website

http://www.ukla.org/
The website of the United Kingdom Literacy Association which is concerned with the promotion of literacy both in school and out-of-school settings.

References

Ackerman, B.P. (1981) 'Young children's understanding of a speaker's intentional use of a false utterance', *Developmental Psychology*, 17 (4): 472–80.
Adams, M.J. (1990) *Beginning to Read: Thinking and Learning about Print*. Cambridge, MA: MIT Press.

Anderson. M. (1993) *Intelligence and Development: A Cognitive Theory.* Oxford: Blackwell.

Bandura, A. (1989) 'Social cognitive theory', in R. Vasta (ed.), *Annals of Child Development*, Vol. 6. Greenwich, CT: JAI. pp. 1–60.

Bates, E. (1976) *Language and Context: The Acquisition of Performatives.* New York: Academic Press.

Bellugi, U., Bihrle, A., Jernigan, T., Trauner, D. and Doherty, S. (1990) 'Neuropsychological, neurological, and neuroanatomical profile of Williams syndrome', *American Journal of Medical Genetics*, 37 (Suppl. S6): 115–25.

Benedict, H. (1979) 'Early lexical development: Comprehension and production', *Journal of Child Language*, 6 (02): 183–200.

Bever, T.G. (1970) 'The cognitive basis for linguistic structures', in J.R. Hayes (ed.), *Cognition and the Development of Language.* New York: Wiley. pp. 279–362.

Bialystok, E., Luk, G. and Kwan, E. (2005) 'Bilingualism, biliteracy, and learning to read: Interactions among languages and writing systems', *Scientific Studies of Reading*, 9 (1): 43–61.

Bishop, D.V.M. (1987) 'The causes of specific developmental language disorder ("developmental dysphasia")', *Journal of Child Psychology and Psychiatry*, 28 (1): 1–8.

Bliss, L.S., McCabe, A. and Miranda, A.E. (1998) 'Narrative assessment profile: Discourse analysis for school-age children', *Journal of Communication Disorders*, 31 (4): 347–63.

Bonvillian, J.D., Orlansky, M.D. and Novack, L.L. (1983) 'Developmental milestones: Sign language acquisition and motor development', *Child Development*, 54 (6): 1435–45.

Bowerman, M. (1982) 'Reorganizational processes in lexical and syntactic development', in E. Wanner and L. Gleitman (eds), *Language Acquisition: The State of the Art.* Cambridge: Cambridge University Press. pp. 319–46.

Bradley, L. and Bryant, P.E. (1983) 'Categorizing sounds and learning to read – a causal connection', *Nature*, 301 (5899): 419–21.

Brown, G.D.A. and Deavers, R. (1999) 'Units of analysis in nonword reading: Evidence from children and adults', *Journal of Experimental Child Psychology*, 73 (3): 208–42.

Brown, R. (1973) *A First Language: The Early Stages.* Cambridge, MA: Harvard University Press.

Brown, R. and Hanlon, C. (1970) 'Derivational complexity and order of acquisition in child speech', in J.R. Hayes (ed.), *Cognition and the Development of Language.* New York: Wiley. pp. 11–53.

Bruner, J. (1974–75) 'From communication to language – a psychological perspective', *Cognition*, 3 (3): 255–87.

Bruner, J. (1983) *Child's Talk: Learning to Use Language.* Oxford: Oxford University Press.

Bryant, P.E. and Bradley, L. (1980) 'Why children sometimes write words they do not read', in U. Frith (ed), *Cognitive Processes in Spelling.* London: Academic Press. pp. 355–70.

Bryant, P.E., MacLean, M., Bradley, L. and Crossland, J. (1990) 'Rhyme and alliteration, phoneme detection, and learning to read', *Developmental Psychology*, 26 (3): 429–38.

Bryant, P., Nunes, T. and Bindman, M. (1997) 'Children's understanding of the connection between grammar and spelling: Linguistic knowledge and learning to read and spell', in B. Blachman (ed), *Foundations of Reading Acquisition.* Mahwah, NJ: Erlbaum. pp. 219–40.

Butler, Y.G. and Hakuta, K. (2008) 'Bilingualism and second language acquisition', in T.K. Bhatia and W.C. Ritchie (eds), *The Handbook of Bilingualism.* Oxford: Blackwell, pp. 114–145.

Capelli, C.A., Nakagawa, N. and Madden, C.M. (1990) 'How children understand sarcasm: The role of context and intonation', *Child Development*, 61 (6): 1824–41.

Carey, S. (1978) 'The child as word learner', in M. Halle, G. Miller and J. Bresnan (eds), *Linguistic Theory and Psychological Reality.* Cambridge, MA: MIT. pp. 264–93.

Carpenter, M., Nagel, K. and Tomasello, M. (1998) 'Social cognition, joint attention, and communicative competence from 9 to 15 months of age', *Monographs of the Society for Research in Child Development* (Serial No. 255), 63 (4): i–vi, 1–143.

Castles, A. and Coltheart, M. (1993) 'Varieties of developmental dyslexia', *Cognition*, 47 (2): 149–80.

Chomsky, N. (1957) *Syntactic Structures*. The Hague: Mouton.

Chomsky, N. (1965) *Aspects of the Theory of Syntax*. Cambridge, MA: MIT Press.

Clark, E.V. (1973) 'Non-linguistic strategies and the acquisition of word meanings', *Cognition*, 2 (2): 161–82.

Cummins, J. (1991) 'Interdependence of first and second language proficiency in bilingual children', in E. Bialystok (ed.), *Language Processing in Bilingual Children*. Cambridge: Cambridge University Press. pp. 70–89.

DeCasper, A.J. and Fifer, W.P. (1980) 'Of human bonding: Newborns prefer their mothers' voices', *Science*, 208 (4448): 1174–6.

DeCasper, A.J. and Spence, M.J. (1986) 'Prenatal maternal speech influences newborns' perception of speech sounds', *Infant Behavior and Development*, 9 (2): 133–50.

Demorest, A., Silberstein, L., Gardner, H. and Winner, E. (1983) 'Telling it as it isn't: Children's understanding of figurative language', *British Journal of Developmental Psychology*, 1 (2): 121–34.

Denes, P.B. and Pinson, E.N. (1963) *The Speech Chain*. Murray Hill, NJ: Bell Telephone Laboratories.

de Villiers, P.A. and de Villiers, J.G. (1979) *Early Language*. Cambridge, MA: Harvard University Press.

de Villiers, P.A. and de Villiers, J.G. (1992) 'Language development', in M. Bornstein and M. Lamb (eds), *Developmental Psychology: An Advanced Textbook* (3rd edn). Hillsdale NJ: Erlbaum. pp. 337–418.

Dore, J. (1979) 'Conversation and preschool language development', in L.B. Cohen and M. Gorman (eds), *Language Acquisition*. Cambridge: Cambridge University Press. pp. 337–62.

Dromi, E. (1987) *Early Lexical Development*. Cambridge: Cambridge University Press.

Ehri, L.C. (1991) 'Development of the ability to read words', in R. Barr, M. Kamil, P. Mosenthal and P. Pearson (eds), *Handbook of Reading Research*, Volume II. New York: Longman. pp. 383–417.

Ehri, L.C. (1995) 'Phases of development in learning to read words by sight', *Journal of Research in Reading*, 18 (2): 116–25.

Ehri, L.C. (2003) 'Phases of acquisition in learning to read words and implications for teaching', in R. Stainthorp and P. Tomlinson (eds), *Learning and Teaching Reading*, British Journal of Educational Psychology Monograph Series II. Leicester: British Psychological Society. pp. 7–28.

Ehri, L.C. and Wilce, L. (1985) 'Movement into reading: Is the first stage of printed word learning visual or phonetic?', *Reading Research Quarterly*, 20 (2): 163–79.

Ehri, L.C. and Wilce, L. (1987) 'Cipher versus cue reading: An experiment in decoding acquisition', *Journal of Educational Psychology*, 79 (1): 3–13.

Eimas, P.D. (1975) 'Speech perception in early infancy', in L.B Cohen and P. Salapatek (eds), *Infant Perception: From Sensation to Cognition*. Orlando, FL: Academic Press. pp. 193–231.

Elliot, A.J. (1981) *Child Language*. Cambridge: Cambridge University Press.

Ervin-Tripp, S.M. (1979) 'Children's verbal turn-taking', in E. Ochs and B.B. Schiefflin (eds), *Developmental Pragmatics*. New York: Academic Press. pp. 391–414.

Fernald, A. (1985) 'Four-month-old infants prefer to listen to motherese', *Infant Behavior and Development*, 8 (2): 181–95.

Flavell, J.H., Miller, P.H. and Miller, S.A. (1993) *Cognitive Development*. Englewood Cliffs, NJ: Prentice Hall.

Frith, U. (1985) 'Beneath the surface of developmental dyslexia', in K. Patterson, M. Coltheart and J. Marshall (eds), *Surface Dyslexia*. Hove: Lawrence Erlbaum. pp. 301–330.

Gathercole, S.E. and Baddeley, A.D. (1993) *Working Memory and Language*. Hove:Erlbaum.

Gleitman, L.R. (1990) 'The structural sources of word meanings', *Language Acquisition*, 1 (1): 3–55.

Goswami, U. (1986) 'Children's use of analogy in learning to read: A developmental study', *Journal of Experimental Child Psychology*, 42 (1): 73–83.

Goswami, U. and Bryant P.E. (1990) *Phonological Skills and Learning to Read*. Hove: Lawrence Erlbaum.

Gough, P., Juel, C. and Roper-Schneider, D. (1983) 'Code and cipher: A two-stage conception of initial reading acquisition', in J.A. Niles and L.A. Harris (eds), *Searches for Meaning in Reading/Language Processing and Instruction*. Rochester, NY: National Reading Conference. pp. 207–11.

Grant, J., Karmiloff-Smith, A., Gathercole, S.A., Paterson, S., Howlin, P., Davies, M. and Udwin, O. (1997) 'Phonological short-term memory and its relationship to language in Williams syndrome', *Cognitive Neuropsychiatry*, 2 (2): 81–99.

Hakuta, K. (1999) 'The debate on bilingual education', *Journal of Developmental and Behavioral Pediatrics*, 20 (1): 36–7.

Hakuta, K. and Diaz, R. (1985) 'The relationship between degree of bilingualism and cognitive ability: A critical discussion and some new longitudinal data', in K.E. Nelson (ed), *Children's Language* (Vol. 5). Hillsdale, NJ: Erlbaum. pp. 319–44.

Hakuta, K., Bialystok, E. and Wiley, E. (2003) 'Critical evidence: A test of the critical-period hypothesis for second-language acquisition', *Psychological Science*, 14 (1): 31–8.

Harley, T. (2001) *The Psychology of Language: From Data to Theory*. Hove: Psychology Press.

Hill, B.P. and Singer, L.T. (1990) 'Speech and language development after infant tracheostomy', *Journal of Speech and Hearing Disorders,* 55 (1): 15–20.

Hoff-Ginsberg, E. (1997) *Language Development*. Pacific Grove, CA: Brooks/Cole.

Horgan, D. (1978) 'The development of the full passive', *Journal of Child Language*, 5 (1): 65–80.

Hurst, J.A., Baraitser, M., Auger, E., Graham, F. and Norell, S. (1990) 'An extended family with a dominantly inherited speech disorder', *Developmental Medicine and Child Neurology*, 32 (4): 352–5.

Johnson, J.S. and Newport, E.L. (1989) 'Critical period effects in second language learning: The influence of maturational state on the acquisition of English as a second language', *Cognitive Psychology*, 21 (1): 60–99.

Johnson, R.S., Anderson, M. and Holligan, C. (1996) 'Knowledge of the alphabet and explicit awareness of phonemes in prer-readers: The nature of the relationship', *Reading and Writing*, 8 (3): 217–34.

Jorm, A. (1983) 'Specific reading retardation and working memory: A review', *British Journal of Psychology*, 74 (3): 311–42.

Juel, C. (1983) 'The development and use of mediated word identification', *Reading Research Quarterly*, 18 (3): 306–27.

Keenan, T. and Evans, S. (2009). *An Introduction to Child Development*. London: Sage.

Keenan, T. and Quigley, K. (1999) 'Do young children use echoic information in their comprehension of sarcastic speech? A test of echoic mention theory', *British Journal of Developmental Psychology*, 17 (1): 83–96.

Laws, G. and Bishop, D.V.M. (2003) 'A comparison of language abilities in adolescents with Down syndrome and children with specific language impairment', *Journal of Speech, Language, and Hearing Research*, 46 (6): 1324–39.

Lenneberg, E., Rebelsky, F.G. and Nichols, I.A. (1965) 'The vocalizations of infants born to deaf and to hearing parents', *Human Development*, 8 (1): 23–37.

Leonard, L.B. (2009) 'Some reflections on the study of children with specific language impairment', *Child Language Teaching and Therapy*, 25 (2): 169–71.

McIntire, M. (1977) 'The acquisition of American Sign Language hand configurations', *Sign Language Studies*, 16: 247–66.

Maclean, M., Bryant, P.E. and Bradley, L. (1987) 'Rhymes, nursery rhymes, and reading in early childhood', *Merrill-Palmer Quarterly*, 33 (3): 255–82.

Malloch, S. (1999) 'Mothers and infants and communicative musicality', *Musicae Scientiae* (Special Issue 1999–2000), 3 (1): 29–57.

Malloch, S. and Trevarthen, C. (2009) 'Musicality: Communicating the vital interests of life', in S. Malloch and C. Trevarthen (eds), *Communicative Musicality: Exploring the Basis of Human Companionship.* Oxford: Oxford University Press. pp. 1–11.

Markman, E.M. (1991) 'The whole-object, taxonomic, and mutual exclusivity assumptions as initial constraints on word meanings', in S.A. Gelman and J.P. Byrnes (eds), *Perspectives on Language and Thought: Interrelations in Development.* Cambridge: Cambridge University Press. pp. 72–107.

Marschark, M. (1993) *Psychological Development of Deaf Children.* New York: Oxford University Press.

Marsh, G., Friedman, M.P., Welch, V. and Desberg, P. (1980) 'A cognitive developmental approach to reading acquisition', in G.E. MacKinnon and T.G. Waller (eds), *Reading Research: Advances in Theory and Practice* (Vol. 3). New York: Academic Press. pp. 199–221.

Mason, J. (1980) 'When do children begin to read: An exploration of four year old children's letter and word reading competencies', *Reading Research Quarterly*, 15 (2): 203–27.

Meier, R.P. and Newport, E.L. (1990) 'Out of the hands of babes: On a possible sign advantage in language acquisition', *Language*, 66 (1): 1–23.

Meisel, J.M. (2008) 'The bilingual child', in T.K. Bhatia and W.C. Ritchie (eds), *The Handbook of Bilingualism.* Oxford: Blackwell. pp. 90–103.

Muter, V., Hulme, C., Snowling, M. and Taylor, S. (1998) 'Segmentation, not rhyming, predicts early progress in learning to read', *Journal of Experimental Child Psychology*, 71 (1): 3–27.

Muter, V., Hulme, C., Snowling, M.J. and Stevenson, J. (2004) 'Phoneme, rimes, vocabulary, and grammatical skills as foundations of early reading development: Evidence from a longitudinal study', *Developmental Psychology*, 40 (5): 665–81.

Nelson, K. (1973) 'Structure and strategy in learning to talk', *Monographs of the Society for Research in Child Development* (Serial No. 149), 38: (1–2): 1–135.

Nelson, K. (1981) 'Individual differences in language development: Implications for development and language', *Developmental Psychology*, 17 (2): 170–87.

Newport, E.L. (1991) 'Contrasting conceptions of the of the critical period for language', in S. Carey and R. Gelman (eds), *The Epigenesis of Mind: Essays on Biology and Cognition.* Hillsdale, NJ: Erlbaum. pp. 111–30.

Orlansky, M.D. and Bonvillian, J.D. (1985) 'Sign language acquisition: Language development in children of deaf parents and implications for other populations', *Merrill-Palmer Quarterly*, 31 (2): 127–43.

Overy, K. (2000) 'Dyslexia, temporal processing and music: The potential of music as an early learning aid for dyslexic children', *Psychology of Music*, 28 (2): 218–29.

Pan, B.A. and Snow, C.E. (1999) 'The development of conversation and discourse skills', in M. Barrett (ed.), *The Development of Language.* Hove: Psychology Press. pp. 229–49.

Perrachione, T.K., Del Tufo, S.N. and Gabrieli, J.D.E. (2011) 'Human voice recognition depends on language ability', *Science*, 333 (6042): 595.

Petitto, L.A., Holowka, S., Sergio, L.E., Levy, B. and Ostry, D.J. (2004) 'Baby hands that move to the rhythm of language: Hearing babies acquiring sign languages babble silently on the hands', *Cognition*, 93 (1): 43–73.

Piaget, J. (1967) *Six Psychological Studies.* New York: Vintage.

Pinker, S. (2007) *The Stuff of Thought: Language as a Window into Human Nature.* New York: Viking Penguin.

Rescorla, L.A. (1980) 'Overextension in early language development', *Journal of Child Language*, 7 (2): 321–335.

Ricciardelli, L.A. (1992) 'Creativity and bilingualism', *The Journal of Creative Behavior*, 26 (4): 242–54.

Shatz, M. and Gelman, R. (1973) 'The development of communication skills: Modifications in the speech of young children as a function of listener', *Monographs of the Society for Research in Child Development* (Serial No. 152), 38 (5): 1–38.

Shaywitz, S.E. (1998) 'Dyslexia', *New England Journal of Medicine*, 338 (5): 307–12.

Silvén, M. (2001) 'Attention in very young infants predicts learning of first words', *Infant Behavior and Development*, 24 (2): 229–37.

Singleton, J.L. and Newport, E.L. (2004) 'When learners surpass their models: The acquisition of American Sign Language from inconsistent input', *Cognitive Psychology*, 49 (4): 370–407.

Skinner, B.F. (1957) *Verbal Behaviour*. New York: Appleton-Century-Crofts.

Slobin, D.I. (1973) 'Cognitive prerequisites for the development of grammar', in C.A. Ferguson and D.I Slobin (eds), *Studies in Child Language Development*. New York: Holt Rinehart. pp. 175–208.

Smith, P.K. (1997) 'Play fighting and real fighting' in A, Schmitt, K.Atzwanger, Grammer, K. and K. Schäfer (eds), *New Aspects of Human Ethology*. New York: Plenum Press. pp. 47–64.

Smith, P.K. and Whitney, S. (1987) 'Play and associative fluency: Experimenter effects may be responsible for previous positive findings', *Developmental Psychology*, 23 (1): 49–53.

Snow, C.E. (1993) 'Bilingualism and second language acquisition: Research findings and folk psychology', in K. Bailey, M. Long and S. Peck (eds), *Psycholinguistics*. Fort Worth: Harcourt Brace Jovanovich. pp. 391–416.

Snowling, M.J. (2000) *Dyslexia* (2nd edn). Oxford: Blackwell.

Stanovich, K.E., Cunningham, A.E. and Cramer, B.B. (1984) 'Assessing phonological awareness in kindergarten children: Issues of task comparability', *Journal of Experimental Child Psychology*, 38 (2): 175–90.

Thompson, J.R. and Chapman, R.S. (1977) 'Who is "Daddy" revisited: The status of two-year-olds' overextended words in use and comprehension', *Journal of Child Language*, 4(3): 359–75.

Treiman, R., Goswami, U. and Bruck, M. (1990) 'Not all nonwords are alike: Implications for reading development and theory', *Memory and Cognition*, 18 (6): 559–67.

Trevarthen, A. (1974) 'The psychobiology of speech development', in E.H. Lenneberg (ed.), *Language and Brain: Developmental Aspects. Neuroscience Research Program Bulletin No. 12*. Boston, MA: Neuroscience Research Program. pp. 570–85.

van der Lely, H.K. and Ullman, M.T. (2001) 'Past tense morphology in specifically language impaired and normally developing children', *Language and Cognitive Processes*, 16 (2–3): 177–217.

Wagner, R.K., Torgesen, J.K. and Rashotte, C.A. (1994) 'Development of reading-related phonological processing abilities: New evidence of bidirectional causality from a latent variable longitudinal study', *Developmental Psychology*, 30 (1): 73–87.

Wilding, J. (1989) 'Developmental dyslexics do not fit in boxes: Evidence from the case studies', *European Journal of Cognitive Psychology*, 1 (2): 105–27.

Yamada, J.E. (1990) *Laura: A Case for the Modularity of Language*. Cambridge, MA: MIT Press.

The Role of Play

 Why you should read this chapter

Play is for many people an essential feature of what it means to be a child and indeed the opportunity to play is regarded as a basic human right for all children. Article 31 of the United Nations Convention on the Rights of the Child states that *'every child has the right to relax, play and take part in a wide range of cultural and artistic activities'* (UNICEF UK, 2013: 1). Play is central to many areas of work with children and young people and there are a number of occupations where play has a central role. These include playwork, which involves the provision of play opportunities for young children, and the work of hospital play specialists who use play methods to help children cope with hospitalisation and medical treatment. It is also given a prominent role in the early years school curricula in England and Wales. Play is therefore not just something enjoyed by children, but also something highly valued by adults who consider it to have enormous developmental potential for children. An understanding of play is therefore essential in any account of child development and this chapter will look at issues such as the nature of play and its role in development, education and therapy.

By the end of this chapter you should

- be aware of the different types of play and their development
- understand the different approaches to defining play
- have a basic knowledge of theories of play
- be able to evaluate the evidence for the role of play in development
- understand the practical issues relating to the educational use of play, particularly in relation to children's perceptions of play and the implementation of play activities in the classroom
- have a basic awareness of the use of play in therapy.

Types of play

Many different activities can count as play. Smith et al. (2011) list a number of different types including **physical play**, **rough-and-tumble play**, **play with objects** and **fantasy play**.

Physical play, as the term implies is physical activity, often without the use of objects, and babies and children engage in these activities because they are enjoyable. Pellegrini and Smith (1998) have proposed that this type of play follows three stages of development. Initially, infants engage in **rhythmical stereotypes,** which are bodily movements such as kicking legs, waving arms or body rocking (Thelen, 1980). This is followed during the preschool years by **exercise play**, whole body movements such as running, jumping and climbing. These activities can be performed alone or with others. This type of play also overlaps and is ultimately succeeded by rough-and-tumble play, which becomes most common during the middle school years. Pellegrini (2011) has noted that babies and children spend much time engaging in these behaviours, with 6-month-old infants spending up to half of their time playfully moving. It is generally accepted that play in children up to the age of 8 involves a significant amount of physical activity (Brown, 2003; Hughes, 2010). Pellegrini (2011) notes that this type of play tends to decline during the primary school years, however, he points out that the notion of a peak in such behaviours in early childhood may not be correct and further research is needed to determine when this peak occurs.

Rough-and-tumble play, as mentioned above, becomes common in the school years and consists of activities such as play fighting and chasing. Smith et al. (2011) suggest that the origins of this type of play may lie in the types of vigorous physical play interactions that take place between toddlers and parents, such as tickling, throwing and the toddler crawling after them. Actual play fighting between children is apparent from the age of 3 onwards. Rough-and-tumble play can be distinguished from other forms of physical play by its social nature (other forms of physical play can be a social or a solitary activity) and by the presence of mock aggression (Hughes, 2010). The friendly, non-aggressive intent in rough-and-tumble play is signalled by smiling and laughter and children can differentiate between real and play fighting (Costabile et al., 1991). Occasionally play fights can turn into real fights, particularly in the case of sociometrically 'rejected' children (see Chapter 8) who misinterpret and respond inappropriately to the usual play signals (Pellegrini, 1988). Smith (1997) has suggested that teachers often over-estimate the tendency of play fighting to become real fighting but this perception is probably based on the small number of aggressive children for whom this is the case. Engaging in rough-and-tumble play does not appear to be linked with greater aggression in later life (Humphreys and Smith, 1984).

Play with objects becomes apparent from the age of around 5 months. Hughes (2010) describes the development of object play. Initially, infants will engage with objects in an exploratory manner, such as feeling them or putting them in their mouth. Gradually, however, infants become less interested in the objects themselves but more in what can be done with them, such as banging them or shaking them to make a noise. This marks the beginnings of usinge objects in a playful manner, a form of play that Piaget (1951) referred to as 'practice play'. From the age of 2 onwards, a number of developments are apparent in play with objects. Toddlers will start to play with two or more objects at the same time and they will also combine objects in play, such as putting beads in a cup or building a tower of two blocks. There is also evidence of wanting to use objects appropriately – a realisation that objects have functions, such as a ball is to be thrown or blocks can be stacked, and this makes objects more interest-ing. A similar progression in the development of object play was also noted by Rosenblatt (1977, cited by Casby, 2003). Initially infants aged 9–12 months engaged in actions such as touching, holding and banging single objects. Between 12–15 months, they engaged in non-conventional coordination of objects (such as hitting toys together). At 15 months, they began using single toys in a conventional manner, such as talking on a toy telephone. At 24 months they began to coordinate the use of two objects (such as brushing a doll's hair), they could represent an absent object (such as putting an imaginary hat on a doll) and use one realistic object as a substitute for another (such as using a block as a car). These latter changes represent the use of objects in fantasy play which will be considered next.

Fantasy play appears from about 12–15 months of age, and marks the beginning of the use of play to represent reality. Fantasy play can be a solitary activity or can involve playing with others, wherein it is referred to as **sociodramatic play**. Piaget (1951) noted incidences of fantasy play in observations of his own daughter at 1 year of age in which she would pick up a piece of cloth, pretend it was her pillow, and lie down with it and pretend that she was sleeping. In general, the earliest acts of this form of play are make-believe acts directed towards the self (Piaget, 1951) and include acting out everyday rituals, such as pretending to eat or go to sleep. The frequency of fantasy play increases markedly from its first appearance (Rubin et al.,

1983), and seems to develop in a distinct pattern consisting of three elements: **decentration, decontextualisation** and **integration** (McCune-Nicholich and Fenson, 1984). A description of these three elements of fantasy play and their development is provided by Hughes (2010). Decentration refers to the incorporation of others into pretend activities, and these others can be parents or objects such as stuffed toys and dolls. Make-believe actions are not directed only towards the self, they can also be directed to others, for example pretending to feed a doll. By the end of the second year, a further development in decentration is noted: dolls or cuddly toys are not just the recipients of pretend actions, they can also become the initiators of actions. Decontextualisation refers to the ability to use one object to represent another, such as pretending a block is a cake or using a stick as a sword. Early in fantasy play, children rely on real objects or realistic substitutes, such as pretending a cloth is a blanket (the cloth is not a blanket but there is some resemblance, making it a realistic substitute). If an object is an unrealistic substitute, children have difficulty using it in a pretend manner, although adults can help by modelling the use of a substitute. By the age of 3, however, children are able to use substitute objects in a manner removed from reality, such as pretending a ball is a comb and going through the motions of pretending to comb their hair with this object. Also, from this age play can involve imaginary objects and actions without the presence of real or substitute objects, although this ability is greater in older children. Overton and Jackson (1973) asked children aged 3–8 to pretend to brush their teeth or comb their hair and found that while most 3- and 4-year-olds used a body part such as a finger as a toothbrush or comb, children aged 6–8 would perform the action by imagining the toothbrush or comb in their hand. Integration refers to the increasing tendency of symbolic play to become organised into patterns. During the first two years of life, children will tend to drift from one activity to another with little connection between them. However, at around 18 months of age children begin to pair up related activities, such as making a teddy bear climb to the top of a tower of blocks and jumping off, and the tendency to engage in these behaviours will increase so that by the age of 2 play involving several actions linked by a single theme are evident.

Smith et al. (2011) have also identified other types of play that have been the focus of research including language play, war toys and war play, video and computer games, and **games with rules**. Overall it is clear that the term 'play' can encompass a wide variety of solitary and social activities.

We have seen that there are many different types of play. The next section will look at attempts to define play; however, before reading this section, try to think about how you would define play. What do you think are the main features of a behaviour or activity that you would consider as play? In what ways would play be different from other activities?

Defining play

Given that there are so many activities that can be regarded as play, are there any defining characteristics that differentiate any form of play from other, non-play activities? Various researchers have suggested ways in which play might be characterised. These approaches are summarised in Table 10.1.

Before going on to look at how play can be characterised, it is important to differentiate play from another behaviour that is sometimes confused with it: **exploration**. The distinction between exploration and play was made by Hutt (1966, 1976) based on observations of young children when presented with a novel object. Initially the children were completely focused on the object, examining its features and wearing a serious facial expression. After a while, however, the children became more relaxed in their behaviour. The initial behaviours toward the object were termed by Hutt as exploration and the later behaviours she called play. Essentially, the children moved from asking '*"what does this object do" to "what can I do with this object"*' (Hutt, 1976: 211). These two types of behaviour could also be distinguished physiologically by heart rate: the children presenting with a variable heart rate during exploration and a calm heart rate during play (Hutt et al., 1989). The distinction between play and exploration is important, and as we will see later in this chapter, particularly in setting up experimental studies on the effects of play.

One approach to characterising play is to specify behaviours that only occur in play, behaviours referred to as **play signals** (Andrews, 2012; Smith et al., 2011). The main signal that we see in children is what has been termed the **play face**, a broad, open-mouth smile, often accompanied by laughter. This expression can be used to invite another to join in play and is also useful during rough-and-tumble play, indicating no aggressive or malicious intent.

Table 10.1   Approaches to defining play

Approach	Definition of play
Play signals	Identify behaviours that only occur in play such as the 'play face'
Play signs	Behaviours that can occur in other contexts but in play they are • repeated • exaggerated • re-ordered • fragmented
Play criteria	For a behaviour to be classed as play, one or more of the following should be present: • intrinsic motivation • free-choice • positive affect • non-literality • active engagement

Not all play will be indicated by play signals and other **play signs** have been proposed. Andrews (2012) and Smith et al. (2011) have pointed out that play can also include behaviours that occur in other contexts, such as running, jumping or manipulating objects. However, when such behaviours are being done in a playful manner they are usually *repeated, exaggerated re-ordered* or *fragmented*. Andrews (2012) and Smith et al. (2011) give the example of a child running up a slope. On its own, this behaviour appears to be being carried out with a purpose. However, if the behaviour is repeated (the child runs up and down the slope several times), exaggerated (the child takes giant steps or jumps), runs just halfway up (fragmentation) or crawls up and then runs down (re-ordering), then we are more likely to agree that the behaviour is indeed play.

Another approach is to identify **play criteria**. Here, play is identified on the basis of one or more specified elements being present. Krasnor and Pepler (1980) proposed such a model of play comprising four elements. Firstly, play should be **intrinsically motivated**, be an end in itself, done purely for the satisfaction of doing it; secondly, the activity should be pleasurable to the child, in other words children should show **positive affect** during their play; thirdly, the behaviour should also show signs of **flexibility** (rules determined by players and not outsiders); and finally, play should be **non-literal**, in other words show an element of 'pretend' or 'make-believe'. It is not necessary for all elements to be present for behaviour to be regarded as play, but the more that are present, the more likely we are to agree that it is play. Rubin et al. (1983) also list these criteria and add **free-choice** (the child has freely chosen to engage in an activity) and **active engagement** (the child must be involved physically and/or psychologically, rather than passively observing the activity). Smith and Vollstedt (1985) tested this notion of play by asking adults to view a video of nursery children at play and asking them to rate specific episodes from the video as playful or not playful. Typically, episodes rated as playful were those in which positive affect, flexibility and **non-literality** were present, and at least two of these criteria had to be present for a judgement of play to be made. However, the intrinsic motivation criterion was not present as a distinguishing feature of play. This could be due to the fact that it is difficult to judge intrinsic motivation from observing behaviour alone. Nevertheless, intrinsic motivation is still regarded as a key characteristic of play, and has also been proposed as a distinguishing criterion by other researchers (see for example Neuman, 1971; Skard and Budy, 2008). Also the point can be made that while some play behaviours are responses to external demands, as in social play, the motivation to engage in the playful situation is itself intrinsic and therefore, a child engaging in a social play activity is intrinsically motivated (McInnes, 2010).

The play criterion approach has the benefit of not trying to attempt a single definition of play and acknowledges that there is a continuum from playful to non-playful behaviour, with pure play being characterised by the presence of all of the criteria. Overall, the view that play is characterised by enjoyment, flexibility and pretence has some support (Saracho and Spodek, 1998). However, it cannot apply to all types of play – for example not all play involves pretence.

It can be seen that there are a number of useful ways to characterise play; but one point needs to be noted about all of these: they are very much based on adult observation of children at play. The views of children themselves as to what is play and what is not are not taken into account. As will be seen later in the chapter when looking at the role of play in education, children's views of play are essential if play is to be used effectively in this setting.

Theories of play

The issue of why children play and its role in development has been considered by many theorists over the years. Early theories stressed the biological significance of play, seeing it as the expression of primitive instincts and promoting physical development. Play has also been considered in terms of its contribution to emotional, cognitive and intellectual development.

Surplus energy theory (Spencer, 1873) saw play as necessary for the discharge of pent-up energy. It argued that nature equips humans with energy which is used in the process of survival and any energy that has not been consumed in this process needs to be released somehow; and in children, this release comes about through play. An opposite point of view was expressed by Patrick (1916) who argued that the purpose of play was the renewal of energy. His basic argument was that play helped children relax when energy levels were low and helped them to avoid boredom while they waited for their natural energy levels to be restored. Hall (1883) saw play as having a cathartic function. His **recapitulation theory** saw development as reflecting the evolutionary history of the human species, and children's play was essentially acting out this history, for example an infant crawling reflected a point in human evolution when humans walked on all fours. Thus play allowed children to play out instincts left over from our evolutionary history. This theory has little support among modern developmental psychologists (Hughes, 2010; Smith et al., 2011). Groos (1901) suggested that play provided the opportunity for the child to exercise and prepare for the tasks of adult life. As can be seen from the previous section children's play activities can involve acting out everyday rituals, and certainly some of the ideas of Groos are at least implicitly reflected in some modern day views of play.

Psychoanalytic theorists such as Anna Freud (1974) see play as cathartic in nature allowing children to explore socially unacceptable feelings and impulses in a safe context, thus reducing the anxiety caused by these. Freud also saw the relevance of this quality of play for its use as a therapeutic tool and began using it in her work with children leading to the establishment of **play therapy** which will be considered later in this chapter.

Piaget (1951) outlined a theory of play in relation to intellectual development. He proposed that play develops through three stages. **Practice play** (from 0–2 years of age) involves mostly repeating physical activity. This is followed by **symbolic play** (from approximately 2–7 years) and marks the beginning of make-believe play. From about the age of 7 onwards, children engage in games with rules: these require the participation of at least two children and can include board games or games in which the children invent their own rules. If you recall from Chapter 4, Piaget outlined two processes contributing to intellectual development: *assimilation* and *accommodation*. In Piaget's view, play was assimilative, it did not facilitate new learning (which occurs through accommodation) but rather allowed children to practise already established skills by repeated execution of known schemas.

Vygotsky (1976) also saw an important role for play in intellectual development but emphasised the importance of pretend play (see Chapter 5). Bruner (1972, 1974) argued that play allowed the practise of new skills and an opportunity for what he called **combinatorial flexibility**, the ability to try out new combinations of behaviours in a safe context. In this way children can acquire new behaviours that can be used in other, less safe contexts.

Berlyne (1969) proposed an **arousal-modulation theory of play**. The basic notion here is that there is an optimal level of basic activity or arousal in the central nervous system and the individual acts in such a way as to maintain this level. The ideal environment therefore should not contain too much or too little stimulation. When an individual is faced with an unfamiliar or confusing environment, the resulting confusion and uncertainty leads to elevated levels of arousal and exploration of the environment is needed to reduce this uncertainty. On the other hand, in an environment where there is insufficient stimulation, this causes lower levels of arousal in the nervous system and the individual will act in such a way as to increase these levels. It is argued that in children play fulfils this role.

Play and development

Smith (2010) has identified three models for the importance of play in development. The first is that play has no role in development; it is just a by-product of the development of other abilities. The second is that play is one of a number of ways in which a child can learn and acquire skills; children can also learn through experiences such as observation, trial and error, and instruction. The third model is that play is essential for many aspects of development in the preschool years and beyond. Smith suggests that it is the third view that is most widely held, a view he terms the **play ethos**.

In terms of providing evidence for the role of play in development, Smith et al. (2011) identify three approaches. The first is to look at what goes on during play to form hypotheses about how this might facilitate development. The second is the use of correlational designs which examine the relationship between levels of play types and developmental outcomes. Finally, there are experimental studies where play experiences are varied or compared against other types of experience or a control group with regard to performance on a measure of development.

The suggestion has been made that pretend play is important for theory of mind development. In pretend play, and in particular in sociodramatic play, children have to take on roles and negotiate roles with other children. They know there is a difference between their own thoughts and feelings and the thoughts and feelings of their character, and the same applies to other children. Hence it is argued that pretend play can develop this ability and enhance a child's social development (Hughes, 2010). Youngblade and Dunn (1995) conducted a study in which they took measures of children's pretend play at 33 months of age and their theory of mind performance at 40 months of age and found significant correlations between the two sets of measures. However Smith (2010) has pointed out that the correlations obtained were small and this is a feature of the results of other correlational studies on this topic.

There have also been attempts to investigate this topic experimentally. Burns and Brainerd (1979) tested the role-taking ability of a number of preschool children (by asking them how each of two characters in a story would feel) and then divided them into a group that engaged in sociodramatic play, a group that engaged in constructive play (in which the children had to work together to make something) and a control group that did not engage in play. Following these interventions, the children's role-taking ability was tested again and it was found that children in the two play conditions improved in their role-taking ability compared to the control group. Dockett (1998) also investigated the effects of sociodramatic play training on theory of mind performance in a group of 4-year-old children compared to a control group. The treatment group did show enhanced post-test performance in theory of mind tests compared to the control group. The experimental studies do indicate a possible causal link between pretend play and theory of mind development; however, the results of the Burns and Brainerd study indicate that it is not just pretend play that can be linked with this ability as they also found a similar beneficial effect of constructive play. Overall, Smith (2010) has concluded that the evidence suggests that pretend play may be helpful for theory of mind, but children can also benefit from experiences other than play.

The role of play in cognitive and intellectual development has also been considered by various researchers. In particular, the role of object play has been of interest. One approach here is to look at the various objects that children play with and consider the cognitive skills they might facilitate (Hughes, 2010). An example is play with blocks. Play with blocks can vary from simple stacking to using many blocks to build complex objects (as in playing with Lego). It has been suggested that playing with blocks can help children to acquire measurement principles through using blocks as arbitrary measures (Schwartz, 2005). As block play also involves the construction of two- and three-dimensional structures, children gain a better understanding of two- and three-dimensional space as well as area and volume (Kersh et al., 2008). Play with blocks has also been linked to development of spatial skills such as visualisation and mental rotation (Caldera et al., 1999).

The issue of play and cognitive/intellectual development has also been investigated using correlational studies. Wolfgang and Stakenas (1985) correlated preschool children's use of different types of toys with performance on the McCarthy Scales of Children's Abilities, a test used to measure intelligence in children. They found that *fluid construction toys* (such as paints and clay) contributed to perceptual performance (measured by tests such as drawing and block building); *structured construction toys* (toys such as blocks that retain their structure and can be used to build something) were related to verbal skills, perceptual performance and memory skills; *microsymbolic toys* (encompassing dolls, toy cars and buildings) were linked to memory skills; and *macrosymbolic toys* (child-size play equipment such as props for dramatic play) were related to perceptual performance, memory and quantitative skills.

 Think of some other toys that young children play with and consider some skills that might be developed through playing with these toys.

Positive correlations have also been found between other aspects of play and cognitive development. Johnson et al. (1982) observed 4-year-old children at play and then gave them cognitive and intelligence tests. They found that constructive play was significantly and positively correlated with intelligence scores. However, no correlation was found between sociodramatic play and intelligence. It has, however, been suggested that imaginative play is related to creativity. Russ et al. (1999) conducted a longitudinal study in which they obtained measures of pretend play in children aged 4 and 5 years of age, and found that the quality and amount of fantasy in early play were predictive of performance in a number of tests of creative thinking four years later. These correlations were independent of intelligence.

Various experimental studies have been conducted to look at the role of play in intellectual and cognitive development. Sylva et al. (1976) looked at problem solving in 3-5-year-olds, using a **lure retrieval task**. This is a task where children are presented with an out-of-reach toy and several sticks and clamps. The sticks can be joined up to create a rake to retrieve the toy. The children were randomly allocated to a 'play' group that was allowed to play with the sticks and clamps, or an observer group that watched the experimenter join the sticks and clamps together, or a no-treatment control group that neither played with nor observed the clamps and sticks. Children were then tested on the lure retrieval task and were also observed as they tried to solve the problem. Sylva et al. found that the play and observe groups were better at solving the problem than the control group and that the playgroup was also more persistent in its attempts to solve the problem. Lure retrieval tasks were also used by Smith and Dutton (1979) who found superior performance in groups that had been exposed to a play condition compared to training and no-treatment groups. However, a similar study by Simon and Smith (1983) found no difference in performance between a play and a training group.

Lure retrieval tasks belong to a class of tasks referred to as **convergent tasks** – there is a single, definite solution. Other experimental studies on play have used

divergent tasks, where there are multiple solutions. Typically, these use tests of 'associational fluency' in which children are presented with an everyday object and asked to think of as many possible uses (standard and non-standard). These types of task have been used to investigate if play facilitates learning and creativity. Again, the typical study here involves children being allowed to play with the objects and compared either with children who complete a different type of task (such as observation) or with a control group. After each treatment, the children are then asked to list as many possible uses for the objects that they can think of. Such studies have been carried out by Dansky and Silverman (1973, 1975), Li (1978) and Pepler and Ross (1981). In general, it has been found that children who were allowed to play with the objects suggested more non-standard uses for them than control or other treatment groups. Dansky and Silverman (1973, 1975) argue that play can engender a 'playful mindset' which facilitates subsequent problem solving.

The studies above are certainly suggestive of a role for play in development, but a number of points need to be borne in mind before making any definite conclusions. Firstly, correlational studies merely indicate that a relation between play and development is present, but they do not allow definite causal connections to be made. If sociodramatic play is correlated with theory of mind performance is it that this form of play facilitates theory of mind or is it that having a theory of mind facilitates engagement in this type of play behaviour? If certain types of object play are related to cognitive skills, do they facilitate cognitive development, or is it that children with certain cognitive skills are drawn to certain types of object play? The results from the experimental studies would, at face value, provide more convincing evidence of causal relations between play and development; however, subsequent reviews of these studies have highlighted a number of methodological flaws (see for example Rubin et al., 1983; Smith and Simon, 1984). In some experiments (such as Sylva et al., 1976), children were not allowed to play with the objects before allocation to groups and hence the point has been made that play in these studies has been confounded with exploration. For this reason the researchers may not have achieved the intended comparison between groups that were allowed to play and groups that were not. Smith and Simon (1984) have also argued that experimental studies of play are beset by experimenter effects such as a lack of double-blind testing procedures, allowing the possibility of unconscious experimenter bias (the manner in which the experimenter interacts with the children may influence performance over and above the experimental treatment). Other problems include a lack of adequate control groups, and general concerns over the ecological validity of the experimental approach (the extent to which such studies can capture the real-life benefits of play). Issues of experimenter and scoring bias have also been identified in experiments using divergent problem-solving tasks (Smith and Simon, 1984). Moreover, in studies using problem-solving tasks, instances have been found where children perform as effectively in non-play conditions (Simon and Smith, 1983; Sylva et al., 1976), again indicating that while play might be useful for development, it is not essential.

Overall, Smith (2010) has suggested that the available evidence does not support the play ethos, and while play can be helpful, children can also learn through other experiences, such as observation and instruction, and through the general effects of socialisation.

Play as an educational tool

In general, the evidence for the role of play in development is mixed. Nevertheless, play is highly valued in early years education, and indeed it can be argued that the play ethos is prevalent here. The notion that play is educationally useful has a long history and can be seen in the educational approaches of Froebel (1906) whose views were influential in the development of the kindergarten and nursery school movement. Froebel took the view that play originated within the child but could be channelled towards learning through adult guidance and provision of appropriate materials. Another early advocate of play in education was Maria Montessori who emphasised the use of constructive play materials and colour and shape matching as a means of promoting learning (Smith et al., 2011).

Moyles (1989) has been a strong advocate for the role of play in education and has stressed the roles of both adult-directed and free play. Central to this is her notion of the **play spiral**. She proposes that directed play can be used to teach children knowledge and skills and that this learning can be consolidated through free play. Repeated directed and free play thus form a spiral of learning:

> *Rather like a pebble on a pond, the ripples from the exploratory free play through directed play and back to enhanced and enriched free play, allowed a spiral of learning ever outwards into wider experiences for the children and upwards into the accretion of knowledge and skills.* (Moyles, 1989: 15)

Another prominent advocate for play in education is Bruce (1991) who has emphasised the value of what she refers to as **free-flow play**. She has specified a list of 12 features that characterise play of this nature:

- using first-hand experiences
- making up rules and being in control
- symbolic representation through the use of props
- choosing to play
- rehearsing the future
- pretending
- sometimes playing alone
- playing with other children and adults
- having a personal agenda which may or may not be shared
- being deeply involved
- trying out recent learning
- coordinating ideas, feelings and relationships.

The more of these features that are present, the higher the quality of the play and the more beneficial the effects are for learning.

In the current early years curricula in the UK, play is accorded a central role. For example, we saw in Chapter 2 that the Welsh Assembly Government in its *Framework for Children's Learning for 3 to 7-Year Olds in Wales* refers to the '*serious business of "play"*'(WAG, 2012: 4) as a vehicle for learning. The centrality of play is not just a feature of early years education in the UK. In Demark, Sweden and other Nordic countries, play is given priority, and up to the age of 6 a child could spend a whole day at nursery engaging in freely chosen play with no curriculum constraints (Brooker, 2011).

Given that the research evidence linking play with developmental progress is not always replicable, lacks ecological validity or is methodologically flawed (Smith, 2010) can this emphasis on play be justified? It has also been pointed out that while early years practitioners espouse the value of play for children's development, this is not always reflected in their everyday practice, resulting in classrooms where children play by themselves and adults do not maximise the developmental potential of the children's play (Bennett et al., 1997).

An essential requirement for implementing play in a useful and productive manner in the classroom is that the activity is seen by the children as play. Earlier in this chapter, defining characteristics of play were considered and the point was made that these were based on adult observations of children at play. However, in this approach, the motives and subjective experience of the child are not accessible to the observer, and what looks like play to the adult may not feel like play to the child (Parham, 1996). One reason for approaching play from the perspective of the adult is a widely held view that young children do not distinguish between work and play (Manning and Sharp, 1977; QCA, 2000).

There have, however, been a number of studies that have attempted to elicit the child's views of play. King (1979) used interviews and observation and found that children described play activities as those that were fun, voluntary, under the control of the child and lacking the involvement of an adult. Activities were defined as work if they were compulsory with adult control and involvement. However, these activities could also be described as fun. Karrby (1989) also used interview and observation methods and found that activities defined as play involved pretence and rules set by children. These could be contrasted with non-play activities which typically were those that were taught, had a specific goal and in which the children were sitting down. These findings have also been found in studies by Robson (1993), Wing (1995) and Keating et al. (2000).

It can be argued that the above findings to a certain extent mirror the findings of studies based on adult perspectives as one can see the roles of positive affect, non-literality and flexibility. However, McInnes (2010) points out that there are limitations in studies using interviews and observations. Interviews with young children can be difficult as they require high levels of concentration on the part of the children, who have to interpret questions, recall activities and talk about them. They may also be constrained by the linguistic abilities of the children, who may find it difficult to get their meaning across and for adults to understand them. In observations, results are based on adult interpretations of behaviour. For these reasons, more recent studies of children's perceptions of play have used an alternative approach.

Alternative studies of children's perceptions of play have used an experimental methodology called the **Activity Apperception Story Procedure** or AASP (Howard, 2002; Howard et al., 2006; Parker, 2007). This is a game-like, photographic categorisation task in which children are presented with photographs of different classroom activities and asked to post each photograph into letter boxes labelled '*play*' or '*work*'. The photographs categorised as 'play' and 'work' can then be examined and features common to those categorised in each way can be identified. The photographs can depict general classroom scenes, as in the studies of Howard (2002) and Howard et al. (2006), or photographs taken from the children's own classrooms, as in the study of Parker (2007). The main advantages claimed for this approach are that it is less subjective than observation and less cognitively and linguistically demanding than interview methods. The 'game' format is also more engaging for young children.

Analyses of the results of these studies show that children do distinguish between play and non-play activities, which can be contrasted with previous views that children do not make such a distinction. Also, there appears to be a clear pattern in the nature of photographs that are categorised as 'play' and 'not play'. Photographs categorised as 'play' tended to depict activities that took place on the floor, activities which the children had chosen and activities that did not involve the direct presence of an adult.

These results suggest some environmental 'cues' – **location**, **choice** and **adult presence** – that can signal an activity as 'play' or 'not play'. The cues of location and adult presence are aspects that have not previously figured in characterisations of play based on adult observation. Why might these cues be important? The rationale underpinning this approach to defining play is based on a theory proposed by Gibson (1979) regarding how we perceive our environments. Gibson argued that we do not perceive objects as such but we perceive what he called their *affordances*, what they can provide or offer. McInnes (2010) elaborates on how this view can be extended to the play situation in which cues are seen as affordances that facilitate play. The cue of location can be seen as a physical or environmental affordance. An activity taking place at a table may constrain children, offering less opportunity to the children for movement and physical activity. The cue of choice – the voluntary nature of an activity – can be seen as social or emotional affordance. Choice is a factor in intrinsic motivation and even the illusion of choice has been shown to increase intrinsic motivation and learning (Swann and Pitman, 1977). Consequently, this cue may be seen as affording children motivation, enthusiasm and perceptions of control. Adult presence may also be seen as social or emotional affordance. It has been found that adult presence in a situation decreases children's participation and that in order to facilitate children taking part the adult needs to be emotionally present, supportive and responsive (Payler, 2007). It may be, then, that adult presence signals a lack of freedom and a sense of control.

Furthermore, it is argued that an activity that takes place on the floor, which is freely chosen (or at least perceived to be freely chosen) and has minimal adult involvement, is more likely to afford an opportunity for play and be approached by the child in a playful manner. This approach to play therefore suggests a manner in which a teacher may implement a play activity in a classroom setting.

The identification of these cues has led to experimental studies comparing children's performance in playful and formal conditions. Thomas et al. (2006) gave children aged 3–5 a jigsaw puzzle to solve and recorded the time taken to complete it. The children were then allocated to a *formal* or *playful* condition in which they were allowed to practise completing puzzles. For the formal condition, children were instructed to do the task, the task took place at a table and an adult was present. For the playful condition, children were invited to participate, the task took place on the floor and an adult was not directly present. Following these conditions, the children were given an immediate post-test in which they were timed in completing the jigsaw puzzle and this test was repeated after a week to separate learning from practise effects. The results showed that while the pre-test completion times of the formal and playful groups were not significantly different, the children in the playful practise condition completed the jigsaw in the immediate post-test significantly faster than the formal group. This improvement in performance was also observed in the delayed post-test phase. Radcliffe (2007) conducted a similar study but used a bead-threading task rather than a jigsaw puzzle. Again she found no initial differences in performance between children but following allocation to a formal or playful practise condition, formal children took significantly longer to complete the task compared to the playful group.

These two studies demonstrated superior performance in children allocated to a playful condition based on manipulation of the types of cues identified as important using the AASP. The argument is that these children were afforded freedom, control and motivation, and hence they approached the task in a more playful manner. But can we be certain that this was the reason for the difference in performance? A further study was reported by McInnes et al. (2009) which not only replicated the procedure employed by Thomas et al. (2006), but also video-recorded the children's behaviour during the procedure. In addition, to eliminate experimenter effects, they used an experimenter blind to the pre- and post-test phases of the study to conduct the delayed post-test. In terms of performance on a jigsaw task, McInnes et al. replicated the findings of the Thomas et al. study, with children in the playful practise condition performing significantly faster in the post-test and delayed test phases. However, McInnes et al. also noted that the two conditions could be differentiated in terms of the behaviour of the two groups of children. Children in the playful condition demonstrated significantly more movement than the formal group. Children in the playful group also engaged in less off-task behaviour and appeared to demonstrate more purposeful problem-solving behaviours as evidenced by behavioural sequences such as *look-rotate-correct placement, look-rotate-undo incorrect placement* or *look-rotate-pick up-not place*. Formal children engaged in more off-task behaviour and demonstrated less purposeful problem-solving sequences (for example a greater frequency of sequences such as *look-rotate-look* or *search-look-rotate*) and more perseverance with incorrect placements. McInnes (2010) also analysed the reliability of these observations and found a high level of agreement (82 per cent) between two independent observers of a sample of these recordings.

These findings have implications for educational practice as they suggest a means for practitioners to create playful environments within a classroom setting that may have beneficial implications for learning. McInnes et al. (2009) also suggest that a benefit of this approach is that practitioners do not need to view different activities as play or not play, but as activities that can be adapted to enable children to approach them playfully. Nevertheless, there are also implications for the behaviour of the teacher. In the above studies, for children to approach a task playfully there needed to be minimal involvement of the teacher and they had to be allowed to choose the activity voluntarily, conditions that will will not always apply in the real-world classroom. However, subsequent research by McInnes et al. (2010, 2011) has also indicated a crucial role for the way in which a teacher interacts with children and manages an activity that can affect whether or not children adopt a playful approach (this topic will be taken up in Chapter 11). Another drawback to the research reported here is that performance is based on a limited range of tasks (jigsaw puzzles and bead-threading tasks) and there is a need for further research on more ecologically valid tasks linked to formal areas of learning, such as language and literacy. However, this line of research does appear to be promising for future studies into the beneficial implementation of play in the early years curriculum.

 Can you think of ways in which a teacher might use the research findings above to implement a playful activity in an area of learning related to the early years curriculum?

Play therapy

Another important practical use of play is its use as a therapeutic tool. **Play therapy** aims to help children and young people suffering from a range of psychological difficulties including depression, anxiety and aggression. It is often used to help children and young people resolve difficult life experiences such as a family breakdown, abuse, trauma, grief and domestic violence. In play therapy, the relationship between a child and a therapist is regarded as paramount in helping to explore, express and make sense of complex and distressing experiences (British Association of Play Therapists, 2011).

The foundations of play therapy can be seen in the work of Freud (1928) and Klein (1932) who used play as a substitute for verbal responses in their therapeutic work with children. Another milestone in the development iof play therapy occurred when Axline (1947) developed an influential model called **non-directive play therapy** (later referred to as **Child-Centred Play Therapy**). This represents a shift away from the psychoanalytic approach of Freud and Klein towards an approach that emphasises a warm and close relationship with the child. The child is provided with a range of play materials and is allowed freedom of expression with these (within certain limits). The therapist provides a warm, accepting and safe environment in which the child takes the lead in directing the therapy sessions; in the meantime the therapist empathises with the child and reflects the child's feelings, as expressed in play back to them. In this way the therapist aims to help the child come to terms with the issues that led the child to the therapeutic intervention in the first place. Many play therapists today adopt approaches based on that of Axline.

A review by Bratton et al. (2005) of a large number of play therapy interventions indicated positive outcomes in the majority of cases, but they recognised that there is a need for more studies to compare the efficacy of play therapy against other forms of therapeutic interventions. Geidner (2008) has also pointed out that evaluations of play therapy tend to be outcome-focused rather than on the clinical and developmental processes involved. This is an important issue as it is one thing to show that play therapy leads to a positive outcome but quite another to explain the reasons for this outcome. Is it because of the specific approach of play therapy, or does it simply reflect, for example, the positive effects of spending time with a warm, caring adult, regardless of the nature of the therapy? Geidner stresses that it is important not just to demonstrate *that* play therapy is effective, but also to indicate clearly *how* play therapy is effective, and the importance of further and carefully controlled evaluations of play therapy has been recognised within the play therapy profession (Frick-Helms and Drewes, 2010).

Chapter summary

- There are many different types of play, each of which follows its own developmental course.
- Attempts to define play have focused on play signals, play signs and play criteria. These attempts to define play are all based on adult observation of children at play. Play should also be differentiated from exploration.
- A number of theories have been proposed as to why children play, but there is no universally accepted theory.
- Play is regarded by many as essential for development (the 'play ethos') but the research evidence does not support this notion. A general consensus is that play can play a role in development, but children can also benefit from other types of experience.

- Play is given a central role in the current early years curriculum in the UK but it is important to think of how play can be implemented practically in a classroom setting. In particular, it is important that an activity is seen by the child as play for an activity to be beneficial.
- Research evidence suggests that children use a variety of cues in their environment, such as the location of an activity, the role played by an adult and whether or not the activity was freely chosen. Activities on the floor, voluntarily chosen by the child and in which the adult does not play a central role are more likely to be seen as play in the context of the classroom. There is some evidence that children's learning is effective under these conditions, but more research is needed using learning tasks related to the early years curriculum.
- Play therapy involves the use of play to help children suffering from a variety of psychological problems. There is some evidence for the efficacy of this approach but there is a need for further research to compare the effectiveness of play therapy against other types of therapeutic interventions, and the reasons for any beneficial effects of play therapy.

Further reading

Andrews, M. (2012) *Exploring Play for Early Childhood Studies*. London: Sage.
A very useful book aimed at any individual using play in their work with children.

Hughes, F. (2010) *Children, Play and Development*. Los Angeles, CA: Sage.
A thorough and readable account of all aspects of play including theoretical, developmental and practical aspects of play.

Useful websites

http://www.playengland.org.uk/
http://www.playwales.org.uk/eng/
There are various organisations working to raise awareness of the importance of play in childhood and providing support to individuals who work with children. The two listed above are the websites for Play England and Play Wales.

http://www.bapt.info/
The website of the British Association of Play Therapists (BAPT), the professional body for play therapists in England, and a source of information about the nature of play therapy and training opportunities in this field.

References

Andrews, M. (2012) *Exploring Play for Early Childhood Studies*. London: Sage.

Axline, V. (1947) *Play Therapy*. New York: Ballantine Books.

Bennett, N., Wood, L. and Rogers, S. (1997) *Teaching Through Play*. Buckingham: Open University Press.

Berlyne, D.E. (1969) 'Laughter, humor and play', in G. Lindzey and E. Aronson (eds), *Handbook of Social Psychology*, Vol. 3. Reading, MA: Addison-Wesley. pp. 795–852.

Bratton, S.C., Ray, D., Rhine, T. and Jones, L. (2005) 'The efficacy of play therapy with children: A meta-analytic review of treatment outcomes', *Professional Psychology: Research and Practice*, 36 (4): 376–90.

British Association of Play Therapists (2011) *Information for Professionals*. Available at: http://www.bapt.info/professionalinfo.htm (accessed 4 March 2013).

Brooker, L. (2011) 'Taking play seriously', in S. Rogers (ed.), *Rethinking Play and Pedagogy in Early Childhood Education*. London: Routledge. pp. 152–64.

Brown, F. (2003) *Playwork: Theory and Practice*. Buckingham: Open University Press.

Bruce, T. (1991) *Time to Play in Early Childhood*. London: Hodder and Stoughton.

Bruner, J.S. (1972) 'Nature and uses of immaturity', *American Psychologist*, 27 (8): 687–708.

Bruner, J.S. (1974) 'Child's play', *New Scientist*, 62: 126–8.

Burns, S.M. and Brainerd, C.J. (1979) 'Effects of constructive and dramatic play on perspective taking in very young children', *Developmental Psychology*, 15 (5): 512–21.

Caldera, Y.M, McCulp, A.D., O'Brien, M., Truglio, R.T., Alvarez, M. and Huston, A.C. (1999) 'Children's play preferences, construction play with blocks and visual-spatial skills: Are they related?', *International Journal of Behavioral Development*, 23 (4): 855–72.

Casby, M.W. (2003) 'The development of play in infants, toddlers and young children', *Communication Disorders Quarterly*, 24 (4): 163–174.

Costabile, A., Smith, P.K., Matheson, L., Aston, J., Hunter, T. and Boulton, M. (1991) 'Cross-national comparison of how children distinguish serious and playful fighting', *Developmental Psychology*, 27 (5): 881–7.

Dansky, J.L., and Silverman, I.W. (1973) 'Effects of play on associative fluency in preschool-aged children', *Developmental Psychology*, 9 (1): 38–43.

Dansky, J.L. and Silverman, I.W (1975) 'Play: A general facilitator of associative fluency', *Developmental Psychology*, 11 (1): 104.

Dockett, S. (1998) 'Constructing understandings through play in the early years', *International Journal of Early Years Education*, 6 (1): 105–16.

Freud, A. (1928) *Introduction to the Technique of Child Analysis* (Trans. L.P. Clark). New York: Nervous and Mental Disease Publishing.

Freud, A. (1974) *The Ego and the Mechanisms of Defence*. New York: International Universities Press.

Frick-Helms, S.B. and Drewes, A.A. (2010) 'Introduction to play therapy research theme issue', *International Journal of Play Therapy*, 19 (1): 1–3.

Froebel, F. (1906) *The Education of Man*. New York: Appleton.

Geidner, J. (2008) 'Developmental science looks at play therapy', *British Journal of Play Therapy*, 4: 4–17.

Gibson, J.J. (1979) *The Ecological Approach to Visual Perception*. Boston, MA: Houghton-Mifflin.

Groos, K. (1901) *The Play of Man*. New York: Appleton.

Hall, G.S. (1883) 'The content of children's minds', *Princeton Review*, 2: 249–72.

Howard, J. (2002) 'Eliciting young children's perceptions of play, work and learning using the Activity Apperception Story Procedure', *Early Child Development and Care*, 172 (5): 489–502.

Howard, J., Jenvey, V. and Hill, C. (2006) 'Children's categorisation of play and learning based on social context', *Early Child Development and Care*, 176 (3–4): 379–93.

Hughes, B. (2001) *Evolutionary Playwork and Reflective Analytical Practice*. London: Routledge.

Hughes, F. (2010) *Children, Play and Development* (4th edn). London: Sage.

Humphreys, A.P. and Smith, P.K. (1984) 'Rough-and-tumble in preschool and playground', in P.K. Smith (ed.), *Play in Animals and Humans*. Oxford: Blackwell. pp. 241–70.

Hutt, C. (1966) 'Exploration and play in children', *Symposia of the Zoological Society of London*, 18: 61–7.

Hutt, C. (1976) 'Exploration and play in children', in J.S. Bruner, A. Jolly and K. Sylva (eds), *Play, Its Role in Development and Evolution*. Harmondsworth: Penguin. pp. 202–15.

Hutt, S.J., Tyler, S., Hutt, C. and Christopherson, H. (1989) *Play, Exploration and Learning: A Natural History of the Pre-school*. London: Routledge.

Johnson, J.E., Ershler, J. and Lawton, J.T. (1982) 'Intellective correlates of preschoolers' spontaneous play', *Journal of Genetic Psychology*, 106 (1): 115–22.

Karrby, G. (1989) 'Children's conceptions of their own play', *International Journal of Early Childhood Education*, 21 (2): 49–54.

Keating, I., Fabian, H., Jordan, P., Mavers, D. and Roberts, J. (2000) '"Well, I've not done any work today. I don't know why I came to school". Perceptions of play in the reception class', *Educational Studies*, 26 (4): 437–54.

Kersh, J., Casey, B.M. and Young, J.M. (2008) 'Research on spatial skills and block building in boys and girls: The relationship to later mathematics learning', in O.N. Saracho and B. Spodek (eds), *Contemporary Perspectives on Mathematics in Early Childhood Education*. Charlotte, NC: Information Age Publishing. pp. 233–52.

King, N.R. (1979) 'Play: The kindergartener's perspective', *The Elementary School Journal*, 80 (2): 80–7.

Klein, M. (1932) *The Psycho-analysis of Children*. London: Hogarth Press.

Krasnor, L.R. and Pepler, D.J. (1980) 'The study of children's play: Some suggested future directions', in K.H. Rubin (ed.), *New Directions for Child Development: Children's Play*, Vol. 9. San Francisco, CA: Jossey-Bass. pp. 85–95.

Li, A.K.F. (1978) 'Effects of play on novel responses in kindergarten children', *The Alberta Journal of Educational Research*, XXIV: 31–6.

McCune-Nicholich, L. and Fenson, L. (1984) 'Methodological issues in studying early pretend play', in T.D. Yawkey and A.D. Pellegrini (eds), *Child's Play: Developmental and Applied*. Hillsdale, NJ: Erlbaum. pp. 81–104.

McInnes, K.E. (2010) 'The role of playful practice for learning in the early years'. PhD thesis, University of Glamorgan.

McInnes, K., Howard, J., Miles, G. and Crowley, K. (2009) 'Behavioural differences exhibited by children when practicing a task under formal and playful conditions', *Journal of Educational and Child Psychology*, 26 (2): 31–9.

McInnes, K., Howard, J., Miles, G. and Crowley, K. (2010) 'Differences in adult-child interactions during playful and formal practice conditions: An initial investigation', *Psychology of Education Review*, 34 (1): 14–20.

McInnes, K., Howard, J., Miles, G.E., and Crowley, K. (2011) 'Differences in practitioners' understanding of play and how this influences pedagogy and children's perceptions of play', *Early Years: An International Journal of Research and Development*, 31 (2): 121–33.

Manning, K. and Sharp, A. (1977) *Structuring Play in the Early Years at School*. East Grinstead: Schools Council Publications.

Moyles, J. (1989) *Just Playing? The Role and Status of Play in Early Childhood Education*. Milton Keynes: Open University Press.

Neuman, E.A. (1971) *The Elements of Play*. New York: MSS Information Corporation.

Overton, W.F. and Jackson, J.P. (1973) 'The representation of imagined objects in action sequences: A developmental study', *Child Development*, 44 (2): 309–14.

Parham, L.D. (1996) 'Perspectives on play', in R. Zemke and F. Clark (eds), *Occupational Science: The Evolving Discipline*. Philadelphia, PA: F.A. Davis Company. pp. 71–80.

Parker, C.J. (2007) 'Children's perceptions of a playful environment: Contextual, social and environmental differences'. BSc dissertation, University of Glamorgan.

Patrick, G.T.W. (1916) *The Psychology of Relaxation*. Boston, MA: Houghton Mifflin.

Payler, J. (2007) 'Open and closing interactive spaces: Shaping four-year-old children's participation in two English settings', *Early Years: Journal of International Research and Development*, 27 (3): 237–54.

Pellegrini, A.D. (1988) 'Elementary-school children's rough-and-tumble play and social competence', *Developmental Psychology*, 24 (6): 802–6.

Pellegrini, A.D. (2011) 'The development and function of locomotor play', in A.D. Pellegrini (ed.) *The Oxford Handbook of the Development of Play*. New York: Oxford University Press. pp. 172–84.

Pellegrini, A.D. and Smith, P.K. (1998) 'Physical activity play: The nature and function of a neglected aspect of play', *Child Development*, 69 (3): 577–98.

Pepler, D.J. and Ross, H.S. (1981) 'The effects of play on convergent and divergent problem solving', *Child Development*, 52 (4): 1202–10.

Piaget, J. (1951) *Play, Dreams and Imitation in Childhood*. London: Routledge and Kegan Paul.

Qualifications and Curriculum Authority (QCA) (2000) *Curriculum Guidance for the Foundation Stage*. London: QCA.

Radcliffe, E. (2007) 'Mathematical development and playful practice'. BSc dissertation, University of Glamorgan.

Robson, S. (1993) '"Best of all I like choosing time". Talking with children about play and work', *Early Child Development and Care*, 92 (1): 37–51.

Rubin, K.H., Fein, G.C. and Vandenberg, B. (1983) 'Play', in P.H. Mussen (ed.), *Handbook of Child Psychology* (4th edn). New York: Wiley. pp. 693–774.

Russ, S.W., Robins, A.L. and Christiano, B.A. (1999) 'Pretend play: Longitudinal prediction of creativity and affect in fantasy in children', *Creativity Research Journal*, 12 (9): 129–39.

Saracho, O.N. and Spodek, B. (1998) 'A historical overview of theories of play', in O.N. Saracho and B. Spodek (eds), *Multiple Perspectives on Play in Early Childhood Education*. Albany, NY: SUNY Press. pp. 1–10.

Schwartz, S.L., (2005) *Teaching Young Children Mathematics*. Westport, CT: Praeger.

Simon, T. and Smith, P.K. (1983) 'The study of play and problem solving in preschool children: Have experimenter effects been responsible for previous results?', *British Journal of Developmental Psychology*, 1 (3): 289–97.

Skard, A. and Bundy, A.C. (2008) 'Test of playfulness', in L.D. Parham and L.S. Fazio (eds), *Play in Occupational Therapy for Children*. St Louis, MO: Mosby Elsevier. pp. 71–93.

Smith, P.K. (2010) *Children and Play*. Oxford: Wiley-Blackwell.

Smith, P.K., Cowie, H. and Blades, M. (2011) *Understanding Children's Development* (5th edn). Chichester: Wiley.

Smith, P.K. and Dutton, S. (1979) 'Play and training in direct and innovative problem solving', *Child Development*, 50 (3): 830–6.

Smith, P.K. and Simon, T. (1984) 'Object play, problem-solving and creativity in children', in P.K. Smith (ed.), *Play in Animals and Humans*. Oxford: Blackwell. pp. 199–216.

Smith, P.K. and Vollstedt, R. (1985) 'On defining play: An empirical study of the relationship between play and various play criteria', *Child Development*, 56 (4): 1042–50.

Spencer, H. (1873) *Principles of Psychology*. New York: Appleton-Century-Crofts.

Swann, J.W.B. and Pitman, T.S. (1977) 'Initiating play activity of children: The moderating influence of verbal cues on intrinsic motivation', *Child Development*, 48 (3): 1128–32.

Sylva, K., Bruner, J. and Genova, P. (1976) 'The role of play in the problem-solving of children 3–5 years old', in J.S. Bruner, A. Jolly and K. Sylva (eds), *Play, Its Role in Development and Evolution*. Harmondsworth: Penguin. pp. 244–57.

Thelen, E. (1980) 'Determinants of amounts of stereotyped behavior in normal human infants', *Ethology and Sociobiology*, 1 (2): 141–50.

Thomas, L., Howard, J. and Miles, G. (2006) 'The effectiveness of playful practice for learning in the early years', *The Psychology of Education Review*, 30 (1): 52–8.

UNICEF UK (2013) *A Summary of the UN Convention on the Rights of the Child*. Available at: http://www.unicef.org.uk/Documents/Publication-pdfs/betterlifeleaflet2012_press.pdf (accessed 4 March 2013).

Vygotsky, L.S. (1976) 'Play and its role in the mental development of the child', in J.S. Bruner, A. Jolly and K. Sylva (eds), *Play, Its Role in Development and Evolution*. Harmondsworth: Penguin. pp. 537–54.

Welsh Assembly Government (WAG) (2012) *Framework for Children's Learning for 3 to 7-Year Olds in Wales*. Cardiff: WAG.

Wing, L. (1995) 'Play is not the work of the child: Young children's perceptions of work and play', *Early Childhood Research Quarterly*, 10 (2): 223–47.

Wolfgang, C.H. and Stakenas, R.G. (1985) 'An exploration of toy content of preschool children's home environments as a predictor of cognitive development', *Early Child Development and Care*, 19 (4): 291–307.

Youngblade, L.M. and Dunn, J. (1995) 'Individual differences in young children's pretend play with mother and sibling: Links to relationships and understanding of other people's feelings and beliefs', *Child Development*, 66 (5): 1472–92.

11

The Role of the Adult

Why you should read this chapter

This book has aimed to provide an overview of basic and applied aspects of development, and in various chapters, reference has been made to the manner in which parents and other adults can influence this process. This chapter aims to draw together some of the theoretical and practical aspects of the role of the adult in child development. Most of the theories of development recognise a role for the adult but in different ways and a brief overview of this will be provided. The chapter will then focus on the ways in which the adult interacts with the child and how this can promote favourable (and less favourable) outcomes in development. The focus here will be on the role of parents and early years practitioners.

By the end of this chapter you should

- be aware of the role of the adult as specified in the various theories of child development
- understand the different styles of parenting that have been identified and the developmental outcomes associated with these styles
- be aware of some recent research findings on the ways in which practitioners interact with children and how these relate to effective learning in early years settings.

Child development theories and the role of the adult

There are various ways in which the adult can influence the development of the child and these are reflected in some of the theories we have come across in this book so far. This section will look briefly at some of these theories in terms of what they have to say about the role of the adult (see also Table 11.1).

Adults assume a key role in learning theories such as those of Skinner (1953). Here the role of the adult is to facilitate development through the processes of reinforcement and punishment. By reinforcement, the adult rewards the child, for example with praise and attention, when the desired behaviours are shown. When the behaviour is reinforced it is likely to reoccur and through this process the adult facilitates the acquisition of new skills in the child. If the child does not show the specific behaviour, it can be shaped by selectively reinforcing approximations to the behaviour until the desired behaviour itself becomes apparent. The notion is that the principles of reinforcement can be applied to all aspects of development whether it is language development, in which the child is reinforced for vocalisations and later for producing correct speech, or desirable behaviour, such as prosocial acts which if reinforced with praise and attention will be repeated.

Social learning theorists such as Bandura (1977) also see a key role for the adult by recognising the roles of observational learning and modelling in learning. The child can observe the adult performing various tasks and can also model themselves on what they observe.

Piaget's is an example of a theory of child development that places less of an emphasis on the role of the adult. For Piaget, children's thinking develops through active exploration of their environments. In Piaget's view, responsibility for learning and development is very much in the hands of children and the role of the adult is largely limited to the provision of a rich and stimulating environment for the child in which development can take place.

Vygotsky sees the adult as playing a central role in the development of the child. Like Piaget, he sees children as active explorers of their worlds. But for him, the key

Table 11.1   Some child development theorists and the role of the adult

Theorist	The role of the adult
Skinner	Facilitates development by reinforcing desired behaviours
Bandura	Adult acts as a role model for child and facilitates the child to learn by observation
Piaget	Provision of a rich and stimulating environment for the child
Vygotsky	Adult facilitates development through direct interaction with child Work with child within zone of proximal development to extend child's abilities beyond what they can achieve on their own

factor promoting development is the process of social interaction between the child and the adult, and this is central to his notion of the zone of proximal development in which adults support and guide children's learning beyond what they are currently capable of achieving on their own. Bruner (1974–75) further developed Vygotsky's ideas through the notion of scaffolding to explain how adults and children can work together in the zone of proximal development.

The role of the parent

Throughout the chapters of this book, there have been examples of how parents are central to the development of their children. We have seen that affectionate and loving care is essential for basic aspects of development such as physical growth and brain development. Children who are deprived of such care suffer restricted growth, as seen in the disorders of non-organic failure to thrive and psychosocial dwarfism, and we came across the effects of neglect and abuse on brain development. In Chapter 4, we saw various ways in which parents can promote cognitive and intellectual development such as through the use of scaffolding as described by Bruner and the provision of a rich and stimulating environment. We have seen in Chapter 10 that provision of certain toys such as blocks may facilitate the acquisition of various cognitive skills. Parents play an important role in language development in numerous ways. The very process of talking to their infant promotes interest in speech and communication. Engaging in acts such as proto-conversations and joint attention with their infant helps to develop early language and communication skills as does the use of infant-directed speech. Later on, they can help the child to further develop their language through the use of expansions and re-casting their children's utterances. In Chapter 8 we saw the many ways in which adults promote emotional and social development in their children. Affectionate and sensitive care helps in the development of secure attachments and emotional regulation. Parents who discuss emotional states and label emotions facilitate the development of emotional understanding in their children and may also help in the acquisition of a theory of mind.

A key aspect that is common to all of these diverse areas of development is the active role of an engaged supportive parent providing a stable and stimulating environment in which the child can develop. However, not all parents will interact in such a positive manner with their children; parents tend to vary in their child-rearing styles and this has been of interest to a number of researchers. The different parenting styles will be considered in the next section.

Styles of parenting

One of the first psychologists to study styles of parenting was Baumrind (1967, 1971) who gathered information on child-rearing by observing parents interact with their preschool children. From her observations, she identified three styles of parenting: **authoritarian**, **authoritative** and **permissive**. Further research on parenting styles was conducted by Maccoby and Martin (1983) who identified two important dimensions on which parents differed: **acceptance/responsiveness** and **demanding/ control**. Acceptance/responsiveness refers to the extent to which parents display support and affection to their children. Demanding/control refers to the amount of control and regulation parents impose on their children's behaviour. An important point about these two dimensions is that they are independent of each other, meaning that parents can vary in the combination of acceptance/responsiveness and demanding/control characteristics displayed. From this observation, and Baumrind's original classification of parenting styles, Maccoby and Martin were able to identify four styles of parenting.

Authoritarian parents were typically low on the acceptance/responsiveness dimension and high on the demanding/control dimension. This parenting style is characterised by a restrictive style in which many rules are imposed on their children and these rules are expected to be obeyed without question. Such parents do not feel the need to explain why it is necessary for the child to comply with their rules and simply expect the child to respect their authority. They will often resort to force and punishment when they encounter resistance from the child. Authoritarian parents will also resort to **psychological control** (Barber, 1996) in order to gain compliance from their children. This includes tactics such as criticism, withholding of affection and attempts to induce shame and guilt. They may also hold excessively high expectations for their children that do not always match their children's developmental level.

Authoritative parents score high in both acceptance/responsiveness and in demanding/control. They are responsive and affectionate to their children. Although they score highly on the demanding/control dimension, they differ from authoritarian parents in several respects. They will place rules and restrictions on their children but are willing to explain the necessity for them and where appropriate will negotiate so that all parties are in agreement. They seek to exercise their control in a more open and democratic manner and will rely on the use of **behavioural control** rather than psychological control to encourage compliance. Behavioural control involves the use of firm but reasonable discipline to regulate their children's conduct and punishing wrongdoing through such means as the removal of privileges or toys.

Permissive parents are high in acceptance/responsiveness but low on the demanding/control dimension. Essentially they are warm and accepting of their children but make little effort to control or regulate their children's behaviour. They will grant autonomy and responsibility for making decisions to their children in areas such as daily routines (mealtimes, bedtimes, television watching), often before they are developmentally ready. Baumrind (1967) noted that some parents tended to adopt this style due to a lack of confidence in their ability to influence their children. Similarly, Oyserman et al. (2005) found an association between a lack of parenting confidence and permissive parenting in mothers with mental health problems.

Uninvolved parents score low in both the acceptance/responsiveness and the demanding/ control dimensions. Often parents who show this style have their own stresses and problems and are so overwhelmed by these that they do not have the time or motivation to devote to child-rearing. Such parents impose few rules and demands but are also unresponsive to their children's needs and emotionally detached. At its extreme, uninvolved parenting would be regarded as a form of child maltreatment called neglect.

Parenting styles and developmental outcomes

Unsurprisingly, an authoritative parenting style is the style that has been linked with the most positive outcomes. In her study, Baumrind (1967) noted that preschool children of parents classified with this style of parenting were contented, self-reliant, confident and had good relationships with their peers and adults. Further research by Baumrind (see for example Baumrind, 1991) found that children from authoritative homes showed high social and cognitive skills in middle childhood and adolescence. Various other longitudinal studies have also linked an authoritative parenting style with positive outcomes in areas such as school achievement, social skills and peer relationships (Deković and Janssens, 1992; Hart et al., 2003; Steinberg et al., 1992, 1994).

Baumrind (1967, 1991) found children of authoritarian parents to be unhappy, insecure and less affiliative towards peers and in middle childhood and adolescence they had generally lower cognitive and social skills compared to children from authoritative homes. Other studies have found a link between authoritarian parenting styles and children's externalising behaviours such as aggression and conduct problems (Hart et al., 2003; Thompson et al., 2003). Deković and Janssens (1992) found that children of authoritarian parents also tend to suffer from peer rejection.

Children of permissive parents are inclined to be impulsive, aggressive, self-centred and lacking in self-control and later in childhood were below average in social and cognitive skills (Baumrind, 1967, 1991). The relationship between permissive parenting and impulsive, low-achieving and rebellious behaviour has been found to be particularly strong for boys (Barber and Olson, 1997, Baumrind, 1967).

Just as it is unsurprising that authoritative parenting is regarded as the most successful parenting style, it is also unsurprising that uninvolved parenting is associated with the most negative developmental outcomes. In the original research by Baumrind (1967) there were no parents whose style was classified as uninvolved but subsequent research has linked this parenting style with a range of adverse outcomes. Children raised in this manner have been found to display externalising problems, such as aggression and temper tantrums in early childhood (Miller et al., 1993), and later on show poor school achievement (Kendal-Tackette and Eckenrode, 1996). In adolescence such children are more prone to criminal and antisocial behaviour, and alcohol and drug abuse (Baumrind, 1991; Pettit et al., 2001; Steinberg et al., 1994).

Can you think of some reasons why authoritative parenting appears to be the most effective parenting style?

The role of the early years practitioner

As we have seen from Chapter 3, recent years have seen a move away from more formal, instructionally based approaches to early education in favour of more interactive, child-centred and play-based approaches to learning and this characterises all of the early years curricula in the UK. While the nature of teaching in such curricula has changed, nevertheless the adult is still seen as having a key role in the early years classroom. Given the more interactive nature of such curricula, it is important that consideration be given to the nature of adult–child interactions and how they affect the delivery of such curricula. The next sections will look at the role of adult–child interactions in the early years classroom, and, given the prominent role assigned to play in the modern curriculum, the nature of interactions between adults and children in the context of play.

Adult–child interactions

There are a number of ways in which the relationship between practitioners and children in the early years classroom can be characterised. One involves the concepts of **classification** and **framing** (Bernstein, 1996). Classification refers to the boundary maintenance between subjects. This is weak where subjects are merged and strong where the boundaries are clearly defined. Framing refers to the relationship between teacher and pupil and the degree of control between them. When framing is strong, then control rests with the teacher, when it is weak, the child is afforded more control. Strong classification and framing denotes a **visible pedagogy** and weak classification and framing denotes an **invisible pedagogy**. Older, more formal approaches to teaching can be seen as examples of visible pedagogy and Emilson and Folkesson (2006) propose that such an approach has the effect of generally reducing children's participation. It is also argued that such approaches result in limited and short-term gains in children's learning, increase stress and anxiety and demotivate children (Stipek et al., 1995).

Research on effective early years practice has indicated that the most effective settings are those in which children are encouraged to choose, plan and control their activities. An example of such an approach was the High/Scope Perry preschool project in the USA. Longitudinal studies of the progress of the children from this project indicated considerable social gains (such as higher school achievement and occupational success) over time compared to children exposed to direct instruction programmes

(Schweinhart and Weikart, 1997). More recently, a study conducted in Northern Ireland by Walsh et al. (2006) compared Year 1 children exposed to the play-based and child-centred enriched curriculum intervention (see Chapter 2) with Year 1 children receiving the more formal early years curriculum in place at that time. They found evidence of a higher-quality learning experience in children exposed to the enriched curriculum, with such children having more opportunities to act independently, being engaged in more challenging activities, and showing higher levels of emotional, social and physical wellbeing. Findings from the *Researching Effective Pedagogy in the Early Years* project, a study of 14 cases of effective early years settings identified in the EPPE project (see Chapter 2), indicated that these settings relied on a combination of adult- and child-led activities (Siraj-Blatchford et al., 2002). In terms of framing, such settings appear to employ framing that is neither strong nor weak.

Another important characteristic of effective early years settings is the language used by adults in their interactions with children. In particular, it has been argued that language which effectively facilitates development is based on *shared problem solving* and the use of *open questions* to the children that seek to extend their thinking. Such an approach forms the basis for what Siraj-Blatchford et al. (2002) refer to as **sustained shared thinking**. These are episodes in which the adult and child work together to solve a problem using intellectual skills and understanding. The interaction is managed by the adult in such a way so that both the child and adult contribute to the thinking that develops and extends the child's existing understanding. Andrews (2012) suggests a number of practices to support sustained shared thinking including:

- Careful observation of the child and listening to what the child is doing.
- Establishing a relationship through effective non-verbal cues such as eye-contact, smiling, nodding and showing genuine interest in the child's actions. Respect is shown for the child's choices and actions through the use of encouraging comments such as '*I really want to know more about this*'.
- Adults repeating what the child has done or thinks might happen and this can serve to affirm the child's actions or summarise them through comments such as '*so you think that will happen?*'
- Adults making suggestions drawing on their own experiences, for example '*when I cook I do it this way*', which still leave choice and power of exploration with the child.
- Offering alternative viewpoints.
- Offering reciprocal responses demonstrating that the adult and practitioner are 'in it together'.
- Modelling thinking: '*Now let me think about this for a minute; perhaps we need to ask advice on how to do this?*'

However, it has been found that use of such language is far from common in educational settings. Wood et al. (1980) found that early years teachers primarily asked closed questions to which they already knew the answers and peer-to-peer dialogue was more extensive than adult-to-child dialogue. Clark (1988) found that teachers working with children under 5 tended to ask simple questions and statements rather than use more complex language interactions. More recently, findings from the EPPE project found that only 5 per cent of all questions asked by practitioners in early years settings were open in nature (Siraj-Blatchford and Manni, 2008; Siraj-Blatchford et al. 2002).

Adult–child interactions in the context of play

The previous section indicates that effective early years settings are those in which children have a degree of choice and control over their activities and the adult interacts with the child in a cooperative and conversational manner. However, the modern early years curricula also require the use of play to facilitate learning.

Despite the prominence given to the role of play in the early years curriculum, it appears that classroom practices do not always reflect this. In the past, it has been found that many teachers are not comfortable with play and child-led activities (Bennett et al., 1997; King, 1978), although it must be acknowledged that these findings predate the introduction of the modern early years curricula in the UK. However, there still seems to be some uncertainty about how to manage play and child-led activities in a classroom setting. There appear to be a range of beliefs ranging from supporting children's play to standing back and not interfering (Spielberger and McLane, 2002). According to Johnson et al. (2005), adult involvement in play activities has been increasing but the quality of this involvement is variable, and is often more concerned with managing and monitoring rather than supporting development. More recently, a study by Martlew et al. (2011) of teachers' experiences of implementing the play-based Curriculum for Excellence in Scotland found that 'active' or 'play-based' learning was interpreted differently by teachers and play in some classrooms was peripheral rather than integral to the learning process.

You will recall from the previous chapter that an important issue in the use of play in education is how children perceive play, and a number of research studies (see, for example, Howard, 2002) have identified 'cues' that children use to differentiate between play and non-play situations. These cues include the location of an activity, whether the activity is voluntary or compulsory and whether or not an adult is involved. A number of experimental studies have been carried out where these cues have been manipulated to create playful learning settings (activity on the floor, children invited to participate and adult not involved) and formal learning settings (activity at the table, children told to participate and adult involved). These studies have indicated that performance on problem-solving tasks is more effective following exposure to playful practice conditions (McInnes et al., 2009; Thomas et al., 2006) and children appeared to be more focused and motivated in their behaviour in the playful practice condition (McInnes et al., 2009). Of particular interest here is the cue of adult presence and the finding that the presence of an adult in an activity tends to signal to the children that the activity is not play. This obviously would have implications for the role of an adult in a play-based curriculum.

However, one feature of these experimental studies was that the cue of adult presence was used in combination with the cues of location and the voluntary nature of the activity. Therefore a formal learning situation was defined in terms of an adult being present *and* being located on the floor *and* the activity being compulsory. What happens if an adult is present but the activity is voluntary and takes place on the floor? A further experimental study was reported by McInnes et al. (2010) which included such a 'playful' condition. This was then compared with a 'playful' condition involving all three cues (adult proximal, activity on floor, voluntary activity) and with two 'formal' conditions (adult present, activity at table, compulsory activity; adult proximal, activity at table, compulsory activity). The task used for this study was a bead-threading task and the time taken to complete it was measured before exposure to the four conditions, immediately after participation in the conditions, and one week later. The behaviour and interactions of the children during the various formal and playful practise conditions was also recorded and analysed. The findings of the study indicated that in all of the conditions in which an adult was present, performance in the task was lower compared to the adult proximal conditions. However, there were also a significantly higher number of adult–child interactions in all the tasks where the adult was present rather than proximal. McInnes et al. suggest that the presence of an adult led to the children losing confidence in their own ability and seeking adult direction and support. This may be a result of adult interaction often being associated with the production of a correct answer or product rather than adult involvement in a child's own play processes.

At first glance, it may be argued that the results of these studies would justify the notion that adults should provide and monitor play activities but should not involve themselves in the play itself. However, McInnes et al. (2010) argue that these findings indicate that it is important for adults to consider the *nature* of their interactions with children and how they might co-construct play situations to be accepted as play partners by the children.

Moreover, while the experimental studies have indicated that adult presence is one of the cues that children use to distinguish play from non-play situations, there are also settings where children do not appear to make use of this cue, and activities in which an adult is present are as likely to be perceived as 'play' as activities in which the adult is proximal or absent. In two recent studies (McInnes et al., 2011; McInnes et al., in press), a setting was identified in which children did not use the cue of adult presence and this was compared with a setting where children did make use of this cue. The two settings were compared in terms of the ways in which the adults interacted with the children including the nature of their involvement in play and the types of language used by the adults in those same interactions. In the setting where children did not make use of the cue of adult presence, it was found that practitioners planned a mix of adult- and child-led activities, but they actively participated alongside children in all activities. In the setting in which children did make use of the cue of adult presence, it was found that while the practitioners also planned for a mix of adult- and child-led activities, they only tended to participate in adult-led activities and left child-led activities to the children. A comparison of the language used by adults and the nature of their interactions with children also revealed differences between the two settings. In the setting where children did not make use of the cue of adult presence, practitioners engaged in more open questions and there were more exchanges with the children based on mutual understanding and shared control, compared to the setting where children did make use of the cue of adult presence.

The results of the studies by McInnes et al. (2011, in press) indicate that in settings where play activities are left to children and where adult–child interactions are based on direct teaching and use of simple language and closed questions, children will use the cue of adult presence to distinguish between play and not play activities. In settings where framing is neither weak nor strong and where adults participate actively in child- as well as adult-led activities and interact with the children in ways which offer choice, control and shared understanding, children are less likely to use the cue of adult presence to make this distinction.

 Can you think of some specific ways in which you might interact with a group of children so that you would be accepted as a play partner in an early years setting?

Chapter summary

- The various theories of child development all recognise a role for the adult in facilitating child development, each theory emphasising a different role.
- Such roles include selectively reinforcing and punishing behaviour (Skinner), acting as role models and facilitating observational learning (Bandura), provision of a rich and stimulating environment (Piaget), and direct interaction and instruction (Vygotsky and Bruner).
- Four different styles of parenting have been identified: authoritarian, authoritative, permissive and uninvolved. Authoritative parenting is associated with the most favourable developmental outcomes.
- Studies of interactions between early years practitioners and children have identified some characteristics of effective interactions, and in particular a style of interaction called sustained shared thinking is regarded as an example of good practice.

(Continued)

(Continued)

- Play is given a central role in the delivery of the early years curricula in the UK, but research indicates that practitioners vary in the ways that they implement and manage play in care and classroom settings, with some practitioners seeing their role to provide and monitor play activities while other practitioners involve themselves directly in play activities.
- Recent research findings have indicated that children use the cue of adult presence to differentiate play from non-play activities: if an adult is present, they are more likely to see an activity as not being play.
- However, the use of the cue of adult presence also appears to be related to the ways in which adults interact with children in the context of play. Where adults involve themselves in child-led activities and interact in such a way that they facilitate perceptions of choice and control in the children, children do not appear to use this cue to distinguish between play and non-play activities.

Further reading

Riley, J. (ed.) (2007) *Learning in the Early Years.* London: Paul Chapman.
A textbook focusing on putting the demands of the early years curriculum into practice.

Whitebread, D. (2012) *Developmental Psychology and Early Childhood Education.* London: Sage.
An account of recent research on early child development and how these findings can be translated into effective early years practice.

Useful websites

http://www.familylinks.org.uk/
There are various organisations that seek to promote effective parenting styles and Family Links is one such organisation.

http://www.ioe.ac.uk/research/153.html
This is the website for the EPPE project and a source of information regarding the ongoing work of this project.

References

Andrews, M. (2012) *Exploring Play for Early Childhood Studies.* London: Sage.
Bandura, A. (1977) *Social Learning Theory.* Englewood Cliffs, NJ: Prentice-Hall.
Barber, B.K. (1996) 'Parental psychological control: Revising a neglected construct', *Child Development*, 67 (6): 3296–319.

Barber, B.K. and Olson, J.A. (1997) 'Socialization in context: Connection, regulation, and autonomy in the family, school, and neighbourhood, and with peers', *Journal of Adolescent Research*, 12 (2): 287–315.

Baumrind, D. (1967) 'Child care practices anteceding three patterns of preschool behavior', *Genetic Psychology Monographs*, 75 (1): 43–88.

Baumrind, D. (1971) 'Current patterns of parental authority', *Developmental Psychology Monographs*, 4, (1, pt. 2): 1–103.

Baumrind, D. (1991) 'The influence of parenting style on adolescent competence and substance use', *Journal of Early Adolescence*, 11 (1): 56–95.

Bennett, N., Wood, L. and Rogers, S. (1997) *Teaching Through Play*. Buckingham: Open University Press.

Bernstein, B. (1996) *Pedagogy, Symbolic Control and Identity* (rev. edn). Lanham, MD: Rowman and Littlefield.

Bruner, J. (1974–75) 'From communication to language - a psychological perspective', *Cognition*, 3 (3): 255–87.

Clark, M.M. (1988) *Children Under Five*. London: Gordon and Breach Science Publishers.

Deković, M. and Janssens, J.M.A.M. (1992) 'Parents' child-rearing style and child's sociometric status', *Developmental Psychology*, 28 (5): 925–32.

Emilson, A. and Folkesson, A.M. (2006) 'Children's participation and teacher control', *Early Child Development and Care*, 176 (3–4): 219–38.

Hart, C.H., Newell, L.D. and Olson, S.F. (2003) 'Parenting skills and social-communicative competence in childhood', in J.O. Greene and B.R. Burleson (eds), *Handbook of Communication and Social-interaction Skills*. Mahwah, NJ: Erlbaum. pp. 753–97.

Howard, J. (2002) 'Eliciting young children's perceptions of play, work and learning using the Activity Apperception Story Procedure', *Early Child Development and Care*, 172 (5): 489–502.

Johnson, J.E., Christie, J.F. and Wardle, F. (2005) *Play, Development and Early Education*. Boston, MA: Pearson Education, Inc.

Kendall-Tackette, K.A. and Eckenrode, J. (1996) 'The effect of neglect on academic achievement and disciplinary problems: A developmental perspective', *Child Abuse and Neglect*, 20 (3): 161–69.

King, R. (1978) *All Things Bright and Beautiful? A Sociological Study of Infants Classrooms*. Chichester: John Wiley & Sons.

Maccoby, E.E. and Martin, J.A. (1983) 'Socialization in the context of the family', in P.H. Mussen (ed.), *Handbook of Child Psychology: Vol. 4 Socialization, Personality and Social Development*. New York: Wiley. pp. 1–101.

Martlew, J., Stephen, C. and Ellis, J. (2011) 'Play in the primary school classroom? The experience of teachers supporting children's learning through a new pedagogy', *Early Years: An International Journal of Research and Development*, 31 (1): 71–83.

McInnes, K., Howard, J., Miles, G. and Crowley, K. (2009) 'Behavioural differences exhibited by children when practicing a task under formal and playful conditions', *Journal of Educational and Child Psychology*, 26 (2): 31–9.

McInnes, K., Howard, J., Miles, G. and Crowley, K. (2010) 'Differences in adult-child interactions during playful and formal practice conditions: An initial investigation', *Psychology of Education Review*, 34 (1): 14–20.

McInnes, K., Howard, J., Miles, G.E. and Crowley, K. (2011) 'Differences in practitioners' understanding of play and how this influences pedagogy and children's perceptions of play', *Early Years: An International Journal of Research and Development*, 31 (2): 121–33.

McInnes, K., Howard, J., Crowley, K. and Miles, G.E. (in press) 'The nature of adult-child interaction in the early years classroom: Implications for children's perceptions of play and subsequent learning behaviour', *European Early Childhood Education Research Journal*.

Miller, N.B., Cowan, P.A., Cowan, C.P., Hetherington, E.M. and Clingempeel, W.G. (1993) 'Externalizing in preschoolers and early adolescents: A cross-study replication of a family model', *Developmental Psychology*, 29 (1): 3–18.

Oyserman, D., Bybee, D., Mowbray, C. and Hart-Johnson, T. (2005) 'When mothers have serious mental health problems: Parenting as a proximal mediator', *Journal of Adolescence*, 28 (4): 443–63.

Pettit, G.S., Laird, R.D., Dodge, K.A., Bates, J.E. and Criss, M.M. (2001) 'Antecedents and behavior-problem outcomes of parental monitoring and psychological control in early adolescence', *Child Development*, 72 (2): 583–98.

Schweinhart, L.J. and Weikart, D.P. (1997) 'The High/Scope preschool curriculum comparison study through age 23', *Early Childhood Research Quarterly*, 12 (2): 117–43.

Siraj-Blatchford, I. and Manni, L. (2008) '"Would you like to tidy up now?" An analysis of adult questioning in the English Foundation Stage', *Early Years*, 28 (1): 5–22.

Siraj-Blatchford, I., Sylva, K., Muttock, S., Gilden, R. and Bell, D. (2002) *Researching Effective Pedagogy in the Early Years* (Research Report 356). London: HMSO.

Skinner, B.F. (1953) *Science and Human Behaviour*. New York: Macmillan.

Spielberger, J. and McLane, J.B. (2002) 'Can too many cooks spoil the broth? Beliefs about the teacher's role in play', in C. Brown and C. Marchant (eds), *Play in Practice: Case Studies in Young Children's Play*. St. Paul, MN: Redleaf Press. pp. 3–19.

Steinberg, L., Lamborn, S.D., Dornbusch, S.M. and Darling, M. (1992) 'Impact of parenting practices on adolescent achievement: Authoritative parenting, school involvement, and encouragement to succeed', *Child Development*, 63 (5): 1266–81.

Steinberg, L., Lamborn, S.D., Darling, N. and Dornbusch, S.M. (1994) 'Over-time changes in adjustment and competence among adolescents from authoritative, authoritarian, indulgent and neglectful families', *Child Development*, 65 (3), 754–70.

Stipek, D., Feiler, R., Daniels, D. and Milburn, S. (1995) 'Effects of different instructional approaches on young children's achievement and motivation', *Child Development*, 66 (1): 209–23.

Thomas, L., Howard, J. and Miles, G. (2006) 'The effectiveness of playful practice for learning in the early years', *The Psychology of Education Review*, 30 (1): 52–8.

Thompson, A., Hollis, C. and Richards, D. (2003) 'Authoritarian parenting attitudes as a risk for conduct problems: Results from a British national cohort study', *European Child and Adolescent Psychiatry*, 12 (2): 84–91.

Walsh, G., Sproule, L., McGuinness, C., Trew, K., Rafferty, H. and Sheehy, N. (2006) 'An appropriate curriculum for 4–5-year-old children in Northern Ireland: Comparing play-based and formal approaches', *Early Years: An International Journal of Research and Development*, 26 (2): 201–21.

Wood, D., McMahon, L. and Cranstoun, Y. (1980) *Working With Under Fives*. London: Grant McIntyre Limited/Publishers.

Glossary

Chapter 1

Adaptation: In Piaget's theory, the notion that just as our bodies are adapted to fit with our environments, our minds are also adapted to fit with our worlds.

Anal stage: The second stage of Freud's theory in which sexual pleasure is focused on processes such as urination and defecation.

Animistic thinking: In Piaget's theory, his observation that children often assumed that inanimate objects have thoughts and feelings, just as they do.

Attachment: The formation of an affectionate bond between the infant and caregiver.

Autonomy versus doubt: The second stage in Erikson's theory in which the child must use their emerging mental and motor skills to become more autonomous and independent.

Basic trust versus mistrust: The first stage in Erikson's theory in which the infant must learn to trust others to care for them.

Behaviourism: An approach to psychology that focuses on observable acts of behaviour as a means to understanding development. This approach also stresses the role of nurture over nature.

Behaviour modification: An approach to dealing with problem behaviours based on the principles of operant conditioning.

Bioecological model: Bronfenbrenner's model of development which sees development as a series of interacting systems with the child at the centre.

Canalisation: The extent to which development is restricted by genetic factors.

Chronosystem: In Bronfenbrenner's model, how time can affect development, such as the age at which a child experiences a particular event.

Classical conditioning: In which learning is seen as the formation of an association between a stimulus and a response.

Conditioned response: A response which was previously a reflex which can be elicited by the presence of a conditioned stimulus.

Conditioned stimulus: A stimulus to which we have learned to make a particular response.

Continuous development: In which development takes place as a gradual accumulation of knowledge, skills and behaviours.

Critical period: In ethology, the notion that there are particular points in the lifespan in which the animal is biologically prepared to acquire a certain pattern on behaviour.

Developmental Stages: Distinct periods in a sequence of development characterised by the presence of a particular set of skills or behaviours and these demonstrate a qualitatively higher level of functioning compared to the skills and behaviours that characterised previous developmental stages.

Discontinuous development: Development proceeds in a series of abrupt changes in which the child moves to a new, more advanced level of functioning.

Ego integrity versus despair: The final stage in Erikson's theory in which we look back over our lives and depending on how well we have resolved the various psychosocial crises, the extent to which we will see our lives as being meaningful and successful.

Ego: In Freud's theory, the part of our personality that seeks to satisfy basic desires in a socially acceptable manner.

Egocentric thinking: In Piaget's theory, his observation that children's thinking was very much restricted to their own point of view.

Electra complex: A conflict experienced by female infants during the phallic stage in which the child desires the opposite sex parent (see also **Oedipus complex**).

Erogenous zones: The different parts of the body involved in sexual pleasure. In Freud's theory, these change with age.

Evolutionary psychology: An approach to psychology that seeks to identify the origins of behaviours in terms of how they may have contributed to survival.

Exosystem: In Bronfenbrenner's model, settings in which the child does not necessarily participate, but which can nevertheless affect development, such as the parent's work environment.

Generativity versus stagnation: The seventh stage in Erikson's theory in which the main concern is to be productive in work or family life.

Genital stage: The stage in Freud's theory in which sexual impulses are re-awakened and the individual must seek to satisfy these in a socially appropriate manner such as marriage.

Id: In Freud's theory, the part of our personality that is driven by basic, instinctual desires and requires immediate gratification of these desires.

Identity versus role confusion: The fifth stage of Erikson's theory in which the individual needs to develop as sense of their own identity.

Imprinting: In ethology, an instinctual, following response in baby birds that keeps them close to the mother.

Industry versus inferiority: The fourth stage in Erikson's theory in which the child has to master various social and intellectual tasks such as learning at school and establishing good peer relationships.

Information processing theories: Theories of development which see development as information flowing through as system and the changes in these processes.

Initiative versus guilt: The third stage in Erikson's theory which occurs around the ages of 3 to 6 years and the task of the child is to develop a sense of initiative, a desire to master their environment but do so in a socially appropriate way.

Intimacy versus isolation: The sixth stage of Erikson's theory in which the task of the adult is to establish a close and loving relationship with another person.

Latent stage: The stage in Freud's theory in which sexual impulses are suppressed and channelled into intellectual and social activities.

Learning theories: Theories of development that stress the role of environmental factors in development.

Learning: Psychological change as a result of experience.

Macrosystem: In Bronfenbrenner's model, the broader social, cultural and political context in which development occurs.

Maturation: Physical and psychological change unfolding according to a genetically programmed 'plan'.

Mesosystem: In Bronfenbrenner's model, this refers to relationships between the various Microsystems and how these can affect development.

Microsystem: In Bronfenbrenner's model, the innermost layer of the model consisting of the child's immediate environment, such as the home or school.

Nature: In the context of the nature-nurture debate, nature refers to the position that development is determined by our genes.

Negative punishment: Undesirable behaviour is punished by withdrawing a desirable stimulus.

Negative reinforcer: Desirable behaviour is reinforced by removing an aversive stimulus.

Nurture: In the contect of the nature-nurture debate, nurture refers to the position that development is determined by environmental factors.

Observational learning/modelling: In Bandura's theory, the individual acquires skills by watching those around them.

Oedipus complex: A conflict during the phallic stage in which the infant desires the opposite-sex parent and resents the same-sex parent.

Operant conditioning: A form of learning in which we come to associate a particular behaviour or response with a particular consequence.

Oral stage: The first phase in Freud's theory in which sexual pleasure is concentrated on the mouth through actions such as sucking.

Phallic stage: The stage in Freud's theory in which sexual pleasure becomes focused on the genitals.

Pleasure principle: The desire of the id to seek immediate gratification of our basic impulses.

Positive punisher: Undesirable behaviour in punished by presenting an aversive stimulus.

Positive reinforcer: The likelihood of a behaviour re-occurring is increased by presenting a desirable consequence such as praise or a reward.

Psychological plane: In Vygotsky's theory, the ability of children to move from doing things with help to doing things on their own.

Psychosexual theory: Freud's theory of development which emphasises the role of sexual desires and impulses, and how these are managed in development.

Psychosocial crisis: In Erikson's theory, a developmental task or conflict experienced at particular points in the lifespan related to biological maturation or the demands being faced by that individual at a particular point in the lifespan.

Punisher: A consequence that decreases the likelihood that a behaviour will occur again.

Reality principle: The desire of the ego to satisfy our desires but in a socially acceptable manner, including delaying gratification.

Reinforcer: A consequence that increases the likelihood that a behaviour will occur again.

Self-efficacy: The individual's beliefs about their competence in dealing with a variety of intellectual and social tasks.

Sensitive period: A point in development in which the child is particularly responsive to environmental influences.

Social learning theory: Bandura's theory of learning which stresses the role of observation and modelling in learning.

Social plane: In Vygotsky's theory, the ability of children to perform tasks with assistance from others.

Superego: In Freud's theory, the part of our personality that contains all of the values and morals internalised from our parents.

Zone of proximal development: In Vygotsky's theory, tasks that a child cannot do alone but can do with assistance from a more experience individual.

Chapter 2

Capacities: The skills which the Scottish CfE aims to develop in children. These are successful learners, confident individuals, responsible citizens and effective contributors.

Children's Workforce Development Council: An initiative launched in 2005 to improve the training and career pathways for graduates working in early years settings. This council was replaced in April 2013 by the Teaching Agency.

Common assessment framework: An initiative arising from Every Child Matters, this is a common assessment scheme that can be used by any professional working with a child or family with additional needs.

ContactPoint: A database set up as part of the implementation of Every Child Matters to facilitate information sharing between agencies working with children and their families. This database was discontinued following a change of government in 2010.

Core Subject areas: In the Scottish CfE, these are health and wellbeing, literacy and numeracy. Teachers are required to ensure that these are incorporated in all curriculum areas.

Curriculum areas: In the Scottish CfE, these are the specific subject topics taught as part of this curriculum. These are arts, health and wellbeing, languages, mathematics, religious and moral education, studies and sciences, social technologies.

Curriculum for Excellence (CfE): The school curriculum for Scotland implemented in 2010. This curriculum covers education from the ages of 3–18.

Early learning goals (EYFS): Specific skills that children should have attained by the end of their reception year. In the current version of the EYFS, there are 17 such goals.

Early Years Foundation Phase: The early years curriculum in Wales for children aged 3–7 years. The phase covers children from nursery to Year 2.

Early Years Foundation Stage Profile: A formal assessment completed for each child in the final term before they reach five. This assessment details the child's progress in relation to each of the early learning goals and an indication as to whether the child is meeting the expected level of development, exceeding the level of development or not meeting the level of development.

Early Years Foundation Stage: A single framework launched in England in 2008 for the provision of care and education for children from birth to five years.

Early Years Teacher: The successor role to the Early Years Professional Status (EYPS).

Early Years Professional Status: Graduates who have followed a specified training pathway that qualified them to take on leading roles in childcare settings. This qualification will be superseded in September 2013 by the role of Early Years Teacher.

Enriched Curriculum: A pilot early years curriculum, based on play and active learning that was implemented in a number of schools in Northern Ireland between 1999 and 2006.

Flying Start: An early intervention programme launched by the Welsh Assembly Government in 2005 aimed at improving the prospects for children in disadvantaged areas. The scheme is funded by the assembly government and implemented by local authorities.

Foundation Stage: The current early years curriculum in Northern Ireland, implemented from 2007 and based on the enriched curriculum intervention.

Integrated Children's Centres: The centres use to deliver Flying Start services in Wales such as childcare, language and play groups and parent support programmes.

Lead professional: An initiative arising from Every Child Matters, this is the professional responsible for coordinating interagency services for children with additional needs.

Learning characteristics: In the Welsh Early Years Foundation Phase, these are three characteristics – playing and exploring, active learning and creating and thinking critically – which are assessed within this phase.

Learning goals: In the Welsh Early Years Foundation Phase, the specific skills children are expected to acquire in each area of learning.

Sure Start Local Centres: The successors to SSLPs following the publication of Every Child Matters. These are tasked with providing support services to children and their families and are controlled by local authorities.

Sure Start Children's Centres: Local groups tasked with implementing the Sure Start Programme through provision of services such as playgroups, postnatal support for mothers, childcare and health education.

Sure Start: An early intervention programme launched in 1998 with the aim of ending child poverty by provision of a variety of support services to children and families living in deprived areas.

Teaching agency: An agency of the Department for Education that oversees training and development programmes for teachers and early education and childcare workers in England.

Chapter 3

Attrition: In longitudinal research, the tendency of some children to drop out of the study.

Bias: In terms of sampling, the possibility that the sample will contain a disproportionate number of individuals with a particular characteristic (e.g. more motivated, more confident, etc.).

Case study: A research study focusing on a specific individual, group or organisation.

Checklist: In the context of observational research, compiling a list of possible behaviours to be observed and noting their presence and absence during the observation period.

Clinical interview: A flexible, open-ended interview, characterised by a conversational style of interaction between interviewer and interviewee with the direction of the interview depending on the responses given by the interviewee.

Cohort effects: In cross-sectional and longitudinal designs, the possibility that performance of the participants may be affected by wider historical or social factors rather than the effects of age.

Conditions: In an experiment, the individual manipulations of the independent variable.

Confidentiality: The researcher restricts access to personal details of the participants.

Control variable: In experimental research, variables other that the independent variable that may also influence the dependent variable and the experimenter, through careful design of the experiment, attempts to make sure that these variables are standardised throughout the experimental situation.

Convenience sample: The researcher obtains a sample by using the participants that are available and willing to participate in the study.

Correlation coefficient: A numerical measure of the strength of a correlation, varying from −1 to +1. The closer the correlation coefficient comes to −1, the stronger the correlation in a negative direction, the closer it comes to +1, the stronger the correlation in a positive direction.

Correlational studies: Studies that aim to investigate if there is a consistent relationship between two variables, but without making statements of cause-and-effect.

Counterbalancing: In a repeated measures design, ensuring that the order of presentation of experimental conditions is varied for the participants. This is done to control against order effects and practice effects.

Cross-sectional design: A research study comparing groups of children of different ages at the same point in time.

Dependent variable: The target behaviour that is measured by the researcher to see if it changes in response to manipulation of the independent variable.

Detailed descriptive notes: In the context of observational research, taking detailed narrative notes of behaviours and the situations in which they occur.

Do no harm: An important ethical principle in which the researcher takes care that participants will not suffer any physical or psychological harm through participation in a research study.

Ecological validity: The extent to which the experimental study applies to real world instances of the behaviour of interest.

Ethnographic approaches: Studies of a cultural group or system.

Event sampling: In observational research, recording each time a specified behaviour occurs and the events preceding and following that behaviour.

Experimental condition: The individual manipulations of the independent variable in an experiment.

Experimental research: An approach to research in which aims to make cause-and-effect statements of relations between behaviours and the factors thought to influence those behaviours.

Field experiments: experiments that take place in a natural setting such as a classroom, play group or clinic.

Grounded theory: An approach to qualitative data analysis that seeks to identify recurring themes or categories of information from the data source, but the identification of these is not guided by any underlying theory and rests on the assumption that the theory is 'grounded' within the data.

Hypothesis: A specific prediction deduced from a theory about what will happen in a specific situation.

Hypothetico-deductive research: An approach to research that involves constructing theories and testing hypotheses derived from those theories.

Independent variable: The aspect of the experimental situation that is manipulated by the researcher.

Inductive research: Research that involves gathering facts and observations in the absence of a guiding theory. Often used for researching areas for which there is little existing information.

Informed consent: The ethical requirement that participants in a study should give consent for their participation on the basis that they are aware of the purpose of the study and what will be required of them.

Longitudinal studies: Studies in which data are collected from the same individuals over a period of time and the individuals are observed or tested repeatedly at various time points over the duration of the study.

Millenium Cohort Study: A long-term longitudinal study tracking the development of a group of British children born at the start of the current century.

Negative correlation: As scores in one variable increase, scores in a second variable decrease.

Operational definition: A clear definition of what constitutes a behaviour of interest for the purpose of a study.

Order effects: In an experiment, the possibility of a participant's performance or responses being affected by their performance or responses in a previous condition.

Participant observation: In observational research when the observer becomes part of the group being studied.

Population: The entire group of individuals to whom a set of research findings are aimed to be applicable.

Positive correlation: As scores in one variable increase, they are accompanied by increases in a second variable.

Practice effects: In an experiment where the same task is used several times, the possibility that improvements in performance may simply reflect participants getting used to doing the task and improving as a result of practice.

Purposive sample: Participants are selected for inclusion in a study on the basis of satisfying a specific criterion.

Qualitative research: A series of approaches to research that do not rely on the collection of numerical data and instead focus more on the content of participant responses such as the language they use or the characteristics of artistic materials produced by the participants.

Quantitative research: An approach to research in which the performance or behaviour of participants is recorded as numerical data which can be subjected to a statistical analysis.

Quasi-experiment: Where the experimenter is not able to directly manipulate the independent variable, but the independent variable varies naturally.

Random allocation: In experimental research with two or more experimental groups, ensuring that all participants have the same probability of being allocated to an experimental condition.

Random sample: Every member of the target population has the same probability of being selected to participate in the study.

Rating scales: Statements in an interview or questionnaire with which the respondents have to indicate the extent to which they agree or disagree with the statement or how typical the statement is of them.

Reactivity: Changes in participant's behaviour that occur as a result of them being aware that they are being observed.

Related design: An experimental design in which all participants are exposed to all conditions of the independent variable.

Representative sample: In the context of observational research, observing a behaviour for a sufficient period of time to observe the typical occurrence of the behaviour in everyday life.

Repeated measures: An experimental design in which participants are exposed to all of the experimental conditions. Also known as a related design.

Sample: The group of individuals who take part in a research study.

Saturation: In grounded theory, the point during the analysis at which no further themes or categories emerge from the data.

Significance levels: The criteria used to determine whether or not a result is statistically significant. A result is regarded as statistically significant if we can show the probability of it occurring by chance is less than or equal to 0.5% (the 0.05 significance level) or 1% (the 0.01 significance level).

Snowballing: An approach to sampling in which the researcher starts with an appropriate participant who is known to them, and this participant then recruits other suitable participants, who in turn recruit further participants.

Socially desirable responses: Responses in an interview that are not necessarily true of the interviewee but represent attempts by the interviewee to present themselves in a favourable light, or tell the interviewer what they think the interviewer wants to hear.

Statistical inference: Making generalisations about the characteristics of a population based on the performance of participants in the sample.

Statistical significance: The probability that a statistical result occurred by chance. If this is very low, then we can assume that the result did not occur by chance and is a result that is likely to apply to the wider target population: we then say that the result is statistically significant.

Statistical tests: A series of statistical procedures that can be applied to numerical data to assess the statistical significance of a set of the research results.

Strange situation: A laboratory-based observational approach to study attachment between infants and caregivers.

Stratified random sample: An approach to sampling in which the target population is divided into a number of key groups (strata) and individuals are selected from each group on a random basis.

Strata: The different groups that may make up a population of interest in a research study. The groups can be based on age, sex, ethnicity, socioeconomic status or other variable(s) of interest.

Structured interview: An interview where all interviewees are asked the same questions, in the same order and using the same wording for each question.

Thematic analysis: An approach to analysing qualitative data sources such as interview transcripts by identifying recurring ideas or 'themes' within the data.

Theory: A set of explanations as to why behaviour occurs.

Time sampling: In observational research, dividing the observation period into a series of smaller intervals and recording the number of times a given behaviour occurs in each interval.

Unrelated experimental design: An experimental design in which each participant is only exposed to one condition of the independent variable.

Chapter 4

Accommodation: In Piaget's theory, the creation of a new schema or modification of an old one when the current schema does not fit with the environment.

Acquisition phase: In the conjugate reinforcement paradigm, the phase during which the infant's leg is attached by means of a cord to a mobile suspended over the cot, so that when the infant kicks, this makes the mobile move. This usually leads to an increase in the rate of kicking.

Adaptation: In Piaget's theory, the process of building schemas through interaction with the environment.

Animism: In Piaget's theory, a limitation of preoperational children in which they attribute thoughts and feelings to inanimate objects.

Assimilation: In Piaget's theory, using existing schemas to make sense of the world.

Automatic processing: Cognitive processes that do not acquire conscious attention and are often beyond our voluntary control.

Baseline phase: In the conjugate reinforcement paradigm, the initial phase of the study in which the infant's normal or baseline rate of kicking is established.

Centration: In Piaget's theory, a limitation of preoperational children in which they can only focus on one aspect of a situation.

Chunking: A method of increasing the capacity of short-term memory by storing several pieces of information as a single unit.

Compensation: In Piagetian conservation tasks, the understanding that when an object or substance is changed in appearance, certain aspects of the change compensate for differences from its original state, and thus the size or quantity of the object or substance remains the same.

Concrete operational stage: The third stage of development identified by Piaget running from the ages of 7 to 11 years of age. This stage is characterised by a more logical and organised pattern of thinking and the ability to use mental operations.

Conjugate-reinforcement paradigm: A method for studying recall memory in infants by getting them to form an association between kicking their legs and making a mobile move, and looking at their ability to retain this association over time.

Context effects: In memory research, the observation that memory performance is better if the circumstances of recall are the same as the circumstances of learning.

Controlled processing: Cognitive processes that require conscious attention and typically involved in skills for which we have yet to acquire full proficiency.

Coordination of secondary circular reactions: The fourth substage of the sensorimotor period during which infants can combine schemas into new and more complex action sequences and used these to solve simple problems.

Deferred imitation: An approach to studying recall memory in infants. The infant is exposed to an action performed on an object (squeezing a toy to make noise). The object is then removed without the infant being allowed to touch it. After a delay, the object is then presented to the infant to see if they will repeat the action witnessed earlier. If the infant shows deferred imitation, then they must have committed that action to memory.

Digit span: A technique for measuring the capacity of short-term memory. The child has to repeat a sequence of digits. With each correct repetition, the sequence length is increased by one digit until the child cannot successfully repeat any more sequences. Digit span is therefore the maximum sequence length that the child can repeat.

Dishabituation: When an infant begins to react to a stimulus again having previously habituated to it, indicating that the infant has recognised a change in that stimulus.

Disequilibrium: In Piaget's theory, a period in which the existing schemas do not match well with reality and children have to rely more on accommodation.

Egocentric speech: Piaget's view that when children talk to themselves during play or other activities this reflects the fact that they are unable to take the perspective of others and talk regardless of whether another can hear them.

Egocentrism: In Piaget's theory, a limitation of preoperational children in which they are unable to see situations from other people's perspectives.

Elaboration: Improving memory performance by creating a shared, meaningful link between two or more items.

Elementary mental functions: In Vygotsky's theory, basic cognitive skills such as memory, perception and attention.

Equilibrium: In Piaget's theory, when the existing schemas provide a good match to reality and children mainly engage in assimilation.

Equilibrium: In cognitive development, periods of stability in which children can get by through assimilating experiences into their existing schemas.

Formal operational stage: The fourth stage of development identified by Piaget running from the age of 11 years onward. This is regarded as the end point of development at which children have acquired the ability to think in more abstract, systematic and hypothetical terms.

Guided participation: Rogoff's proposal that rather than learning through formal instruction, children learn and acquire skills by being involved from an early age in the everyday activities of their society and learning through support from more experienced partners.

Habituation: When an infant no longer reacts to a new stimulus.

Habituation-dishabituation paradigm: A technique for studying recognition memory in infants. Involving presenting a novel stimulus to an infant until the infant no longer reacts to it, and then presenting a changed version of the stimulus to see if the infant reacts, thereby indicating a recognition that the stimulus is different from the previous presentations.

Higher mental functions: In Vygotsky's theory, cognitive skills in the child that are acquired as a result of interaction with more experienced members of their society.

Hierarchical classification: The ability to divide objects into meaningful classes and subclasses.

Hypothetico-deductive reasoning: Solving a complex problem by firstly coming up with a 'theory' which describes all of the dimensions of a problem and possible factors that might affect the outcome, deducing testable 'hypotheses' from the theory and testing these hypotheses which will result in the theory being supported or amended.

Immediate retention phase: In the conjugate reinforcement paradigm, the phase in which the mobile is disconnected from the infant's foot and the rate of kicking is measured. If the rate of kicking stays the same as during the acquisition phase, the infant is regarded as recalling that kicking their foot makes the mobile move.

Inability to conserve: Preoperational children's lack of understanding that certain aspects of an object or substance can remain the same despite changes in physical appearance.

Infantile amnesia: Our inability to remember events from infancy.

Internalisation: In Vygotsky's theory, the process by which children move from the social to the psychological plane.

Invention of new means through mental combinations: The final substage of the sensorimotor period marking the beginning of the child'd ability to think using mental representations.

Long-term memory: Our permanent knowledge base which does not appear to have any limits in terms of its capacity or duration. Information in long-term memory is highly organised and thought to form an associative network in which related units of information are stored together.

Mature strategy: When children use a memory strategy spontaneously, apply it to a variety of tasks and use of the strategy yields positive results.

Memory strategies: Techniques for improving memory performance.

Metamemory: Our own knowledge and insights into how our memories work and our own memory abilities.

Object permanence: In Piaget's theory, the realisation that objects continue to exist even when they cannot be seen, a realisation acquired during the sensorimotor period.

Organisation: Improving memory performance by grouping items into meaningful categories.

Organisation: In Piaget's theory, cognitive change that occurs as a result of the child linking schemas together to create an interconnected system.

Preoperational stage: The second stage of development identified by Piaget spanning the ages of 2–7 characterised by a growth in representational ability.

Primary circular reactions: The second substage of the sensorimotor period characterised by infants gaining increasing control over their behaviours and repeating behaviours that lead to interesting consequences.

Processing efficiency: A view of memory development that proposes that the total capacity of the information-processing system is fixed but this is divided between operating space and storage space. As children get older, they are able to devote fewer resources to operating space and therefore have more resources for storage space leading to an increase in memory ability.

Production deficiency: A phase in memory strategy development during which children have the capacity to use a strategy but don't use it spontaneously, but they can be instructed to use it with positive effects.

Propositional thought: The ability to evaluate the logic of a statement (or proposition) without referring to real-world circumstances.

Psychological plane: In Vygotsky's theory, the ability of children to move from doing things with help to doing things on their own.

Reciprocal teaching: An educational application of Vygotsky's theory in which small groups of peers discuss a subject providing each other with instruction that is beyond their individual ability but within zone of proximal development.

Reflexive schemas: The first substage of the sensorimotor period during which infants practice and gain control over basic reflexive behaviours.

Rehearsal: Learning a list of items by constant repetition of the items using overt or covert speech.

Reversibility: The ability to mentally arrange the steps in solving a problem in reverse order to return to the starting point.

Scaffolding: This is a process whereby adults adjust the amount and type of support they offer to the child. As the child begins to acquire the skill, the amount of support and instruction is reduced.

Schema theory: An application of Piaget's notion of the schema to early childhood education and involving the identification of patterns underlying different behaviours and once this pattern or schema has been identified, using this to devise learning experiences for the child.

Schemas: In Piaget's theory, these are mental structures created by children to make sense of experience.

Secondary circular reaction: The third substage of the sensorimotor period during which infants gain further control over their actions and seek to repeat events caused by their actions.

Sensorimotor period: The first stage of development identified by Piaget, spanning the first two years of life. During this stage, the child moves from mainly reflexive behaviours to acquiring the ability to think using mental representations.

Sensory register: A memory store that preserves basic sensory details such as visual images of sounds for a very brief period.

Seriation: The ability to arrange objects according to a quantitative dimension such as size or length.

Short-term memory (aka working memory): A memory store which acts as a sort of mental workspace that allows us to retain information for brief periods while we operate on this information.

Social plane: In Vygotsky's theory, the ability of children to perform tasks with assistance from others.

Sociocultural Theory: Vygotsky's theory of development which emphasised the role of social and cultural factors in development, and the role of more knowledgeable and skilled members of society transmitting knowledge and skills to children through their interactions with them.

Stage: In Piaget's theory, when schemas are qualitatively similar.

Strategy inefficiency: A phase in memory strategy development in which children attempt to apply a strategy but do so in an inefficient and inconsistent manner.

Transitive inference: The ability to recognise relations between objects in serial order, such as understanding that if A is greater than B and B is greater than C, then A is greater than C.

Tertiary circular reactions: The fifth substage of the sensorimotor period during which infants can repeat and vary new actions and imitate more complex behaviours.

Utilisation deficiency: A phase in memory strategy development during which a strategy is used but with no positive effect.

Chapter 5

Age of viability: When the foetus reaches 22–25 weeks of gestation it has a chance of survival if born prematurely and given intensive care.

Amnion: A protective membrane formed from the cells of the trophoblast.

Amniotic fluid: The fluid within the amnion that helps to maintain a stable temperature and protects the developing organism from jolts caused by the mother's movements.

Blastocyst: The zygote after four days, a hollow fluid-filled ball.

Brain stem: The structures in the brain that control basic physiological processes such as reflexes, respiration and digestion.

Cephalocaudal trend: Physical growth and motor skill development proceeding in a head-to-toe direction.

Cerebral hemispheres: The two sides of the brain which control different functions.

Cerebral lateralisation: The specialisation of the left and right hemispheres for controlling different functions.

Cerebrum: The left and right hemispheres of the brain.

Chorion: A structure that forms from the trophoblast during the germinal stage which forms a second protective layer for the developing organism.

Corpus callosum: A set of fibres which link the left and right hemispheres of the brain.

Directed reaching: Attempts by infants from 3 months of age to reach for objects which are more coordinated and efficient and involve increased eye, head and shoulder control.

Dynamic Systems Theory: An approach to the development of motor skills that sees new skills as a reorganisation of existing skills into more effective ways of exploring the environment which allow infants to achieve desired goals.

Ectoderm: The layer of the embryonic disk that will become the skin and nervous system.

Embryo: The developing organism after two weeks.

Embryonic disk: The cells on the inside of the blastocyst which will go on to form the new organism.

Embryonic stage: The second stage of prenatal development which lasts from the third to the eighth week of pregnancy.

Endoderm: The layer of the embryonic disk that will become the digestive and respiratory systems.

Experience-dependent placticity: Modification of synapses or the development of new ones based on the specific learning experiences of the individual.

Experience-expectant plasticity: The development of synapses that respond to experiences that are expected and common in the human species.

Fine motor skills: Small sequences of movement such as reaching and grasping.

Frontal lobe: The region of the brain imvolved in the planning and regulation of behaviour.

General growth curve: The general pattern of physical growth in childhood – rapid growth in infancy, a slow but steady pace in childhood followed by a rapid growth spurt in adolescence.

Germinal stage: The first stage of prenatal development covering the first two weeks after conception.

Glial cells: Cells responsible for nourishing the neurons and for the process of myelination.

Gross motor skills: Actions such as crawling and walking which allow a child to move around their environment.

Growth hormone: A hormone produced by the pituitary gland in the brain which is responsible for the growth of all body tissues except the central nervous system and genitals.

Limbic system: A set of brain structures involved in emotional responses and memory.

Mesoderm: The layer of the embryonic disk that will become the skeletal and muscular systems.

Myelination: The coating of neurons with a fatty substance called myelin which improves the efficiency of the transmission of neural impulses.

Neural tube: Formed during the embryonic stage when the ectoderm folds over and eventually becomes the spinal cord.

Neuron: The basic unit of the brain and nervous system.

Neuronal death: Neurons that connect with each other crowd out the remaining neurons which then die.

Neurotransmitters: Chemical substances which transmit information by crossing the synapses.

Nonorganic failure to thrive: A growth disorder in infants caused by a lack of parental love, infants with this disorder show similar symptoms to children suffering from malnutrition.

Occipital lobe: The region of the brain responsible for visual processing.

Palmar (or ulnar) grasp: A clumsy grasping action in infants in which the fingers close against the palm.

Parietal lobe: The region of the brain responsible for bodily sensations.

Pincer grasp: Use of the thumb and index finger to explore and manipulate objects.

Placenta: The structure which allows oxygen and nutrients to be transferred from the mother's blood to the embryo.

Plasticity: In the early stages of development when the different areas of the brain are not yet committed to a specific function and are receptive to the experience of the individual.

Prereaching: Poorly coordinated attempts by newborn infants to reach for objects in front of them.

Proprioception: A sense of movement and location arising from bodily sensations such as muscle contractions.

Proximodistal trend: Physical growth and motor skill development proceeding from the centre of the body outward.

Psychosocial dwarfism: A growth disorder in young children caused by emotional deprivation which interferes with the production of growth hormone.

Synapse: The tiny gap between each neuron where the neural fibres come close together but don't meet.

Synaptic pruning: The brain disposes of the synaptic connections of neurons that are not regularly stimulated.

Temporal lobe: The region of the brain involved in language, hearing and smell.

Teratogens: Factors that can have an adverse effect on the development of the unborn child.

The fetal stage: The third stage of prenatal development which lasts from the nine weeks to birth.

Thyroid-stimulating hormone: A hormone which prompts the thyroid gland in the neck to release thyroxine, a substance necessary for brain development and for growth hormone to have its full impact on body size.

Trophoblast: The cells on the outside of the blastocyst which will go on to form the structures that will protect and nourish the developing organism.

Umbilical cord: The structure that links the placenta to the developing child.

Villi: Finger-like structures that develop from the chorion that burrow deep into the wall of the uterus leadng to the development of the placenta.

Yolk sac: A structure which forms during the germinal stage and is responsible for the production of blood cells.

Zygote: A single cell formed by the fusion of an egg and a sperm cell.

Chapter 6

Adolescent onset conduct disorders: There are no significant behavioural problems in childhood and delinquent and antisocial behaviour emerges at the onset of adolescence.

Behaviourally inhibited temperament: A temperamental style in infants and children that causes them to be upset by unfamiliar experiences and a desire to withdraw from these.

Callous-unemotional traits: An interpersonal style characterised by a lack of guilt and empathy, callous use of other people to achieve one's goals and high levels of proactive and reactive aggression.

Child Behaviour Checklist: An instrument measuring levels of psychopathology in children and adolescents that can be completed by parents, teachers or adolescents.

Childhood onset conduct disorder: Conduct problems that are present from the preschool years onwards and problem behaviours tend to increase in frequency and severity through the course of childhood and on into adolescence.

Co-morbidity: The co-occurrence of two or more disorders at the same time.

Continuity: In the context of developmental psychopathology, factors related to the re-occurrence of a disorder in childhood.

Developmental pathways: In developmental psychopathology, the aspects of development that lead to the emergence of disorders in children.

Developmental psychopathology: The study of developmental processes that contribute to or protect against psychopathology.

Diagnostic and Statistical Manual of Mental Disorders (DSM): A system for the classification of psychological disorders that takes a categorical approach to diagnosis.

Discontinuity: Factors relating to preventing the re-occurrence of a disorder in childhood.

Echolalia: A feature of autism characterised by repetition of what other people say with no intention to understand or communicate.

Elimination disorders: Problems related to the eliminative functions such as bedwetting (enuresis) and uncontrolled bowel movements (encopresis).

Equifinality: Where different developmental pathways can lead to the same outcome, such as depression in one child occurring as a result of bereavement whereas depression in another child occurred as a result of neglect.

Externalising problems: Psychological problems such as aggression and where distress is expressed in external behaviours.

Factors that promote self-esteem and self-efficacy: A protective mechanism which helps children to feel that they can deal with their problems, such as school achievement.

Internalising problems: Psychological problems such as anxiety and depression where the suffering is expressed internally.

Masked depression: The notion, currently not accepted, that children masked out their depression with somatic complaints or acting out behaviours.

Multifinality: An adverse event resulting in different outcomes for different children, such as a neglect leading to aggression in one child and depression in another.

Opening of opportunities: Turning points in a child's life that offer the chance to reduce the impact of risk factors, such as staying on a school and acquiring qualifications that lead to more opportunities in later life.

Pervasive developmental disorders: Disorders in which a wide variety of functioning is disrupted.

Prosody: The normal rhythms of speech which can be used to understand the meaning intended by the speaker. Children suffering from autism have difficulty in using such speech signals.

Protective factors: Factors that act as a buffer against the development of problems when faced with the various risk factors.

Protective mechanisms: How a given set of factors protect against psychopathology.

Qualitative departures from development: Where behaviours that would not be expected in normal development are apparent.

Quantitative departures from development: Where there is more or less of a behaviour present than would normally be expected, such as more anxiety, or less language.

Reduction of negative chain reactions: A protective factor which prevents a vicious cycle of adverse circumstances and psychopathology.

Reduction of risk impact: Factors that act as a buffer for a child exposed to a risk factor, such as a caring relationship with an older sibling compensating for an uncaring or dysfunctional parent.

Risk factors: In developmental psychopathology, any factor that increases the likelihood that a child will develop a disorder.

Strengths and Difficulties Questionnaire: A brief screening instrument for identifying psychological problems in children and adolescents. There are two forms, an informant version that is completed by parents or teachers, and a self-report which can be completed by adolescents.

Systematic desensitisation: A behavioural approach to treating anxiety which aims to substitute a fear response with relaxation through gradual exposure to the feared object or situation.

Tic disorders: Disorders involving involuntary movements or vocalisations, such as in Tourette's syndrome.

Token economy: A behavioural intervention for promoting positive behaviour. Each time the child behaves in a desirable manner, a token is awarded and once a certain number of tokens has been achieved, these can be 'exchanged' for a reward such as a toy or engaging in a fun activity.

Vulnerability factor: In developmental psychopathology, any factor that increases the likelihood that a child will succumb to a risk factor.

Chapter 7

Acute illnesses: Illnesses characterised by a rapid onset and a short duration.

Anoxia: Deprivation of oxygen during the birth process.

Apgar scale: A method for assessing the health of the newborn infant by examining Appearance, Pulse, Grimace, Activity and Respiration.

Breech position: When foetus is positioned for birth in a feet or buttocks first position which can lead to complications in the birth process.

Chronic illnesses: illness that are characterised by a slow onset and a long duration. These can include respiratory diseases such as asthma or metabolic diseases such as diabetes. Typically there is no cure for such illnesses, they have to be managed over the course of the lifespan through the use of medication, and changes to lifestyle in terms of diet and physical activity.

Contagion (Bibace and Walsh's model): The second stage in children's understanding of illnesses in which children believe that they can get sick through physical proximity to other people but not through touching them.

Contagion: A method of disease transmission in which contamination is spread between individuals.

Contamination (Bibace and Walsh's model): The third stage in children's understanding of illnesses in which illness is caused by physical contact with an individual or object that is 'bad' or 'harmful' to the body.

Contamination: A method of disease transmission in which an object becomes negatively affected through contact with another.

Disengagement coping: A strategy for coping with chronic illness through use of strategies such as avoidance and denial.

Hypothyroidism: A deficiency in the production of thyroid hormone which can lead to poor growth and mental impairment.

Immanent justice: The belief that illness or accidents are a consequence of misbehaviour.

Internalisation: The fourth stage in Bibace and Walsh's model of children's understanding of illnesses in which children still consider the cause of illness to be external but the mechanism of transmission is ingesting 'germs' through inhalation and swallowing.

Isolette: A special type of bed used to care for premature infants.

Low birth weight: Infants below their expected weight at birth. See also preterm infants and small for date infants.

Phenominism: The first stage in Bibace and Walsh's characterisation of children's understanding of illness in which the causes of illness are explained in relation to spatially or temporally remote external events that co-occurred with the illness.

Phenylketonuria (PKU): The inability of the body to process a particular type of amino acid (a building block for proteins) which if undetected can lead to brain damage and learning difficulties.

Physiologic: The fifth stage in Bibace and Walsh's model of children's understanding of illnesses in which children realise that while illnesses have external causes, it is internal, physiological processes that give rise to the symptoms.

Placental abruption: When the placenta becomes detached from the wall of the uterus leading to an interruption of the blood supply to the infant.

Prematurity: When an infant is born before a full 38 weeks of gestation.

Preterm infants: Infants born before their due date but of a normal weight given the amount of time spent in the uterus.

Primary accident prevention: Measures to prevent accidents happening at all.

Primary control or active coping: A strategy for coping with chronic illness that involves attempts to change the source of stress or one's response to the stressor. Strategies used here include seeking social support and taking active steps to deal with the symptoms.

Psychophysiologic: The sixth stage of Bibace and Walsh's model of children's understanding of illnesses in which children continue to think of illness in terms of internal physiological processes but are also now aware that there may be psychological causes of illness as well, and thoughts and feelings can influence what goes on in the body, such as stress causing a heart attack.

Secondary accident prevention: Strategies to minimise the effect of an accident if it does happen.

Secondary coping: A strategy for coping with chronic illness in which children seek to adapt to their situation through acceptance, cognitive restructuring and positive thinking.

Small for date infants: Infants below their expected weight taking into account the length of the pregnancy. Some of these are full-term babies but below their expected birth weight, others are seriously underweight premature babies.

Tertiary accident prevention: Strategies to minimise the outcome of injury resulting from an accident.

Three E's' of accident prevention: Education to raise awareness of accident risks any ways to avoid them, **engineering** to make the environment safer and **enforcement** which involves applying legal sanctions against risk taking behaviour.

Chapter 8

Associative play: Play in children in which there are some basic interactions such as sharing toys and commenting on each other's activities.

Attachment Q-set (AQS): An observation-based technique for assessing attachment in young children.

Attachment: The strong and affectionate bond between the infant and caregiver.

Average children: Children who are not as liked as popular children but not as disliked as rejected children.

Belief-desire psychology: The realisation by children that other people hold beliefs about the world as well as desires.

Categorical self: When children begin to categorise themselves on the basis of characteristics such sex ('boy' or 'girl'), age ('baby', 'boy') and even goodness and badness ('I good girl').

Controversial children: Children who are liked by many of their peers but disliked by many others.

Cooperative play: Play characterised by a high level of interaction between children involving joint activities such as playing formal games, engaging in pretend play in which each child takes on a role or building things together.

Desire psychology: The realisation by children that just as they have desires, so do other people and this can be used to explain and predict behaviour in others.

Difficult infants: Infants who show difficulty in establishing regular routines, are slow to accept new experiences and have a tendency to cry and fuss often.

Easy infants: Infants who are sociable, quickly establish regular routines and adapt easily to new experiences.

Emotional regulation: The processes by which we manage our emotions and adjust them to a comfortable level so that we avoid extremes of emotions.

False belief task: A task used to assess the presence of a representational theory of mind in children.

First-order beliefs: Attempts to understand what another believes.

Goal-corrected partnership: The final phase of attachment development which begins at around 2 years of age. The attachment relationship is now more reciprocal in nature.

Goodness of fit: A model proposed by Thomas and Chess to explain how infant temperament and parenting received by the infant can act together to influence an outcome.

Higher order mental states: Understanding that an individual can have beliefs about a third person.

Horizontal plane: The nature of peer relations in children referring to the fact that the relationships are on a more equal footing than relationships with adults.

Insecure-avoidant attachment: An attachment style characterised by the infant being unresponsive to the parent and showing no overt signs of distress when the parent departs. During the reunion episodes, the infant fails to respond to the parent and often actively avoids the parent.

Insecure-disorganised attachment: An insecure form attachment style that appears to be a combination of the avoidant and resistant attachment styles. The infant appears to be confused about whether to avoid or approach the caregiver. During the reunion episodes, they may appear confused or freeze, or they may begin to approach the caregiver only to move away as the caregiver draws near.

Insecure-resistant attachment: An attachment stylein which the infant will fail to explore the room before separation and is distressed when the parent leaves. During the reunion episodes, the infant shows an ambivalent attitude to the parent, seeking contact yet also simultaneously showing resistant behaviour such as struggling when picked up and being generally difficult to sooth.

Internal working model: A mental representation of the nature of the individual and their relationship with others formed as a result of early attachment experiences.

Maintenance of proximity to a discriminated figure by means of locomotion as well as signals: Also known as 'clear cut attachment'. The third phase of the development of the attachment relationship which runs from approximately 7 months. Infants now have a clear preference for individuals with whom they are familiar (parents, grandparents, a particular care worker) and will seek physical proximity and contact with those individuals and become upset when they leave.

Multiple emotions: Experiencing several different emotions in response to the same event.

Neglected children: Children who receive few nominations in the 'like' or 'dislike' category and are essentially ignored by their peers.

Non-social solitary play: When a child plays alone, or watches other children play but does not join in.

Orientation and signals directed towards one (or more) discriminated figures: Also known as 'attachment in the making'. The second phase in the development of the attachment relationship which runs from approximately 2–7 months of age and marks the beginning of the infant beginning to differentiate familiar and unfamiliar people. Infants are more likely to smile at the primary caregiver and be comforted by them when distressed.

Orientation and signals without discrimination of figure: Also known as 'preattachment'. The first phase in the development of the attachment relationship, as described by Bowlby, which takes place over the first 6–8 weeks of life. At this stage infants emit behaviours such as smiling, grasping and crying that will bring them into contact with adults who will care for them, however they do not yet show a preference for the primary caregiver over other.

Parallel play: Children playing alongside each other, using the same toys but not interacting with each other.

Peer groups: Groups of children who interact frequently, have a sense of membership, and have norms governing the behaviour of members.

Personal agency: The realisation by infants that they can have an effect on their surrounding environment.

Popular children: Children who are liked by many of their peers and disliked by few.

Rejected–aggressive children: Children suffering peer rejection who display high levels of aggression, are impulsive and have a poor capacity for emotional regulation.

Rejected children: Children who are disliked by many and liked by few.

Rejected-withdrawn: Children suffering peer rejection who tend to be socially anxious, withdrawn and submissive.

Representational theory of mind: When children understand that a belief is a representation of reality but not reality itself.

Second-order beliefs: The understanding that a person can have beliefs about a third person.

Secure attachment: An attachment style in which infants use the parent as a secure base for exploration, may or may not be upset when the parent leaves, but are happy when the parent returns and actively seek contact. If distressed during the separation, their distress is relieved upon the return of the parent.

Self-conscious emotions: Emotions such as guilt, envy, embarrassment and pride which are related to damage or enhancement to the sense of self.

Slow to warm-up infants: Infants who are in between the easy and difficult categories, slow to adapt to new experiences, but with repeated exposure will gradually 'warm up' and adapt.

Social referencing: The use of other people's emotional expressions to respond to situations that are uncertain and ambiguous.

Sociometry: A technique for measuring peer relations in children in which a group of children in a setting such as a school are asked to nominate several students that they like or dislike.

Stranger anxiety: A distinct fear of unfamiliar people seen in infants from around the ages of seven months, characterised by crying, whimpering and attempts at avoidance.

Strange situation: A laboratory-based observation technique for measuring the security of attachment.

Temperament: Individual differences in the general behavioural and emotional characteristics of an infant.

Theory of mind: The ability to attribute mental states to others and use these to explain their behaviour.

Vertical plane: The nature of relationships between children and adults in which children are less powerful.

Visual cliff technique: This consists of a set up of two tables with a gap in between them and the gap is covered with Perspex. Usually when a baby is placed on a table, they will usually appear reluctant to cross onto the glass surface as it appears to be a drop. This technique is used to study perceptual development and the use of social referencing in infants.

Chapter 9

Analogy: A strategy for reading new words based on words already known: The child comes to realise that words that sound similar also have similar spelling patterns.

Babbling: When infants combine vowel and consonant sounds into syllables and repeat them producing sounds such as '*babababa*'.

Categorical perception: The ability to perceive differences between phonemes such as /b/ and /d/ but without noticing variations within a single phoneme.

Communicative musicality: A characteristic of mother-infant interactions in which the mother's speaking voice has a distinct musical quality with clearly discernable rhythms and melodious patterns and the infant mirrors these qualities in response.

Comprehension exceeding **production:** A phase in language development when children know more words than they can actually produce.

Consolidated alphabetic phase: The final phase in Ehri's model of reading development during which fully connected spellings of more and more words are retained and spelling patterns that recur across different words become consolidated, leading to greater speed and accuracy in word recognition.

Constraints: In the context of learning word meanings, a proposal that rather than consider all the possible hypotheses about the meaning of a newly encountered word, children only focus on a limited range of possible meanings.

Cooing: The production of soft, low vowel sounds in infant such as oo which occurs around one month of age.

Developmental dyslexia: A diagnosis made when children fail to acquire reading skills despite normal cognitive development and adequate opportunities to develop reading skills.

Early sequential bilinguals: Children who learned their first language before they learned their second language but learned the second language relatively early in childhood.

Expansions: When parents expand a child's utterance into a longer and more complex sentence.

Expressive children: Children who acquire many terms useful for social interaction.

Fast mapping: The ability of children to acquire word meanings very rapidly, often only a single brief exposure.

Full alphabetic stage: The third phase in Ehri's model of reading development in which children are able to form full connections between the letters in a word and their sounds.

Infant-directed speech or **motherese:** This is the form of speech that is often used by adults to talk to a baby and has a distinct 'musical' quality characterised by use of exaggerated intonation and pitch and is used to attract a baby's attention.

Interactionist theories: A view of language development that see language as an innate ability but further developed by social interaction experiences.

Joint attention: A process in which adults also follow the infant's line of vision and comment on what the baby sees.

Language acquisition device (LAD): An innate system proposed by Chomsky for the acquisition of language.

Language acquisition support system (LASS): A proposal by Bruner that parents use a collection of strategies to facilitate language development in the child.

Late sequential bilinguals: Children who learned their second language in adolescence or later.

Learning theory: A view of language development which stresses the role of environmental factors such reinforcement and imitation.

Metalinguistic awareness: An understanding of the nature of language.

Mutual-exclusivity constraints: In learning word meaning, a strategy of assuming that a new word applies to an object for which a word is not already known.

Naming explosion: A phase in language acquisition that occurs around 18 months of age characterised by a rapid acquisition of words.

Nativist theory: A view of language development which sees language as an innate ability.

Observational learning and imitation: In the contect of language development, the view that children acquire words and phrases by listening to others and imitating their behaviours.

Onset and rime: Sound units in a word that are larger the individual phonemes, but smaller than a syllable. The onset of a syllable consists of the opening consonant or consonant cluster, the rime component contains the vowel and succeeding consonants.

Operant conditioning: In the context of language development, the view that when children make a vocalisation they are **reinforced** (e.g. they receive praise and attention) leading them to repeat these behaviours.

Operating principles: A proposal by Slobin that children possess a set of inbuilt cognitive strategies which can be applied to the task of language acquisition.

Overextensions: When for example, the word 'cat' is applied not just to cats, but also to dogs, and other four-legged animals.

Over-regularisations: An error made by children in which they treat all words as regular words, examples include the use of such words as 'runned', 'sheeps', 'wented', etc.

Parameter setting: When the language acquisition device infers a rule or parameter about a language, such as the basic order of words in that language, the rule becomes fixed and is used to interpret further speech.

Partial alphabetic phase: The second phase in Ehri's model of reading development in which children begin to use their emerging alphabetic knowledge to make connections between some of the letters in a word and their sounds.

Phonemes: The individual speech sounds that make up a language.

Phonological awareness: Understanding of the sound structure of spoken words and the use of this to process spoken and written language.

Phonological dyslexics: A proposed sub-group of dyslexic children who are poor at reading regular words or nonwords.

Phonological recoding: Identifying the sounds represented by the letters in a printed word and blending them together to recognise the word.

Phonology: The basic sounds that make up the words of a language.

Poverty of the stimulus: A criticism of learning theory accounts of language development based on the observation that when a child is reinforced for producing a correct utterance, they do not receive direct feedback on what was correct about their speech.

Pragmatics: Understanding the communicative aspects of language such as knowing how to communicate intentions, taking into account other peoples's perspectives and understanding how meaning can also be communicated through tone of voice, and understanding differences between literal and intended meanings.

Pre-alphabetic phase: The first phase in Ehri's model of reading development in which reading is largely visually based and does not involve any use of letter-sound rules.

Proto-conversations: Give-and-take communications between infants and caregivers such as games of 'peekaboo'.

Protodeclarative pointing: The infant's use of gestures to bring an object to another's attention.

Protoimperative pointing: The infant's use of pointing to make a request, such as pointing to a toy that is out of their reach.

Reading–age controls: A comparison of normally developing readers and dyslexic readers in which the normally developing readers are younger than the dyslexic readers but of the same reading ability.

Recasting: When parents rephrase a child's utterance providing a grammatically correct example.

Referential children: Children who acquire lots of object names.

Say-mean distinction: The understanding that people don't always say exactly what they mean.

Semantics: The meanings of words on their own and in sentences.

Sensitive period: In the context of language development, a period when the brain is especially ready to process language.

Shaping: In the context of language development, when parents selectively reinforce children for producing vocalisations that approach real words. When children start producing sentences, they are reinforced for producing grammatically correct sentences.

Simultaneous bilinguals: Children who learned their first and second languages at the same time (e.g. having parents who speak different languages in the home).

Specific language impairment: A diagnosis made when a child's language lags behind other areas of development, and does not appear to be related to wider learning disabilities, hearing loss, neurological problems or impoverished language environment.

Surface developmental dyslexics: A proposed sub-group of dyslexic children who typically can read regular words but have great difficulty with irregular words.

Syllable: An independently articulable segment of a word.

Syntactic bootstrapping: A strategy of paying attention to the way a word is used in a sentence to infer meaning.

Syntax: Rules relating to the correct ordering of words in sentences, for example the ordering of nouns and adjectives.

Telegraphic speech: The nature of children's initial two-word utterances which consist of nouns, verbs and adjectives, and tend to omit words such as articles ('the'), prepositions (e.g. in, on), conjunctions (e.g. and) and inflections (endings to denote plurals or tenses).

Underextensions: When a child uses a word in a very restricted way such as using the word 'car' to refer only to the family car, and not to other cars.

Universal grammar: The set of features common to all languages (e.g. all languages contain concepts such as subject, object and verb). This grammar is contained within the language acquisition device.

Whole-object constraints: In learning word meanings, a strategy of assuming that names refer to whole rather than parts of objects.

Chapter 10

Active engagement: A proposed characteristic of playful behaviour meaning that the child must be involved physically and/or psychologically, rather than passively observing the activity.

Activity Apperception Story Procedure: A game-like, photographic categorisation task in which children are presented with photographs of different classroom activities and asked to post each photograph into letter boxes labelled '*play*' or '*work*'.

Adult presence: In the context of play, when children use the presence of an adult to define an activity as play or not play.

Arousal-modulation theory of play: A theory of play that proposed that in an environment where there is insufficient stimulation, this causes lower levels of arousal in the nervous system and children's play serves the purpose of increasing stimulation to an optimal level.

Choice: In the context of play, when children use the voluntary or compulsory nature of an activity to define it as play or not play.

Combinatorial flexibility: Bruner's view that play facilitated the development of new skills by affording the ability to try out new combinations of behaviours in a safe context. In this way children can acquire new behaviours that can be used in other, less safe contexts.

Convergent tasks: Tasks with a single, definite solution.

Decentration: In the context of the development of pretend play, the incorporation of others into pretend activities, and these others can be parents or objects such as stuffed toys and dolls.

Decontextualisation: In the context of the development of pretend play, the ability to use one object to represent another, such as pretending a block is a cake or using a stick as a sword.

Divergent tasks: Tasks where there are multiple solutions.

Exercise play: Whole body movements such as running, jumping and climbing.

Exploration: In the context of play, the initial behaviours of children toward an object before they start playing.

Fantasy play: The use of play to represent reality. Fantasy play can be a solitary activity or can involve playing with others.

Flexibility: In the context of defining play, an activity in which rules are determined by players and not outsiders.

Free-choice: A proposed characteristic of playful behaviour meaning that the child has freely chosen to engage in an activity.

Free-flow play: A list of 12 characteristics of play proposed by Bruce that are beneficial for learning.

Games with rules: Piaget's third stage of play development which involves the participation of at least two children and can include board games or games in which the children invent their own rules.

Integration: In the context of the development of pretend play the increasing tendency of symbolic play to become organised into patterns.

Intrinsically motivated: An activity should be an end in itself, done purely for the satisfaction of doing it.

Location: In the context of play, when children use the location of an activity to define it as play or not play.

Lure retrieval task: A task where children are presented with an out-of-reach toy and several sticks and clamps. The sticks can be joined up to create a rake to retrieve the toy.

Non-directive play therapy: (Also known as **Child–Centred Play Therapy**): An approach to play therapy that emphasises a warm and close relationship with the child.

Nonliterality: For the purposes of defining an activity as play, it should show an element of 'pretend' or 'make believe'.

Physical play: Physical activity, often without the use of objects, and babies and children engage in these activities because they are enjoyable in themselves.

Play criteria: Defining behaviours as play on the basis of one or more specified elements being present.

Play ethos: The view that play is essential for all aspects of development.

Play face: A broad, open-mouth smile, often accompanied by laughter. This expression can be used to invite another to join in play and is also useful during rough and tumble play indicating no aggressive or malicious intent.

Play signals: Behaviours that only occur during play.

Play signs: Behaviours that can occur in other context, but are playful if they are repeated, re-ordered or fragmented.

Play spiral: The proposal by Moyles that adult-directed play can be used to teach children skills, free play can be used to consolidate these skills and repeated cycles of directed and free play can be used to form a spiral of learning.

Play therapy: The use of play to help children and young people suffering from a range of psychological difficulties including depression, anxiety and aggression.

Play with objects: The use of objects in play, encompassing a number of behaviours, including exploration of the characteristics of objects, incorporating them into fantasy play, and real or imagined use of such objects.

Positive affect: In the context of defining play, an activity should be pleasurable to the child.

Practice play: The initial stage of play development proposed by Piaget which involves mostly repetition of physical activity.

Recapitulation theory: An early theory of play which saw development as reflecting the evolutionary history of the human species, and children's play as essentially acting out of this history.

Rhythmical stereotypes: Bodily movements such as kicking legs, waving arms or body rocking.

Rough-and-tumble play: Activities such as play fighting and chasing.

Sociodramatic play: Pretend play involving play with others.

Surplus energy theory: An early theory of play which saw play as necessary for the discharge of pent-up energy.

Symbolic play: Piaget's second stage of play development marking the beginning of make-believe play.

Chapter 11

Acceptance/responsiveness: The extent to which parents display support and affection to their children.

Authoritarian parents: Parents who are low on the acceptance/responsiveness dimension and high on the demanding/control dimension. This parenting style is characterised by a restrictive pattern in which many rules are imposed on their children and rules are expected to be obeyed without question.

Authoritative parents: Parents who are high on the acceptance/responsiveness dimension and on the demanding/control dimension. They are responsive and affectionate to their children. They place rules and restrictions on their children but are willing to explain the necessity for these and where appropriate will negotiate with them. They seek to exercise their control in a more rational and democratic manner.

Behavioural control: The use of firm but reasonable discipline to regulate children's conduct and punishing wrongdoing through means such as removal of privileges or toys from the children.

Classification: In a classroom setting, the maintenance of boundaries between subjects. This is weak where subjects are merged and strong where the boundaries are clearly defined.

Demanding/control: The amount of control and regulation parents impose on their children's behaviour.

Framing: In a classroom setting, the relationship between teacher and pupil and the degree of control between them. When framing is strong, then control rests with the teacher and in weak framing, the child is afforded more control.

Invisible pedagogy: Classroom settings in which there is weak classification and framing.

Permissive parents: Parents who are high in acceptance/responsiveness but low on the demanding/control dimension. Essentially they are warm and accepting of their children but make little effort to control or regulate their children's behaviour.

Psychological control: Parent's attempts to gain compliance in the children through the use of tactics such as criticism, withholding of affection and attempts to induce shame and guilt in their children.

Sustained shared thinking: Episodes in which the adult and child work together to solve a problem using intellectual skills and understanding, and the interaction is managed by the adult in such a way so that both the child and adult contribute to the thinking that develops and extends the child's existing understanding.

Uninvolved parents: Score low in both the acceptance/responsiveness and demanding control dimensions. Such parents impose few rules and demands but are also unresponsive to their children's needs and emotionally detached from them.

Visible pedagogy: Classroom settings in which there is strong classification and framing.

Index

Page references to Figures or Tables will be in *italics*